Wesleyan University, 1831–1910

Wesleyan University 1831–1910

Collegiate Enterprise in New England

David B. Potts

Wesleyan University Press

Distributed by University Press of New England
Hanover and London

Wesleyan University Press
Distributed by University Press of New England,
Hanover, NH 03755

© 1992 by Yale University
Reprinted by arrangement with Yale University Press
Wesleyan University Press paperback 1999

CIP data appear the end of the book
Printed in the United States of America   5   4   3   2   1

For Betsy

Contents

Illustrations

Photographs courtesy of Wesleyan University Archives unless otherwise noted.

Preface

"Is there an interesting story to tell?" asked the mentor from my dissertation years upon hearing I had embarked on this new project. When that question comes from Bernard Bailyn, it clearly implies two more pointed queries: Can a rich, empirically based analysis be developed? Will the analysis make a significant contribution to current interpretations? With gratitude for the standards set by his scholarship, I have tried to provide an affirmative answer to my mentor's question.

While working toward this goal I benefited from the extensive research on Wesleyan history completed by my predecessors. Sixty years ago Carl F. Price '02 produced *Wesleyan's First Century*, featuring profiles of each presidency and an account of the centennial celebration. In 1943 the board of trustees commissioned George Matthew Dutcher, a member of the faculty since 1901, to write a history of the university. They substantially reduced his teaching load. He retired three years later and continued work on the project. When failing health brought his efforts to a close in 1949, he had produced a typescript of more than twelve hundred pages. This undocumented, partially revised manuscript covered Wesleyan's origins and first decade. Work resumed on the project a decade later when Albert E. Van Dusen '38 agreed to plan a multi-volume history and to write the first volume. At that time he was associate professor of history at the University of Connecticut and also served as Connecticut state historian. In 1969 Willard M. Wallace '34, a faculty member with twenty-five years of service, agreed to prepare a second volume. It was to cover the years 1887–1967. He subsequently extended his text to 1982. Although my essay constructs the story of Wesleyan in an entirely different fashion, anyone who consults the Price volume and the typescripts of my more recent predecessors, available in the Wesleyan University Archives, will see my indebtedness to the information and insight found in their writings.

It is fitting that historical study of a college or university be a continuous process and the work of many hands. History has much to say about our collective identities and destinies. Art that it is, history also speaks from many angles of vision. A richly textured understanding of an institution best emerges from the writings of a succession of individuals and generations.

My generation of institutional historians enjoys a new opportunity to place the story of a particular college or university in the larger context of the history of American higher education. During the past two decades American historians have produced an impressive body of monographic scholarship on a variety of topics, periods, and regions in the three hundred fifty years of our collegiate history. This scholarship provides the institutional historian with many new and interesting questions and with many comparative reference points. My history of Wesleyan attempts to reap the full benefits of current scholarship.

Analytical opportunities are largely defined, of course, by the nature and extent of records available at the institution itself. Wesleyan's virtually complete files of official records and university publications, supplemented by extensive manuscript collections, reflect the caring stewardship of many librarians, scholars, and others taking the initiative to acquire, preserve, and organize the documents of sixteen decades. This enterprise acquired a new stature in 1963 with the appointment of John W. Spaeth, Jr., Robert Rich Professor of Latin, Emeritus, as university archivist. His meticulous scholarly work in this capacity is particularly well evidenced in the cataloguing of the Fisk Papers. Elizabeth A. Swaim became university archivist in 1972. While continuing to serve as special collections librarian, she diligently gathered imperiled documents from remote locations and resolutely guided the collection through three moves during reorganization, renovation, and expansion of Olin Library. Largely due to her highly professional service, the archives are now well organized and easily accessible in an environment conducive to their long-term preservation and scholarly use.

A major portion of the sources for Wesleyan's history, however, resides far beyond the campus. Hundreds of calls and letters to supplement many research trips yielded generous help from alumni, librarians, local historians, and others. College archivists, particularly at Amherst, Williams, and Yale, cheerfully and competently responded to each new question.

Members of the campus community who assisted are also so many that only a few can be designated. Betsy Potts provided text management, research assistance, and an eye for economy of prose. Her skills, empathy, and encouragement were invaluable. Portions of the manuscript in early drafts benefited from critical readings by Jeffrey Butler, Paul Mattingly (New York University), and Jack Paton. Bill Barber and Elizabeth Swaim read all six chapters in a most rigorous and helpful manner. Leon Marr managed the trustee data base with patience and precision. John Wareham assisted with photography, William Van Saun with graphs, and Karen Kratzer with the campus map. Lesley Gordon volunteered for the Civil War roster and produced a first-rate study. Among the ten Wesleyan students working with me at various times, Amy Mortimer, Deirdre Stiles, and Stuart Svonkin engaged the largest and longest projects. Olin Library's staff generously shared their full range of expertise and took supportive interest in the evolving analysis.

In 1986 Wesleyan made an extraordinary commitment to scholarship and institutional self-understanding. With trustee approval President Colin Campbell took an action that, to the best of my knowledge, is unprecedented in the annals of college and university histories. He provided generous support for long-term, full-time work by a historian preparing an institutional history to meet a single standard: successful peer review for publication by a scholarly press. His successor, William Chace, reaffirmed that commitment and extended it with funding needed to complete the present volume. Wesleyan's understanding, trust, patience, and sustenance are deeply appreciated.

I am grateful for help supplied during the past four years by a host of generous people within and beyond the Wesleyan family. They taught me the many ways in which writing an institutional history can be a congenial collegial enterprise.

Introduction

This book is written primarily as a contribution to scholarship on the history of American higher education. Wesleyan is viewed as one of the several hundred liberal arts enterprises woven into the cultural and economic fabric of a young nation. The potential for analysis in a regional context is explored most fully, drawing upon historical studies of nearby institutions to illuminate events at Wesleyan and to augment understanding of how liberal arts colleges developed in nineteenth-century New England. Many opportunities are pursued to extend boundaries of contextual analysis far beyond those usually drawn by institutional histories.

This book is also written as the first volume of an institutional history. It assumes the special responsibilities of the institutional historian for richness and reliability of detail concerning when and how each organization within the institution began. It seeks to include all the significant events and to introduce all the important individuals connected to those events. The text and notes, as approached through the index, are intended to serve as reference sources for accurate answers to specific questions. Use of the index for reference purposes is essential because information on a person, group, event, or topic may appear in two or more places in the text, depending upon where data will best serve the developing analysis. The most important objective as institutional history is to relate all this information in a manner that fosters within the Wesleyan community new levels of institutional self-understanding.

Consideration of how to tell the story so as to serve the complementary purposes of scholarship and institutional self-understanding led to the concept of collective identity as a basis for organization. Analysis of long-term shifts in the way Wesleyan has functioned, has viewed itself, and has been regarded by others divided 160 years into four major periods. From 1831 to 1870 Wesleyan was a local evangelical enterprise promoted by a town that provided land and buildings and by a few Methodist clergy and laymen who extracted very limited support from a denomination having only a nascent interest in higher education. From

1870 to 1910 almost all of Wesleyan's attributes were decidedly Methodist. Then came a half-century as a prestigious New England liberal arts college. Rapid growth in financial resources from the mid-1950s to the mid-1960s brought a decision in 1962 to become a "little university." In this fourth identity Wesleyan recruited a highly diverse student body, enlarged the faculty to include many important scholars, and established doctoral studies in a few fields of science and in ethnomusicology.

Specific years—1870, 1910, 1962—separating one period from another mark a point where events and other developments confirm that a new version of the institution's identity has become well defined and publicly affirmed. The revised identity may take decades more to reach its fullest flowering. Each divide is preceded by several decades of preparatory changes in at least some of the components of institutional identity: legal (charter), demographic (trustees, faculty, students, and alumni), programmatic (curriculum and extracurriculum), rhetorical (common values expressed in speech and writing), visual (architectural), and associational (ties with other institutions). In the plate tectonics of institutional change, preparatory movement leads to a point where a new identity supersedes that which previously prevailed.

This approach and periodization yield large and interesting why questions at the points of transition. Why was Wesleyan founded in 1831 as a joint enterprise of Middletown and Methodists? Why did Wesleyan become a more thoroughly denominational college in the late nineteenth century? Why did the Methodist institution become a prestigious New England liberal arts college by 1910? Why did the prosperous liberal arts college decide to become a "little university" in 1962?

The first three of these questions determine the selection of information, shape the narrative, and drive the analysis of this volume. To capture the ebb and flow of events and lives in the complex collective biography known as institutional history, the style chosen is that of an analytical narrative. The analytical agenda includes efforts to report accurately a host of basic facts; to identify, reconstruct, and explain important changes; and to place major developments in regional and national contexts. The narrative devotes less attention to presidencies than do most institutional histories. There is less use of category and theory than in most scholarly monographs. Answers to large why questions are provided in the web of tales told rather than weighted lists. This approach may put considerable burden on the scholarly reader to proceed slowly and thoughtfully, but it also provides ample room for interpretation differing from that of the author.

By traveling in comprehensive fashion from the 1820s to 1910, this book departs from the mode of monographs written during the last two decades on institutions such as Harvard, Dartmouth, Yale, and Princeton.[1] Rather than focusing on a particular person, group, event, or intellectual topic, this analysis of Wesleyan seeks to explore all facets of institutional life. And the span of years covered is close to a century, as compared to the half century or so found in the Ivy League monographs. Although monographic in research depth and sustained argumentation, this work paints on a larger canvas. It is similar in scope to volume one of the recent institutional history of Middlebury College, which covers the period from 1800 to 1915.[2] Perhaps it is appropriate that analysis of Wesleyan, a college bearing the name university, transcends boundaries of established scholarly blueprints.

This book can be read swiftly for pleasure, using the summary paragraph or two at the beginning of each chapter as a plot summary. But it is hoped that most readers will find benefits in pacing themselves so as to reflect on the large amount of research and interpretation packed into almost every paragraph. For such a reading, the start of each chapter provides a map of analytical trails to be traveled. And the notes often serve as an extension of the text, continuing conversations with historians, with those having a special interest in Wesleyan, and with others who may wish to pursue additional information on a particular topic.

American colleges and universities rarely apply to themselves as collective entities the central liberal arts injunction for individuals: seek self-knowledge. History is a powerful tool for self-understanding, yet few institutions have recent scholarly histories to illuminate their present and future. My work attempts to demonstrate that such histories are possible through patient, almost archaeological digging that reconstructs enough of a picture to permit substantial analysis. The task is long, hard, and expensive. Clarity, complexity, and understanding gained, however, are well worth the investment.

1 An Enterprising Spirit: Middletown and Methodists

*W*esleyan University emerged from the enterprising efforts
*of prominent citizens in Middletown, Connecticut, and from the evangelical
efforts of leaders in the Methodist denomination. By late 1828 conditions favored
the founding of a college to be nurtured by Middletown and the Methodists.
Skillful matchmaking united local promoters and regional church organizations.
The agreement they forged in contractlike manner stipulated that Middletown
would provide land, buildings, and a large portion of the initial funding. The
Methodists, in return, would sponsor a college in Middletown, raise a minimum
initial endowment, guarantee ample local representation on the board of trustees,
and put the college in operation by a certain date.*

*Similar alliances between a town and the denominational sponsors of a liberal
arts enterprise produced dozens of new colleges in Jacksonian America. In this
decentralized manner citizens of the young nation sustained a tradition of liberal
learning that extended back through the colonial colleges to Oxford and Cambridge, and from there back to the teaching and writing of the ancient Greeks.
Willbur Fisk's inaugural address in September 1831 defined this link between a
local enterprise and the heritage of liberal education.*

Local Aspirations

Middletown in the 1820s was attempting to recover from several decades
of economic and social reversals. During the eighteenth century, the

town developed from a stable farming community into a bustling river port of artisans and merchants engaged in extensive international trade. In 1784 Middletown, along with Hartford, New Haven, New London, and Norwich, attained incorporation as a city. By 1790 Middletown was nearing the zenith of its trade with the West Indies and was Connecticut's largest city. But Jefferson's embargo from 1807 to 1809, the three years of British blockade during the War of 1812, intense political and religious conflicts, and better opportunities attracting young men to the West greatly slowed the city's economy and growth, particularly by comparison with its rivals, Hartford and New Haven.[1] The 1820s were thus a time for new strategies to reestablish local prosperity.

Several steps to stimulate economic growth occurred in the early and mid-1820s. Completion of substantial buildings for commercial pursuits gave Main Street a more "businesslike appearance." Residents improved major streets with sidewalks and the planting of shade trees. A second local bank opened and a second weekly newspaper began publication. Some of the modest manufacturing enterprises went beyond an emphasis on textiles and started to produce light machinery.[2]

When the possibility of becoming a college town appeared in 1823, citizens pursued this opportunity with vigor. Moving in the wake of Congregational disestablishment achieved through Connecticut's Constitution of 1818, Episcopalians were about to break Yale's exclusive hold on higher education in the state. A group of Episcopal ministers and laymen in Connecticut, led by Bishop Thomas Church Brownell and joined by several members of other denominations, obtained a charter for Washington (later Trinity) College in May 1823. The charter authorized trustees of the new institution to locate it in "such town in this State, as they shall judge most expedient." In the bidding competition that followed, a committee of twenty-three prominent citizens organized Middletown's efforts. A letter to the *American Sentinel* in August 1823 summarized what was at stake:

> It is believed that no opportunity equally favourable with that presented by the location of the College in our City, to promote its prosperity, is soon to be expected. . . . The extension of our markets by increasing the demand for our agricultural productions; the employment of laborours and mechanics; the increase of mercantile business; the education of our children at home, and at a comparatively trifling expense; and the improvement of the state of society, by the residence among us of the men of talents and

learning connected with the College; are advantages too obvious to require illustration, and too important to be regarded with indifference.

Similar economic arguments made in a New Haven newspaper, where "Yale College now scatters annually about $150,000," were reprinted by the *Middlesex Gazette* for the edification of Middletown readers. A special town meeting in March 1824 approved $20,000 worth of proceeds from the town quarries in Chatham (now Portland) as an offer to Washington's trustees in return for location of the college in Middletown. An additional $18,000 in subscriptions raised that spring enabled Middletown to outbid Hartford by $4,000 and to offer almost double New Haven's bid. Middletown's offer also included almost fourteen acres of land for the campus. The Hartford-oriented bishop and trustees, however, voted on 6 May 1824 to take the second-ranking proposal.[3]

Middletown quickly rebounded from this reversal into the arms of a masterful promoter, Captain Alden Partridge. Partridge was looking for a better location to expand his American Literary, Scientific, and Military Academy, opened in 1820 in Norwich, Vermont. A man of enormous energy and will who loved military dress and drill, Partridge served from 1815 to 1817 as superintendent of the United States Military Academy at West Point. After several episodes characterized by questionable ethical judgment, arbitrary action, and general flamboyance (including the arrest of his faculty for plotting against him and his own arrest for disobeying orders originating from President James Monroe), Partridge was court-martialed, convicted of insubordination, and forced to resign from the army in 1818. He recovered from this setback at age thirty-two by launching a career as educator of citizens who, in a nation lacking a large standing army, would be prepared to serve in times of crisis as soldiers and military leaders. Less than a week after the loss of Washington College to Hartford, a Middletown newspaper advocated use of the college subscription to make Partridge (who was also being recruited to teach mathematics and engineering at Washington College) "a handsome offer."[4]

News of Partridge's academy in Vermont began to appear in the Middletown papers. In terms similar to those employed a year earlier for the effort to obtain Washington College, direct appeals by local promoters of relocation argued:

Whether we view an Institution of this kind in reference to its literary or pecuniary advantages, it is certainly an object of far greater importance than anything that has ever yet, or probably ever will be presented for our acceptance. The mechanic will find constant employ, the merchant an increased demand for his goods, and the farmer a constant and ready market for his produce. This School, on a fair calculation, will bring into our town at least $50,000 annually, which will add so much to our general stock of wealth.

By July the local press reported that some "respectable inhabitants" were "exerting themselves to raise sufficient funds to locate this institution in the city of Middletown."[5]

The group raising subscriptions and negotiating with Partridge in July and August 1824 included many of those who had worked to obtain Washington College. At a town meeting on 2 August 1824, assembled citizens appointed the leading promoters as a committee to purchase land and erect buildings for the academy. The committee received authorization to use Middletown's rights to brownstone from the Chatham quarries for the purpose of obtaining building materials. Stones not used in construction of the academy facilities could be sold to defray quarrying, transportation, and construction costs. Total value of stone and proceeds from sale of stone was not to exceed $10,000.[6]

Intensive efforts to raise an additional $22,500, finish negotiations with Partridge, and purchase land for the campus were completed in little more than a month. Partridge gave a well-received lecture on his "system of instruction" to a large audience. Shares sold at $30 each entitled the shareholder to an interest in the academy property in the proportion that the amount paid bore to $32,500. On 6 September 1824 committee members used some of the proceeds to purchase almost twelve acres of prime land from Nehemiah Hubbard for $3,000. With full Masonic pomp and political oratory, the town celebrated on 20 October 1824 the placing of a cornerstone for the first of two buildings to be constructed for Partridge's academy.[7]

Much to Middletown's delight, the academy quickly established itself as a prosperous local enterprise. Stockholders gained a charter from the Connecticut General Assembly in May 1825. The charter incorporated this group as "proprietors" of the academy and authorized them to select trustees. The committee of promoters transferred title for the land and buildings to this new corporation. Partridge moved his five-year-old enterprise from Vermont during the summer, and the academy officially opened in Middletown in September. The first catalogue listed almost three hundred students, drawn from nineteen states and studying a range of subjects extending from languages to engineering and from bookkeeping to dancing. The youngest students were ten years of age; the oldest were in their early twenties.[8]

Partridge was an entrepreneur with a sharp eye for publicity opportunities. Through public lectures and student exhibitions he kept his enterprise before the attentive eyes of Middletown citizens. He invited a distinguished Harvard scholar, George Ticknor, to serve at the public examination of students in the summer of 1826. Ticknor declined. The captain advertised his system of instruction throughout the Northeast and beyond when he regularly marched large groups of cadets on excursions to New Haven, New York, Boston, Washington, D.C. (mostly via steamboat and stage), and Niagara Falls.[9] Partridge's students were a veritable moving billboard.

Although enrollments at the academy continued at a high level for the first two years, financial problems began to appear by the spring of 1826. Virtually all readily available local resources had been exhausted in providing land and the original buildings. A bold attempt to gain federal funds had failed. Pressing needs for a library, scientific apparatus, and endowment funds led academy trustees to petition the Connecticut General Assembly in May 1826 for permission to conduct a lottery that would raise $40,000. The legislature deferred action. When resubmitted a year later, along with an ambitious request for authority to grant degrees, the petition met a similar fate. Continued consideration of these requests ended in the spring of 1828, when discouraged academy trustees withdrew their petition. Forced back on its own resources, Middletown attempted a local subscription drive for funds to purchase educational equipment. The academy, however, was beginning to lose some of its early luster. Partridge was often away, especially in the South, promoting satellite academies based on his ideas for military education. During his absences discipline declined. A visit in July 1827 from the sharp-tongued Anne Royall, a writer of travel books, resulted in a scathing description of the academy in her *Black Book* (Washington 1828). She found the academy filled with undisciplined "ruffians" living "knee-deep in dirt." Partridge she dismissed as "one of the most consummate clowns that ever undertook to keep a school." Shortly before Royall's visit, the peripatetic Partridge reopened his previous facility in Norwich, ostensibly as a "primary school" to prepare students for the institution in Middletown.[10] The academy stockholders had good reason to become nervous.

Trustees of the academy announced a reorganization in June 1828, placing governance in the hands of the faculty. They named a faculty member as superintendent, promised to make monthly visitations, and left Partridge with undefined "general supervision." That summer the students dissolved their literary society and made provisions for disposal of its library. Enrollment dropped sharply in the fall, and Partridge left for Washington. He would soon return to Vermont, where his academy would in 1834 become Norwich University.[11] By late fall of 1828 it was apparent that the academy's days in Middletown were numbered.

Despite the ill-fated effort in 1824 to acquire Washington College and the more recent problems with a volatile Captain Partridge, Middletown in late 1828 remained a resilient, enterprising city of almost seven thousand residents. The Connecticut branch of the Bank of the United States, established in Middletown in 1817, had been lost to Hartford in 1824. But the Middletown Savings Bank, founded in 1825, reported a sound fiscal condition. Planning started for a new county courthouse (completed in 1832). Almost-daily steamboat service made Middletown readily accessible for commerce with Hartford, New York, and Boston. Eleven small factories employed nearly four hundred people. Across from the academy grounds on High Street, Heth Camp opened his Palestine Garden in late August. For twelve and one-half cents admission one could stroll through gardens of plants brought from the Holy Land and enjoy refreshments. A few blocks north, work began in the closing weeks of the year on a magnificent Greek Revival home for the China merchant, Samuel Russell. Down the hill near Main Street, Methodists held Christmas services in their new church adorned with an imposing Greek facade.[12] The academy buildings would soon be vacant, but not for long.

Denominational Development

Methodism grew rapidly in early decades of the nineteenth century. During the 1820s the denomination's membership surpassed that of its nearest rival, the Baptists. By the 1840s Methodist membership easily exceeded the combined total for Presbyterian, Congregational, Episcopal, Lutheran, and Reformed churches. This growth occurred by means of centralized church organization directing the evangelical efforts of itinerant ministers. Weekly local meetings of small groups known as classes sustained a strong discipline and piety between ministerial visits. Even the laymen conducting these meetings received their appointments from the church hierarchy.[13]

Education to promote evangelical ends received renewed attention within the dynamic Methodist bureaucracy of the 1820s. Few Methodist ministers had much formal schooling. But they could see a broad range of Americans placing increased value on education. They could also anticipate that members of the denomination would soon seek schools where their children might advance in educational status and social standing. The General Conference of 1820 urged the establishment of literary institutions within the territory of each annual conference. Bishops obtained the authority to create new roles for Methodist clergy by assigning preachers to serve as teachers and educational administrators in schools and colleges. Such alternatives to long-term service in a settled pastorate appeared throughout American Protestantism during the first few decades of the nineteenth century. Achievement and esteem became available to the ordained in such areas as missions, the religious press, and a host of other denominational agencies. For the few well-educated Methodist ministers such as John P. Durbin, Stephen Olin, and Willbur Fisk, education became a desirable calling, especially when health deficiencies precluded a career of arduous circuit riding.[14]

In 1828 the quadrennial national meeting of Methodist leaders assembled in Pittsburgh heard a report from Willbur Fisk, chairman of its committee on education. An 1815 graduate of Brown University, Fisk had briefly studied law and served as a private tutor before being licensed as a Methodist preacher in 1818. After various assignments in Vermont and Massachusetts, Fisk began in 1825 his highly successful principalship of Wesleyan Academy, Wilbraham, Massachusetts. This thoughtful, articulate man in his middle thirties was well prepared to lead his denomination in addressing issues of educational policy and priorities. His report surveyed recent progress in founding Methodist academies and colleges and urged new efforts. Noting that "revivals of religion have been so frequent in our literary seminaries," Fisk asked: "If God smiles on our undertakings, shall we not proceed?" He found "the minds of both ministers and people are more awake" to the subject of education than ever before. As Fisk accurately sensed, his denomination was inclined to heed his counsel against establishing a national Methodist university. The Methodists in 1828 were poised to embark on a decade of local collegiate activity that would yield a dozen institutions affiliated with their denomination.[15]

In a much broader context, 1828 marked the beginning of "the Methodist age" in American religious life. From this year to the eve of World War I, Methodist religious enthusiasm, belief in the importance of human agency and will, and romantic faith in individual and social perfection permeated the leading Protestant denominations and the larger culture. Important shifts in American political life, symbolized by Andrew Jackson's election in 1828, were a part of the same new patterns in the cultural and social fabric of the young nation.[16] A time of accelerating economic, political, and evangelistic enterprise supplied much common ground on which Middletown and the Methodists could meet.

Forging an Alliance

Laban Clark, matchmaker between local academy trustees and the Methodist denomination, came to Middletown in 1828. At age fifty, this seasoned circuit rider in New England, Canada, and New York was a staunch Jacksonian Democrat entering an area where Old Hickory's election that fall would not be well received. Clark's administrative duties as presiding elder of the New Haven district kept him in close touch with Middletown during the next three years. He demonstrated a sharp eye for building relationships with enterprising local leaders, despite their political preferences, and soon made Middletown his home for the remainder of a ministerial career and then a retirement extending into his ninety-first year.[17] Later venerated as patriarch of the New York East Conference (formed in 1849 from sections of the New York Conference, including western Connecticut) and honored as president of Wesleyan's trustees from 1831 to 1868, Clark arrived at a particularly opportune time.

Heman Bangs, the thirty-eight-year-old Methodist preacher in Middletown, and his congregation were in the midst of constructing their new brick church. When assigned to this pastorate in 1827, the tall, plain, and blunt Bangs found Middletown's Methodists to be "dull and lukewarm," lacking a parsonage, and meeting in a dangerously deteriorated facility. A season of revivals soon increased membership, and Bangs's energetic leadership stimulated a decision in January 1828 to proceed with replacement of the old building. Despite the reluctance of local banks to assist in funding and the lack of credit with Middletown's "men of money," Bangs and his congregation completed construction in time for a dedication service on New Year's Day 1829. In the process, Bangs earned local respect for Methodist enterprise and established friendly relations with local leaders.[18]

Willbur Fisk preached the dedication sermon. A highly successful revival under his guiding hand at Wesleyan Academy in the early spring of 1828 had brought enrollment and his principalship to a high-water mark. The reputation of this young preacher-educator from Massachusetts, Clark recalled many years later, "drew the attention of the citizens and the house was filled to overflowing." Fisk spoke with the "peculiarly flexible and sonorous" voice of "a charming singer," using a variety of tones to provide vivid expression for "moral emotions." His "eloquence threw a charm upon the whole population of the city and awakened new views of Methodism and its capabilities."[19]

The local leaders who soon began to see the Methodists as potential tenants for Middletown's almost vacant academy facilities were men of considerable personal resources and strong civic-mindedness. Samuel D. Hubbard and William L. Storrs, for example, were sons of merchants successful in the West Indies trade of the late eighteenth century. Through inheritance or their own success as lawyers, merchants, manufacturers, and investors in local and western lands, trustees of the academy and like-minded supporters had the means to help establish a college. Their lives also reflected a broad range of public interests and an educational perspective transcending denominational boundaries. Several, such as Elijah Hubbard and George W. Stanley, led efforts to attract Washington College and then Partridge's academy as well as the campaign to establish Wesleyan University in Middletown. In the 1840s Samuel Hubbard worked to bring rail service to Middletown. Four of these prominent citizens held important political offices at the local, state, or national level. Both Hubbards had terms as mayor of Middletown, Stanley was state's attorney for Middlesex County, Storrs was a chief justice in Connecticut, and Samuel Hubbard served as United States congressman and briefly as postmaster general. Non-Methodists among these local promoters constituted a third of Wesleyan's twenty-one original trustees. Four held membership in First Church of Christ (Congregational) and three in Church of the Holy Trinity (Episcopal). Henry L. DeKoven's son attended Wesleyan in the 1830s and became an Episcopal clergyman; Jonathan Barnes's son graduated in 1848 and entered the Congregational ministry. Six of the seven were graduates of Yale.[20]

Early in the spring of 1829, these local leaders initiated the process of founding a college in Middletown affiliated with the Methodist denomination. Partridge's enterprise was pursuing a rapid retreat to Vermont. Stockholders discussed what to do with their investment in land and buildings on High Street. In one of the discussions someone suggested that the Methodists be engaged to found a college, perhaps by offering these enterprising evangelicals an opportunity to buy the property at less than half its value. An observer of this initiative noted that stockholders saw a distinct advantage in founding a college "under the patronage of the Methodists." Since such an institution would not be seen as a threat to the established markets for Yale and Washington among the Congregationalists and Episcopalians, there would probably be little legislative opposition to granting a charter. By early April a few Methodist leaders such as Laban Clark expressed interest.[21]

On behalf of the academy proprietors, Clark carried to the annual meeting of the New York Conference a proposal for sale of the facilities. Methodists responded with actions designed to gain control of the process. The conference, meeting in Troy that May, appointed a small delegation to consider establishing a college. They invited the New England Conference to do likewise. New England's delegation, appointed in June, included Willbur Fisk. He worked closely with Clark to coordinate work of the joint committee. This group soon established a competition "to get as many and as large bids as possible" for the location of a Methodist college. The deadline for submitting proposals to the committee was 2 December.[22]

Briefly an initiator, Middletown soon became a bidder. The academy trustees, after consultation with Clark, Fisk, and a few other Methodist leaders, offered the land and buildings on a contingency rather than a reduced-cost basis. These facilities, valued at more than $30,000, would be deeded for use by a college sponsored by the Methodist conferences if the Methodists first raised a significant endowment to provide for the institution's permanency.[23]

Middletown leaders worked during the summer and fall of 1829 to revise and augment the proposal. A more realistic assessment of what funds could be obtained within the denomination soon reduced by one-third the $100,000 originally required for endowment. Continuing concern among Methodists about their capacity to raise funds, and growing competition from other towns and cities preparing bids (especially Bridgeport and Troy), led to further reduction of the stipulated amount to $40,000. To help the Methodists meet the endowment requirement, academy trustees prepared a resolution for the town meeting of 16 October at which it was voted that the town subscribe to the purchase of four hundred shares of stock in "the Wesleyan College or University to be located in Middletown." The stock was to be purchased in five annual $2,000 installments. Individual subscriptions, such as one for $500 from Samuel Hubbard and another for $250 from the Episcopal minister, raised approximately $8,000 more from Middletown and vicinity.

Lyceum and Dormitory, built in
1824–25. This woodcut, a view of the
campus probably sketched in the summer
of 1835, is the best available for envision-
ing the buildings Middletown offered to
the Methodists in 1829. The Lyceum
(*left*) provided space for classrooms,
library, and chapel; the Dormitory
accommodated about one hundred
students.

Ready with an offer worth more than $50,000 in land, buildings, and
endowment subscriptions, Middletown leaders pressed the joint committee for a definite decision.[24]

On 3 December 1829 the committee made its choice in favor of Middletown. The explicitly contractual arrangement between Middletown
and the Methodists to be placed before the annual conference meetings
in the spring had specific terms. The conferences would sponsor a college to be opened in Middletown by 1 October 1831 with a minimum
endowment of $40,000 and a board of trustees having one-third of its
members selected by the academy trustees (the group representing Middletown residents incorporated in 1825 to hold property housing Partridge's school in Connecticut). Through commitments by the proprietors
of the academy, other individual residents, and the city, Middletown
would provide fifteen acres of land, two stone buildings with ancillary
structures, books, chemical apparatus, and approximately $18,000 in

subscriptions to purchase stock in this new enterprise. Townspeople had doubts that spring about Methodist capacity to raise their portion of the endowment, but the New York and New England conferences made their commitment of support by ratifying the agreement in May 1830. The newly constituted New Hampshire and Vermont Conference cast a similar vote in late June. On 13 May 1830 Elijah Hubbard, acting for the academy trustees, notified Partridge that he must clear out his military uniforms and other equipment to make way for the Methodists.[25]

Constructing an Institution of Broad Purpose
Organization of the new collegiate enterprise proceeded according to plans formulated by the joint committee and endorsed by the conferences. Published in the summer of 1830, these plans reflected important choices with regard to name, funding, and governance.[26]

Selection of a name occurred without any recorded discussion or debate. Reference to the prospect of founding "a Wesleyan University" appeared in the *Middlesex Gazette* in July 1829. Knowledge of Wesleyan Academy in Wilbraham may have led logically to employing this adjective for an institution of higher education patronized by Methodists. Additional rationale could derive from John Wesley, chief founder of Methodism in mid-eighteenth-century Britain, being a graduate of Christ Church College, Oxford University. Usage of the term *university* was more puzzling. Noah Webster's new *Dictionary* of 1828 defined a university as "an assemblage of colleges" or a "universal school" teaching "all branches of learning" through "the four faculties of theology, medicine, law, and the arts and sciences." This definition derived from British and European practice generally guided American institutions prior to Wesleyan's founding. Harvard College did not become Harvard University until 1780, adding a long-anticipated medical school the following year. Yale College delayed designation as Yale University until 1887, belatedly recognizing professional and graduate programs developed decades earlier. There were a few deviations, however, from standard usage. Without much justification until several years later, for example, Brown began designating itself a university in 1804. Knowledge of this case, plus vague aspirations for professional schools held by a few of Wesleyan's founders, may be the most important reasons why the boundaries of current terminology were so boldly exceeded in Middletown. With a final flourish long before that made in founding the Johns Hopkins University (1876), the name acquired the definite article and settled status by late 1829 as the Wesleyan University.[27] Many colleges in nineteenth-century America changed their name at least once. Despite periodic discussions of the matter over the next 150 years, the decision of Wesleyan's founders would be revised only by dropping "the" during charter revisions made in 1870.

Funding for the proposed college included plans for raising an endowment, the interest from which would supplement revenue produced by tuition and fees. Methods chosen for raising endowment funds at Wesleyan (and most other colleges of the day), however, actually diminished tuition income. A purchaser of stock in Wesleyan (initially at $25 per share and by 1833 at $100 per share) received for any students he or she sent to Wesleyan a tuition rate reduced by 10 percent of the amount thus contributed. With tuition at $36 per year, a $100 stock purchase cut tuition revenue from each such student by more than 25 percent. A minister contributing this amount acquired lifetime rights to send his own or any other minister's son tuition-free. Longer-term arrangements were even more generous. A full-tuition "scholarship in perpetuity" cost $500 and created a drain on tuition revenues that could continue for generations unnumbered. Even allowing for 6 percent interest on the funds contributed as endowment, the net tuition discount offered by these various incentives ranged from 11 to more than 80 percent. Such means to raise endowment yielded a very modest sum while contributing to future financial woes.[28]

To hold the endowment funds and other assets of the college and to supervise its operations, the founders set up a governance system chosen from two available models. Although they differed in structure, both models stood in the American tradition of colleges governed not by their faculties but by "representatives of the civil society that supported and protected them." Most widely used among such peer institutions as Amherst, Williams, Trinity, Middlebury, and Union was the single-board-of-trustees model established by Yale in 1701. A dual-board approach evolved at Harvard between 1636 and 1650. This structure also prevailed at William and Mary (1693), Brown (1764), and Bowdoin (1794). At Brown, in an arrangement well known to Willbur Fisk, the corporation consisted of two branches. The fellows had authority to confer degrees and took responsibility for supervising financial and educational operations on a daily basis. The trustees had more general oversight duties and met annually with the fellows. Wesleyan adopted a dual-board structure similar to that at Brown.[29]

Wesleyan's Joint Board of Trustees and Visitors (hereafter usually referred to as the joint board) originally consisted of twenty-one trustees (fourteen initially appointed by the patron conferences and seven by the academy trustees) and twenty-one visitors (elected annually by the patron conferences). The self-perpetuating trustees held and managed all college property. The visitors joined with the trustees to supervise all other operations of the college.[30] In the choice of a dual and therefore large board of governance, Wesleyan initiated a proclivity for large boards that would not be broken until 1959.

Election and convening of the joint board proceeded in the summer of 1830 with typical Methodist organizational skill. The elections conducted by the academy trustees and by the three patron conferences covering a six-state region were completed between mid-May and mid-July. All but one of the twenty-one trustees and twelve of the twenty-one visitors attended the first meeting of the board, held 24–26 August 1830 in the Lyceum, one of two buildings constructed for the academy. Subsequent attendance patterns confirmed this early indication that the trustees, more so than the annually elected and often changing visitors, would be the primary source of stability, continuity, and guidance for the young institution.[31]

Actions taken at the first meeting of the joint board clearly established a pattern of trustee leadership and an acknowledgment of the Middletown-Methodist alliance. George Stanley, a Middletown Congregationalist, served as secretary. The six trustees appointed to the prudential committee, a group entrusted with oversight of most affairs of the college during intervals between annual meetings of the joint board, included two more local Congregationalists, Samuel Hubbard and Isaac Webb. Recognition of the other two major constituencies occurred with the election of Laban Clark (New York Conference) as president of the board of trustees and the election of Willbur Fisk (New England Conference) as president of the college.[32]

Appointment of a committee to apply for a charter was the final major action taken at this first meeting. Five trustees, including Fisk, Clark, Stanley, and Henry DeKoven (a Middletown Episcopalian), plus one visitor, guided these efforts. They petitioned the General Assembly in May 1831 for incorporation of the joint board in order "to promote the general welfare" by establishing "a Collegiate Institution of the highest grade" that would "offer the means of a liberal education to youth." The petition cited evidence of substantial local and ecclesiastical support for the venture. Virtually without opposition, the bill of incorporation received favorable action from both houses. Governor John S. Peters gave final approval to the charter on 26 May 1831. (See appendix 1.) Wesleyan was ready to join the approximately three dozen private liberal arts colleges already granting bachelor's degrees and to become an early participant in the unprecedented wave of American college founding that began in the 1820s and crested in the 1850s.[33]

Just before this growth surge in higher education, the Dartmouth College case of 1819 signaled full recognition of colleges as corporations with legal status and beneficial private-enterprise roles in economic and cultural development of the young nation. Incorporated colleges obtained the same legal standing as entrepreneurial ventures establishing canals, turnpikes, and manufacturing companies. From 1830 to 1860 new colleges appeared at an average rate of five dozen per decade. Most were local enterprises affiliated with a religious denomination.[34]

Methodist-affiliated higher education at the time of Wesleyan's founding was in the early stages of a slow and shaky start. The three Methodist colleges operating in spring 1831 were less than a decade old; none survived beyond the Civil War. Madison College in western Pennsylvania closed a year after Wesleyan opened. The demise of Augusta College (Kentucky) occurred in the late 1840s, and that of LaGrange College (Alabama) in the late 1850s. Colleges starting with or acquiring Methodist sponsorship after 1830, however, rarely failed. Almost three dozen were in operation by 1860.[35]

Local colleges with denominational affiliations worked hard in the 1830s to avoid the stigma of sectarianism. Charters often included stipulations similar to those found in Wesleyan's: "the religious tenets of any person" must not be made "a condition of admission to any privilege in said university" and there must be no "religious test" employed in the appointment of the president, faculty, or other officers. Curricula rarely included courses in theology or other subjects that might suggest sectarian indoctrination. Trustees often named colleges for the towns that successfully bid for them. Use of a person's name was occasionally the politic choice. As part of an effort to forestall opposition to their charter petition before the Virginia legislature, Methodist founders of Randolph-Macon (chartered in 1830 and opened in 1832) chose a name honoring two prominent political figures, one of whom was a nominal Baptist and the other an adherent of Muhammadanism who later turned to high-church Anglicanism.[36]

Often reflected in charters, curricula, and names, the predominantly public rather than sectarian purpose of antebellum colleges regularly found expression in speeches that linked these local enterprises with the

Willbur Fisk, Wesleyan's first president, 1831–39.

time-honored tradition of liberal learning. This was an era of great respect for the power of oratory. Ties between elevated educational aims and local enterprise appeared most dramatically in the spoken and subsequently published inaugural addresses delivered by college presidents.

Connecting with a Tradition

Willbur Fisk's task on 21 September 1831 was to unite the entrepreneurial achievement of Middletown and Methodists with the tradition of liberal learning that similar local and denominational forces helped to disseminate across a vast, rapidly developing young nation. In effecting this union he had to address important sensitivities among an audience that included relatively uneducated Methodist church leaders and Yale-educated Middletown trustees. He also had complex choices to make between contemporary versions of the liberal education tradition expressed recently and nearby with great vigor in the Yale *Reports* of 1828 and in the new curriculum introduced by Eliphalet Nott at Union College that same year.

"The spirit of reform is abroad, and is reconnoitering the whole field" of education, Fisk told the "numerous and respectable" audience gathered to hear his inaugural address. This reference reminded his more knowledgeable listeners about the ideas advocated by a handful of reformers publicly promoting curricular revision at several American colleges and universities in the 1820s. Reformers challenged the predominance of required classical studies in the undergraduate curriculum. They introduced new curricular pathways to the bachelor's degree, providing options for students to select nonclassical subjects for study in depth. Such reorganizations of the curriculum were briefly attempted at the University of Virginia and Harvard in 1825, and at the University of Vermont and Amherst two years later. A wide-ranging discussion of reform ideas in higher education occurred at a meeting of "literary and scientific gentlemen" convened in New York City in 1830 to help with planning for the institution that would become New York University. All these efforts produced publications. It is particularly clear that Fisk was conversant with ideas emanating from the last-mentioned gathering, to which he was invited but was unable to attend.[37]

By far the most successful reformer in instituting and sustaining curricular alternatives to the traditional required studies for the bachelor of arts degree was Eliphalet Nott of Union College. As president from 1804 to 1866 of a college that in the late 1820s was one of the three largest in the country, Nott was a force to be reckoned with in antebellum higher education. His oration before Union's Phi Beta Kappa society in 1824 advanced a "cheering hypothesis" concerning science. The word *science* at this time often referred to any organized body of knowledge and principles; Nott's address particularly referred to new discoveries and ideas in "physical science" and "political science." Science, in the sweeping vision of Nott, served as the "handmaid of religion." Recent rapid gains in scientific knowledge had immense potential "to increase human knowledge and perfect human virtue" throughout the world. By the mid-1820s Nott had greatly augmented the resources for teaching natural science at Union. In 1828 he introduced a separate science curriculum with no classical studies beyond the first year. Where other colleges offered a less-esteemed bachelor of science degree for such studies, Union took the revolutionary step of awarding the traditional bachelor of arts degree. Willbur Fisk passed through Schenectady, New York, on his way to the General Conference of 1828. Although he did not stop to meet Nott, Fisk almost certainly had encountered his ideas and reputation by 1831.[38]

Through education, "the youthful mind is disciplined," Fisk told his entering students, recently recruited faculty, and others gathered in the new Methodist church near Main Street to hear his inaugural address. Fisk was a strong supporter of mental discipline. His address at the opening of Wesleyan Academy in 1825 clearly endorsed exercise of the reasoning faculties through "intellectual labour and close thinking." Mental discipline achieved through rigorous exercise of the mental faculties was broadly accepted as an indispensable goal of antebellum education.[39] But the means to achieve this goal were a subject of intense debate.

The single most influential document in the literature of nineteenth-century education, a defense of mental discipline achieved primarily through study of mathematics and the classical languages and literature, appeared less than three years before Fisk prepared his address and less than thirty miles to the south of Middletown. Responding to a suggestion that Yale consider deleting "study of the dead languages" from the required course of study, Yale's trustees asked the faculty for a report on this issue. This two-part report and that of a trustee committee were published in late 1828 as *Reports on the Course of Instruction in Yale College.* Benjamin Silliman reprinted the document for even broader distribution in the January 1829 issue of the *American Journal of Science and Arts.* The *Reports* presented a carefully constructed treatise on mental discipline as "the foundation for a superior education," the best route to "professional distinction," and the means for exerting "a commanding influence in society." More important, the authors identified study of classics and mathematics to be the most effective and thus highly "practical" and essential part of a liberal education.[40]

Yale spoke with the authority of tradition and success. Nott and other reformers beckoned with an alternate view combining immediate practicality and a dazzling view of the future. Fisk had choices to make. Middletown's most venerable newspaper had found the Yale *Reports* to be "equally luminous, eloquent, and profound." Almost a third of the trustees were Yale graduates. Even the campus plan was patterned after the row-of-buildings configuration instituted at Yale in the late eighteenth century. Methodists, on the other hand, were not oriented to the professional-success message from Yale, were especially suspicious of formal professional training of ministers, and were inclined to short-term rather than long-term pragmatism in pursuit of evangelical ends. They had spoken in 1830 of instituting short courses at Wesleyan as alternatives to the traditional classical course, perhaps even using them for instruction in agriculture and in the "mechanical and useful arts." Fisk was probably the only minister in the New England Conference with a college degree.[41] What tone and direction would he select for the infant college?

Arriving on campus 18 December 1830, Fisk had ten months to make arrangements for opening the college. He spent much time raising funds, recruiting faculty, and preparing the facilities. By August, however, he clearly articulated the primary link he would establish between this nascent local enterprise and Western civilization's tradition of liberal learning. "I have done educating youths for *themselves*," he wrote to a former educational colleague, "my . . . object . . . will be hereinafter to educate all I can get *for the world*."[42]

Emphasis on social responsibility and on careers oriented to civic service, an enduring characteristic of Wesleyan, began on the college's first day of operation. This distinguishing element in the oratorical approach to liberal education as traced by Bruce A. Kimball had roots in the teachings of Isocrates; received extensive development by Cicero and other Romans; traversed the Middle Ages, Renaissance, and Reformation in the writings of Augustine, Erasmus, and Luther; appeared in gentlemanly garb at the British universities during the sixteenth century; and migrated to their American offspring in the colonies. A concern for values and for active, virtuous citizenship was quite muted, however, in the Yale *Reports* and writings of reformers in the 1820s. Although sharing the respect for mental discipline, individual development, and scholarly discovery found in these contemporary documents, Fisk argued that "nothing is more important than the spirit of benevolence." The philosopher portion of the liberal arts tradition—a strand of thought Kimball associates with the self-sufficient, endless search for truth and the dialectical pursuit of knowledge found in Plato, Socrates, Enlightenment thinkers, and modern experimental scientists—would clearly be subservient to that of the orator. Wesleyan would stand with the orator, placing primary emphasis on noble virtue, commitment, and action to make a difference in the world.[43]

Fisk presented his carefully chosen connection to the tradition of liberal learning with the force of logic and example. Observers of Fisk as a speaker and preacher portrayed him as "a lucid, cogent reasoner, a chaste, elegant speaker, . . . and an affable, interesting man." Even when stimulating a revival meeting with "a clear and forcible argument," his "manner was calm, his voice not loud, his gestures few." The case Fisk made in his inaugural address for education to effect "the final renovation of our world" reflected in its explicitly connected chain of thoughts a manner of exposition probably gained through his legal studies. Additional persuasive power came from personal example. Fisk was deeply involved in social reforms, particularly in the temperance and antislavery movements.[44] His career was a powerful illustration of the benevolence he advocated.

In order to "supply . . . men who will be both willing and competent to effect the political, intellectual, and spiritual regeneration of the world," Fisk envisioned a college of great energy and enterprise. The student was to be "enterprising," "vigorous in his constitution," and a person of "self-dependence." He would be prepared for "passing from one employment to another." Faculty should be "energetic and enterprising in their character," accountable for the quality of their teaching, and responsive to salary incentives that stimulated them "to make extra exertions for the world." Fisk espoused an academic Arminianism fully in harmony with his Methodist Arminianism, assigning great importance to the role of human responsibility, will, and effort.[45]

While advocating benevolence fueled by enterprise and equipped by liberal education, Fisk reasoned his way to several consistent but controversial positions on curriculum, classification of students, and degrees. His deviance from the doctrines of the Yale *Reports* was most striking. Mental discipline, he argued, must be achieved in a manner that educated men most effectively "for the good of the world." Since "the mind is suitably disciplined by being exercised in those studies that are most essential to our happiness and usefulness," classical languages should be de-emphasized or removed in order to assign primary importance to "modern literature, the natural and exact sciences, and application of the sciences to the useful arts."[46]

By basing his more controversial ideas on such appealing general principles, however, Fisk probably evoked little discomfort or discontent in an audience that listened "with great attention and deep interest." His experience as principal and fund-raiser in Wilbraham had sharpened skills of appealing to "a benevolent public." Middletown patrons could find in Fisk's views reassuring support for the position stated within the denomination earlier that year: Wesleyan University was not designed in any way to "inculcate Methodism." And what a welcome change for the town in moving from the flamboyant and volatile promoter they had experienced in Captain Partridge to the thoughtful and refined preacher now speaking to them with "candor . . . and good sense." The Methodists of New York and New England, in turn, could feel favored by a denominational leader of national repute who had recently declined other offers of top positions within the church and higher education. In the thirty-nine-year-old Fisk, they had a beloved colleague who was "at once devout and scholarly."[47]

Fisk's inaugural address appeared in the *Methodist Magazine*, and the Methodist press published excerpts. The trustees ordered three thousand copies printed for distribution.[48] Under the banner of benevolent enterprise so integral to the spirit of Jacksonian America, Willbur Fisk skillfully launched the Wesleyan University.

2 An Earnest Education

*V*alues defined in the oratory, writings, and lives of the first five presidents shaped much of Wesleyan's early identity. In an age when Americans paid close attention to oratory as high art and exciting entertainment, college presidents had an unusual opportunity to set the tone for an institution. The campus community at Wesleyan rarely exceeded 150 students and faculty in any year from 1831 to 1870. Presidents usually taught a few classes and administered discipline. They were a powerful presence on a daily basis. Using their substantial influence both on campus and off, they portrayed Wesleyan as an evangelical Protestant college committed to liberal arts education. Rigorous intellectual training in Wesleyan's family-like setting, they argued, would prepare enterprising students to become contributors to the commonweal, particularly through careers as clergymen and educators.

Consistent with these aims, an evangelical faculty began building a professional identity. They included scholarship in the emerging career of college teaching. They sustained traditions of liberal learning, especially through use of the recitation method to foster intellectual development. They expected strengthened intellect would serve evangelical ends. The educational experience faculty designed and supported had broad boundaries, extending from the required sequence of courses in classical and mathematical studies to the literary societies, student publications, and oratorical exhibitions. A large majority of their students entered this focused educational program from humble backgrounds, earnestly en-

gaged the range of educational resources, found time for pleasant diversions despite an intensive work schedule, and emerged as graduates holding an unusually high level of religious belief and commitment to careers of service.

Fundamental Values

Willbur Fisk defined Wesleyan's educational enterprise within the context of evangelical Protestantism. He saw the greatly expanded religious enterprises of the Christian church as a "striking feature . . . of the present age." Using worldwide opportunities provided by connecting links of commerce, travel, friendship, and literature, the kingdom of Christ was "gaining strength, and enlarging its operations." Education was "second only to Christianity itself in carrying on this work." Drawing "youths of the greatest promise for extensive usefulness . . . from a Protestant community," Wesleyan had a role to play in the Christianizing of America and the world.[1]

In working to achieve this goal, Wesleyan would be neither sectarian nor secular but eminently serviceable "in reference to the public good." Fisk's college would stress not the particularity of a denomination but rather the partnership of Methodism in advancing a Protestant culture. Like other Protestant leaders of his time, Fisk worked to attain "an orderly, well-mannered, and moral society based on a broadly Christian system of values and code of behavior." Neither the partnership nor the definition of Christian included Catholics,[2] but entrepreneurs of all religious persuasions could easily view the stable society to be shaped by evangelism as an asset to the free-enterprise economy.

The depth of Fisk's piety gave a special force to his definition of collegiate mission. His conversion experience in 1817 was one of profound emotion and enduring effect. From that point on he was particularly admired for the deep vein of evangelical piety that ran through all his performances. A student recalled his face as "a perpetual benediction." The logical locutions of his inaugural concluded with a succinct expression of the sentiment driving his thoughts: "We burn with the inexpressible desire to contribute something toward changing the current of this world's fashions and maxims, toward purifying its spirit, and elevating its moral and intellectual character."[3]

Liberal education at Wesleyan during Fisk's presidency served his desire to produce "faithful, intelligent, enterprising, benevolent men . . . trained up, and sent forth to be leaders in the great enterprises of the day." Regulations governing chapel attendance served this purpose by requiring a student in the mid-1830s to attend daily morning and evening prayers. On Sunday he also had to attend a late-morning chapel service and an afternoon service at a church of his choice in Middletown. For the most pious pupils, a variety of regular voluntary gatherings such as meetings of the Missionary Lyceum supplemented this schedule. Revivals embraced both town and campus in 1834 and 1837. The most notable religious element in the curriculum was Fisk's teaching as professor of moral science and belles lettres. His courses for juniors and seniors in evidences of Christianity and in moral philosophy applied Christian beliefs to a wide range of ethical and political issues.[4]

Fisk's choice of textbooks for moral science underscored his definition of a broadly Protestant college. Like so many other presidents of antebellum colleges, he first employed the work of William Paley, an Anglican archdeacon who provided a nonsectarian approach to the gospels. When it appeared in 1835, the text by Francis Wayland, a Baptist and president of Brown, replaced that of Paley. Wayland described himself as a moderate Calvinist but stressed a "consistent piety" rather than theological distinctions.[5] At the time of Fisk's death in early 1839, Wesleyan was a college committed to serving the goals of an evangelical era.

During the next two years, while Augustus William Smith served as acting president, the joint board elected and courted Stephen Olin as Fisk's successor. Olin accepted election on condition that his health would be sufficient to the task. After extensive travel in Europe and the Middle East failed to ameliorate the pulmonary disorders persisting throughout his career (as they did with Fisk), he decided in early January 1841 that he was unable to assume the presidency. A few weeks later the board elected Nathan Bangs. With the opening of the winter term in mid-February 1841, he began the task of perpetuating "the holy and vigorous impulse" given to the young college by its first president.[6]

At age sixty-two Bangs had a wealth of evangelical experience. His career included service as missionary in Canada, book agent, and editor of Methodist publications. When elected to Wesleyan's presidency, this self-educated native of Connecticut was corresponding secretary of the denomination's missionary society. A leading figure in the New York Conference, he knew Wesleyan from its inception and chaired the joint board from 1833 to 1841. Among his several books on Methodist doctrine and church practice, the four-volume *History of the Methodist Episcopal Church* went to press just before he assumed presidential duties. Tall, tireless, and forceful to the point of being blunt, Bangs was a seasoned defender of the Methodist denomination. He occasionally placed Wesleyan in the larger context of evangelical efforts by those "cultivating the American vineyard, . . . planting and nurturing trees of righteousness for the glory of God and our country's welfare." Yet his primary focus, much more so than that of Fisk, was upon Wesleyan's identity as a college specifically serving the Methodist church.[7]

Where Fisk's inaugural explored a wide expanse of educational ideas, Bangs presented a discourse on why the Bible should be introduced as a regular subject of study at the college level, particularly at Wesleyan. The Bible, he argued, contained a wealth of knowledge and truth "in our own tongue." Thus it was eminently suited for initiating students "into the knowledge of any and all the branches of useful and ornamental literature, without borrowing a single feather from heathenism to decorate their brow." Bangs also advocated introducing preprofessional studies at Wesleyan for ministers, doctors, lawyers, and teachers. As his presidency began, the joint board established three new professorships: Biblical literature, law, and pedagogy. According to Bangs, Wesleyan "should be made what its name implies—a university."[8]

The Bangs presidency, like the new professorships, was short-lived. Bangs stood in the shadow of Olin's reputation. As Olin's health improved in 1842, students began to feel he had a superior claim on the presidency. They found that Bangs, who lacked a college degree, was somewhat deficient in scholarly stature for the presidency of a college with high aspirations. A student described him as "destitute of a liberal and thorough education" and his appointment as "a painful necessity." There also was some feeling in the New England Conference that Wesleyan was too oriented toward the New York Conference; the Bangs presidency personified this imbalance. Bangs therefore came to be viewed as a president who gave Wesleyan an identity too parochial in its patronage and mission, lacking in educational prestige, and overly expansionist in its curricular development. Under heavy pressure from student dissatisfaction, Bangs resigned in August 1842. The joint board immediately turned to Olin.[9]

Stephen Olin was a towering force in the service of evangelical goals. His distinctive physique and strength of intellect were vividly recorded in the diary of John Quincy Adams when Olin preached before the House of Representatives on 5 January 1845. He was "a man upwards of six feet tall, framed for a ploughman or a wood cutter with an anxious, deeply thoughtful, not unpleasing countenance, sprawling limbs and great awkwardness of gesticulation. But he preaches without notes, with uninterrupted fluency, plain but very appropriate language, close argument, well-chosen and at times elegant elocution." Adams reported

Stephen Olin, Wesleyan's third president,
1842–51

that those in the crowded House chambers were "chained in attention for an hour and a quarter." Frequently away on fund-raising trips and often debilitated by illness, Olin did not teach regularly. But it is easy to understand, given Adam's description, why Olin's informal encounters with students and his occasional sermons and addresses made him "eternally influential" in the lives of many graduates. His baccalaureate exhortations enjoined students to become evangelically and thoroughly religious. "Write the name of Christ upon your banner," he urged the graduating class of 1848. For Olin, Wesleyan had an evangelical mission to serve church and country.[10]

Enlisted in this cause were the fullest powers of intellect. Unlike Bangs, Olin had all the expected credentials for a college presidency. Son of a Vermont judge, he briefly studied law before entering Middlebury College. After graduating with top honors in 1820 he taught at an academy in South Carolina, became a Methodist preacher, and then held an appointment for seven years as professor of ethics and belles lettres at Franklin College (later the University of Georgia). In 1834 he became the first president of Randolph-Macon College in Virginia. Health problems, which plagued his career from college days onward, ended his active service in this capacity after three years. Yet his reputation as a scholar among the Methodists grew steadily. His attempt to regain strength through travels in Europe and the Middle East from summer 1837 until the autumn of 1840 yielded his most substantial scholarly work, *Travels in Egypt, Arabia Petraea, and The Holy Land* (1843). Reelected to the Wesleyan presidency at the same meeting where Bangs resigned, the forty-five-year-old Olin brought to Wesleyan in September 1842 a widespread reputation for extraordinary mental powers and a firm belief that intellect, guided by religious principles, would prepare young men to be "agents and co-workers with Divine Providence in all His gracious and benevolent operations."[11]

Olin's evangelical exhortations had specific roots in his belief that Methodists must be more zealous and diligent in saving souls by spreading the Gospel at home and abroad. His more general support for cooperation among all Christian denominations found expression through his participation in the founding of the Evangelical Alliance (1846), an international association established in London. For Methodist and non-Methodist students alike, Olin's preaching carried the force of "luminous argumentation and . . . deep evangelic pathos." Listening to his sermons, which could extend for more than two hours, was "like standing under Niagara." A former faculty member recalled "his burning thoughts and glowing emotions pouring themselves forth in a mighty torrent, his gigantic form trembling and every nerve quivering." Among student listeners "hard hearts melted, eyes wept that were unused to tears, and many a young man vowed new allegiance to Christ." When Olin died of typhoid fever in August 1851, students expressed their veneration for him as a man of "liberal and intelligent piety."[12] Olin effectively sustained and strengthened the evangelical dimension of Wesleyan established by Willbur Fisk.

The search for Olin's successor occurred in a decade of American church history when denominations such as the Methodists were busy consolidating recent advances in the structure and status of their missionary and other enterprises. Cooperative evangelical emphases of earlier decades were somewhat muted by increasing religious diversity, theological debates among denominations, and organizational splits over the slavery issue.[13] The era of heroic evangelical leaders was passing. Wesleyan's joint board turned to candidates noted primarily for their scholarly credentials.

In October 1851 the joint board decided to offer Wesleyan's presidency to Rev. John McClintock, editor of the *Methodist Review*. This thirty-seven-year-old graduate of the University of Pennsylvania had served for twelve years as a professor at Dickinson College. His widely used textbooks in Greek and Latin signaled the highly productive scholarly career that would follow. His standards for the *Review* clearly exceeded those suggested by his good friend and correspondent Stephen Olin. McClintock declined, however, on grounds that his health would be inadequate for performance of presidential duties.[14]

Turning to another scholar, one who had demonstrated administrative abilities while serving as acting president a decade earlier, the board at its annual meeting in August 1852 elected Augustus Smith. One of Fisk's original appointments, Smith was the senior member of the faculty. His impressive textbook, *An Elementary Treatise on Mechanics* (1849), would be republished seven times during a span of more than three decades. Smith immediately accepted the appointment.[15]

Smith was, at age fifty, a man of slight and infirm physique known for his urbane and scholarly ways. He and his wife received high praise for their warm and refined style as hosts to students, faculty, trustees, and townspeople. Above all else, Smith achieved respect as a precise scholar. A graduate of Hamilton College with highest honors in 1825, Smith had more than a quarter-century of teaching experience. In addition to his achievement as an author, he was an educator who read far beyond his fields of mathematics and astronomy and was a teacher enthusiastically praised by alumni.[16]

But Smith was a layman, poorly equipped to sustain the evangelical tone set for Wesleyan by his predecessors. Unable to use the pulpit, he also lacked talent as a platform speaker. He did not even attempt an inaugural address. At a time when his counterparts at Yale, Trinity, Amherst, Williams, and Middlebury were ordained, Smith found his appointment described as "an experiment." His slim margin of victory over Rev. Joseph Cummings presaged the short-term nature of this departure from the ministerial norm that persisted at Williams until 1872, Middlebury until 1885, Amherst until 1890, Yale until 1899, and well into the twentieth century at Brown, Dartmouth, and Trinity.[17]

Smith worked in his quiet way to encourage evangelical activities, suggesting to the committee on education of the General Conference in 1852 that "the prayers of the whole evangelical church be enlisted simultaneously in behalf of the unconverted in our colleges." He cited evidence in 1854 of a high level of piety among students at Wesleyan. His own piety was unquestioned. Yet he was unable to emerge from the long shadows cast by Fisk and Olin. He rarely wrote for or achieved mention in the Methodist press. A correspondent quoting Smith's views in the *Christian Advocate* during the fifth year of his appointment showed no awareness that he was the president of Wesleyan. With influential faculty opposition and with students expressing the opinion that Wesleyan was "asleep" and needed a president who by his energy and talents would "command the support and confidence of the world" beyond the campus, Smith submitted a forced resignation in August 1857. His success in obtaining endowment funds and setting high academic standards earned recognition for bringing Wesleyan "a kind of solid and uniform prosperity." His devoted efforts on behalf of Wesleyan were deemed insufficient, however, in bringing "an increase of influence and strength commensurate with the growth of the country and with the expectations of its founders."[18]

Joseph Cummings '40, elected president on the same day the joint board accepted Smith's resignation, brought to the position a capacity for vigorous evangelical as well as educational and administrative leadership. He was Wesleyan's first alumnus to serve as president, and he had studied under the influence of Fisk. Son of a Methodist minister, Cummings occupied pulpits of important churches in Boston and nearby towns for seven years. Before that period he gained experience as a teacher and principal at Amenia Seminary, a strong academy of the

New York Conference located near the border of northwestern Connecticut. When selected by Wesleyan's board, Cummings had completed three years as president of Genesee College, near Rochester. He finished his work there and arrived at Wesleyan in March 1858.[19]

Students enthusiastically greeting their new forty-one-year-old president encountered a formidable figure. Cummings was "a man of magnificent proportions—tall, erect, and massive." He was the first Wesleyan president to enjoy excellent health. His "incessant industry" drew upon an extraordinary level of energy. He taught freshman composition as well as senior moral philosophy, supervised the construction of buildings in addition to raising the money for them, and organized an extracurricular Bible class while also preaching whenever the occasion required.[20]

A powerful pulpit orator, in technique perhaps the equal of Olin, Cummings gave his "thoroughly practical and evangelical" sermons in a "full, sonorous, penetrating" voice. Instead of an inaugural address, Cummings delivered the baccalaurate sermon at the commencement of 1858. His plain preaching style built to climactic calls to action. Like his occasional brief writings, his sermons were known more for elevated sentiment than for profound thought. His baccalaureate sermons were not published and probably not even written out in any finished form. Reports on their content make it clear, however, that each graduating class heard from Cummings "the notes of a bugle summoning to the front a new battalion of armed volunteers in the great struggle for the general triumph of truth in the earth."[21]

Students heard the call to evangelical duty throughout their undergraduate years. For the unconverted it was an exhortation to experience and profess a commitment to Christ. For those already publicly professing Christian faith, the message came from a man who saw himself and the Methodist church deeply involved in extending the kingdom of Christ throughout the country and the world. Like many of his colleagues at Yale and other New England colleges, Cummings saw his converted students as "agents of the millennium," each one equipped by scholarship to see more fully "the power, wisdom and goodness of his Creator." Through scholarly study of history and the material world, he argued, the march of human progress and the unity of God's design became ever more clearly revealed. These revelations served as a guide and a spur to action. In response to the social problems and issues frequently discussed by Cummings, Wesleyan students were expected to pursue "a manly and practical Christianity."[22]

And with unrelenting action. A close friend gave the appropriate simple summary view of Cummings: "The watchword of his life was duty." From early in his career, through seventeen years of leadership at Wesleyan, and right up to the end of his third presidency (1881–90 at Northwestern), Cummings kept his focus on action, achievement, and accountability. As he lay close to death from heart failure at age seventy-three, Cummings uttered his last words to his physician: "Has my record been a good one? It will be accepted, will it not?" In terms of sustaining at Wesleyan the energetic evangelism of his teacher, Willbur Fisk, the answer was clearly affirmative.[23]

Closely linked to the evangelical ends promoted by Wesleyan's first five presidents was the educational process of mental discipline. Fisk's inaugural address strongly supported "the vigorous exercise and manly growth of the intellect." In order to pursue benevolent enterprises each Wesleyan student would need a mind "so trained, that, like a ship in good trim, it would answer to its helm, and adjust itself to its circumstances, however variable the winds and the currents in the stormy sea of life." Bangs made a similar connection in his baccalaureate sermon of 1841: "Learning disciplines and expands the mind; religion sanctifies the heart and purifies the affections, and by uniting them, the young man is prepared to enter upon the duties of life with that enlightened judgment and pure motive which will guide and guard him in all his pursuits." Intellectual acquisition and discipline, Olin told the graduating class of 1848, "qualify an immortal spirit the better to perform its functions; more perfectly to understand and more keenly to enjoy all that God shall reveal or enjoin through the long annals of an endless life." Although Smith did not publish thoughts on the relationship, he probably agreed with his successor, Cummings, who viewed "mental exercise" as a means "through which the soul is improved and brought nearer to God."[24]

Establishing intellectual rigor as a central element in the educational ethos of mid-nineteenth-century Wesleyan was of highest priority for Stephen Olin. Fisk balanced a suitable discipline with the importance of "useful and practical wisdom" found in subjects such as modern literature. Bangs justified Bible study as "demanding the highest efforts of the mind" but saw this text as equally useful in many other ways. Olin emphasized a single dimension of learning, fully in agreement with the Yale *Reports*. He approached educational issues with a frequently expressed belief that "mental discipline . . . is the fundamental principle, the *beau ideal* of education, on which both teacher and learner should fix a steadfast eye." Those who taught and studied at Wesleyan during his presidency knew that "a high and finished classical discipline was his ideal for our own college."[25]

Olin's two immediate successors sustained this affirmation of analytical thinking more by example than exhortation. Smith was remembered as a teacher who expected the full concentration of students on a difficult mathematical problem until it was fully understood. He chose an "analytical approach" for his textbook because this method would develop and strengthen "more of the mental faculties." Students of Cummings recalled the classes in moral philosophy taught by this "large, burly man of rather stern and forbidding aspect" as "debating clubs" where he "taught us to think." One recalled his classroom as "an intellectual gymnasium where on the bars of logic and metaphysics he trained the muscles of the mind." From Fisk's inaugural of 1831 to addresses in 1870 of leading trustees such as Daniel Curry and Orange Judd, mental discipline was a value Wesleyan used to define its educational enterprise.[26]

To guide young men along the arduous pathway of an evangelical vision served by constant mental discipline required close attention to matters of governance. Student ages ranged from twelve to thirty. Almost all resided in a single building. Problems of governance were constant and complex. Although Wesleyan did not have the frequency of student disorder and occasional rebellion found at Yale, Amherst, and most other New England colleges in the years from 1800 to 1860,[27] the disciplinary philosophies and skills of three of the first five presidents encountered severe tests.

Perhaps mindful of student disorders at colleges such as Brown, where several outbreaks contributed to the departure of a rules-and-regulations-oriented president in the mid-1820s, Fisk and Olin publicly proclaimed a paternalistic approach to governance. For Fisk, the best government for a college was patriarchal rather than one based on a code of statute laws. "The student," Fisk said, "should feel that he is offending against his father and friend, and against the peace and prosperity of the community, in which he has a common interest." Olin, too, saw the limits of campus codes, advocating instead a "nearer approximation to that parental discipline which Nature has prescribed for the government of youth." Olin's approach was to hold students "accountable for their conduct upon the common obligations of morality and duty."[28] Both men had the stature and sensitivities to achieve a high level of success with paternalistic approaches in the years from 1831 to 1851.

Bangs and Smith, however, were measured by the paternalistic stan-

dard and were found lacking. Bangs paid tribute to the fatherly solicitude of Fisk and was welcomed by students as a new president
"conciliatory in his intercourse with those with whom he is called immediately to act, apt to listen and to yield, as well as to teach and to
guide, efficient in government, full of the overflowing love of a parent."
Yet within a year students came to view him as heavy-handed in disciplinary matters. Probably in part for this reason, more than fifty students signed a letter to him in May 1842 asking him to resign. This
action became a disciplinary incident in which fourteen signers who
refused to recant were suspended. On the day of their departure a cheering group of about fifty students escorted all but one of the offenders to
the boat. The raucous escorts gave three groans for Bangs and broke
windows upon their return to campus. Most students talked about leaving. Bangs's resignation came about six weeks later. Smith's resignation
in 1857 also derived in part from issues related to paternalistic governance. Praised as teacher, president, and disciplinarian by a senior-class
spokesman at the 1856 commencement, Smith rapidly lost his paternalistic hold on student enthusiasms during the 1856/57 academic year. In
the heated presidential campaign of fall 1856 a few members of the
mostly Republican student body asked for leaves in order to work for
the election of John C. Frémont. When Smith denied these requests,
his affiliation with the Democratic party left him open to charges of
partisanship. He was also probably held accountable for the unpopular
faculty decision, disputed by students in the fall of 1856 and spring of
1857, to seat students alphabetically in daily chapel rather than by class.
The petition of August 1857 signed by sixty-two students asking the
joint board to replace him asserted that he "had failed to command
respect or even attachment" amid a growing "disregard, amounting to
contempt, of College Rules."[29]

A student selected to give the oration welcoming Smith's successor in
1858 gave rhetorical expression to expectations for a paternalistic presidency. "We look to you," he told Cummings, "for impulses to the noblest
of lives—for mental, social, and moral stimulation." Asking for "a
father's interest" in the religious education of students, the orator posed
the central question: "Will you, sir, take the place of those we have left
in our distant homes?" Cummings's reply was not recorded, but he
appeared to have met this standard until the mid-1860s. After a brief,
relationship-damaging clash with students in 1864 over the dress code
for chapel, Cummings got into serious trouble a year later. He had a
sharp tongue in dealing with students who asked for exceptions to es-

tablished practice and norms. A student summarily expelled for resisting Cummings's verbal onslaught received widespread support from the student body. Fifteen sophomores protested by leaving campus in early June. The matter went to the joint board in a student petition asking them to investigate and to either replace Cummings or restrain his arbitrary and insulting ways. A large and skillful committee of the board saved the day by mediating the conflict in a manner that gently found reason for blame and praise on both sides, leaving all parties reasonably satisfied. Cummings then preached an excellent baccalaureate sermon, presided with great dignity at commencement, announced three major gifts for endowed funds, and went on to be remembered as a president who had "a personal and tender interest" in students. He "encouraged the despondent, visited the sick, prayed with the penitent, and pleaded and labored with the erring."[30]

The core values articulated and exemplified by Wesleyan's presidents from 1831 to 1870 shaped the educational enterprise through its three major components. Faculty, drawn almost entirely from the evangelical ranks, worked intensively to discipline young minds in a pious, fatherly manner. The curriculum, in its formal and in its faculty-supported informal aspects, kept a sharp focus on developing intellectual skills within a context of evangelical awareness and paternalistic oversight. Students, most of whom had made public professions of their faith, pursued mental discipline in many settings and chose careers reflecting the "tone and character" imparted to their minds by the educational program.[31]

Professors

Faculty, according to Willbur Fisk, "should be men of learning, apt to teach, unimpeachable in their life, gentlemanly and winning in their manner, industrious in their habits, energetic and enterprising in their character, interested in their work, and faithful in the performance of their duties." It went without saying that Wesleyan's professors, like those at similar antebellum colleges in New England, should also be pious. In 1835 the faculty pledged themselves to "pursue our occupation under a deeper sense of our responsibility to Heaven," seeking the religious improvement of students by instruction, conversation, and personal example. Recruiting his faculty largely through church networks, Fisk had only a very limited number of well-educated Methodists available. The six hired during his presidency were not all Methodists and were very young. By the middle of Wesleyan's first decade Fisk was in his early forties; the other faculty ranged in age from mid-twenties to

early thirties. At a time when even Harvard's faculty had about 90 percent from a single denomination (Unitarian), a Methodist argued in 1839
that all faculty at Methodist-affiliated colleges should be members, pref-
erably clergymen, of the denomination. Although ministers remained a
minority of Wesleyan's professors, the faculty soon became thoroughly
Methodist, with all members piously committed to their calling. President Cummings in 1866 saw the teacher as "the most direct co-worker
with God." This description fit both the faculty he knew as a student in
the Fisk years and those he recruited up to 1870.[32]

Appointments of successors to the original faculty reflected a strong
tendency to choose alumni. Similar trends occurred at Amherst, Williams, and Middlebury. In three of the four central areas of Wesleyan's
curriculum, recent graduates replaced faculty who began teaching at
Wesleyan in the 1830s. The position in classics occupied by Daniel D.
Whedon (Hamilton '28) was filled by Harvey B. Lane '35 in 1843, and
then, in Latin, by Calvin S. Harrington '52 in 1861. Augustus Smith
(Hamilton '25) turned mathematics over to John M. Van Vleck '50 in
1853. William North Rice '65 arrived in 1868 anticipating the retirement in natural science of John Johnston (Bowdoin '32). The only appointment during Stephen Olin's presidency, Charles K. True (Harvard
'32) in moral science and belles lettres, the position originally held by
Fisk (Brown '15), had to be defended against criticism for hiring from
outside the Wesleyan family.[33] By 1870 alumni held five of seven professorships. The other two were occupied by the soon-to-retire John Johnston and by James C. Van Benschoten (Hamilton '56), appointed in
1863 in Greek and modern languages.

The predominance of alumni on the faculty supplied a strong motive
for strenuous service. With distinctive loyalty and local experience, they
were ready to assume the staggering breadth of responsibilities assigned
to professors of this era. Harvey Lane's student experience with the
entire Wesleyan curriculum permitted him to begin his teaching career
as assistant professor of mathematics and natural philosophy and then
become professor of Greek and Latin languages. Joseph Cummings
taught small segments of ethics, psychology, evidences of Christianity,
political economy, international law, the United States Constitution, and
rhetoric. Faculty attended and helped to conduct morning and evening
prayers; some also taught voluntary Bible classes. If unmarried, they
lived in the dormitory. In general, they gave close scrutiny to each student, making themselves "fully acquainted with his habits and attain-
ments," taking "a kind personal interest in his welfare," and making sure

"no one escapes their solicitude." For this intense paternalism faculty received both praise for their dedication and sympathy for being overworked.[34]

Despite this diversity of duties assumed for alma mater, the faculty began to build a sense of independent professional identity. A major role in selecting their own members provided the foundation for professional stature. Provision for this prerogative appeared at the start. A draft of articles for organizing Wesleyan in 1830 articulated the key role for faculty in selection of their membership. They would initiate nominations for appointment, subject to final election by the joint board. Consistent practice and bylaws adopted by the joint board in 1859 confirmed this role. The faculty started to record minutes of its meetings in 1835, and an early instance of collective action came in 1845 with regard to salaries. A letter addressed to the board noted that salary payments during the last few years had usually been from one to three terms in arrears and advised the board to obtain loans from other sources. Almost a decade later the faculty found their salaries "inadequate for support" and suggested increases. In both cases the board responded with the requested action. Although faculty compensation at Wesleyan in the mid-1860s fell below that of talented ministers, salaries did keep pace from 1831 to 1870 with those at Amherst and Williams, far exceeded those at Middlebury, and stayed close behind those at Yale.[35]

Additional steps to acquire a distinct and respected status for the academic profession included research and writing for publication. Presidents Fisk and Olin set an example in the 1830s and 1840s for publication of argumentative and analytical work. Fisk's sermons, addresses, and positions on theological and social reform issues frequently made their way into print. His *Travels on the Continent of Europe* sold out four printings in less than four weeks, helping the publishing firm of Harper & Brothers through the depression years of 1838–39. Olin, in addition to sermons, addresses, and articles in the Methodist press, published a two-volume travel book that included findings important enough to engender a dispute in the *North American Review* and elsewhere. The issue was whether he had given proper credit to the work published two years earlier by a major Biblical scholar. Except for a few addresses and articles in Methodist journals and Joseph Holdich's biography of Fisk, little came from the pens of most other faculty prior to 1850. The roots of a scholarly tradition can be found by this date, however, in John Johnston's half-dozen brief reports and notes in the *American Journal of Science and Arts*, in the pioneering inclusion of analytical chemistry in his textbook of 1840, and especially in the clear, concise, closely reasoned text on mechanics, published by Augustus Smith in 1849.[36]

Published contributions to American cultural life during the next two decades were modest. Works by and about Olin appeared posthumously in the early 1850s. Johnston and Smith prepared revised editions of their textbooks. Van Vleck, brought to the faculty by Smith, produced annual reports on the positions of the moon and Saturn. Rice, his admiring student,[37] began teaching in 1868 as Wesleyan's first faculty member with a doctoral degree and as author of an article on Darwinian theory. Harrington published an annotated edition of three comedies by Plautus in 1870. Cummings, author of various reviews, addresses, sermons, and articles in the Methodist press from the mid-1840s to mid-1850s, found that a campus-building presidency combined with substantial teaching left little time for writing. His annotated textbook edition of Butler's *Analogy* did not appear until 1875.

The influence of German universities, providing models of academic expertise achieved through specialized research within a discipline, arrived at Wesleyan in the 1860s. Direct knowledge of this professional example entered the Harvard and Yale faculties in the 1820s and those of Amherst and Williams in the late 1850s. Wesleyan's first German-trained teacher, Van Benschoten, joined the faculty in 1863. His Methodist faith weighed heavily not only in Wesleyan selecting him but also in his choice of Wesleyan over a competing offer from Union College. He added an archaeological dimension to the teaching of Greek and gave analytical lectures. Although not a publishing scholar, Van Benschoten used his travel and study abroad to bring a new awareness of contributions that current research and international scholarly contacts could make to teaching. And he advised Rice to study in Germany. In 1867, Rice obtained Yale's first Ph.D. in geology, accepted appointment to the Wesleyan faculty, and received a year's leave of absence to study at the University of Berlin. Also on leave to study in Europe that year was Fales H. Newhall '46, appointed in 1863 as professor of rhetoric and English literature and instructor in Hebrew.[38]

Study abroad did not inspire notable research achievements by any of these three. Van Benschoten had health problems and devoted his scholarly talent and energy to being a Christian teacher. Newhall suffered from illness that ended his career less than a decade after his return. Rice dispersed his vast professional energies in dozens of directions. But these young professors did set the example of pursuing graduate study as preparation for the emerging career of college teaching, thus advancing the nascent tradition of scholarship nurtured by Smith, Johnston, and Van Vleck.[39]

Calls for higher levels of faculty scholarship came directly from the denomination during the 1860s. The *Methodist*, a weekly published in New York City, spent much of the fall of 1864 urging greater scholarly productivity from faculty at Methodist-affiliated colleges in order to elevate the cultural life of Methodism. Joseph Cummings found himself in an uncomfortable defensive position and responded in a manner leaving him vulnerable to suggestions that he was not sufficiently vigorous in recruiting faculty with the highest scholarly potential, even if this meant hiring a few non-Methodists. At the New England Methodist Centenary Convention in 1866 the paucity of publications by Wesleyan faculty had to be defended again.[40]

Creating a sense of professional identity amid the early influence of a German-university research model and the expectations for books to serve denominational purposes, Wesleyan faculty kept a clear focus on sustaining the traditions of liberal learning. The oratorical tradition, with its concern for enduring values, found strong expression in science classes as well as those in the humanities. The philosophical tradition of searching for ever-elusive truths found expression most frequently in the emphasis on mental discipline as preparation for intellectual discovery.

Clues to the Christian outlook framing the early study of science at Wesleyan begin with John Johnston's great respect for James Dwight Dana's geological scholarship. Johnston praised Dana's famous textbook of 1863 for its historical approach outlining "a grand development of events which have taken place in regular order . . . all this, of course, under the control and continued superintendence of the same Divine Mind that in infinite wisdom originally called matter into being, and gave it its properties and laws." This "of course" was probably an explicit premise in Johnston's teaching of science at Wesleyan for four decades, and it clearly was a bedrock assumption in classes taught by his student and successor, Rice. For Rice, "a fact must take its place in a broad philosophy of life or throw light on a principle of nature or a moral truth." In teaching Latin and Greek, Whedon found opportunity in the 1830s to "dispense precepts of integrity," "store the youthful character with generous sentiments," and effect "moral elevation." In the 1860s Harrington sustained this approach to classical literature, editing a Latin text that "abounded in moral lessons." He thought Wesleyan "should be as pure as the pulpit" in its doctrine and piety.[41]

While maintaining this version of the oratorical tradition, faculty vigorously perpetuated the philosopher's commitment to training of the intellect. Their chief tool was the recitation method, through which they held students accountable for mastery of daily assignments. Students had a vocabulary for these encounters. To stumble through with weak responses to the instructor's probing questions was to "fizzle." Total lack of preparation produced a "smash." In the hands of recently graduated tutors, recitations at larger institutions may have involved little beyond rote learning.[42] When conducted by a faculty such as Wesleyan's, this method was a powerful stimulus for development of analytical skills.

Fisk questioned his students closely but supportively to determine how well they understood the assigned reading. Interjecting supplementary information or observations, he kept the mind of the student constantly alert. Olin supported recitations over lectures because they could "introduce the teacher to an intimate acquaintance with the intellectual peculiarities of his pupils, and enable him to accommodate his instruction to the wants of every mind." Olin designed assignments "to throw the student upon his power of analyzing his thoughts" and render him "more capable of making a clear and connected statement" of what he knew. Assessing the achievements of Olin's entire faculty, the visiting committee conducting annual examinations in 1848 reported: "It is obvious to the committee the pupils are here taught to *think* and *reason*. Their recitations are not a mere parrot's part of uttering words without comprehension of their meaning. They are trained to analyze, to classify, to compare, and to judge." This daily intellectual exercise served "to discipline and stimulate the mind as to enable and dispose it to conduct its processes of thought and investigation as to bring it to the discovery of hidden truths."[43]

Educational Program

The curriculum employed by faculty in this manner was quite simple and stable up to 1869. Greek, Latin, and mathematics, the subjects thought to provide maximum mental discipline, commanded all of the classroom time of freshmen and sophomores and about two-thirds of the four-year course of study for a bachelor of arts degree. Instruction in natural science during the junior and senior years included brief introductions to biology, chemistry, physics, astronomy, geology, and physiology. Astronomy was taught with a new French telescope purchased by President Fisk during his trip to Europe in 1835–36. Rhetoric, logic, and moral philosophy rounded out a curriculum considered by the examining committee in 1845 "to compare advantageously with those of the best American colleges."[44]

Efforts to extend the curriculum beyond traditional areas of liberal arts study were generally short-lived. Proposals made in 1832–33 within the joint board to establish schools of medicine and law received only brief consideration, probably because of the costs involved. Conferences in New England wanted Wesleyan to establish a theological school in the early 1840s, including professorships in Hebrew, Biblical literature, and ecclesiastical history. Financial realities and the arrival of the curricular conservative, Olin, as president in 1842 thwarted implementation of these plans. The New England Methodists soon chartered a theological institute in New Hampshire, and Wesleyan offered future ministers only the courses in Hebrew, begun on a fee basis in 1838 and continued as electives. Augustus Smith blocked efforts of a few faculty in the mid-1850s to introduce courses in Biblical studies and theology. Soon after the arrival of Joseph Cummings in 1858 and James Van Benschoten in 1863, Wesleyan offered instruction for students with a ministerial career in mind, but only on an informal basis. Also outside the regular curriculum, law instruction was offered for about five years in the 1840s on a fee basis by a local trustee, William Storrs. Similarly, classes in pedagogy could be obtained for a few years in the early 1840s from Alfred Saxe '38, principal of Middletown's new high school.[45]

Few students showed interest in other alternatives to the classical curriculum such as modern languages or the course of study leading to a bachelor of science degree. Despite Willbur Fisk's call for more emphasis on modern languages and his hiring of Jacob F. Huber in 1831 to teach them, low enrollments in this optional study made it necessary for Huber to take on administrative duties in order to justify his salary. This professorial position lasted little more than a decade. From the mid-1840s to the early 1870s, modern languages received minimal attention. The bachelor of science and English literature course permitted students to avoid Greek and Latin, obtaining the B.S. degree in about three years rather than four. First conferred in 1838, this degree was earned by about 10 percent of the graduates during the next six years and by only 2 percent from 1845 to 1870. All but a handful of students and parents invested in the traditional B.A. curriculum.[46]

Attention to individual needs and preferences proceeded within this settled and comprehensive curricular structure. The faculty examined students individually for admission and then placed them at appropriate levels of instruction in each department. In response to "wants of the community" a few changes occurred in 1850: a term of civil engineering was introduced in the fall of senior year, and modern language instruction was offered, for an additional fee, during two terms as an alternative to a course in the required curriculum.[47]

In the fall of 1869, just a few years after Harvard granted its sophomores, juniors, and seniors a substantial degree of freedom to select courses, Wesleyan introduced choices for juniors and seniors that made even Latin, Greek, and mathematics elective. Stimulated by suggestions in the report of the examining committee in 1866, faculty and trustees addressed issues of curriculum revision for a few years and then moved decisively to meet what Joseph Cummings described as "increasing demand for modern languages and for science in a college curriculum." Similar curricular reforms did not occur at Amherst, Williams, Middlebury, or Yale until the 1880s.[48]

The budding curricular plans for interest-driven academic achievement had precursors in certain activities established long before 1869 to supplement formal instruction. Student literary and debating societies were integral parts of the learning environment, approved and supported by the faculty and trustees. Like their counterparts at colleges such as Amherst and Williams, the societies at Wesleyan began within months of the opening of the institution. Philorhetorian (founded as Philorhetorean Lyceum in 1831) and Peithologian (so designated beginning in 1833 when Adelphian, dating back to 1831, changed its name) were Wesleyan's principal and competing societies before 1860. Issues debated at the weekly meetings ranged from capital punishment, slavery, and women's rights to the dangers and benefits of reading novels. The faculty permitted these meetings to be scheduled during the required evening study hours and set aside rooms in college buildings for the meetings and library of each group.[49]

Through donations and purchases, students built up society libraries of several thousand volumes. Their collections of contemporary journals, works of history, and recent literature complemented the more classical and theological acquisitions of the college library. Members of one society had access to resources of the other. Since almost all students belonged to either Philo or Peitho, the literary society libraries joined the college library and the Missionary Lyceum library in providing a range of collections to be used for course-related reading, preparation for debates, research for writing essays or orations, and other purposes. When the literary societies faded out of existence in the late 1860s, their libraries became part of the college library. Various patterns of decline, demise, and transfer also occurred during these years at Harvard, Brown, Yale, Middlebury, and other New England colleges. In their antebellum years of peak vitality, however, societies offered a welcome relief from solitary study. Within "their cheerful, well-furnished" quarters, students extended the curriculum's commitment to mental discipline through "a temperate, healthy collision of mind to mind."[50]

Intellectual activities in harmony with Wesleyan's educational goals also occurred through the sponsorship of other organizations. In the Eclectic Society (1837) members wrote essays and critiques delivered at the weekly meetings, with each essay also subject to oral criticism. A student in 1861 found this process to be "excellent drill for composition." The Mystical Seven (1837) cultivated wit through a mixture of elaborate ritual, epistolary exuberance, and literary exercises. It became a senior honor society in the late 1860s, about the time when its rival, Skull and Serpent (1865) appeared. The Xi Chapter of Psi Upsilon (1843) started with literary exercises and later moved toward an emphasis on extemporaneous speaking. The Gamma chapter of Phi Beta Kappa (1845), ninth oldest chapter in the nation, sponsored disputations, conversations, and communications on literary and scientific topics at its meetings in the late 1840s. The Cuvierian Society (started in 1836 as the Natural History Society) included faculty and residents of Middletown during its decade or so of scientific discussions, papers, and collection-building. The Missionary Lyceum (1834), intending to be "a moral force in the work of evangelizing the world," sponsored an ecumenical variety of speakers prior to its demise around 1870.[51] Often using specially designated rooms in college buildings and including faculty in their activities, these groups gave students ample opportunity to read, investigate, argue, and write.

Student publications of note began in 1840 with the *Classic; or College Monthly*, carrying student and faculty essays, poems, and other writings. Beset with constant financial problems, it lasted for two years. The yearbook, *Olla Podrida*, published its first issue in November 1858 and soon evolved from a newspaper format to octavo. Along with the outburst of student newspapers started at Yale, Harvard, Williams, Amherst, and Trinity in the first few years after the Civil War, Wesleyan's

Argus appeared on 11 June 1868. Promising to portray accurately "the spirit of college life and thought" in issues published every three weeks,[52] this source of campus and alumni news became the latest example of the many student enterprises working hand in hand with a curriculum emphasizing critical thinking and communication skills.

Oratorical performances provided one test for how effectively the formal curriculum, supplementary curriculum, and faculty fostered these skills. Almost every student prepared an oration, occasionally in Greek or Latin, for either the sophomore exhibition, held in the fall, or the junior exhibition, held in the spring. Seniors also had exhibitions in the late fall during Wesleyan's first decade, but senior orations were soon required only as part of the commencement program. Topics were as varied as those found on the literary society agendas. The addresses, usually delivered before an interested public at Middletown's Methodist church, sometimes received detailed critical reviews in the religious and local press. In the 1850s praise for good performances took immediate and tangible form when "ladies in the galleries responded to the eloquence of the orators by throwing bouquets in rich abundance."[53]

The ultimate test occurred in annual public examinations of all students at the end of the academic year. A committee of "literary gentlemen" selected by the faculty spent several days conducting these assessments of individual achievement in each subject. Gabriel P. Disosway, a graduate of Columbia and a prolific contributor of articles in the religious and secular press, often served as chair of the committee in the 1830s and 1840s. President Jeremiah Day and Professor Benjamin Silliman of Yale were invited to assist with the examinations of 1835. In 1860 the committee to examine seniors included clergymen of several denominations, and a Congregational minister served as chair. Committees primarily observed while the faculty administered rigorous oral examinations. They did not hesitate to require additional study for those students failing to demonstrate proficiency. Even the best student in the mid-1860s found the examinations very demanding. Committees also applied their critical scrutiny and comments to student orations and compositions, admissions standards, content and emphases in the curriculum, teaching effectiveness of each faculty member, and instructional facilities and apparatus. Citing their experience with examinations at Harvard and other institutions, committee members in the 1860s expressed high regard for the levels of achievement they found at Wesleyan. But they also called for still-higher levels of scholarly attainment by students and faculty. In general, these committees found Wesleyan's educational program, with its emphasis on thinking skills, "well adapted to make the men who shall be adequate to the exigencies of the interesting age in which we live."[54]

Students

Who were the students engaging a traditional curriculum and collaborating with faculty and trustees to foster literary societies that extended the range of Wesleyan's educational program? The one hundred to one hundred fifty enrolled annually from the mid-1830s to 1870 were usually described as a self-motivated, "enterprising class of young men," all but about 10 percent of them drawn "from the industrious classes." Most came from small towns and prepared at nearby academies, the predecessors of public high schools. To the dismay of Wesleyan presidents and examining committees concerned with balanced budgets and educational quality, these cost-conscious students frequently chose to cover the freshman subjects at academies close to home. They thus delayed college entrance until they could qualify, through entrance examinations, as sophomores. Like other newer "interior colleges" of New England, Wesleyan attracted a large segment of older students. Although some Wesleyan students entered at age fourteen, the mean age at graduation for the period 1842–71 exceeded twenty-four. It is highly probable that the positive correlation between mature student ages and humble family backgrounds found in studies of similar New England colleges is equally valid for Wesleyan. Compilations of age at graduation during the 1850s also indicate that Wesleyan's students were somewhat older and poorer than those at Amherst and Middlebury, and considerably so compared to students at Bowdoin and Williams.[55] It is also likely that Wesleyan exceeded all other New England colleges on both dimensions from 1831 to 1870.

For these enterprising, mobile students attending antebellum colleges in steadily increasing numbers, enrollment in higher education was an ambitious and well-considered decision. Some Wesleyan students, such as the 15 percent from Middletown listed in the catalogue of 1832, might see the college primarily as a convenience. Most, however, came from considerable distances. New York supplied more students than the combined totals for Connecticut and Massachusetts. The trip from New York City in the early 1840s took twelve hours by steamboat or nine hours by steamboat to New Haven, train to Meriden, and stage to Middletown. Fales Newhall, arriving from Saugus, Massachusetts, in 1843, recalled Middletown coming into sight around a bend in the Connecticut River. There was a "wild flutter" in his "student soul" upon seeing Wesleyan's buildings "rising above the cloud of summer foliage" and representing "the goal of my boyish aspirations." The liberal education Newhall sought was touted as "a *marketable* commodity," an investment parents could make in an "imperishable, ever rising stock." With less than 2 percent of New England's white males of college age enrolled in higher education, the bachelor's degree was becoming a badge of distinction in careers such as teaching and the ministry.[56]

College was serious business. Students coming from families where they were "brought up to work" followed a schedule of required chapel services, recitations, and study hours that filled each weekday from before sunrise until about nine in the evening. A considerable number were licensed preachers, who served nearby pulpits on Sundays in order to meet college expenses. A report in the mid-1850s noted that no less than three out of four students earned part or all of their college expenses by teaching school in the winter. This economic necessity led so many students to seek and receive permission to leave before the end of fall term and to return after the start of spring term that the three-term calendar was revised in 1842 and 1858 to accommodate those who taught. Due to scholarships, few students paid the tuition of eleven or twelve dollars per term, and most earned enough to cover other expenses.[57]

Hardworking students still managed to find time for social enterprises that served purposes other than extending the curriculum. Eclectic (1837), the local fraternity, and Psi Upsilon (1843) soon had competition from four more chapters of national fraternities: Chi Psi (1844), Delta Upsilon (1850), Alpha Delta Phi (1856), and Delta Kappa Epsilon (1866). Literary exercises formed a part of their activities, but these were primarily social organizations, soon established as successors to the fading literary societies. While "the recitation room furnishes substantials" noted the *Olla Podrida*, fraternal societies provide "the ornaments of education."[58]

Breaks from busy schedules were also used for exercise. Probably as early as 1831 students had informal games of "football," playing by kicking rather than carrying the ball, on land just south of the original college buildings. A freshman in 1862 found "the violence of the exercise and the excitement of the game . . . just the thing to discipline [a student's] muscles and direct his mind." Ice skating on Pameacha Pond was also popular throughout the early years. For the more adventurous there were occasional opportunities to skate up the Connecticut River to Hartford. Stephen Henry Olin '66 reported in 1864 that he covered the twenty miles in an hour and twenty minutes. He returned by train. The nearby river offered additional opportunities for rowing and sailing. Probably influenced by the example of boat clubs formed at Harvard and Yale and by America's first intercollegiate sports competition, a crew race in 1852 between Harvard's club and two from Yale, Wesleyan students established boat clubs in the late 1850s. More than half of the Wesleyan student body belonged to these organizations in the late 1860s. The opening in early 1864 of Wesleyan's first gymnasium, a frame structure behind College Row, stimulated enthusiasm for indoor exercise.[59]

Intercollegiate competition began with a baseball game against Yale in late September 1865. Amherst and Williams had initiated such competition in 1859, and various campus baseball clubs appeared at Wesleyan in the early 1860s. Under Stephen Henry Olin's leadership and a Greek name suggested by James Van Benschoten, Wesleyan's Agallian Base Ball Club lost the eight-inning game in New Haven by a score of 39–13. About fifteen hundred spectators gathered in Hartford in 1866 to watch Olin's team, wearing as club colors a lavender ribbon, play against a team from Waterbury. "You can't imagine," Olin wrote to his mother, "the excitement and pleasure of a hard-fought game of ball."[60]

Pranks and politics provided additional outlets for student energies. Faculty minutes record occasional incidents requiring disciplinary action for rowdy and disrespectful behavior, but the low frequency of disorder at Wesleyan as compared to other campuses offered further testimony to the general seriousness of purpose among its enterprising students. In campus politics, however, large segments of the student body played major roles in forcing the departure of two presidents and in creating a serious challenge to a third. National political issues also received frequent attention, particularly the debate over slavery. Richard S. Rust '41 even met part of his college expenses as one of the first antislavery lecturers in Connecticut. On several occasions he was mobbed. Before graduating he compiled a book of essays and poems advocating emancipation that included two contributions by William Lloyd Garrison and two of his own. As the North-South conflict deepened, students followed the Buchanan-Frémont presidential contest in 1856 with great interest.[61]

Word of the South's firing on Fort Sumter elicited an immediate out-pouring of Unionist support. Joseph Cummings's patriotic speeches and similar impromptu efforts by students were followed by drills and orga-nization of the Wesleyan University Guards. Receipt of letters from worried parents, however, tempered Cummings's subsequent talks. No-tice came that the only enlistment option was a minimum of three years or the duration of the war. Volunteer numbers dwindled. The fourteen students who signed up that spring joined with volunteers from Mid-dletown and vicinity to form the nucleus of Company G, Fourth Con-necticut Infantry, a regiment later reassigned to First Connecticut Artillery. But an increasing number of students enlisted in the next year or two, often with units from their hometown areas. During the war years 32 percent of Wesleyan undergraduates entered active service, a proportion probably exceeding that found at Amherst, Williams, and Yale.[62] The educational program, already well adapted to meet individ-ual circumstances of attainment and leaves for employment, experienced no major disruption.

Elements of stability in student life during Wesleyan's first four de-cades were numerous. Except for age range, the student body was homo-geneous. More than half the students were New Englanders, and about a third were from New York. Few came from below the Mason-Dixon line, the western states, or foreign countries. Three students from Puerto Rico attended during the 1841–42 academic year, and four black stu-dents enrolled, one briefly in 1832 and the other three in the late 1850s and early 1860s. Wesleyan's first black graduate was Wilbur Fisk Burns '60, son of the Methodist bishop of Liberia. A German Jew who had converted to Methodism and a Catholic who left before the end of his first year provided in the early 1860s rare contacts with religious tradi-tions outside the ranks of evangelical Protestantism. Of those inside the ranks, probably about half in the early years were Methodists, with the proportion increasing to 60 percent by 1870. Approximately one-third of the students were licensed preachers. At least three out of four young men attending Wesleyan during these early decades were, by public declaration of their faith, "professors of religion." A poll of forty col-leges in 1867 showed Wesleyan to be at the top in percentage of students professing religion. Periodic revivals on campus and in Middletown, often as a result of the national day of prayer for colleges each February or March, helped keep these numbers high.[63]

Bonds developed through shared piety, common backgrounds, and

Wilbur Fisk Burns '60, Wesleyan's first black graduate, returned to his native Liberia, where he practiced law and became a government official

daily contacts of residential life found expression and nurture through singing. Wesleyan's tradition as a "singing college" had roots in the vitality of Methodist hymnody. By the 1850s students were composing songs (or at least lyrics to be sung to familiar tunes) for various public occasions. Among the transitory glee clubs organized for special occasions from the mid-1840s through the 1860s, a club in 1862 made the first public tour of Wesleyan singers. A class song noted with emotive foresight at the junior exhibition of 1858: "We'll cherish this bond with affection fond, the Time shall but make it dearer." The truth in this observation can be seen in formation of the Alumni Association in 1836 (just three years after the first graduation), the periodic class reunions starting in the late 1860s, and the concurrent formation of alumni clubs in major cities. For the evangelical, earnest, energetic, Republican, white, male student body drawn from humble families in the Northeast, the 1850s and 1860s were "a time of hand shaking and good fellowship, and of great expectations."[64]

Wesleyan's expectations for career goals came in early and enduring fashion from highly influential presidents. Having called in 1831 for "men who will take the field . . . in the service of the world," Fisk described his students near the end of the decade as "scores of young men who are destined to act a public part in life." Olin addressed Wesleyan students as young men with a destiny to fulfill and expected them to be "chief actors in all the great enterprises of their generation." With these lofty goals before them it is not surprising that students and faculty showed little interest for the short-lived manual labor shop set up in the mid-1830s. Woodworking offered meager earnings, and there were many other college activities better suited to preparation for high callings of public service.[65]

Career choices of Wesleyan graduates reflected a belief that "the true remedial system for the amelioration of the condition of man . . . is found in the union and diffusion of knowledge and religion." More than half of the graduates of the 1830s and 1840s became educators (33.1 percent) or ministers (25.2 percent). These two occupations claimed 60 percent of the graduates in the 1850s and 1860s, with the percentage of educators waning (18.6 percent) and that of ministers waxing (41.4 percent). The demand for pedagogues and pastors within the swelling Methodist population was strong. Through correspondence and contacts, Fisk and his successors were busy one-man placement agencies. In keeping with Fisk's view that other occupations could also be pursued in a manner serving the public good, a constant percentage of graduates during the first four decades entered the fields of law (16 percent), medicine (5 percent), and business (12 percent).[66]

Compared to colleges such as Amherst, Wesleyan in the four decades preceding 1870 produced ministers and teachers at an unequalled rate (almost 60 percent of all graduates). Amherst's portion of graduates entering the ministry during these four decades (41 percent) exceeded Wesleyan's (34 percent), but by the 1860s Amherst's declining annual percentage was surpassed by the steadily ascending one at Wesleyan. And Wesleyan's portion of educators, although dropping steadily, still stood at 25 percent for the entire period. Amherst's was slightly more than 10 percent. Wesleyan was a premier source of well-educated young men committed to service in churches, schools, and colleges.[67]

The record of this service became a central element in Wesleyan's understanding of itself. Throughout the 1860s alumni supplied biographical information for the first *Alumni Record*, published in 1869. Orange Judd '47, tireless collector and compiler of these data, noted in his preface the volume's utility for alumni, "cementing them more strongly as a body." His largest hope, however, was that "this work will serve a useful purpose in showing the *vast amount of work* already accomplished by our Alma Mater, although but a little over a third of a century old." Through this publication the fruits of an evangelical educational enterprise devoted to cultivating mental discipline and an inclination to service could be seen in "the writings and teachings and preachings of the graduates."[68]

3   *Entrepreneurial*
    Strategy: From Town
    to Denomination

*T**he resourcefulness and resilience of collegiate enterprises met severe tests from 1830 to 1870. Wesleyan developed ways to survive local economic reversals, two major depressions, divisive public issues, a war, epidemics, proliferation of rival colleges, and dubious institutional funding devices. Adjustments in the style of presidential leadership, changes in the composition of the governing board, and cultivation of alumni support brought resources to compensate for diminished local and state funding. Denominational donors came to the fore. Once a struggling local enterprise, Wesleyan by 1870 was a regional Methodist college of substantial resources. A charter revision in that year confirmed the arrival of a late nineteenth-century denominational identity.*

Hazards

Local adversities led to declining financial support from Middletown. The generous local funding for establishing the college could not be sustained in a community struggling to make the transition from a mercantile to an industrial era. That shift yielded only modest gains in Middletown's population growth and prosperity by 1870, particularly when compared with other cities in Connecticut. Reflecting a lack of development in large-scale industry, Middletown's population ranking among Connecticut cities dropped from third in 1830 to sixth in 1870.[1]

Hopes for a brighter future had been closely tied to ill-fated efforts to bring a major rail line through the city. In 1835 the Hartford and New Haven Railroad studied three possible routes, one of which included Middletown. Despite promotional and financial efforts by prominent Middletown citizens, the route selected in 1836 was the most direct of the three. Running through Meriden, the tracks traversed considerably less difficult terrain than the proposed way through Middletown, ten miles to the east. The line opened in 1839. An extension to Springfield in 1844 linked tracks from New Haven to Boston, and completion of a final segment between New York and New Haven in 1849 opened rail travel between the region's two major cities.[2]

Meriden's economy reaped large benefits. Middletown mounted a second effort. The most direct route (or "air line") between New York and Boston passed almost exactly through Middletown's industrial district. Promoters of the new venture gained incorporation in 1846 for what would later become the Boston and New York Air Line Railroad. But a series of political and financial obstacles delayed the start of construction until 1853 and postponed completion of the project until 1873. By that time chances for successful competition with the Shore Line between New York and Boston were greatly diminished. The Air Line struggled for survival until the turn of the century, before slipping into local-line status. Passenger service ended in 1928.[3]

A third effort brought limited rail access to Middletown and Wesleyan in March 1850. Unable to obtain legislative authorization in the mid-1840s to build the necessary bridge over the Connecticut River for the Air Line, Middletown leaders sought a charter to construct tracks intersecting the New York to Boston line at Berlin, seven miles north of Meriden, and then continuing westward to New Britain. As in previous cases, Hartford interests opposed the request. Middletown emerged from this legislative battle with authorization to build only a nine-mile branch line from Berlin to the north end of the city, about one mile from campus.[4]

Travel time from Boston and New York to Wesleyan in 1850 had decreased to about five hours. This was a significant reduction compared to the time required in the early 1830s: approximately twelve hours overnight by steamboat (in seasons when the river was navigable) from New York and two days by stage from Boston. Balanced against this long-awaited benefit, however, was the protracted claim that railroad issues made on the time and financial resources of Middletown's leaders.[5] By mid-century the limits of local attention to Wesleyan and of local support for this educational enterprise were increasingly clear.

Constraints created by ebbs in the national economy presented additional challenges for Wesleyan. In early 1837 Willbur Fisk initiated a major fund drive. He needed to balance Wesleyan's accounts after his extensive purchases of books and scientific equipment in Europe, and he had ambitious plans for the first endowed professorship and for a president's house. With the momentum from his widely reported travels and celebrated return, Fisk achieved a promising start in obtaining subscriptions from individuals and congregations in New York City. The panic of 1837 hit with full force that spring. Subscribers were unable to pay on schedule. Bills were due. By early 1838 a discouraged Fisk predicted he would be able to collect less than one of every ten dollars pledged. The protracted depression, lasting years after his death in 1839, was a major reason why Wesleyan's assets during his presidency grew little beyond those accumulated to launch the college in 1831.[6]

With the depression reaching its low point in 1843, followed by only gradual recovery until the end of the decade, Wesleyan pursued a policy of retrenchment. Despite "the all-pervading pecuniary embarrassments of the country," Acting President Augustus Smith and the faculty took the position in 1840 that there should be no lowering of admissions standards. Enrollments declined and so did the size of the faculty. Partly due to "the existing financial state of the country," Stephen Olin reported in 1847, the college still strained under its heavy burden of debt. Three years later Olin noted the elimination of even the low-paying position of tutor.[7]

An upswing in the economy, fund-raising, and enrollments in the early 1850s enabled Augustus Smith to report in 1855 a reduction of indebtedness, prompt payment of salaries, and a few badly needed building repairs. The panic of 1857, however, greeted Joseph Cummings just weeks after his election to the Wesleyan presidency. Lingering effects of the subsequent brief depression led him to suspend efforts in 1859/60 to raise $50,000 for new buildings. The Civil War deferred such tasks for several more years and reduced values of land in Illinois, Missouri, Wisconsin, and Tennessee that Wesleyan sold in the 1860s.[8] Prime times for building a college's resources between 1830 and 1870 were few and far between.

Controversial social issues tested the young institution almost from the start. The rights of African-Americans in the North became a pressing campus concern in the fall of 1832, with the enrollment of Charles B. Ray. This young boot maker from Massachusetts entered Wesleyan with plans to become a Methodist minister. Less than two months after he arrived on campus, Ray left. Assessing the controversy, pressure, and hostility created by the college's few students from the South and some of those from New England, Wesleyan's first African-American student decided to move on to New York City. He later became editor of the *Coloured American*, a leader in the black convention movement, and founding minister of a Congregational church that served an area of lower Manhattan where a substantial number of blacks lived in poverty.[9]

President Fisk and the trustees had a major issue to address. Fisk, who had been the principal when Ray entered the academy at Wilbraham two years earlier, now tried to make plain to hostile Wesleyan students "the inconsistency and illiberality of their views." He promised protection to Ray. Soon after Ray left, Wesleyan's trustees passed a resolution "that none but male white persons shall be admitted as students of this institution." Perhaps abetted by this resolution, a small group of hostile students again held sway in 1833. They harassed and threatened Amos Beman, son of the minister of Middletown's African Methodist Episcopal Zion church, when he went to the dormitory room of an abolitionist student three times each week to obtain tutoring assistance. The joint board rescinded its exclusionary resolution in 1835, but much damage had already been done.[10]

Condemnation and criticism lasted for several years. William Lloyd Garrison's *Liberator* printed an account of the Ray case, labeling it a "scandalous affair." A speaker at the annual meeting of the New England Anti-Slavery Society in 1833 condemned this "disgraceful" Methodist conduct. The counterpart society in New York heard Ray speak in 1836 of the "heartless prejudice" he experienced at Wesleyan. A Methodist merchant in Boston wrote to Fisk in 1837 threatening to withhold payment on a subscription to Wesleyan because he had heard blacks were excluded.[11]

Although Fisk successfully reassured this donor, he kept himself and Wesleyan in the midst of heated debates over slavery from 1835 through 1838. Fisk opposed slavery, but also denounced the abolitionists as revolutionaries who spread "the poison of schism" and threatened to "dismember the Church of Christ." He and his faculty colleague Daniel Whedon advocated voluntary colonization of American blacks in Africa as a long-term solution. In response to letters on this topic sent by Whedon to the Methodist press, Garrison found Wesleyan in 1835 to be "one of the strongholds of Southern despotism." Even more damaging than the tangles with Garrison was the long, bitter, and exhausting battle Fisk fought with fellow New England Methodists, and a few in

New York City, over the issue of abolition versus colonization. A Boston editor worried that abolitionists might harm the college in retaliation against Fisk. An abolitionist put the onus on Fisk, arguing that he had "no right to indulge his love of controversy to the injury of the university." The argument cited as evidence the alienation of prospective students and at least one wealthy donor.[12] Only Fisk's stature within the denomination as a person of unquestioned piety and integrity kept this debate from seriously hurting the college.

Within Connecticut, the conservative stance taken by Fisk (and the similar position taken in the 1840s by Olin, a former slaveholder) probably found wider acceptance. Like Fisk, Jeremiah Day, Yale's president from 1817 to 1843, belonged to the American Colonization Society (1817). Abolitionists of both races were threatened or attacked during the 1830s in Norwich, Hartford, Middletown, Meriden, Torrington, New Canaan, and Norwalk. Hostile demonstrations terminated plans for a manual labor college for African-American men in New Haven in 1831 and closed a school for young African-American women in Canterbury in 1834.[13]

More than two decades passed before another African-American student enrolled at Wesleyan. Charles H. Gardner n1859, who entered in the fall of 1855, left during his senior year. Wilbur Fisk Burns entered in 1856, and Thomas F. Barnswell '62 in 1859. By 1860, when Burns became Wesleyan's first black graduate, about two dozen African-Americans had earned degrees from colleges such as Middlebury, Amherst, and Bowdoin, beginning in the 1820s, and Oberlin in the 1840s. As Burns received his diploma "there was a slight demonstration in the audience, but whether it was designed to express approbation for the graduation of a colored student or otherwise, it would be impossible to say." Implying that even Connecticut should be ready for the first graduation of a black person from one of its colleges, this newspaper account noted that "Wesleyan University has only done what would be done now in any Northern college."[14]

Threats and problems related to disease appeared with the start of Wesleyan's second year. The European cholera epidemic reached New York City in the summer of 1832 and spread throughout the nation that fall. Wesleyan had to reassure an apprehensive public. A newspaper notice published in September said Wesleyan was untouched by the illness and "none may hesitate to send their sons immediately." Although there were no cases on campus, "the ravages of the Cholera and the consequent derangement of business" in New York City did deliver a serious blow to fund-raising through most of the academic year 1832/33.[15]

Persistent health problems occurred with regard to Wesleyan's first four presidents, particularly Fisk and Olin. The pulmonary disorders shortening the adult lives of both placed considerable constraints on fund-raising and other operations at several points in the college's first two decades. Fisk's European trip, largely devoted to restoring his health, yielded benefits in public relations and in purchase of books and scientific equipment at favorable prices. Assignment to Wesleyan of proceeds from the book Fisk wrote about his travels, however, barely compensated for costs of the trip. The European gifts acquired for Wesleyan in cash, books, and minerals probably amounted to less than $2,000. More important, the almost fifteen months he was away, beginning in early September 1835, represented a lost opportunity on American shores during a prime time for presidential fund-raising prior to the panic of 1837. Olin, too, had health-related restrictions from the start of his presidency. Just as prosperity returned to the nation in the late 1840s, his illness placed severe limitations upon resource-building activities.[16]

Competition from other educational institutions posed a constant threat, beginning in the 1830s and reaching a peak with the chartering of Boston University in 1869. A Methodist editor worried as early as 1833 about "the inexpediency of multiplying collegiate institutions under our patronage." Although the closest of the five other Methodist-affiliated colleges in 1834 were Allegheny and Dickinson in Pennsylvania, Wesleyan competed for financial support in Massachusetts and upstate New York with Methodist academies. Critics of a plan to establish near Syracuse yet another college under Methodist patronage called in 1836 for restraint in order to give Wesleyan "the united support of all the northern Methodists." By 1845 the denomination patronized eleven colleges dividing up a total enrollment of only six hundred young men. The General Conference issued a call for restrictive action. Stephen Olin had ample reason to express concern when he learned of plans in the late 1840s to found Genesee College in an area of upstate New York from which Wesleyan had been accustomed to receive a considerable number of students. Methodist donations to Wesleyan from this region also diminished due to a movement led first by Presbyterians and then by Baptists to found the University of Rochester. Local pride and interest tended to prevail over denominational loyalties.[17]

Rivalry between Methodists in the New York and Boston areas sometimes stimulated support for Wesleyan but could also prove to be quite damaging. Methodists in Massachusetts threatened in 1854 to found their own college unless Wesleyan received better support from New York. By 1862 Methodists in New York City were talking about founding their own university near that city. Joseph Cummings spoke in a pained and blunt manner a few years later of "the strong local feeling that has ever constituted a great embarrassment to our educational interests." He worried about a potentially damaging blow to the agreement forged by Wesleyan's founders for partnership between the two cities. "Interested parties," according to Cummings, sought "to divert attention from this our oldest college, and to establish two others—one near New York and the other near Boston." Cummings was especially critical of reluctance in New York to match generous pledges from his own New England Conference. A half-million-dollar offer from a donor in the latter region, he feared, was now lost to Wesleyan due to lack of reciprocity from New York, the college's home conference.[18]

By 1864 a major donor and trustee from the Boston area, Lee Claflin, was working to bring a Methodist theological school to that city. Plans for a Methodist university began brewing in the late 1860s and soon engaged the attention of Claflin and two other Wesleyan trustees, Jacob Sleeper and Isaac Rich. In the spring of 1869 the *Argus* lamented this Methodist tendency to be "influenced more by *local* than by *general* ideas," but to no avail. Chartered 26 May 1869, Boston University opened its College of Liberal Arts four years later. More serious than the competition for students represented by this new institution (or by Syracuse University, opened under Methodist auspices in 1871) were the consequences for fund-raising. Boston University, not Wesleyan, would realize the subsequent substantial gifts of Claflin (who died in 1871), almost $700,000 from the estate of Rich (who died in 1872), and more than $500,000 from Sleeper (who died in 1889).[19]

Discounts on tuition, combined with a dearth of endowment in the early decades, produced additional financial stress. Operating expenses and acquisition of property and equipment absorbed all the money raised by the sale of scholarships and stock in Wesleyan. Not until the late 1840s did any funds begin to function as endowment. A large number of students by 1839 paid no tuition because a parent or friend had purchased a scholarship. Others received a tuition discount calculated at 10 percent of every dollar donated through purchase of stock by a sponsor. By the mid-1840s these discounting schemes prevented Wesleyan from realizing almost half of the potential tuition income. Responding to competition from other Methodist colleges for students and for funds, Cummings announced in 1858 the sale of "cheap scholarships." Fifteen years of tuition ($36 per year) could be purchased for $50; fifty years for $100 (one-fifth the amount charged for perpetual scholarships in the 1830s). He also apparently implemented an idea suggested by his predecessor; tuition for needy students who had no scholarship patrons was simply waived. In a few years, he predicted, Methodist colleges would no longer charge tuition. Annual aggregate tuition income at Wesleyan in the 1860s averaged less than $150; annual expenditures for faculty salaries alone averaged more than $11,000.[20]

Large increases in endowment became imperative to sustain annual operations. Funds held to function as "permanent" endowment in 1855 amounted to less than $10,000. Over the next five years endowment funds increased by more than $100,000 (including a large portion in notes and subscriptions), yielding income in 1860 of almost $9,000. By 1870 an endowment of $342,000 produced annual receipts of $24,000.[21]

Yet deficits for all but a few of those years were larger than ever. During Wesleyan's first four decades income met expenditures only in the years from the late 1840s to mid-1850s and again for a few years in the mid-1860s. Indebtedness went from $7,000 in 1836 to almost $25,000 in the mid-1840s. A reduction to about $15,000 was achieved around 1850, but subsequent deficits brought the amount to almost $30,000 in 1869. Annual interest paid on that debt was often equivalent to more than one-eighth of the faculty salary budget.[22]

Defaults on pledges periodically elevated the level of financial strain. Pledges to endowment by conferences and individuals were usually difficult to collect. Donors often gave interest-bearing notes rather than cash. Interest on these notes might be received for several years, and then financial reversals would preclude payment of either interest or principal. Final collection was slow and uncertain. Of the $100,000 subscribed to the Centum Millia campaign in the mid-1850s, only about $76,000 had been realized fifty years later. The note for $100,000 given by a trustee, Daniel Drew, was a large segment of the endowment in 1870. After he went bankrupt in 1876, the trustees granted his request to be released from this obligation.[23]

Deferred maintenance was an almost constant source of stress. The two original buildings had been heavily used and abused before Wesleyan assumed ownership. The prudential committee had to pay immediate attention to repair of facilities. Retrenchment budgets in the 1840s left much to be done during the next decade. An alumnus noted in 1856 that "the whole premises are in need of repairs and improvements." Soon after his arrival in 1858, Joseph Cummings reported that the instructional and dormitory facilities "have too much the aspect of a declining institution." To catch up on maintenance he even offered to assume the teaching responsibilities for an unfilled faculty position (in addition to his own courses) if the board would spend on repairs and improvements the salary thus saved. The amount spent for repairs in the last year of Smith's presidency was $280, but in the first five years of Cummings's presidency the average annual maintenance expenditure exceeded $2,000. Those same years brought a return of sizable deficits.[24]

Amid the hazards of discounts, dearth of endowment, deficits, debts, defaults, and deferred maintenance there were a few small blessings. Wesleyan escaped contagion during the national cholera epidemics of 1849 and 1866, as well as that of 1832. Where Williams lost half of its dormitory space to a fire in 1841, the only conflagration at Wesleyan up to 1870 destroyed just two small barns connected with the Boarding Hall. No enrollment drops of crisis proportions occurred such as those at Amherst from 1837 to 1846, Middlebury in the late 1830s, and Williams in the 1860s. There even were occasional windfalls of favorable publicity, such as Frederick Hall's report of his visit to campus in 1838. A well-experienced academician and scientist living in Washington, D.C., Hall gave glowing testimony to the quality of facilities, faculty, presidential leadership, and location of Wesleyan. First published in the *National Intelligencer*, this account appeared in his book of 1840. Given the attack on Partridge and his academy little more than a decade earlier by another visitor from Washington, Middletown and the Methodists probably breathed a sigh of relief.[25]

Ceremony, Structure, and Support

Presidents, trustees, and alumni played major roles in helping the fragile young institution navigate the often choppy seas from 1830 to 1870. Two presidents of substantial public stature, not only within the denomination but far beyond, were succeeded by two who met needs for administrative acumen and a more pronounced denominational identity. Composition of the board of trustees shifted from one reflecting the local-enterprise aspect of early Wesleyan to one almost totally Methodist. Alumni became better organized and more influential. These adaptations of institutional leadership and support permitted traditions of liberal learning to persist and prosper.

Through publications, positions taken in national debates, and oratorical accomplishments, both Fisk and Olin achieved broad public recognition for themselves and Wesleyan. Fisk was not only a leading Methodist but also an important temperance advocate and a member of the executive committee of Connecticut's new Board of Commissioners for the Common Schools. Fisk's reputation as an educational thinker led President Wayland of Brown to recommend that the new president of a Baptist college in Maine seek his advice. Olin was one of the great preachers of his time, was widely known in the South as well as his native North, and had an international orientation through his prominent role in the Evangelical Alliance. Among the honorary degrees each received was one from Brown for Fisk in 1835 and one from Yale for Olin in 1846.[26]

Both presidents understood well the role of ceremony, public position, and honorary degrees in building Wesleyan's reputation. Commencements were a particularly opportune time to celebrate the liberal arts and to build a positive institutional image. "These public occasions," Fisk noted, "accomplish much for the cause of education. They give a popular character and a general interest to the subject, and invest our seminaries of learning with a public sympathy." At Olin's last commencement there was an overflow audience of "hundreds of gentlemen and ladies from all parts of the State, together with many distinguished names from this city and other places, including Governor Seymour, Professor Benjamin Silliman of Yale and others."[27]

Celebrity speakers at various events sponsored by literary societies during graduation week served as a link between colleges and American cultural life. Just months before his conversion to Catholicism in 1844, Orestes A. Brownson gave an address on social reform from the perspective of a free-thinking Democrat. Henry Ward Beecher, the Congregational denomination's premier preacher, spoke in 1851. The largest stirring of public interest resulted from Ralph Waldo Emerson's address in 1845 on "The Function of the Scholar." In the eyes of Methodists, Emerson's "most *ethereal*" transcendentalism "appeared like a confused heap of broken sunbeams." Olin tried to immunize students just before Emerson's visit by treating transcendental faith with scorn and sarcasm in his baccalaureate sermon. He portrayed transcendentalists as "aristocratic aspirants after a graceful piety," who "commonly wander into that cold region of unfruitful speculations." He rebuked these "persons of literary tastes and polished manners" for the "wretched fastidiousness" that separated them from the simple and pure piety of the masses. As Emerson spoke three days later, Olin responded with laughter to some of the thoughts presented. He also wrote to Emerson immediately afterward, requesting that several statements in his address be toned down prior to possible publication, lest they give "much pain to many of our patrons" and "so inflict serious injury upon our Institution." Wesleyan weathered the hazards of heresy and reaped publicity benefits as host for this star from the national lecture circuit. The urban press, secular as well as denominational, took note.[28]

Honorary degrees served two major purposes. Wesleyan most often used them to build relations with Methodist conferences. Recipients of honorary master's and doctor's degrees were usually Methodist ministers and educators in Methodist academies. Closely attuned to public sentiments disparaging narrow sectarianism, Wesleyan also used these degrees to underscore the college's larger evangelical and civic role. Non-Methodist recipients included prominent ministers from Hartford and Middletown. At Wesleyan's third commencement a Baptist received the D.D. degree. Horace Bushnell, a leading Congregational minister and theologian, was similarly honored in 1842. The peak of commencement ecumenicalism probably occurred in 1845. Seated in a large oak armchair reputed to have been used in the late seventeenth century by Governor John Winthrop, Stephen Olin presided at festivities in which honorary degrees went to a Baptist and two Congregationalists. Two of them were ministers in Middletown; the third was a professor at Yale.[29]

The value of ceremony and symbol did not escape those who presided after Fisk and Olin. When Cummings wore a cap and gown at the commencement of 1858, an observer found this "added much to the dignity and impressiveness of the scene." Yet Smith and Cummings also began to develop many administrative aspects of the presidency. Smith prepared the first extensive analysis of Wesleyan's financial condition, promoted planning for the first major campaign to fund unrestricted endowment, and managed the college's investments.[30] Cummings created an entirely new level of organizational development.

Achieving an attractive and orderly campus was high on Cummings's early agenda. During his first year in office, vines were cut away from North College, heaps of ashes removed, soil graded, and footpaths replaced by sidewalks. Just a hint of student disorder reported in the New York press in 1859 brought a swift denial from the president and reassurance regarding the "good order, faithfulness, and diligence" of Wesleyan students. Using a dormitory room as his office, Cummings worked there evenings to ensure proper decorum.[31]

Cummings continued his quest for more orderly administration in July 1862 by advocating publication of a new code of rules for students and an updated catalogue of library holdings (to replace the one compiled in 1837). His systematic approach to financial assets of the university included endorsing fund accounting and stipulating that there be no use of permanent funds to finance repairs; using a "judicious lawyer" to collect unpaid subscriptions; writing off worthless subscriptions carried on the books for many years; selling off western land of uncertain worth; and acquiring land to provide for future campus expansion. In building formal and well-scheduled connections with important constituencies, Cummings paid particularly close attention to Methodist conferences and the alumni.[32]

The large and unwieldy joint board of trustees and visitors was Cummings's most persistent concern. Throughout the decade preceding charter revision in 1870, one of his major goals was to reduce the governance structure to a single board of trustees. He also questioned lifetime trusteeship, advocating election for terms of five (and later three) years to produce a more active and effective board. Most important, he pushed for appointment of "men of the right kind of influence" and wealth. Even the most finely tuned organization had continuous need for funding.[33]

Changes in the board of trustees during Wesleyan's first four decades were as important as the shift from presidents of evangelical stature to presidents with stronger administrative and denominational focus. Twenty-one trustees named in the charter of 1831 received authority to acquire, hold, and manage the college's property. They had the right to fill vacancies on the board and to increase their number to a maximum of thirty-nine. A board of visitors, elected by patron Methodist conferences and not to exceed the number of trustees, met with the trustees to elect the president and faculty, establish rules and regulations for the college, prescribe the course of study, and give general oversight to conduct of the institution. Although the powers of the joint board were much broader than those of its trustee component, the trustees were by far the most important group in the making of policy and the long-term guidance of Wesleyan. Elected annually by various conferences, visitors had a high rate of turnover. Trustees were more regular attenders at the annual meetings of the joint board and also met separately to deal with financial matters. Trustees dominated the prudential committee, established by the joint board to deal with governance matters that required action during the interval between annual meetings.[34] Much about Wesleyan's identity is reflected in the changing composition of the board of trustees and the prudential committee.

Trustees from Middletown played a major role in Wesleyan's first few decades. A majority of the original board of trustees lived in or near the city. Most of these local members were not Methodists. Congregationalists and Episcopalians from Middletown composed a third of the board until 1843, gradually diminishing to about an eighth in 1870. The total Middletown contingent declined from one-half to one-quarter of the board during the first four decades, continuing downward to one-tenth in the 1890s.

Trustees from Boston and New York established a strong presence in the 1850s. By the late 1860s the number from New York was double that of Boston, with the latter group moving to found its own university. The percentage of trustees from the New York City area would continue its growth, reaching a pre-1910 high point in 1902.

Methodist ministers and wealthy Methodist businessmen also grew in number and influence during the first four decades. Ministerial presence on the board grew from 28.6 percent in 1831 to 40 percent in 1871. Methodist businessmen, mostly from the New York City area, more than doubled their numbers in the 1860s. With this impetus from efforts by Cummings to build a board of wealth and influence, businessmen on the board would reach a nineteenth-century peak of 58.7 percent in 1879.

Changes that made the trustees less local, more urban, and more Methodist in orientation eventually affected the composition of the prudential committee. To a larger extent than any other governing group, this committee of seven-to-nine members looked out for the daily welfare of Wesleyan during the earliest decades. Usually composed entirely of Middletown trustees and a conference-appointed visitor or two residing in the city, the committee included at least two and sometimes as many as four non-Methodists. This component dropped to one in 1871, when the prudential committee was succeeded by the executive committee. Three of seven members on the new committee were wealthy businessmen from Boston and New York.[35]

As the presence of Yale-educated local trustees waned, Wesleyan's own graduates began pressing for influence and representation on the board. Organized 23 August 1836, the alumni devoted most of their efforts in the first few decades to planning periodic class reunions and making small gifts to the college. In the mid-1850s, however, the group began addressing major issues of Wesleyan's finances and leadership. Just one year after noting in 1856 that alumni were a "powerful element of strength" in Wesleyan's future, Augustus Smith felt that force when a committee appointed by the alumni recommended a change in the presidency. And the Alumni Association made its feelings on representation clearly known when calling upon the board in 1856 to make adjustments so that alumni would "no longer be passed by in the appointment of Trustees."[36]

The trustees placed this communication on file but took action a year later to serve both old and new constituencies. To fill the position open due to Samuel Hubbard's death, the trustees appointed an alumnus who lived in Middletown. The next day the joint board elected Wesleyan's first alumnus president. Soon after his arrival Cummings became the third alumnus elected to trusteeship. (Schuyler Seager '36 served as a trustee from 1844 to 1851.) Another graduate also attained election to the board at that meeting in 1858. Continuing to fill Middletown vacancies with graduates and to elect minister-educators from alumni ranks, the trustees increased alumni representation to almost a quarter of the board by 1862. The charter revision of 1870 gave alumni the right to elect five trustees. In 1883 alumni became a majority of the board.[37]

Alumni also became more active during the 1860s in raising funds, publishing biographical information on Wesleyan graduates, and organizing clubs in major cities. Their first project was to establish an endowment for purchase of library books. Then they successfully urged the faculty to nominate the campaign's major donor for an honorary degree. In 1869 they pledged a substantial amount toward completion of Memorial Chapel. From initial data collection in 1860 until publication of the first *Alumni Record* in 1869, the Alumni Association encouraged and supported this "more perfect history of the Alumni." Boston alumni met in 1867 at the Revere House, the city's most prestigious hotel, for their first annual dinner, replete with songs, toasts, and a report from the president. New York's club initiated a similar annual event two years later, gathering for a meal and an evening of camaraderie at Delmonico's, a highly fashionable restaurant. Joseph Cummings had begun the decade with a strong desire "to connect as clearly as is possible with the Institution the interests and sympathies of the Alumni." By 1870 these links were well forged.[38]

Changes with reference to alumni and trustees at Wesleyan in the years from 1831 to 1870 fit, in most respects, the pattern emerging among New England colleges. Wesleyan's Alumni Association (1836) was preceded by similar organizations at Williams (1821) and Yale (1827), and followed by those at Amherst (1842) and Harvard (1842). Alumni began electing overseers at Harvard in 1866, and the practice of electing trustees soon spread to Williams (1868), Wesleyan (1870), Yale (1871), and Amherst (1874). Clergy constituted a little more than one-third of Wesleyan's trustees in 1870, about the same proportion as that found at Williams and close to the average percentage for a group of fifteen private colleges located mostly in the Northeast.[39]

Unlike the general trend in this group from 1860 to 1900, however, Wesleyan's ministerial component waxed rather than waned. Clergy on Wesleyan's board would reach a peak of 50 percent in 1892. Wesleyan's contingent of businessmen grew from 16 percent higher than the fifteen-college average in 1860 to 20 percent higher in 1880. A corresponding dearth of lawyers and physicians placed Wesleyan's board by 1870 increasingly in the hands of Methodist clergy and wealthy laymen from business backgrounds who were devoted to building an ever-stronger denomination. Almost 83 percent of the board in 1870 came from these two groups.[40]

Shifts in the style of presidential leadership, the composition of the trustees, and the role of alumni brought new levels of organization-mindedness to Wesleyan by the late 1850s. Alumni became quick to criticize any lack of efficiency in the conduct of the presidency. Noting that Wesleyan alumni constituted a powerful influence in the church, Joseph Cummings worked with the joint board to keep denominational constituencies well informed through regular visits and reports. In the mid-1850s the board directed that printed annual financial reports be prepared and distributed to the patron conferences. The board also called for an annual report from each academic department. The first *Alumni Record* assigned an identification number to each graduate. This provided an efficient means of assembling and cross-referencing data on alumni, particularly with regard to family relationships.[41] Most of these and other changes in organizational orientation were closely related to the fundamental question of what sources of financial support would sustain this enterprise of liberal learning.

Citizens, Methodists, and Alumni

Middletown was the primary source of assets used to found Wesleyan. Land and buildings worth more than $30,000, endowment subscriptions of about $18,000, chemical apparatus, and almost a fifth of the 2,750 volumes in the original library came from Middletown. Nonlocal contributors had, by late 1833, provided only about $30,000 in endowment subscriptions. Noting that the patron Methodist conferences had nearly 100,000 members, a New York Conference minister was astonished at the low level of denominational support. It is clear why Fisk used his inaugural address to observe with gratitude how "the finger of divine Providence pointed to Middletown" as a location. "But for this aid from without," he explained to British Methodists several years later, "our own church could not have commanded the means for commencing of the University."[42]

Some of the funding from Middletown, however, was almost lost in the swirling currents of Jacksonian politics. In 1833 Wesleyan's prudential committee sought payment of Middletown's $10,000 subscription authorized four years earlier by citizens attending a town meeting. Referred to a committee at the town meeting of 7 October 1833, this request soon stirred a controversy. A meeting of "Mechanics and Farmers," perhaps an incipient Working Men's party such as those that flowered briefly in the Northeast during this period, passed resolutions opposing payment of the $10,000 to Wesleyan and advocating that it be used instead to support common schools.[43]

Spirited debate raged in the local newspapers. Opponents of the grant, claiming "strict principles of Republicanism," argued that Wesleyan trustees were "already embracing a large portion of the wealth, legal talent, and personal influence in the town." These critics objected to using public resources for an institution benefiting only a minority of residents. Supporters of the grant countered that Wesleyan, like Partridge's academy, brought large financial benefits distributed throughout the local economy and provided (during the term breaks) teachers for the common schools. Opponents argued that the town meeting of 1829 had lacked legal authority to make such a grant. Supporters appealed to the city's sense of honor, noting an obligation incurred by a large majority vote taken at a well-attended public meeting. To the opposition's argument that the burden of support for Wesleyan should chiefly rest on the Methodist denomination, Willbur Fisk responded that Methodists already showed signs of meeting their responsibility. Conference academies served as a major source of students.[44]

The opposition was strong. It was probably based in the growing ranks of Jacksonian Democrats, who would seize control of the Connecticut legislature from the Whigs in 1835. A compromise was needed, particularly one that would defuse the issue of additional tax burden to support an institution educating a tiny minority. At a special town meeting 25 November 1833, citizens considered a proposal for leasing to Wesleyan Middletown's interest in proceeds from the town quarry in

Chatham (now Portland) until the sum realized reached $10,000. The assignment of these rights was not to extend beyond forty years. It was not much of an overstatement for one Wesleyan supporter to claim that default on the original grant "would probably prove fatal to the University." Severely threatened, the alliance between Middletown and the Methodists survived by a vote of 214 to 169.[45]

Although quarry proceeds would come in slowly, reaching $9,000 in 1861, the Middletown vote enabled Wesleyan to certify that it now had the $40,000 in valid endowment subscriptions required by academy trustees for transfer of the land and buildings to the Wesleyan trustees. This transfer occurred in late December 1833. Middletown had delivered the resources of critical importance to establishing the college.[46]

Middletown's role in Wesleyan finances for the next two decades was more that of a lender than a donor. Annual deficits, initially covered by using funds intended for endowment, soon necessitated loans from Middletown banks. By the mid-1840s new loans from this source enabled liquidation of older indebtedness. Buildings and grounds originally given by Middletown served informally as security for these loans.[47] Middletown thus helped Wesleyan muddle through the long depression following the panic of 1837.

Contributors from Middletown responded with modest gifts when asked in 1855 to help the Centum Millia campaign reach its goal. Even with contributions of $1,000 from Laban Clark and $500 from the faculty, Middletown's subscriptions amounted to less than $5,000. Samuel Russell's $300 led local gifts from non-Methodists, as compared to those of Methodist laymen in New York (Daniel Drew, $5,000) and Boston (Isaac Rich, $20,000; Lee Claflin, $10,000; John Gove, $7,500). Two years later Rich nominated his former pastor, Joseph Cummings, to succeed Augustus Smith, a Middletown resident during his quarter century of service as faculty member and then president. All that the three long-term local non-Methodist trustees who attended the meeting could do was join forty-four other prominent Middletown citizens the next day in expressing their "deepest regret and surprise" at Smith's forced resignation. Their public letter stated concern that the joint board's action could have a negative effect on future relations between college and community.[48]

Smith's successor expressed frustration with Middletown's potential donors in 1863 while struggling to raise from local sources a major part of the $3,500 needed to construct a gymnasium. He reported the prevailing opinion that Middletown did not properly appreciate the advantages conferred by Wesleyan. This opinion, he claimed, "has greatly embarrassed us and kept from the Institution a large amount of funds." There was talk in late 1862 of removing Wesleyan to Worcester or Boston. Despite a few signs of economic revival in the mid-1860s, most Methodists probably viewed Middletown as a once-prosperous city now "sadly in need of rejuvenation" and no longer able to provide support commensurate with Wesleyan's needs.[49]

State aid during the years from 1834 to 1854 almost equaled the value of land and buildings deeded to Wesleyan in 1833 by Middletown proprietors. Approaching state legislatures for assistance to collegiate enterprises essentially local and evangelical in nature was a common practice in antebellum America. Distinctions between public and private institutions, established in the Dartmouth College Case of 1819, were seldom if ever employed to define separate sectors of higher education until after the Civil War. A long-established American practice of unfettered, pragmatic competition for government resources and favors prompted Dartmouth College trustees to plan a petition for state aid just a few months after Chief Justice John Marshall announced the Supreme Court's decision. The pattern of occasional special governmental concessions and grants of money or land that benefited almost all colleges prior to 1800 would continue for at least another half century.[50]

When Wesleyan in 1833 first petitioned the state legislature for an appropriation, there was ample precedent near at hand. Yale received more than half of its total gifts during the eighteenth century from the General Assembly and obtained a bank bonus of $7,000 in 1831. A grant to Washington (later Trinity) College that same year amounted to $11,500. The Massachusetts legislature helped Williams to survive with grants worth about $53,000 from 1793 to 1823 and responded to Willbur Fisk's petition by granting half a township of land to Wesleyan Academy in 1828.[51]

Two of the grants to Wesleyan came through use of the bank bonus device. After an unsuccessful first effort to obtain state aid, Wesleyan petitioned in 1834 for $20,000 to endow a Connecticut Professorship of Intellectual, Moral, and Political Science. Apparently sensing that a bill for a direct grant would not be politically viable, those in the legislature working for Wesleyan's petition employed a method that could garner support from both parties. For the Whig majority favorable to a strong banking system, bank charters to which provisions to aid higher education were added might be quite appealing. Minority Democrats might be more inclined to tolerate such charters if the corporate privilege granted came with a price, a fee assessed for an educational enterprise that might otherwise tap the general treasury.[52]

The legislative pathway was complex and hazardous. Efforts to amend a bill chartering the Stamford Bank with provisions for payment of a $5,000 fee to Wesleyan survived an attempt to cut the amount in half. The fee of $15,000 for Wesleyan attached to the charter for the Manufacturers Bank at Farmington was almost diverted to subsidize start-up costs of the Connecticut Silk Manufacturing Company. After several legislative maneuvers the final amount for Wesleyan in the charter was $10,000. Since this bank never went into operation, Wesleyan received as a result of the 1834 legislative session only the $5,000 from Stamford. The other antebellum bank bonus for Wesleyan was $2,000 paid by the Middlesex County Bank for authorization granted in 1851 to increase its capital stock.[53]

Of far greater importance was the $10,000 grant made in 1839. Willbur Fisk's plea for state aid, published in pamphlet form after his death and distributed to all members of the General Assembly, began by making the case for a "pressing need." Wesleyan's financial "embarrassments . . . endanger its existence," he claimed, and derived in large part from lack of dormitory rooms to accommodate increased enrollment. Fisk saw tuition from additional students as the means to eliminate annual deficits threatening survival of his young college. Except through state aid, he saw no immediate prospect to finance construction of new student housing. Middletown had done its part, and the number of students exceeded the capacity of the dormitory donated by town residents.[54] Methodists were giving only small amounts, usually for scholarships that further reduced tuition income. The national financial depression was too severe to hope for large gifts from individual sources.

Fisk's pamphlet also appealed to "friends of equal rights and privileges," noting grants made to Yale and Washington. He demonstrated the cultural benefits to the state from colleges, especially in strengthening the common schools. His most telling argument, however, was an analysis of "pecuniary profit" to residents of the state if Wesleyan had buildings that would enable enrollment to double. Almost 80 percent of Wesleyan's students, each of whom spent about $250 per year, came from beyond Connecticut's borders. Increased enrollment would bring more money into the state. Lack of help from the legislature, he warned, might cause removal of the institution to New York. While assistance to Wesleyan hung in the legislative balance, there was talk of removal to

Troy, Poughkeepsie, or Rhinebeck.[55] What better way could be found to anchor Wesleyan in Connecticut than with a grant for a building?

Governor William W. Ellsworth, a Whig, opened the General Assembly session in 1839 with a message that included praise for the recently deceased Fisk and support for aid to Wesleyan. A petition campaign the previous year, although unsuccessful in persuading a retrenchment-minded General Assembly to grant funds for additional college buildings, probably built a presumption with some legislators that Wesleyan was next in line among the state's colleges and was entitled to assistance. The new petition boldly requested $30,000; the initial amount considered by the House was $24,000. Opposition to this level of funding led to a series of maneuvers by Middletown's representative, Dr. Charles Woodward, to create sufficient support for a grant of $10,000. A Congregationalist and a Democrat, Woodward spoke of Wesleyan as "not exclusively sectarian" and as beneficial to the public interest. In the key action, taken by the House on 23 May, aid to Wesleyan won approval by the slim margin of ten votes. Most of the $10,000 financed construction of a new boarding hall.[56]

Wesleyan's final grant from the state prior to 1870 facilitated movement beyond local and state funding into an era of denominational and alumni support. Enacted in 1854, the bill authorized a conditional grant of $10,000. Middletown citizens contributed only a small portion of the $90,000 that had to be raised in order to receive the legislative grant. This prospect of state assistance primarily served to stimulate higher levels of Methodist donations.[57]

Support from Methodists left much to be desired prior to the mid-1850s. Appeals to the Methodist constituency in the 1830s and 1840s balanced several themes. Assurances that Wesleyan would not "inculcate Methodism" accompanied appeals to denominational loyalty. Use of the college to advance the denomination was advocated along with reminders of Methodist responsibility to help "create a republic of letters among the American people." Except for narrowly Methodist appeals during the brief presidency of Nathan Bangs, Wesleyan urged Methodists to consider their responsibility "to the public, to ourselves, and . . . to . . . the cause of evangelizing the world." Despite costly efforts of agents carrying these appeals and lofty goals into the various conference districts, Willbur Fisk found that Methodist contributions to education and to Wesleyan in particular were as "meager as the leakage of a miser's purse." When close to death in 1839, Fisk spoke to faculty members of "his fear and regret that the Church generally was not sufficiently alive to the interests of the University." Olin's travels in the 1840s from conference to conference and church to church to establish an endowment of $60,000 achieved but limited success. The portion of annual operating expenses covered by gifts and by income from gifts made by Methodists inched up from about 40 percent in the 1830s to about 50 percent of Wesleyan's severely retrenched budget in the late 1840s.[58]

A heightened sense of denominational identity, organization, and purpose appearing in American religious life of the 1850s and 1860s brought Methodists into a much closer nurturing relationship with Wesleyan. Structural signs of this dawning era of denominationalism can be found in the final breakup of cooperative organizations sponsored by Presbyterians and Congregationalists. Loosely gathered denominations such as the latter began to organize on a national level. Baptists extended operations of the state conventions to bring formerly local colleges under their oversight. Methodists moved toward more complex organization by including laymen in meetings of the General Conference and by establishing a national board of education. Mobilized for competition, American churches by 1870 had entered a period of "intense denominational rivalries."[59]

Consideration of removing Wesleyan to a location where it might receive greater denominational (and local) support was one sign of growing Methodist interest in the college. Timely grants from the state legislature in 1839 and 1854, practical considerations in abandoning valuable land and buildings, legal restraints, and emotional ties to a campus holding the "sacred dust" of Fisk and Olin kept Wesleyan in Middletown. Another indication of denominational attentiveness to Wesleyan's needs in the 1850s was greater effort made by Methodist academies to direct their graduates toward the university. Joseph Cummings noted success in this endeavor by the mid-1860s.[60]

Methodist leaders also showed a quickening interest in certain details of denominational presence on campus. The self-perpetuating board of trustees, as compared to one that might be elected by patron conferences, was viewed as anomalous for "a denominational institution." The *Christian Advocate* noted that none of the three orators addressing the student societies at the commencement of 1858 was a Methodist. The level of piety among students appeared insufficient in the early 1860s. Statistics published in 1867 facilitated close scrutiny of the number of conversions and potential ministers at Wesleyan as compared to other colleges.[61]

Calls for a stronger Methodist educational system became more insistent in the 1860s. Leadership on this issue came from George R. Crooks, editor of the *Methodist*. Advocating a configuration of regional Methodist universities, Crooks saw them as "Methodist institutions . . . holding the *Methodist* name . . . culturing *Methodist* piety and . . . chiefly of *Methodist* patronage." Such institutions would help meet the denomination's pressing need for better-educated ministers. As Methodists moved from a period of evangelism to one of culture, he argued a few years later, the denomination needed ever-better organization and the creation of high level "literary centers." Other Methodist leaders sensing the increasing wealth and education of church members agreed. A "thoroughly cultured ministry" would be required lest "the pulpit . . . be behind the pew in intellectual power." As Methodists competed with other denominations, ministers must lead with intellect as well as piety.[62]

Wesleyan's change of presidents in 1857 served well the movement to link denominational development with improved education of ministers. Election of a scholarly layman five years earlier had distressed churchmen fearful of a plan "to drive a religious predominance from the University." Cummings's credentials were more ministerial than scholarly, and he brought the desire and skill to bind church and college more closely together. An aspirant to high denominational office, Cummings entered upon his duties in 1858 with strong backing from ministerial colleagues. "It is necessary in various ways," he told the joint board in 1860, "to cause the attention of the church to be directed towards the Institution." In his first annual report he informed the board that regular Sunday preaching had been restored on campus and called for construction of a new chapel. He established a voluntary theology class and supported such study in conjunction with the three-year bachelor of science course as preparation for the ministry. Acknowledging the difficulty of gaining nonlocal support, he nonetheless worked hard to cultivate conference interest and to tap denominational fund drives such as that in 1866 for the centenary of American Methodism. His proposals to restructure the board, increase faculty positions, construct and equip facilities, and enlarge the endowment were consistently couched in terms of "the church has the right to demand," the "wants of the church," the "honor of our church," and "our interests as a Denomination." Excellence was necessary to attract and retain the young men of the church.[63]

Solicitation of denominational support for Wesleyan and other Methodist colleges during the Cummings presidency (1858–75) probed for deep-seated denominational instincts. Comparisons with funding for

Congregational colleges demonstrated a need to be ever more competitive. "Surrounded," as it was, "by powerful colleges of other denominations," Wesleyan needed large increases in endowed funds. Pleas for financial support tried to evoke fear and guilt in Methodist parents, who would "wrong their children" by sending them to schools and colleges under the direction of other denominations. Such students would become "estranged from the church of their fathers." Despite "the intimate relation between the prosperity of the Church and our literary Institutions," yield for Wesleyan from the centenary campaign fell "far short of expectations." Methodists were under considerable pressure to redeem themselves and advance the denomination by providing funds and students for Wesleyan.[64]

Responses in the form of small contributions from church members during the 1850s and 1860s were nearly the same as those of the two prior decades. About $30,000 of the $76,000 realized from the Centum Millia campaign of 1853–55 came in donations of modest amounts. Sale of cheap scholarships and the centenary fund drive in the 1860s may have brought in as much as $40,000 more for general endowment from the denominational rank and file. It was major gifts from a few wealthy Methodists that raised the level of denominational support for Wesleyan. By the late 1860s these large contributions had significantly increased the portion of Wesleyan's endowment income attributable to denominational donors. Methodist money supplied approximately 70 percent of annual operating costs.[65]

Methodist laymen accumulating wealth in the financial centers of Boston and New York became increasingly important to Wesleyan from the mid-1840s to 1870. The first few serving as Wesleyan trustees began attending board meetings regularly in the late 1840s. Enough were present in 1855 for the denominational press to take note. Joseph Cummings had a keen sense of individual riches developing in the denomination and urged that "wealthy men should be connected with the Corporation." He cultivated their continuing support through such means as naming of endowed chairs for the donors and having portraits of benefactors painted for display on campus. He supported the lay representation movement that brought some of Wesleyan's trustees into conference meetings previously limited to clergy. In 1869 a layman from Boston presided at Wesleyan's annual trustee meeting; two years later a layman from New York filled that position. Along with many other colleges in post–Civil War America, Wesleyan would be financed principally by new urban wealth.[66]

Methodist philanthropists who served on
Wesleyan's board of trustees were instrumental in linking the college to new
urban wealth. *Clockwise from upper left*:
Jacob Sleeper, Isaac Rich, Orange Judd,
and Daniel Drew.

Major contributors to Wesleyan from Boston included Jacob Sleeper, Lee Claflin, and Isaac Rich. Beginning in the mid-1840s, Sleeper collected and forwarded a steady stream of annual contributions from the Boston area. Many were from donors of less than $100, but his own gifts in the $500 to $1,000 range headed the list. With a fortune gained in the manufacture of clothing and then increased through investments in real estate, Sleeper gave the bulk of his annual income to hundreds of churches, institutions, and needy individuals, most of them related to the Methodist denomination. For fifty-nine years this gentle, unassuming man served his local church as superintendent of the Sunday school. A close friend and advisor to Olin, Sleeper tried to keep the weary president's spirits up in hard times. As winter approached in the late fall of 1845, Sleeper sent Olin an overcoat.[67]

Isaac Rich acquired his wealth in the fish business and then real estate. Befriended in boyhood by Willbur Fisk, Rich kept a portrait of Fisk in his reception room and named one of his finest ships the *Willbur Fisk*. Rich wanted to be a minister, but the desired call never came. As a layman, however, he contributed much time and wealth to Methodist enterprises. His first large gift to Wesleyan, made in the mid-1850s, was followed by three others after Cummings became president. A bequest of $10,000 to Cummings indicated their close friendship. This man of "beautiful and vivacious countenance" was Wesleyan's most generous early donor, contributing from 1846 to 1872 a total of about $150,000.[68]

Whereas Rich often used a matching-gift approach to philanthropy, Lee Claflin preferred to make a capstone contribution that enabled a specific goal to be reached. He showed his high regard for Fisk by naming one of his sons Wilbur Fisk Claflin. With initial prosperity from production of leather, boots, and shoes, Claflin invested successfully in western land, banking, coal mining, and shipping. Constantly concerned with his spiritual shortcomings, he worked hard on his piety and his benevolences. He helped many needy individuals; supported Methodist churches, societies, and schools; and provided critical funding to colleges for African-Americans. From the mid-1840s to the mid-1850s he gave about $18,000 to Wesleyan.[69]

The fourth self-made Methodist millionaire of meager schooling in Wesleyan's early financial history gained and lost his fortune in New York. Daniel Drew took a considerable interest in Wesleyan, attending more than a dozen annual trustee meetings from 1848 through 1870. His grandson, Daniel Drew Chamberlain, joined him on the board in 1865 at age twenty-six. With an extraordinary "mixture of piety and rascality," Drew built Methodist churches and Drew Theological Seminary using money gained from unscrupulous stock manipulations. Like other major donors, Drew gave interest-bearing notes to Wesleyan for his endowment subscriptions that began in 1855 and reached a total of $100,000 in 1868. By 1871, when he started down the road to financial disaster, he had paid about $14,000 in interest on his notes. Before the notes became worthless in 1876, he sent another $30,000 in small gifts and interest.[70]

Two other important laymen from New York, Oliver Cutts and Charles C. North, were generous donors in the 1860s. Captain Cutts engaged in trade with Haiti and owned a plantation in Port-au-Prince. He pledged $25,000 in 1863 to endow a chair, paying the professorial salary for more than a decade. There is no record that he paid the principal. North, also a successful merchant, gave Sunday exhortations at Sing Sing Prison, was a founder of Drew Theological Seminary, helped plan American Methodism's centenary celebration of 1866, and served on the Methodist board of education. Contributions by North and his wife to a variety of Wesleyan projects in the 1850s and 1860s reached several thousand dollars. He wrote lengthy articles on Wesleyan's finances in the late 1860s and became president of the board of trustees in 1871.[71]

Joining these denominational donors was a group that in a few decades would be ready to succeed them. Wesleyan alumni, like the group of major contributors, had particularly active members drawn from Methodists in New York City. By the mid-1850s some prominent graduates viewed with approval Wesleyan's growing denominational identity. They were now sufficiently numerous and established to be seen as "a new ground of hope" for building the university's future prosperity. Their first major fund-raising effort, begun in 1863, was to create an endowed fund for purchase of library books. Responding to Isaac Rich's offer of matching funds in 1864 toward construction of a library building, the alumni reached their goal of $25,000 by July 1865.[72]

Foremost among alumni supporters in the 1860s was Orange Judd '47. Judd's pledge in 1869 to provide a new science building received acclaim from Charles North as "the first large gift rendered to our University by one of her own sons." Sensing an important transition toward alumni leadership in gifts to Wesleyan, North pointed out that previous large donations had come "from successful businessmen, who, having been denied a liberal education for themselves, were happy in laying the foundation for others." Judd's generosity as an alumnus emanated from

Methodist activism, scientific and journalistic acumen, and short-term success as a New York investor. His compilation and publication of Wesleyan's first *Alumni Record* in 1869 supplied evidence of the benefits that graduates had bestowed upon the denomination. His innovative and successful Sunday school publications, *Lessons for Every Sunday in the Year*, prepared with the help of Julia M. Olin and James Strong, appeared in four volumes during the early 1860s. Before beginning to amass wealth as an agricultural editor and publisher, Judd had studied analytical and agricultural chemistry at Yale. While building his *American Agriculturalist* from a circulation of less than 1,000 in 1856 to more than 100,000 in 1864, he had also served as agricultural editor of the *New York Times*. Subscription and advertising revenues invested in a Long Island railroad enterprise brought him sufficient resources to state that he would fund construction of a first-rate academic facility for Wesleyan. But financial reversals from subsequent losses in the railroad venture, publishing, and real estate speculation led to bankruptcy in 1883. Judd had paid $65,000 of his pledge. Wesleyan used $36,000 in endowment funds to cover the balance of costs for Judd Hall.[73]

In 1870 Judd stood at the center of a network of support that would sustain Wesleyan in the coming decades. Just two years before, Daniel Drew and Isaac Rich were called forward at commencement and cheered because of their service "for the Church." With newly won prominence and praise as an alumnus, Judd joined Drew at the second annual New York City alumni dinner in 1870. The widows of Olin and Fisk attended, President Cummings spoke, and toasts were given "in pure water." Churchmen, campus leaders, and committed urban alumni converged at the Astor House in a celebration of Wesleyan's bright future.[74]

Equipping the Educational Enterprise
There was much to celebrate in the acquisition of campus resources between 1831 and 1870. Purchase of small parcels of land to supplement the twelve acres that would be transmitted in 1833 by trustees of the academy began less than two months after receipt of the charter. This process continued for the next four decades, slowly shaping an almost square campus that extended westward from High Street to the base of Foss Hill. A narrow strip stretched over Foss Hill and included the college cemetery created in the late 1830s. Thought first given in 1832 to planting trees on the barren grounds where Partridge drilled his cadets yielded action in the next decade. "Waving young trees" planted by students in 1841, an observer noted, were associated with "all halls

of classic learning, from the days of Plato and his Academy." By 1858 an abundance of trees obstructed a front view of the buildings. Perhaps trimmed or thinned out during subsequent years, the trees were found to "stand at judicious intervals" by 1863. Ivy on the walls of buildings was noted as early as 1849, and "asphaltum walks" were installed by 1870. The campus projected a general air of neatness and comfort.[75]

From the earliest years, a substantial portion of the college's meager resources went toward the purchase of scientific apparatus and mineral collections. The excellent telescope Fisk ordered in Paris in 1835 was replaced in 1869 with a new instrument surpassed in the United States only by the one used at Harvard. "A most splendid orrery," bought in 1837 for $2,200 was progenitor of state-of-the-art apparatus for astro- nomical study listed in the catalogue of 1869/70. Expenditure of more than $7,000 in 1868 to purchase the Shurtleff Cabinet of shells, birds, and botanical specimens greatly enhanced Wesleyan's collection of min- erals, fossils, and other materials for study of natural history.[76]

Books also received high priority right from the start. "A library we must have," Willbur Fisk declared in 1831, and he worked hard to build the collection. Starting with probably more than one thousand volumes from the academy library and another five hundred from "an association in the city," Fisk soon obtained free documents from the Library of Congress, purchased a private library at a highly favorable price, and received the gift of a smaller personal collection. On his European trip he bought several hundred volumes of the latest standard French scientific works and some texts in classical literature. He also received various books donated by British Methodists. The well-diversified col- lection described in a published catalogue of 1837 was soon augmented by Fisk's bequest of classical works from his personal library. By 1840 the college and literary society collections totaled about ten thousand volumes, a few thousand more than could be found at Williams and a few thousand less than at Amherst. The collection grew only slightly during hard times in the 1840s and was passed in size by that of Wil- liams. Substantial increases in the 1860s, aided in part by acquiring the library of Troy University when its doors closed, brought the collection to almost twenty thousand volumes in 1870. Wesleyan ranked about twentieth among the nation's college and university libraries.[77]

Middletown and the state of Connecticut played the major roles in providing campus buildings built before 1865. Some of these structures dated back to the days of the academy. Construction of the Lyceum (called Chapel Building from 1862 until September 1871 and then South

College) began in October 1824 and was completed the next spring. The Dormitory (called North College after September 1871) was built at the same time. Just months prior to receiving from Middletown proprietors the deed to these brownstone buildings in late 1833, Wesleyan purchased Old Boarding Hall (1825), a brick structure on the southeastern edge of the campus privately constructed and operated to serve the academy and then Wesleyan. It was sold and demolished in 1847/48. In 1835 the brick building built by Partridge behind the Dormitory was purchased from him for $175. Used as a chemistry laboratory until 1871, it was demolished in 1907.[78]

In addition to the Lyceum and the Dormitory, major buildings constructed before 1865 were the President's House (1837, later known as the Dean's House), the Boarding Hall (1839, known as Observatory Hall from 1868 to 1927), and Old Gym (1864). Completed at an expense, including barn and fences, of about $6,750, the new home for Willbur Fisk (and his successors until 1904) modestly took its place among other Greek Revival houses on High Street. More than a third of construction costs were covered by royalties from Fisk's *Travels*, with the stipulation that 6 percent interest on this amount be paid annually to his widow. Funds granted by the Connecticut General Assembly paid for the Boarding Hall, placed southwest of the two brownstone buildings. This frame structure later contained dormitory rooms as well as a dining hall. When Joseph Cummings provided half the funds needed (by covering the teaching assignments of a faculty member on leave as well as his own), an observatory tower was added in 1868. Subsequently known as Observatory Hall, the building was razed in 1927 to make way for Harriman Hall. Middletown donations helped fund construction of the Old Gym, also located behind College Row until moved in 1897.[79]

Middletown began College Row in the mid-1820s; Methodists completed it almost a half century later. The plan to align academic buildings in a row facing an open area originated in the early days of Partridge's academy. Following the example set by Yale, similar configurations appeared at Amherst and other New England institutions in the early nineteenth century. Up through the mid-1850s plans persisted to erect a building south of the Lyceum in a style that would "correspond with the exterior" of the Dormitory in size and scale. Such a building would contain a chapel and other needed facilities. These aspirations to symmetry were replaced by an arrangement in the late 1860s placing a church at the center of a longer row.[80]

College Row as it appeared on the letterhead of stationery printed in 1875. Begun with two academy buildings constructed in 1824–25, this row of brownstone buildings was completed with Judd Hall and Memorial Chapel, both dedicated in 1871.

Like Fisk, Joseph Cummings called for more buildings early in his presidency. Cummings argued that buildings in good repair had major ethical and churchly purposes. "There is a moral influence in well arranged buildings," he told the trustees, "that cannot otherwise be secured. In all our institutions the buildings do much of the teaching whether for good or for evil." New buildings, he argued, would also serve "our interest, honor, and duty as a church" by attracting Methodist young men and thus helping to retain them within the denominational fold.[81]

Methodists responded to appeals from Cummings with gifts to build three brownstone buildings extending in a line south from the Dormitory and the Lyceum: Rich Hall (1868), Memorial Chapel (1871), and Judd Hall (1871). Built with a gift of $40,000 from Isaac Rich, the new library had a Gothic Revival style complementary to that of the chapel constructed by its side. The almost $70,000 for construction of Memorial Chapel came in response to appeals based on denominationalism and patriotism. Leadership provided by the Ladies' Centenary Association called for contributions that would make the chapel a monument to the century of American Methodism celebrated in 1866. This "earnest and enterprising" group of women, whose husbands were faculty, trustees, alumni, and friends of the college, wrote hundreds of letters to raise money through small donations. The Army and Navy Union, organized in 1866 by Wesleyan alumni who served on the Northern side, solicited gifts for a chapel to honor the almost three hundred Wesleyan alumni who had served in the Civil War (thirty-one of whom lost their lives). Judd Hall, one of America's first buildings designed exclusively for comprehensive undergraduate instruction in science, was already partially constructed when the cornerstone was laid 5 May 1870. Among the miscellany of items deposited in the cornerstone were: photographs of Judd, Rich, Drew, and Cummings; newspapers and journals from New York City and the Methodist press; Judd's *Alumni Record*; reports to the annual conferences and their minutes; and the Methodist *Discipline*.[82] College Row was complete. Thanks to new Methodist wealth, Wesleyan was a well-equipped college with prospects of a bright academic and financial future.

Methodist Majorities
All that remained was to recognize the growth of Wesleyan's denominational identity by revising the charter of 1831. The amended charter of 1870 replaced the joint board of trustees and visitors with a single board of trustees not to exceed forty members. Although a majority of the forty possible positions would be filled through election by the trustees, each of the thirteen patron Methodist conferences was entitled to appoint at least one trustee. Another five positions were to be filled by graduates elected by alumni. But the crucial revision provided that "at all times the majority of the trustees, the president, and a majority of the faculty shall be members of the Methodist Episcopal Church."[83]

Approval of the charter by the trustees, visitors, and the Connecticut General Assembly came without discernible dissent. The outgoing joint board was primarily preoccupied with provisions for election, especially those to meet longstanding alumni concerns. The sentence stipulating a Methodist president and Methodist majorities in the new board of trustees and in the faculty was offered late one evening at the end of joint board deliberations. Rev. Daniel Curry '37, editor of the *Christian Advocate*, made the motion. The next morning the joint board unanimously approved the full text of the proposed charter revisions, including this amendment. Connecticut's legislature authorized these revisions 2 June 1870.[84]

Curry was a highly influential Methodist minister in New York City from 1862 to 1887. He worked closely with wealthy Methodist laymen and was a widely recognized leader in the Alumni Association and the

New York Wesleyan alumni club. Tall, muscular, intellectually combat-ive, capable in debate of striking "Titanic blows in offensive and defen-sive warfare," and an untiring advocate of denominational objectives in higher education, Curry was a formidable force on the joint board. His sense that it was time to place a clearly Methodist stamp upon the insti-tution's charter drew upon many years of experience in alumni and trustee affairs. Perhaps no one thought it prudent to challenge him; probably no one thought it appropriate to object. With the exception of one passing mention of the provision assuring Methodist control, ac-counts of the charter change in the local and denominational press did not even note this part of the document. By 1870 Wesleyan and many other colleges could easily assume a denominational identity.[85]

4 Denominational
Support and Influence

*W*esleyan's ties with the Methodist denomination sustained *a peak of intensity from 1870 to 1890. Methodist donors serving on the almost totally Methodist board of trustees carried Wesleyan through times of financial hardship. Departures and arrivals of clerical presidents reflected fluctuations in support for each from leading lay donors and from the denomination. Coeducation began in 1872 primarily due to Methodist advocacy and traditions. The family and educational backgrounds of students were Methodist to a very large extent. Students exhibited a seriousness of academic purpose and often pursued careers of service yielding direct benefits to the denomination.*

Close connections with wealthy laymen, ministerial conferences, secondary schools, and families of the Methodist church shaped the way Wesleyan described itself and appeared in the eyes of its constituencies. Historical sketches of the college stressed Methodist origins, with little or no mention of roles played by Middletown and the Connecticut legislature. The Methodist press in New York and Boston consistently viewed Wesleyan as "mother of us all." A self-image rooted in Methodism persisted into the early years of the twentieth century. Important public events on campus up to 1906 gave ample recognition to Wesleyan's identity as a denominational, although not sectarian, college.

Metropolitan Methodists

Isaac Rich's death in Boston on 13 January 1872 marked a turning point in Wesleyan's relations with Boston Methodists. Less than four years earlier the partnership of Boston and New York in support of Wesleyan found dramatic expression at the dedication of Rich Hall. After funding construction of this library building and donating a portrait of New York's Daniel Drew to grace the interior, Rich persuaded Drew that they should each give notes for $100,000 toward Wesleyan's endowment. Announcement of these gifts to the audience gathered at the new building prompted applause, cheers, stamping of feet, waving of handkerchiefs, tears of joy, and the singing of "glory hallelujah." A year later Rich made his will, partly at the urging of Rev. Gilbert Haven '46, a promoter of the new Boston University. It was well known that Rich retained a deep interest in Wesleyan while developing a commitment to the Methodist university recently chartered in his city. Contents of the will were not yet known to those who attended the memorial service in Boston for Rich on 21 January. His close friend Joseph Cummings preached the sermon. A rumor claimed that the estate would go to Wesleyan. When the complex provisions of the will became public almost a week later, they suggested "a strong debate between Middletown and Boston." The net result, however, was clear. Rich's wealth would launch Boston University.[1]

Boston's presence on the Wesleyan board dwindled in the 1870s. Lee Claflin died in 1871. John W. Lindsay '40, the first dean of faculty at Boston University, left the board in 1875. Jacob Sleeper attended one meeting during the decade and resigned in 1879. Only modest levels of support would come from Methodists in Connecticut, most of it from a few wealthy laymen in Hartford, Bristol, and Meriden.[2] The success of Boston University, virtually ensured by Rich's bequest, left the financial fate of Wesleyan almost entirely in the hands of Methodists in metropolitan New York.

One month after Rich's death, Daniel Drew hosted the annual New York Wesleyan alumni club dinner at his home on Union Square. The more than one hundred graduates assembled at this lavish event heard a poem celebrating Wesleyan's benefactors. Acknowledging the past generosity of Rich, Sleeper, Orange Judd, and "that prince of brokers, generous Daniel Drew," the poem identified three laymen who would lead the next generation of major donors to Wesleyan: Oliver Hoyt, Andrew Stout, and George Seney n1845. Two lesser figures completed this prescient poetic inventory. All pursued business interests in Manhattan or Brooklyn; most were deeply involved in Methodist enterprises.[3]

As members of the nation's largest Protestant denomination, these men were part of the dramatic growth of membership and wealth in Methodist ranks during the late nineteenth century. Northern Methodist membership rose from 1.3 million in 1870 to 2.7 million in 1900. Once a denomination of rural residents with meager means, Methodism participated fully in the late nineteenth-century growth of America's urban middle class. Some Methodists in major cities became very wealthy. Indications of this "age of Methodist affluence" included new church edifices of impressive size and architectural detail. Tents at camp-meeting grounds yielded to neat frame cottages and the atmosphere of middle-class summer resorts. By 1890 church leaders noted with concern that increased wealth in some Methodist families produced transfers of membership to denominations of even greater wealth and social prestige.[4]

Methodists of means who remained within the denominational fold helped to finance vigorous evangelical competition. Opponents in this struggle included Catholics, Congregationalists, and Baptists. Continuing to build denominational strength in this time of religious rivalry, Methodists developed an elaborate structure of national agencies devoted to missions, publishing, and various benevolent enterprises. Competing to some extent even among themselves, Methodists founded new institutions of higher education (Boston University, 1869; Syracuse University, 1870; Vanderbilt University, 1872) and attempted to strengthen ties to older colleges (for example, Wesleyan, Dickinson, and Randolph-Macon). Churches and individuals responded to calls for "a loving and loyal denominationalism" in education. Prompted by arguments for combating the "godlessness" of state universities, they contributed to nearby Methodist institutions.[5]

Despite Methodism's highly bureaucratic control over ministers and local churches, attempts at centralized direction of schools and colleges were late and ineffective. The board of education, chartered in 1869 as an agency of the denomination's national governing body, the General Conference, reported with frustration in 1884 on the major continuing problem. Because "the work of establishing and endowing institutions of learning is local and sectional," the report observed, "for a long time practical difficulties were encountered in devising methods to incorporate their work harmoniously into our connectional system." These difficulties persisted. Even the collection of annual data on schools and colleges suffered from lack of local cooperation. The university senate, a loosely organized confederation of Methodist colleges formed in 1892 under the authority of the General Conference, made only halting progress in the establishment of standards for accreditation of Methodist-sanctioned institutions. Wesleyan cooperated with the board and the senate, but neither body offered a direct link to wealth within the denomination.[6]

Wesleyan tied itself closely to Methodism primarily through trustees rather than church polity. The only formal link to church structure in the revised charter of 1870 authorized each of the thirteen patron conferences to elect a member of the board. The conferences regularly selected one of their clerical colleagues for this position. And Wesleyan's president, also a Methodist minister, served ex officio. The geographical, denominational, and occupational characteristics of one-fourth of the fifty-five-member board from 1880 to 1910 thus remained static. The forty-one other positions were filled through election by trustees (thirty-one) and by alumni (ten). Shifts in geographical and occupational characteristics within this group of board members began to develop in the 1860s and yielded peak levels of Methodist businessmen and lawyers around 1880. The vast majority from these two occupations lived or worked in New York City and its environs. In the fall of 1879 the forty-one nonconference trustees included fifteen Methodist businessmen and two lawyers from New York City. Another eight of the nonconference trustees were Methodist ministers, including two who resided in New York City and worked closely with the metropolitan laymen on behalf of denominational enterprises. Rev. Daniel Curry, for example, joined with Oliver Hoyt in the mid-1860s to lead the committee that planned events to celebrate the centenary of American Methodism. Out of this celebration came the founding of Drew Theological Seminary, whose board of trustees from 1870 to 1910 included eighteen laymen and nine ministers from the New York City area who served concurrently on Wesleyan's board. In the city where American Methodism began and now maintained headquarters for national and international agencies, in the state where Methodists were unusually numerous and wealthy, in the denominational context of almost familylike relationships among clergy and philanthropists, Wesleyan gained support as "the mother of our denominational institutions" and "the crown and glory of our Church."[7]

Metropolitan Methodists on Wesleyan's board began in the 1870s to link trustee operations more closely to the city. The trustees first elected a New Yorker as president of the board in 1871, and leadership from the city continued for the next forty years. Finances of the college, once supervised by treasurers of the board who resided in Middletown, became in 1877 the responsibility of metropolitan trustees. A charter amendment in 1878 authorized the board to hold special meetings in the city. (Regular meetings in this location, except for the annual meeting, received similar sanction in 1905.) The board's executive committee, previously composed primarily of trustees from Middletown, became in 1892 the much larger general executive committee, with a sufficient number of board leaders from New York to give them a controlling influence.[8] Wesleyan's board had changed a great deal since the pre–Civil War years when Middletown's non-Methodist laymen such as Samuel Hubbard watched over the financial needs of the college.

Firmly connected to New York City, Wesleyan's prospects began in the 1870s to wax and wane along with the fortunes of a few metropolitan laymen. Tremors from the panic of 1873 rapidly traversed the ninety miles from Wall Street to High Street. Wesleyan's first generation of large donors from New York—Daniel Drew, Orange Judd, and Oliver Cutts—headed into hard times, forcing them to default on notes to Wesleyan. Loss of interest payments on these notes left Wesleyan in June 1876 with annual income on notes and investments reduced by 40 percent, an annual deficit equal to about half the annual operating budget, and indebtedness equal to almost half the endowment. To permit introduction of an enlarged curriculum and to meet increased operating costs due to three buildings recently completed, the trustees borrowed more money from the Middletown National Bank; sold endowment securities; almost doubled tuition, room rent, and fees; reduced faculty salaries by 10 percent; and solicited special subscriptions at annual board meetings to help cover deficits. This form of passing the hat among board members met with sufficient success in 1878 for the group to stand and sing the doxology. But there was urgent need for longer-term strategies. One was to stem erosion of endowment by adopting a charter revision in 1878 prohibiting further use of endowment funds to meet current expenses. Another was to increase the size of the board in 1879 from forty to fifty-five, including five elected by alumni (in addition to the five alumni positions created by the charter revision of 1870). Most important was the decision to seek sustained assistance from urban sources. The board relieved Cyrus Foss from some of his teaching responsibilities and put him on the road. Foss, who came from a New York pastorate and began his presidency in 1875 with two years of near despondency over Wesleyan's finances, returned to the city and sought help from wealthy Methodists.[9]

Oliver Hoyt, a leather merchant who served as president of the board for ten years in the 1870s and 1880s, heard the call and led the trustees in reducing annual deficits. Entering the leather business in 1844, Hoyt by 1870 had a partnership with his brothers Mark and William that operated seven tanneries in Pennsylvania. All three became millionaires. Oliver's high level of activity within Methodism included support for missions, education, and temperance. Gifts to Wesleyan, first from Oliver, then William and to a lesser extent Mark, reached a total of well over $150,000 by 1903.[10]

Andrew V. Stout, a former parishioner of Cyrus Foss at St. Paul's, joined Hoyt to form the "royal team" of benefactors who helped Wesleyan through the 1870s. About a month after Drew filed for bankruptcy in 1876, Stout stepped forward with a gift of $40,000 to endow a professorship. He became the host for the annual reunion of New York alumni in 1877, entertaining more than one hundred grateful graduates at his mansion on Madison Avenue. Starting as a school teacher in 1831, Stout invested a portion of his modest salary in real estate. After ventures in the 1840s as a wholesale merchant in leather and as a manufacturer of shoes, he organized the Shoe and Leather Bank of New York in the mid-1850s. Stout was president of the bank for twenty-eight years. Like Oliver Hoyt, he gave substantial sums for Methodist missions and education.[11]

George I. Seney raised levels of Methodist philanthropy dramatically in 1880, doubling Wesleyan's endowment through a series of gifts that totaled $250,000 in a single year. After a slow but sure rise through the banking ranks in Brooklyn and New York City to presidency of the Metropolitan Bank in the late 1870s, Seney became a major figure on the national scene in railroad development and speculation from 1879 to 1884. He benefited from the panic of 1873 and the subsequent depression which enabled northern investors to acquire southern railroad lines. Seney liberally watered stock as he and a few other investors took control of the East Tennessee, Virginia, and Georgia Railroad in 1881 and the Richmond and Danville in 1883. In a bold and shrewd ploy, he and Calvin S. Brice headed a syndicate that built the "Nickel Plate" (New York, Chicago, and St. Louis Railroad) line parallel to that of William H. Vanderbilt. Using the threat of selling out to Vanderbilt's chief competitor, Jay Gould, or possibly letting the line go into receivership and operate at low rates, Seney and his cohorts maneuvered Vanderbilt into buying them out at a price yielding large profit. Son of a Methodist minister, Seney spent his freshman year at Wesleyan (1841/42) and graduated from New York University in 1846. He donated more

George Ingraham Seney n1845. Seney
served on the board as a representative
of the New York East Conference,
1871–88.

than a million dollars to denominational enterprises, including Emory
University as well as Wesleyan. His gifts were the major source of funds
responsible for establishing the Methodist Episcopal Hospital of Brooklyn, and he was active in a wide range of denominational affairs.[12]

The brief panic of 1884 burst Seney's bubble and deprived Wesleyan
of $250,000 in additional funds he had pledged or intended to give.
Seney was one of four major Wall Street players who precipitated the
panic. One fled to Canada. Two went to jail. Seney's use of bank funds
to speculate in railroad stocks rendered his Metropolitan Bank vulnerable to falling stock prices. The bank closed in mid-May. Seney submitted his resignation. He immediately transferred to the bank $1.5 million
in personal assets, including his home in Brooklyn and a large collection
of paintings. With help from others on Wall Street, the bank reopened
and paid its depositors in full. Wesleyan fared less well. The roller-
coaster ride of reported endowment—up in the late 1860s with pledges
from Judd, Drew, and Cutts, down in the late 1870s due to their financial
reversals, up in the early 1880s with the rising fortunes of Seney, down
again in 1884 by 20 percent when he defaulted on subscriptions—left
an annual budget once again lacking the income to meet expenses.[13]

The "financial cyclone" of 1884 prompted resumption of 10-percent
salary reductions for faculty and another year of relief from teaching by
the president so he could devote most of his efforts to fund-raising.

During the next few years trustees resumed their practice of passing the hat to cover annual deficits, moved to modernize investment policies, and appointed a finance committee to audit and monitor all accounts. When the panic of 1893 brought several more years of hard times, the trustees were better organized to respond and had a significantly larger endowment due to major contributions from two new metropolitan donors, both of whom had important links with Methodists.[14]

Daniel Ayres n1842 made unanticipated gifts to Wesleyan in 1889 that provided $300,000 in endowment to support programs in science. This pioneering plastic surgeon was the son of a well-known Methodist layman in Brooklyn. Ayres entered Wesleyan in 1838, leaving at the end of his junior year to seek more advanced instruction at Princeton under Joseph Henry. After graduating from Princeton and obtaining his M.D. from New York University, he taught at Long Island Medical College and provided medical care for wealthy families. Although he was an Episcopalian, Ayres served as one of the first trustees of the Methodist hospital in Brooklyn. He made liberal donations to medical and other institutions. His contributions to Wesleyan increased the endowment to more than $1 million, putting Wesleyan near the top of New England colleges when ranked according to interest-bearing funds.[15]

Daniel B. Fayerweather's bequest provided another pleasant surprise in 1890. Most of the $225,000 for Wesleyan from this estate came during the years 1892–98. Fayerweather had no previous connection with Wesleyan. He attended a Congregational church. Advised by a Congregational clergyman, he prepared a will in 1884 that named twenty colleges or universities (and Union Theological Seminary) as beneficiaries. Most of these institutions had ties with the Congregational or the Presbyterian denomination. Fayerweather's knowledge of and regard for Wesleyan probably came through the Hoyt brothers. These Methodist philanthropists gave the young shoemaker his start in the leather business when they hired him in the mid-1850s and soon made him a partner. He and two partners established a new firm in 1870 that would bear his name and become, by the time of his death in 1890, the largest hide and leather business in New York City. Oliver Hoyt, who helped to launch this successful career, was president of Wesleyan's board when Fayerweather made his will. In distributing his millions made in the "Swamp," as the leather district near the Brooklyn Bridge was called, Fayerweather had ample reason to put the Methodist college in Connecticut on his list of favored liberal arts institutions.[16]

In the mid-1890s Wesleyan's endowment continued to compare favor-

John Emory Andrus '62, Methodist
multimillionaire and Wesleyan trustee
(1889–1934), supported renovation and
expansion of campus facilities

ably with those of other New England colleges. Although tuition income (after tuition reduction grants were made) covered less than 4 percent of annual expenditures, deficits ran at the modest level of $3,000, equivalent to little more than one faculty salary. Any cash-flow problems were met by short-term personal loans from John E. Andrus '62, who succeeded William Hoyt as treasurer of the board in 1892. Wesleyan's biggest need, given expanding enrollments and program growth, was in the area of facilities. A portion of the unrestricted bequest from Fayerweather funded construction of a gymnasium.[17] Other building projects elicited support from new Methodist donors.

Andrus attended Wesleyan at the behest of his father, a Methodist minister. From his graduation in 1862 until the late 1880s he had little contact with the college or the denomination. He was busy in New York becoming rich. A quick start on the way to wealth came through manufacture of medicines, especially alcohol-based elixirs. While steadily enlarging this business, he wisely invested his profits in real estate ranging from New York to Minnesota to Florida. He also became a major shareholder in Standard Oil of New Jersey and several other successful corporations. This tall, austere, tobacco-chewing tycoon joined the Wesleyan board when his son William entered as a freshman in 1889. His reconciliation with the Methodist church occurred a year later, and he sustained a high level of involvement in denominational enterprises for the next four decades. For Wesleyan he provided funds to renovate the original dormitory, North College (1893); to develop an enclosed athletic field (1898) complete with a grandstand (1902); and to cover about one-quarter of the construction costs of a new classroom building, Fisk Hall (1904). These contributions plus those made toward the library fund and reduction of annual deficits up to 1910 easily exceeded $75,000.[18]

Charles Scott, with help from his son Charles Scott, Jr., '86, provided Wesleyan with a physics building. The John Bell Scott Laboratory (1904) memorialized another son, who graduated from Wesleyan in 1881 and died in 1898 of an illness contracted while serving as a chaplain in the Spanish-American War. Scott came to Philadelphia from Ireland at age two, attended public schools, and entered the saddlery business in the 1840s. He soon became a partner and prospered from high demand during the Civil War. In the mid-1870s he turned to the manufacture of car springs and built the second largest business of this type in the nation. A lifetime Methodist, Scott served on the boards of several denominational enterprises. The gifts he and his son made to Wesleyan from 1878 to 1910 reached a total of about $135,000.[19]

Five other Methodists responded regularly to Wesleyan's need for large contributions. George G. Reynolds '41, a Brooklyn lawyer and judge, led this group. He gave almost $100,000 prior to 1911, including major contributions toward construction of the Eclectic fraternity house (1907). One-time major donations or bequests of at least $5,000 during the years 1870–1910 came from more than a dozen individuals having important ties to Methodism. Many smaller donors joined these wealthy Methodists in supporting Wesleyan through denominational campaigns, particularly the Twentieth Century Thank Offering at the turn of the century. Contributions made through churches to this multipurpose campaign could be designated for Wesleyan. Small donations to the thank offering, including several thousand dollars from the Middletown Methodist church, provided approximately 20 percent of the funding for Fisk Hall. Dedicated in 1904 with appropriate churchly ceremonies, this brownstone building and Scott Laboratory gave architectural testimony to an era when all but a fraction of the approximately $2 million raised to save, sustain, and enlarge Wesleyan came through Methodist connections.[20]

Of the dozen largest contributors, who provided three-fourths of this total, ten made their fortunes in the New York City area. Nine were active in a variety of denominational enterprises. They served on boards for missions and Methodist hospitals, superintended Sunday schools, and attended the annual and quadrennial conferences that determined denominational policies. Some, such as Oliver Hoyt and George Seney, were lifelong friends. Seney and Andrew Stout (along with another trustee, Bishop Edmund S. Janes) had summer residences in Bernardsville, New Jersey.[21] The network of metropolitan Methodists extended from churches in Manhattan, Brooklyn, and Yonkers to the campus in Middletown.

Presidents and Patrons

Wesleyan presidencies, as Joseph Cummings learned in the mid-1870s, took many of their cues from this network. Cummings had his career roots in the New England Conference, particularly in the Boston area. His former parishioner, Isaac Rich, nominated him for the Wesleyan presidency in 1857, and Boston philanthropy led by Rich provided a major portion of resources accumulated during the Cummings administration.[22] Cummings also raised funds in New York, but by 1873 the founding of Boston University and the death of Rich rendered his position vulnerable. Boston would no longer be a major source of funds to sustain an expanded physical plant and an expanding curriculum. The New York trustees who dominated Wesleyan's board needed a president who could tap their metropolis for a doubling of the endowment.

Rumors of a Cummings departure appeared in 1873, the same year that tensions between the president and the faculty required attention from the board. For several years faculty members had smarted under the sharp, sarcastic tongue of a president who thought they did not work with sufficient diligence and efficiency. This "perpetual series of insults" reached a breaking point in 1873 when Cummings called for the trustees to establish a new code of rules governing faculty work and to require annual reports from each professor. Faculty also resented the merely "reluctant assent" Cummings gave to the enlarged curriculum they formulated in 1872/73 while he was on leave of absence to travel in Europe. And after the panic of 1873, Cummings advised the trustees to exercise even greater caution in implementing this ambitious program. The major issue raised by faculty, however, was the related matter of a change of administration being "absolutely essential to the prosperity of the College." Advancing arguments salted with threats of resignation, faculty members told trustees that Cummings lacked "elements of outside popularity which are necessary to make friends for the College."[23]

Cummings submitted his resignation in January 1874 and again in June. But he did so in such a manner as to elicit board refusals to accept. By April 1875 a report at the New York East Conference defined the issue as a disagreement between the trustees and faculty. Two months later the faculty's assessment acquired additional weight from hard realities. The board confronted yet another annual deficit, mounting indebtedness, and a meager endowment that had grown only slightly in the last five years. The trustees informally sent emissaries to Cummings requesting his resignation. Cummings complied. They immediately made plans for a campaign to increase the endowment. A month later they selected a highly popular minister from New York City to serve as president and to lead that campaign.[24]

Cyrus David Foss '54 came to the Wesleyan presidency at age forty-one from fifteen years of pastorates in some of the most prestigious Methodist churches of Brooklyn and Manhattan. His "straight, strong body" of almost six feet in height, eyes of unusual brightness, dignified manner, and winsome smile combined to create a commanding pulpit presence. With "remarkable sweetness of voice," he preached well-organized, "luminous" sermons. He was a familiar, urbane figure in "the chief households of metropolitan Methodism," and his parishioners at the half-dozen churches where he held appointments included Daniel Drew, Andrew Stout, Bishop Janes, and Charles North, president of Wesleyan's trustees when they elected Foss. Oliver Hoyt experienced conversion under the preaching of Foss's father. Intimately connected with Wesleyan's trustee and alumni constituencies, this skillful expositor and advocate of Methodism was the unanimous choice of the search committee and the board. His powerful Methodist associates then persuaded him to take the position, despite its salary level 40 percent below what he received as one of the city's "princely preachers."[25]

The inauguration of Foss on 26 October 1875 was Wesleyan's first major event of this type since Willbur Fisk's induction in 1831. More than a dozen trustees from metropolitan New York attended. The recently opened Air Line Railroad reduced their travel time to less than four hours, and a special train for their return enabled them to stay at evening festivities until almost eleven. A "brilliant assembly" of trustees, faculty, students, alumni, and citizens filled the new chapel. Noah Porter, the venerable and conservative president of Yale, offered the opening prayer. Speakers consistently pursued the event's goal of "rallying friends of the institution to new zeal and combined efforts for its advancement." The student speaker bluntly noted Wesleyan's current financial "crisis." Handing the college keys to Foss, his weary predecessor's parting blessing was that they might "be symbols of your power to open the hearts of the wealthy, the powerful, the generous, and secure new resources." The alumni speaker reminded his audience of Foss's popularity in Methodist circles and his "sacrifice of personal comfort" in accepting this new denominational assignment. On behalf of the trustees, George Reynolds asserted Wesleyan's "claims upon the church especially for an ample, nay a munificent equipment" and his anticipation that the appointment of Foss would enhance those claims.[26]

Expectations soared as Foss stood to address an audience that included the widows of Fisk and Olin. Although valedictorian of his class and briefly teacher and principal at Amenia Seminary, Foss had no professional experience in higher education. Yet few doubted his abilities as a thoughtful and polished speaker. In terms that echoed the Yale *Reports* of 1828, Foss defined liberal arts education as "foundation work," the "thorough training and rich furnishing of the mind" that enable graduates to handle "distant duties and uncertain perils" and move along "the road to eminence." Employing concepts similar to those used by other college presidents in late nineteenth-century New England, he advocated a curriculum that would "make not specialists, but men." Study of the liberal arts at a "Christian college" would "develop an all-sided noble character," one reflecting physical health, intellectual vitality, spiritual depth, and ethical awareness. Closing his "earnest, plainly intelligible, and decidedly impressive" address with appropriate praise for faculty, expression of faith in students, and hopes for a few millionaires some day among the alumni, Foss used a quotation to remind the trustees of their responsibility. "The first question is money," his unnamed source asserted. "There is money enough in the Church. We are to command it."[27]

In search of funds and students, Foss spent much of his five-year presidency intensively cultivating the thirteen annual conferences that had a patron relationship to Wesleyan. Moving from rostrum to pulpit to campground, he found it "useful to the University . . . to show myself at such places." This "wandering life" and the "begging" that "goes very much against my grain" soon left him deeply fatigued and discouraged, with "no heart for the long financial pull before the college." Under pressure to pledge annually almost 10 percent of his salary to the endowment fund campaign, he turned to his mother for assistance. The financial retrenchment of 1877 further reduced his disposable income through a 10-percent reduction in all salaries. After the board refused to accept his resignation that year, he dutifully continued his best efforts.

He seized every opportunity to "plough" with major donors such as Oliver Hoyt, William Hoyt, and Andrew Stout. Through or perhaps with Oliver Hoyt he probably cultivated Hoyt's good friend, George Seney. The first of Seney's major gifts arrived in October 1879. When elected to the denomination's highest honor in 1880, Foss resigned from the presidency with a sense that Wesleyan's finances "have vastly improved." He served as bishop (and as a trustee of Wesleyan) until his death in 1910.[28]

John Wesley Beach '45 became Wesleyan's seventh president with the backing of his friend George Seney, the wealthiest member of the board. At the time of his appointment Beach was presiding elder of the New York district (embracing parts of Manhattan, Brooklyn, and Long Island). His prior denominational service included twenty-five years of pastorates in the New York and New York East conferences, preceded by three years as principal of Amenia Seminary. Remembering with high regard Beach's administrative achievements at Amenia in the early 1850s, Seney thought this studious, fifty-year-old minister had superior qualifications for the Wesleyan presidency. The board moved with unusual dispatch to elect him on 22 June 1880. Immediately afterward Seney announced his second gift of $50,000 to the endowment in order "that the administration of Dr. John W. Beach be no financial failure."[29]

The new president, admired by Seney for his manliness, was of average height and build. His sermons, delivered in clear, correct prose with a deep bass voice, tended toward the philosophical and abstract. Congregations listened to him "with respect and often with interest, but much as they would listen to a professor whom they did not quite understand." Introspective and reserved, Beach rarely spoke up in conference meetings and other public settings. He had a firm sense of duty, however, and was not one to flinch when under attack. Early in life Beach concluded that he was not "cut out for popularity."[30]

Beach devoted less than full attention to maintaining good relations with various constituencies. Among the patron conferences, even the crucial New York East heard very little from him on behalf of Wesleyan. When he did attend, his influence was not strong. He missed some annual meetings of the alumni clubs in New York and Boston. His baccalaureate sermons drew praise for their substance, but much greater acclaim went to other speakers at commencement-week events. Appearances on campus by Beach's two immediate predecessors elicited expressions of public affection rarely if ever accorded to him.[31]

The distance between Beach and Wesleyan undergraduates grew

steadily after an incident in 1881. A freshman football game against Trinity started at 3 P.M., despite a faculty rule prohibiting such weekday contests at this hour. Members of the team cut class in order to play. Spectators increased the number of absences. With the game well under way and Wesleyan leading, Beach learned of this activity, appeared on the field, and abruptly ended the game by confiscating the ball. He was hissed to his face by angry students, and about fifty students expressed their displeasure with three groans for the president. The *Argus* found his manner of discipline in this and previous episodes to be unfortunate and lacking in good judgment. In 1883 Beach purchased a home about a quarter mile from campus, making the president's house available as a residence for women students. Alumni found this new location for presidential receptions "a little strange." Students criticized a decision by which "the presidential mansion has degenerated into a female dormitory." Tensions mounted as students came to view Beach as an indiscriminate and harsh disciplinarian with devious ways of investigating misbehavior and prowling around the campus at night to prevent disorder. In early March 1887, Beach was "rotten egged" by the students. The eggs may have missed their mark, but a petition from almost 80 percent of the senior class to the trustees in early May was clearly on target in demonstrating the profound alienation between Beach and the large majority of students.[32]

Beach's perceived liabilities, as catalogued by the student petition and the report of a special committee appointed by the board at its June meeting, went far beyond matters of discipline. His relations with faculty were "strained and inharmonious." Enrollments for the last three years were static or even slipping a bit. But the major problem resided in the raising of funds within Wesleyan's denominational constituency. When Seney's financial reversals stopped his gifts in 1884, the board put increasing pressure on Beach to find new resources. The value of endowed funds, however, actually declined over the next three years. The Alumni Association at its annual meeting of 1887 appointed a committee with a majority of Methodist ministers to investigate. The committee's resolution calling for a change in the presidency passed by a vote of 100 to 1. A large committee of the board appointed for the same purpose concluded that Beach "has failed to command for his administration the approval and confidence of those most concerned for the welfare of the university." The board voted 23 to 4 to request Beach's resignation. When he characteristically refused, they declared the office vacant as of July 1. Seney was present but lacked the financial leverage to protect his friend. Beach stayed in Middletown, serving for the remainder of his career as presiding elder of the New Haven and then the New York district. Seney left the board in 1888.[33]

Coeducation

Denominational ties that deeply influenced the board and presidencies at Wesleyan in the late nineteenth century also shaped the student body. This was particularly the case with regard to the advent of coeducation. Admission of women in 1872, when assessed in national and regional contexts, reflected the power of advocacy rooted in the denomination and the compelling precedent of well-established Methodist educational practice.

In the decade after Appomattox, the issue of higher education for women received a great deal of public attention. The need for workers during the Civil War greatly increased the number of occupations at least partially open to women. The work force in 1870 included almost two million women. Male war casualties increased the number of women required to support themselves. As more women sought a college education, campus debates and the popular press explored two major issues. Could women meet the mental and physical demands of hard study? Would women, men, and society most benefit from separate colleges for women or from coeducational institutions?[34]

Collegiate coeducation began in the West at the time early models for separate women's colleges appeared in the East and the South. Oberlin first admitted women to the regular B.A. course in 1837 (the same year instruction began at Mount Holyoke), and was the most frequently cited example of coeducation. The Oberlin plan, however, was more compromise than clarion call. Although almost all the classes women attended were coeducational, fewer than 20 percent of the women graduates up to 1867 earned the B.A. degree. A large majority received a diploma from the four-year "ladies course," which omitted Greek, calculus, and most of the Latin required for a B.A. degree. When extolling this two-track approach to a group of educational leaders in mid-1867, James H. Fairchild, president of Oberlin, emphasized the wholesome influence of women students upon their male peers, noted a downward trend in the already small percentage of women seeking the B.A. degree, and found this trend quite natural and appropriate given the separate sphere of duties to which women would "properly be called." Usually guided by considerations of economic expediency and established sex roles, experiments in coeducation spread the Oberlin model through much of American higher education in the post–Civil War decades.[35]

Consideration of coeducation at Wesleyan probably began in July 1867. One week after Fairchild's extensive report on Oberlin to the gathering in Springfield, Illinois, Arthur B. Calef '51 presented a paper on "Education of Women" to Wesleyan's board. There is no record of what this Middletown attorney said to his fellow trustees, but his paper apparently introduced the resolution: "That in consequence of the demand for the higher education of women the course of study in this University shall be open to females as well as males." The board referred this resolution to a committee that included Calef, Isaac Rich, and Oliver Hoyt, with instructions to report at the next annual meeting.[36]

The committee made no report, and the quiet, indirect manner in which the issue was handled over the next four years suggests the sensitive nature of such a proposal at this early date in the movement for coeducation in New England. Although college-level coeducation in the region began with the opening of Bates in 1863, advocates of educating men and women together usually met strong resistance at long-established New England colleges. From the early 1870s to the founding of Radcliffe in 1894, Harvard refused demands and then a financial inducement for coeducation at the undergraduate level. Bowdoin, Dartmouth, Trinity, and Yale did not even accord serious consideration to movement in this direction.[37]

Proposals and requests for coeducation appeared at seven New England colleges in 1871. Evidence of a coordinated effort to raise this issue throughout the region's campuses is lacking. It was probably not coincidental, however, that the closely related movement for women's suffrage reached an early peak in 1871–72. Testifying before a Congressional committee in January 1871, Victoria Woodhull used the recently passed Fourteenth Amendment to argue that "the broad sunshine of our Constitution has enfranchised all." But women's rights advocates found more darkness than light on the New England collegiate front during the next few years. The Society of Alumni at Williams initiated a debate on coeducation that led only to a negative vote in this organization two years later. A proposal for coeducation presented in July by Henry Ward Beecher to Amherst's trustees met defeat in November at the next board meeting. Middlebury trustees also discussed the issue, but not until 1883, when enrollment had dropped to thirty-seven, would the first women be admitted. Brown rejected applications from three women that fall and did not provide instruction for women until 1891. Only Colby, the University of Vermont, and Wesleyan decided in 1871 to join Bates as coeducational institutions.[38]

In this chilly climate for coeducation in New England, Wesleyan's treatment of the issue minimized debate. After Calef's resolution of 1867 there is no indication of the topic being discussed during the next four years. Implicitly, coeducation probably became part of the process of revising the charter. The trustees appointed a committee on charter revision in 1868 and spent a large portion of the annual meeting in 1869 working on a text that created a single governing board, specified denominational control, and provided for election of some trustees by patron conferences and by alumni. Calef was a key figure in this process. By the time the board approved the text in 1869 and accepted in 1870 the new charter as passed by the state legislature, proponents of coeducation held the high ground. They could argue that every opportunity had been afforded those who opposed admitting women to propose a charter clause stipulating that a Wesleyan education was available only to males. No opponents of coeducation shouldered this burden of advocating male exclusivity.[39]

The stage was thus set for Orange Judd to place before the newly organized board of trustees its first policy decision. His resolution at the meeting of 19 July 1871 stated "that there is nothing in the Charter or By-Laws which precludes the admission of ladies." After much discussion, the trustees referred this matter "with power" to the executive committee and the faculty. Since these groups were led by strong advocates of coeducation, there was little reason for surprise when both soon authorized the president to announce that Wesleyan was ready to admit women.[40]

Why did significant opposition fail to mobilize at Wesleyan during the years 1867–71? Where enrollments at Colby and the University of Vermont were at a low point prior to coeducation decisions, those at Wesleyan were healthy and increasing. Wesleyan's president, although a supporter in principle of coeducation, predicted that coeducation would bring at least short-term reductions in overall enrollment at a time of financial stringency. Surely more was at work than the initiative and the skillful management of charter revision by a local Congregational trustee.[41]

The move for coeducation at Wesleyan drew much of its strength from five Methodist alumni in positions of great influence. Orange Judd was one of Wesleyan's two largest benefactors. While the new science building named for him was under construction, a rumor circulated predicting his daughter would enter Wesleyan in the fall of 1870. On the day before he made his motion for coeducation, Wesleyan honored him at the dedication of Judd Hall. On the morning of the trustee vote, Judd presented his motion to the board, presided at the Alumni Association meeting where a unanimous vote endorsed coeducation, and joined with a majority of trustees that afternoon to obtain the action enabling coeducation to begin in 1872. Joseph Cummings, who had served as a vice-president at the Female Suffrage Convention held in Hartford in 1869, viewed coeducation as a "great characteristic of the educational work and spirit of Methodism." Gilbert Haven, editor of *Zion's Herald*, served with Calef and Cummings on the joint board committee to revise the charter. He used columns of the *Herald* to support coeducation at Wesleyan and elsewhere. A good friend and ministerial colleague of his made the motion through which the Alumni Association endorsed coeducation. In combination with Methodist alumni on the faculty such as John Van Vleck and William North Rice, these proponents of coeducation had considerable leverage in opening Wesleyan's doors to women.[42]

Advocates of coeducation at Wesleyan had their roots in a denomination moving toward serious consideration of ordination for women. Maggie Newton Van Cott received a preacher's license in the New York Conference in 1869. Many interested ministers of the New England Conference attended a service in Springfield, Massachusetts, at which she preached in early 1870. More than a dozen other women obtained local preacher's licenses during the 1870s. The General Conference of 1880 blocked a substantial effort to ordain women, but the movement beginning shortly before Wesleyan became coeducational developed important male allies for women working to expand their sphere of activities within the denomination. Gilbert Haven, for example, gave earnest support both to coeducation at Wesleyan and to the ordination of women.[43]

The most important single influence leading Wesleyan to coeducation at a time when Amherst, Brown, Middlebury, and Williams decided to the contrary was Methodism's well-established practice of educating young men and women together. Gilbert Haven and others could trace Methodist support for coeducation at the precollege level to Willbur Fisk's principalship of Wesleyan Academy in the mid-1820s. Of the more than two dozen Methodist colleges and universities in 1870, all but four were coeducational. The number of coeducational Methodist colleges in 1870 was more than double that of any other denomination.

The first women graduates received their degrees in 1876. *Clockwise from upper left*: Jennie Larned, Phebe Almeda Stone, Angie Villette Warren, Hannah Ada Taylor.

Recent decisions in favor of coeducation qualified DePauw for the Methodist group in 1867, Northwestern in 1869, and Allegheny in 1870. Charters for new coeducational universities to open in the years 1871–75 under Methodist control would soon expand the list by three: Boston University, Syracuse University, and Vanderbilt University.[44] As Wesleyan entered its most Methodist years, the adoption of coeducation was a denominationally logical step.

The "four brave ladies" who entered Wesleyan in 1872 resolutely engaged the demanding tasks of a pioneering group. Angie Warren Perkins '76 recalled the importance of having three others to combat loneliness and find ways to "enjoy our work and the facilities offered us." The college provided no campus housing for women until a decade later. The first four encountered discrimination when trying to rent rooms in town. After a long search finally seemed to yield results, the owner told them the next day that she "couldn't take lady student boarders." The novelty of their presence was more than local. Bates, Colby, and the University of Vermont, the three colleges in New England where coeducation preceded Wesleyan's "experiment," had only one woman each continuing from the previous spring term. "We realized we must be very dignified," Perkins remembered, "for all New England was watching us."[45]

Male observers in the student body, faculty, and alumni saw Wesleyan as engaged in "a trial" to test the system of coeducation in an eastern environment. Given "a fair field and a generous competition," the "Wesleyan ladies" must prove themselves worthy. The best orator of the pioneering four, Jennie Larned '76, experienced particularly close scrutiny in this context. In the prize competition among sophomores, her declamation received praise as "a very creditable one" that "will, no doubt, furnish a new argument to the friends of coeducation." Carrying the future of coeducation thus placed upon her shoulders, she entered the junior exhibition the following spring, only to hear muted male acclaim that her speech "may, perhaps, furnish an argument to the advocates of coeducation." All was redeemed by her senior oration at the 1876 commencement, however, which "won golden opinions from all, and proved conclusively that intellectual culture is not incompatible with ladylike grace and refinement."[46]

In contrast to such high drama, everyday relations between men and women students during the first two decades of coeducation at Wesleyan reflected a general spirit of wary accommodation. Women were a tiny minority for the first two decades, always constituting less than 10 percent of the annual enrollment. Almost 45 percent came from homes within a twenty-mile radius of Middletown. They made full use of the unrestricted academic opportunities open to them, accommodated themselves to exclusion from class day exercises and election to senior class office (up to 1885), and summoned an astute forbearance in the face of other provocations. Denied access to the gymnasium, they probably gained exercise through walks. They may even have organized a baseball team in the early 1890s. Denied access to fraternities, they initiated Greek-letter organizations for women: Sigma Rho (1875), which lasted about a year; Sigma Pi (1880), which became Kappa Alpha Theta (1883–87). Male students labeled their female peers "quails," a term widely used before coeducation to describe unmarried, desirable young women who were "legitimate prey." Wesleyan men occasionally acknowledged and applauded the academic success of individual women, but a large majority consistently voted against coeducation when polled on this topic. With grudging tolerance, male undergraduates usually made the distinction that women at Wesleyan "though with us, are not of us."[47]

Despite this atmosphere of ambiguity and accommodation, women received support from important sources and achieved a large measure of academic success. Wesleyan presidents in the 1870s and 1880s gave assistance to the advancement of women. Foss added his voice to that of Cummings in the women's rights movement, endorsing the principle of equal pay for equal work. Beach testified to the benefits of coeducation, and his move to a new home in 1883 freed the president's house for use as the first women's dormitory. When that building reverted to its former use in 1889, the trustees purchased Webb Hall (known thereafter to male students as the "Quail Roost") to provide a larger rooming facility and social center for women students. The "manhood scholarships" established by George Seney in 1882 to reward academic achievement gave substantial financial support to about half the women enrolled in the late 1880s. Initiating a persisting pattern of disproportionate academic success compared to male achievements, Wesleyan's first four women graduates (receiving the B.A. degree in 1876) also earned election to Phi Beta Kappa.[48]

As alumnae, the forty-three women graduates of Wesleyan from 1876 through 1892 continued to encounter the mixture of constraints and opportunities present during their undergraduate days. Newspaper announcements in the early 1880s for the annual dinner of the Boston Wesleyan alumni club specified that "ladies are not invited." Although a report on the dinner of 1882 explained that "the discrimination was intended only to embrace the ladies of the families of the alumni, and not the lady graduates themselves," the article also noted that no alumnae attended. In 1886, however, Angie Warren Perkins gave one of the brief addresses at the alumni commencement dinner. Five years later Anna Van Vleck '79 ran for election to the board of trustees. The Alumni Association voted to reappoint the two male incumbents, but Mary Graham '89 gained appointment to the association's nominating committee in 1893.[49]

Patterns of matrimony and employment revealed limitations rooted in the feminine ideal of Victorian culture, particularly the notion of women's domestic duties and its clearly implied choice between marriage and career. More than half of Wesleyan's women graduates, 1876–92, remained single and pursued careers. Of the twenty who did marry, only three had careers while married. The rest were about evenly divided between those who worked prior to marriage and those never employed. Almost two-thirds of those with careers were educators, usually at the secondary level. A Methodist newspaper expressed the hope in 1873 that women educated at Wesleyan would teach in Methodist schools. Only four who graduated prior to 1893, however, took positions in the denomination's institutions. Undaunted, the same newspaper reaffirmed its support of coeducation in 1890, declaring that Wesleyan women "are demonstrating every day the wisdom of the vote which opened the halls of [the college] to them."[50]

Methodist Students
Methodist influences that made Wesleyan available to young women also brought most of the male students to campus. Wesleyan faced serious competition in the early 1870s when the denomination's new universities in Syracuse and Boston began drawing students from the same Methodist families previously oriented toward Middletown. At the urging of Joseph Cummings, the trustees moved to meet the challenge of new recruiting techniques employed by these competitors within Wesleyan's traditional territory. In 1873 the board authorized Cummings and the faculty "to make any such arrangements they may deem proper with any Conference Seminary or Preparatory School, to increase the intimacy of such schools with the Wesleyan University." The proportion of Wesleyan students who entered from these Methodist secondary schools rose from about one-third in the 1870s to a high of just over half in 1890. Printed appeals directed largely at the denominational constituency also probably helped raise to a high of almost 25 percent in

1880 the segment of entering students whose fathers were Methodist ministers. From the mid-1870s to the mid-1880s various reports indicated that more than 80 percent of the students were Methodist (see accompanying graph). This peak percentage for Wesleyan exceeded the approximately 75 percent Congregationalist tally at Amherst and was distinctively high for Methodist colleges in the late nineteenth century.[51]

These students of the 1870s and 1880s probably listened receptively to baccalaureate sermons and other presidential calls to lives of strenuous Christian benevolence. Cummings, Foss, and Beach frequently explored the themes of evangelical duty sounded by their predecessors. Foss saw the United States as destined to be "the great evangelizer of the world." Colleges should aid in this enterprise by being "professedly Christian" and by infusing the educational process with moral principle and religious belief. Their "learned and Christian" faculty must educate "the whole man"—intellect, imagination, and heart—for careers of Christian service. With characters thus cultivated, students were expected to engage energetically "the duties you must do . . . as citizens, legislators, leaders of the thought and life of communities, states, nations perhaps." Beach went even farther down the Arminian road in urging "practical godliness" as the highest and most essential form of Christian life. To the ears of some Methodists his words came close "to exaggerating the place of works and external efforts in character-building." Student responsibility in "the work of making the world better," however, remained just as clear as in the days of Fisk.[52]

Pervasive efforts to sustain piety among students were particularly intense during these decades. The trustees pushed hard in the early 1870s to institute and sustain required Sunday services in the new chapel. Some even wanted the New York East Conference to establish a Methodist parish on campus. Students had to attend a Sunday morning service in Middletown and an afternoon service on campus. Required daily chapel preceded classes on other days of the week. Students frequently used these brief services to read in preparation for the day's classes. Although inattention and occasional disorder also prevailed on other campuses in these years, morning prayers remained at Wesleyan, Amherst, Williams, Yale, and most other New England colleges until well into the twentieth century. Dissent occasionally voiced at Wesleyan was mild compared to the student efforts to abolish chapel requirements on other campuses. Faculty contributions to campus religious life in the 1880s included voluntary Methodist class meetings conducted each week by four professors. Beginning in 1886 Wesleyan brought in a prom-

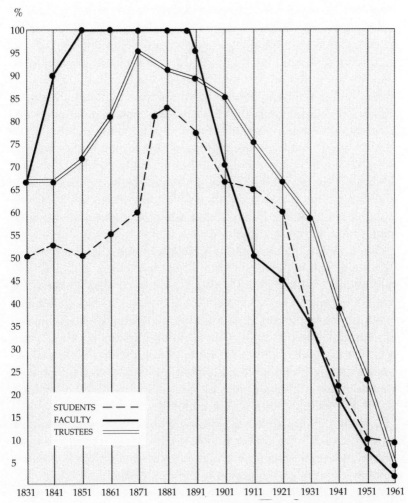

%

100
95
90
85
80
75
70
65
60
55
50
45
40
35
30
25
20
15
10
5

STUDENTS – – – –
FACULTY ▬▬▬▬
TRUSTEES ══════

1831 1841 1851 1861 1871 1881 1891 1901 1911 1921 1931 1941 1951 1961

Percentage of students, faculty, and
trustees who were Methodist, 1831–1961.
Wesleyan's most demographically denominational years were 1871–91.

inent visiting preacher for the nation's annual day of prayer for colleges. Major campus revivals occurred in 1875, 1880, and 1895. Alumni prayer meetings, initiated in the late 1880s, became a regular part of commencement-week activities. In the 1890s almost 90 percent of Wesleyan's students publicly professed the Christian faith.[53]

The hold of Methodist-hued religious activities on a large segment of the student body may explain Wesleyan's late entry into the intercollegiate YMCA movement. Beginning with a broadly Protestant emphasis in 1858, this movement spawned student YMCAs on more than forty campuses before 1877, when it established a national organization. The Christian Association organized at Wesleyan in 1878 by a traveling representative of the national network quickly faded from view. Not until 1885, twelve years after the YMCA took hold at Williams, did students at Wesleyan establish a unit that would last.[54]

Consistent with the central role Methodists played in the temperance movement, however, Wesleyan faculty and students soon found ways to support this cause. Professor Calvin Harrington ran for Congress on the Prohibition party ticket in 1875. Known primarily for his contributions to Methodist hymnody, he was no more successful than this generally ineffective political organization. Joseph Cummings ran for governor of Connecticut under the same banner and with the same result in 1876, when he was no longer president but still on the faculty. Interest in the issue persisted among students. In 1888 formation of the Prohibition Party Club attracted about fifty students.[55]

Some of the social aspects of campus life, especially fraternities and a sorority, provided diversions from the deep religious concerns of these decades. With the antebellum literary societies extinct by 1870, fraternities at Wesleyan grew in influence during the next twenty years. Acquisition of chapter houses, which began at Williams in the late 1850s and at Amherst in the mid-1870s, proceeded at Wesleyan primarily in the early 1880s. Observers for the Methodist press noted in 1884 that each of the four Wesleyan chapters of national fraternities had "an elegant, costly, and nicely furnished house for literary purposes." Eclectic, the local fraternity, brought the total to five. Students began to live in fraternities that year. About 15 percent of the male students roomed in this manner in the late 1880s, with each house being "under the supervision of a capable matron." Membership in fraternities at this time included almost 90 percent of the men; almost 80 percent of the women belonged to Kappa Alpha Theta, a sorority organized in the early 1880s. As at Amherst, the fraternities in these years continued to function

Students from the class of 1889, posing
with the Douglas Cannon they fired at
midnight 22 February 1886

much as the literary societies did, including literary exercises in their
weekly meetings and taking turns in sponsoring a public oration during
commencement week. A critic anticipated the coming "exchanges of a
broad forensic culture for a mere good fellowship tending to conviviality." A supporter may have confirmed the early stages of this process in
1891 when assuring Methodist readers that, unlike "society houses" at
other colleges, those at Wesleyan "are not places of dissipation. On the
contrary, they exert a refining social influence."[56]

The Douglas Cannon scrap became in these years more than an annual diversion from academic and evangelical intensity. It began to
emerge as the most enduring and celebrated saga in Wesleyan's history.
The firing of cannon to observe anniversaries of important events in the
nation's history was a common practice in antebellum America. With
several cannon remaining on campus from the days of Partridge's military academy, and others available from a local militia company,
Wesleyan students easily obtained the artillery to conduct such observances. A cannon firing at sunrise on 4 July 1858 is the first recorded
event of this nature. When a change in calendar brought the academic
year to a close in June rather than in August for the next few years,
Washington's birthday became Wesleyan's annual day for patriotic ex-

pression. From 1859 through 1866 various cast-iron cannon were fired in the early morning hours almost every February 22 by either the freshman or sophomore class. In 1867 the freshmen fired a new brass cannon borrowed from the Douglas Battery, a local militia organization. By this year the event was a contest between the freshman class, bearing responsibility for firing a cannon on February 22, and the sophomores, charged with foiling this effort by spiking the cannon or by some other means. Shock waves from a particularly heavy charge broke most of the library windows in 1869. This led to faculty action that banned the cannon salute from campus. Although honoring this rule from 1870 to 1893, enterprising freshmen usually managed to produce a volley within earshot of the college grounds at the appointed early-morning hours. Compared to the stirring public event it became in the 1890s, however, the cannon scrap during these off-campus years "was carried on mainly by a few wild spirits in each class and was frowned upon by many students and the Faculty as a perfectly useless nuisance."[57]

The collegiate custom of "rushes" pitting freshmen against sophomores might occur at any time of year. As with the firing of the Douglas Cannon, freshmen were expected to earn and defend the right to carry walking canes. Cyrus Foss described one episode to his mother in late May 1877: "We have had a very rough and exciting cane-rush here today, between the entire Freshman and Sophomore classes right in front of our house. I captured three canes, and separated the pale and ragged combatants with much difficulty." A decade later Foss's son wrote home about a similar encounter during the intermission of a football game. The clash involved about forty freshmen urged on by the juniors and an almost equal number of sophomores incited by the seniors. Although "for about fifteen minutes the wool flew," he reported, afterward "everybody agreed that it was a very gentlemanly and well conducted rush."[58]

At the center of the rush in 1887 was Wesleyan's superintendent of buildings and grounds, Harlow B. Raymond. He was a powerful force for law, order, and general campus decorum from 1863 to 1910. Known with respect and affection by generations of students as "Doc" Raymond, he contributed a variety of talents to Wesleyan. He supervised the construction that completed College Row. He kept a stock of bell clappers on hand to thwart periodic pilferage that threatened timely calls for early morning prayers and classes. Little escaped his watchful eye during the evening hours ripe for mischief on or against college property. His efforts to raid a clandestine post-curfew card game in the dormitory room of Arthur E. Sutherland '85 in 1882 inspired a ritual chant used at alumni gatherings for decades after his retirement. With functions that included those later performed by deans of students and alumni secretaries, this all-purpose administrator earned inclusion along with the president and faculty in class albums compiled by seniors in the late nineteenth century.[59]

The students enrolled from 1870 to 1890 under the vigilant care of Doc Raymond had good reason to pursue extracurricular activities in moderate, restrained fashion. For a large majority, Wesleyan represented a unique opportunity to advance from backgrounds of modest means. Many delayed entry until it became financially possible to pursue their goals. The average age at graduation continued to exceed twenty-four well into the 1890s. The description of young men at Wesleyan in the early 1870s as "generally poor" carried little overstatement. About half in the early 1880s came from families of farmers, ministers, and educators. The fathers of another 10 percent were tradesmen. Only about 15 percent were sons or daughters of merchants and manufacturers.[60]

Most of these students needed and received financial assistance. Although Wesleyan's tuition was less than half that at Yale, Amherst, and Williams in 1870, and remained well below that charged by most New England colleges in the 1880s, hardly anyone even paid the stated rate. The president had authority from the board to release up to one hundred students from payment of tuition. Methodist education societies and conferences sponsored many preministerial students. Seney scholarships (awarded to more than forty students annually in the late 1880s) covered the additional costs of attending, such as room and board. A few students in the 1870s also received loans from the Ladies University Education Society. This organization of faculty wives and interested townspeople began building a loan fund in 1858 through contributions and special events. There was no lack of financial assistance to help any resolute student acquire the "cultural currency" for building a successful career.[61]

Drawing upon thirty-five years of experience as a faculty member, John Van Vleck noted in 1889 the continuities in student attributes since the 1850s. "The general character of the students of Wesleyan," he observed, "is much the same as in the earlier years of its history. Very few of them are wealthy, many of them are poor, and the large majority come to seek an education with the earnest purpose that must characterize those who must depend upon themselves." Alumni and Methodists in these years took great pride in the hard-striving Wesleyan student who was "determined to get an education" through "vigorous mental activity," was informed and concerned regarding the most important social and religious issues of the day, and rarely engaged in the various forms of college rowdyism found on other campuses.[62]

Career choices of these students briefly perpetuated earlier patterns but then began to reflect new trends. The surge of those entering the ministry during the 1860s continued into the 1870s before declining from half the graduates of 1863–72 to one-fourth of those receiving degrees in the years 1880–89. The number and percentages of Wesleyan alumni from the 1870s who became Methodist preachers still easily exceeded comparable calculations for the 1830s or 1840s. As a matter of general interest, the *Argus* printed long lists of annual assignments for ministers within the patron conferences. The *Alumni Record* compilation for the classes up through 1881 yielded impressive statistics on Wesleyan's half century of contributions to American Methodism. Almost half the graduates had served as ministers, nine out of ten in pulpits of the Methodist denomination. Total years of teaching, often in Methodist schools and colleges, came to 5,738 (as compared to 8,540 preaching years). With the diminished percentage of male graduates entering the ministry upon graduation in the 1880s came corresponding increases of those engaged in education and business. But an increase of commitments to missionary work, as well as the cumulative record since 1831, enabled Wesleyan to continue its claims upon the gratitude of the denomination well into the twentieth century.[63]

A Past to Serve the Present

In the years when Wesleyan most fully forged and tapped its denominational connections, faculty, alumni, and friends began to write its history. This was also the time when leaders of the Methodist press intensified their calls for Methodists to emulate members of other denominations by sending their children to colleges of their own religious persuasion. Pleas for denominational loyalty included tributes to the benefits of liberal education but tended to stress religious benefits to students, parents, and the Methodist church. Noting the "army of Methodist students" attending forty-three colleges and universities of the denomination in 1885, James M. Buckley n1860, editor of the *Christian Advocate*, called for substantial increases in their ranks. A more favorable ratio of students to members of the denomination, he argued, would increase the ability of Methodists "to do our part in the future work of the world." These hopes for Methodist development and Wesleyan's desire for church support probably shaped the emerging historical view of Wesleyan's denominational identity.[64]

The story of Wesleyan's beginnings appeared in print at least eleven times in the fourteen years prior to celebration of the semicentennial in 1881. Eight Methodist authors created these accounts. Where each began his story and how he reached the point of connection in 1829 between Methodists and Middletown provided the first indicator of how much emphasis an account would place on the denomination's role in Wesleyan's first half century. Four of the authors started with the early efforts of American Methodists to found educational institutions. Three led off with the military academy of Captain Partridge or Middletown's unsuccessful competition with Hartford for Washington (now Trinity) College. The author of three accounts tried both approaches. Most of the eight authors then developed an explanation of how local and denominational activities in the story intersected in 1829. The typical explanation tended to diminish the role of Middletown by characterizing the connection point as an "accident" resulting from a "trifling conversation" in which a Middletown stockholder in the academy "sportively suggested" that the Methodists might want to purchase the land and empty buildings at a bargain price. The two accounts that characterized the connection as a thoughtful and logical encounter, in which Middletown approached the Methodists, had little influence on subsequent renditions of Wesleyan's early years.[65]

Once beyond the chance provision of facilities for a denominational movement toward higher education, the story had little reason to include non-Methodists in subsequent developments. Ignoring the six Yale graduates from Middletown, one author claimed that few of the trustees "had any very intelligent idea of a college at all." Only the two accounts making a purposeful connection between Middletown and the Methodists mentioned local citizens and trustees of the college by name. None of the eleven renditions included reference to important grants received from the Connecticut General Assembly from 1834 to 1854.[66]

In these accounts Rev. Laban Clark emerges as the dominant and virtually sole source of initiative and nurture for the fledgling enterprise. In most renditions Clark quickly seizes the moment of opportunity and stimulates serious consideration of an agreement between Middletown and the Methodists. Through his "vigor and enthusiasm" he becomes the "Father of Wesleyan University." The litany of Methodist heroes that follows — Fisk, Olin, Rich, Seney, and others — completes the story of Wesleyan's first half century. Conclusions are then as factually incomplete and denominationally slanted in the first rendition ("This is certainly a very remarkable and favorable exhibit of the denomination in its educational efforts.") as in the tenth (Methodist "sacrifice, labor, and expenditure" made Wesleyan "a good investment for the Methodist Episcopal Church.").[67]

In the historical address at the semicentennial celebration in 1881, Rev. James M. King '62 placed upon this inspirational story of denominational initiative and achievement the imprimatur of a milestone event. He also demonstrated the standard version's utility. His remarks closed with a quotation from Olin about Wesleyan's legitimate demands upon the denomination. Methodists should instinctively view Wesleyan as belonging to them, Olin had argued, "just as the churches and ministry are theirs." After King's speech the Methodist press faithfully continued the previous decade's portrayal of Wesleyan as "the mother of our denominational institutions" and "mother of us all." The picture of Wesleyan as a "denominational institution" dependent upon the patronage of the Methodist church also persisted. As presented in popular print and public events at the turn of the century, Wesleyan's identity still had much to do with being "eminently a child of the church."[68]

Portents of Change

Public events regularly used the story of Wesleyan's origins as formulated during the peak years of denominational consciousness. Even though this account endured, a comparison of the semicentennial celebration in 1881 with the Wesley Bicentennial observance held at Wesleyan in 1903 reveals early signs of change. Wesleyan's denominational era itself would soon begin fading into history.

The semicentennial exercises had an almost totally Methodist orientation. After the welcoming remarks from President Beach, Bishop Edward G. Andrews '47 presented a statistical analysis to show that Methodists could and should send even more of their sons and daughters to Wesleyan, a college designed so that "the general spirit and manner of Methodism should pervade its philosophy and its worship." He also called for increased faculty scholarship that would produce "a fountain of true and sanctified knowledge" to which "ever-increasing numbers of our ingenuous youth will resort." The historical address proudly identified Wesleyan as "an epitome of the relations of American Methodism to higher education." Bishop Foss gave the concluding oration. A college such as Wesleyan, he argued, must sustain daily prayers conducted in the spirit of Fisk and Olin. It must always provide an important place in the curriculum for the Bible, ethics, natural theology, and Christian evidences. Above all, there must be a perpetuation of "dear old Wesleyan's goodly succession of . . . learned and Christian instructors" always ready to offer "positive theistic and Christian teaching." Only the poem presented by Stephen Henry Olin '66, recently elected by alumni to the board of trustees, moved outside the Methodist context and concluded with a call for Wesleyan to achieve a "broader fame." Honorary doctorates awarded at commencement the following day went to four Methodist ministers and a professor at Drew Theological Seminary.[69]

Whereas Wesleyan in 1881 rejoiced in the unprecedented benefactions of George Seney, the Methodist multimillionaire, the campus mood in 1903 reflected several years of financial difficulty. Hopes for major support from the denomination were fading. The Twentieth Century Thank Offering announced by Methodist bishops in November 1898 had a goal of $10 million for education. Wesleyan's president and several trustees held positions within this national effort. Encouraged by prospects for help from the denomination, Wesleyan's board authorized in 1899 a drive to raise $1 million for endowment and $150,000 for an academic building. Influential alumni joined the president in using the Methodist press to promote Wesleyan as a donor-designated beneficiary of gifts to the thank offering. Funds received by June 1903, however, were less than $60,000. Even with subscriptions paid later, the total would not reach one-tenth of the goal. Using the Wesley Bicentennial as a springboard, the trustees would soon try again to raise $1 million from within the denomination in the name of its founder. The second effort would also yield about one-tenth of the desired amount.[70]

Plans for the Wesley Bicentennial celebration at Wesleyan led to scholarly if not financial success. The 1881 call by Bishop Andrews for more faculty scholarship had one clear answer in development of the four-day program in 1903. From the earliest conceptions it was apparent that the celebration would be "not narrow and sectarian, but . . . broadly religious and educational." Wesleyan's president and faculty members planning this event made sure it would celebrate John Wesley as a "great reformer and scholar," whose heirs in America, Fisk and Olin, "first made Methodism a recognized force in the thoughtful and scholarly life of the country." Speakers distinguished for their ability to present a wide-ranging analysis of the man and his times were chosen without restriction as to denominational affiliation.[71]

The special ceremonies began on a hot Sunday afternoon in late June at the Middletown Methodist church. Invited guests included representatives from more than three dozen institutions of higher education.

The audience received assurance at the start that the occasion "rises above a mere Methodist celebration." Two Methodist scholars presented learned addresses on Wesley and the Methodist movement. The featured speaker on Monday evening was Caleb T. Winchester '69, Wesleyan's widely acclaimed professor of English literature. Drawing upon research for his biography of Wesley, Winchester described a prodigious reader, prolific author, keen logician, and cultured gentleman with scholarly tastes and an open mind. At the alumni luncheon the next day, President Charles W. Eliot of Harvard presented a toast linking Wesley to John Harvard in their advocacy of freedom and their "non-conformist catholicity." Before a capacity crowd at the North Congregational Church that evening, President Woodrow Wilson of Princeton delivered a broadly conceived analysis of John Wesley's place in history. Through superb statesmanship, Wilson argued, Wesley did much to lead the regeneration of his times.[72]

Commencement capped the festivities. To provide sufficient capacity for an unusually large attendance of alumni and guests, the Middlesex Opera House substituted for the Methodist church used in earlier years. Initiating a new practice for this annual ceremony, the Wesleyan faculty wore academic robes. After addresses by an Episcopal and a Methodist bishop, the president of Dartmouth College, William J. Tucker, gave the concluding speech. One of the early advocates of Protestant liberalism, this Congregational minister had instituted a modern college presidency at Dartmouth in the 1890s. Under his leadership Dartmouth doubled its enrollment in the previous decade and would soon have more than a thousand students. Tucker displayed a keen sense of Wesleyan's needs in 1903. Continuing the bicentennial's tendency to carry John Wesley beyond denominational boundaries, Tucker moved him farthest of all. Wesley made an unintended but major contribution to scholarship and higher education, Tucker asserted, because one long-term result of the Wesleyan revival "was a vast accession of mental power to the Anglo-Saxon race."[73]

The ceremonies closed with the awarding of honorary degrees. A committee led by Stephen Henry Olin had reported to the trustees in mid-May the names of recommended honorands. Olin was a ubiquitous worker among alumni and trustees helping Wesleyan to achieve the broader fame he called for in 1881. Moving with ease in the upper levels of culture and society in New York City, Olin had also moved from the Methodist circles of his famous father to those of the Episcopal church. Witty and urbane, he served as toastmaster in 1903 at the alumni luncheon. It was no doubt with pleasure that he watched the scholarly and ecumenical Wesley Bicentennial celebration conclude with almost half of the seventeen honorary doctorates being conferred on prominent non-Methodists.[74]

Although counterbalanced at this major event, the continued practice of giving honorary degrees to Methodists was one of several signs of Wesleyan's continued efforts to maintain strong ties to the denomination. As on two previous occasions, the college had helped in 1888 to host the annual meeting of the New York East Conference. Prominent Methodists frequently occupied the campus pulpit on important occasions. Ceremonies in 1904 to dedicate the two new academic buildings, Fisk Hall and Scott Laboratory, followed Methodist form and practice. The latter ceremony closed with singing of a Methodist hymn composed for the dedication of Judd Hall in 1871. Wesleyan's appeals "to Methodists who are interested in advancing scholarship within the church," however, had limited resonance in many reaches of the denomination at the dawn of a new century.[75] While celebrating Wesleyan's Methodist connection, the Wesley Bicentennial of 1903 also served as an early parting tribute to an identity that would soon recede into the institution's past.

5   *Methodist Professors*
    Becoming Academic
    Professionals

*S*cholarly celebration of a scholarly John Wesley in 1903 was no accident. Wesleyan's faculty, chief planners for this event, had created an intellectual community that would soon help carry the college beyond its denominational identity. From 1870 to 1910 they brought to almost full realization their conception of professional roles as scholars and college professors. Their growing sense of expertise and professional authority guided a major revision of the curriculum in 1873. When they determined the time was right, they effected a second reshaping of graduation requirements in 1908. Controlling access to their professional group, they recruited a faculty that had, by the new century's first decade, a decidedly more scholarly and less denominational orientation. Their recruiting influence even included the hiring of a long-term president fully supportive of faculty goals.

Professional opinions, scholarly analyses, and research findings engendered serious opposition within some segments of the denomination at the turn of the century. Three senior faculty members encountered early rumblings of a Methodist moralism and fundamentalism that gained strength after 1900. By 1905 it was clear that pursuit of professional autonomy and scholarly ideals cast serious doubt on the future viability of Wesleyan's denominational affiliation.

A Sense of Profession

Leadership in the development of a clear sense of professional identity and mission came from four faculty members whose careers spanned all but a few of the years between 1870 and 1910. John Monroe Van Vleck '50, mentor for the other three, began teaching mathematics and astronomy at Wesleyan in 1853. Experience gained during two years as an assistant in the Nautical Almanac Office, Cambridge, Massachusetts, gave him a keen sense of professional scholarship. Although his own research contributions were limited to preparation of annual astronomical tables, he supplied the guiding spirit in building a curriculum and faculty committed to the norms of scholarly investigation. William North Rice '65 began teaching geology and natural history in 1868. Caleb Thomas Winchester '69 assumed the duties of librarian a year later and became Olin Professor of Rhetoric and English Literature in 1873. Each of these three held appointments at Wesleyan for fifty-one years. Wilbur Olin Atwater '65 taught chemistry for more than three decades until disabled by a stroke in 1904. All but Van Vleck were sons of Methodist ministers, and all four were loyal, active members of the denomination.[1]

Recruitment of Atwater in 1873 marked the beginning of colleagueship among the four and included expression of their hopes for integrating service to scholarship with service to their denomination. After obtaining his Ph.D. at Yale's Sheffield Scientific School in 1869 and completing two years of study at German universities, Atwater began his career as a professor of agricultural chemistry at East Tennessee University. The few available teaching jobs in this new field were generally at institutions in remote locations. Finding Knoxville to be "away out of the world," Atwater took a position at the University of Maine. The hunting and fishing in Orono were good, but he continued to regret being "so far away from society and from scientific centers." Through correspondence with Rice, his college classmate and fraternity brother, Atwater learned that Wesleyan's professor of natural science was about to retire because of failing health. Expressing sentiments that probably helped him to obtain the appointment at Wesleyan, Atwater told Rice of his enthusiasm for "teaching and propagating scientific truth" and for the "deal of good that can be done by such chaps as you and I in influencing the thought of our church and our times." Modern science and enlightened Methodism might go hand in hand.[2]

Pursuing its dual mission for scholarship and denomination, the faculty worked with Wesleyan's trustees to enlarge and delineate spheres of professional prerogative. Definitions of faculty responsibilities and authority resided in the rules and regulations adopted by the joint board in 1831 and were presumably incorporated in the bylaws adopted in 1833. New editions of the trustee bylaws appeared in 1859, 1884, 1894, and 1911.[3]

The two central professional prerogatives established in 1831 were reaffirmed in all bylaw revisions up to 1911. Control over access to the "permanent" professional group at Wesleyan took the form of a stipulation that every nomination by the president to the trustees for appointment at the rank of professor or associate professor required concurrence of the senior faculty. Creation of the Academic Council in 1892 gave additional foundation and focus to the role of full professors in decisions on hiring, retentions, and promotion. Control over changes in the curriculum took the form of placing initiative for such changes in the hands of the faculty. Ultimate authority for appointments and curricular revision rested with the trustees, but prerogatived preeminence in these two areas resided with the academic professionals.[4]

Exclusive authority replaced shared authority in three other areas of faculty responsibility. The rules and regulations of 1831 assigned to a joint committee composed of the faculty and the annual outside examining committee the decisions on recommending candidates for earned degrees. Any role actually played by the examining committee soon faded. Honorary degrees, according to the bylaws of 1859, "may be conferred on those recommended by the President and Faculty as well worthy of the honor." The revision of 1884 dropped any reference to the president having a role in this process. Up to 1884 government of the college (covering the day-to-day regulation of campus life) was "vested in the President who shall be aided and sustained by the Professors." The bylaws of 1884 made governance a responsibility shared by "President and Professors . . . provided that every act of executive administration shall have the concurrence of the President." Although retaining this veto power for the president, the bylaws of 1894 simply stated that "the government of the University shall be vested in the Faculty."[5] The incorporated institutional context within which academic professionals worked continued to give legal authority for final decisions on degrees and institutional policy to the board of trustees. Wesleyan's faculty by 1894, however, had broad and well-defined institutional roles that recognized their expertise as professional educators.

Beyond these central functions, a daunting array of duties crowded into weekly faculty meetings and the daily lives of professors. In 1875 a faculty member envisioned the day when Wesleyan's instructors, "relieved in some measure from routine drudgery, should be not middlemen but producers in the economy of thought."[6] To achieve this goal, the faculty worked throughout the years 1870–1910 to reduce time spent on matters peripheral to emerging concepts of professional expertise and priorities.

Weekly faculty meetings presented a constant challenge to wise and efficient use of faculty time. New items such as the regulation of intercollegiate athletic contests extended agendas already strained by routine administrative matters. The number of participants quickly doubled, as full-time teaching appointments rose from six professors and a teacher of elocution in 1870/71 to eight professors, two instructors, and four tutors in 1880/81. When the faculty roster reached twenty (ten professors, four associate professors, two instructors, and four tutors) in 1890, a committee attempted to "devise some plan by which the routine work which comes before the Faculty may be lightened." The committee apparently recommended more standing committees. By 1896 there were fifteen committees for a faculty of twenty-five. Imposition of a one-hour-fifteen-minute limit on meetings, perhaps to encourage brief committee reports, simply spawned motions to extend beyond that limit.[7]

Faculty made larger gains in reducing the time they devoted to formal religious exercises. The required Sunday services instituted in 1871 at the insistence of trustees had little support in supplying the pulpit from a faculty in which only three members besides the president were ministers. Even with the president carrying much of the load, the faculty voted in 1883 to abolish these Sunday afternoon campus services. Students were then required to attend a Sunday morning service at churches of their choice in Middletown. Faculty action in 1874 also eliminated weekday evening chapel services and established a schedule to lighten the faculty load for attending and conducting the required morning services. Half of the professors were assigned to Monday, Wednesday, Friday and half to Tuesday, Thursday, Saturday. By 1890 responsibility for morning chapel rested with the president and volunteers.[8]

Partial divestment of intercollegiate athletic supervision took much longer. Hardly a year passed from 1880 to 1900 without athletic questions frequenting the agenda. May the baseball team schedule a weekday afternoon game? Might the football team practice in the early afternoon in late November? Should the track team be permitted to start a weekday home meet at 3 P.M.? Would team members be excused from a day of classes for a regatta in New York, or a football game in

Philadelphia? What if the game were scheduled for Thanksgiving morning, thus conflicting with church services? How could appropriate limits on absences be developed that would also resolve requests for permission to travel from the glee, mandolin, and drama clubs? What steps must be taken to prevent the use of nonstudents playing under assumed names or of students who had played professionally? Should a high board fence be built near the playing field to make charging admission more feasible?[9]

One solution was to refer such issues to the standing committee on athletics (which would soon also oversee the musical clubs), established in 1892. Another was to obtain regulation by association. In 1885 Wesleyan joined the Intercollegiate Football Association, founded by Princeton, Harvard, Yale, and Columbia nine years earlier. Increasingly outmatched, Wesleyan withdrew from this disintegrating league in 1893 and joined Amherst and Williams in 1899 to establish a league with more stringent rules for participants. The most important step to reduce the number of athletic items requiring faculty deliberation came in 1903. Not long after wrestling with the question of whether the baseball team should be permitted to play on Good Friday, the faculty probably not only endorsed but welcomed the formation of an athletic supervisory organization similar to those established at Amherst in 1890 and Williams in 1897. The Wesleyan University Athletic Council, composed of three faculty, three alumni, and three students, regulated most aspects of intercollegiate athletics, including schedules. The solution was partial. In 1906 the faculty was still acting to tighten eligibility requirements for athletic teams and the glee and drama clubs, to stop early afternoon football practice in November, and to prohibit attendance at classes while "wearing football suits."[10]

Student discipline, the ever-present drain on time and energy of college faculties in nineteenth-century America, created a need for devices to delegate responsibility. In the 1870s tutors, hired on the condition they remain single for the year and live in the dormitory, assumed the tasks of evening "guard duty" previously assigned to faculty. The creation of an honor system in 1893 removed from the faculty agenda the investigation of occasional cases of using "skids" in exams or other instances of cheating. Student-written regulations formulated in 1900 for the annual cannon scrap reduced the number of disciplinary actions resulting from this event. Hazing, attendance deficiencies, instances of a "low grade of scholarship," and assorted manifestations of "untrustworthiness of character" kept a substantial caseload on the faculty agenda up to 1910, but the burdens of in loco parentis were somewhat lightened.[11]

Even clearer gains were evident by 1900 with regard to textbook selection and library management. Reliance upon individual expertise began to save time expended on collective action. In 1890 the faculty moved from annual votes on instructor recommendations for changes in course readings to an arrangement where instructors merely reported such changes to the committee on courses of study. The first step in reducing oversight of the library came in 1871, when the annual vote on a list of books to be purchased for the library yielded to the assignment of book-ordering decisions to individuals according to their areas of teaching responsibility. Development of the position of librarian in the mid-1890s from a part-time to full-time appointment with senior faculty status provided for management of the library. In 1898 the faculty voted to give up their respective keys to the library.[12]

The miscellany of faculty professional lives at the turn of the century was still substantial. Faculty continued to take major responsibility for making sure that records of alumni, faculty, and trustees were well kept and periodically published. To the tasks of preparing each year's catalogue and a semiannual summary of Wesleyan news published for off-campus readers, faculty added in 1909 the production of a weekly bulletin listing on-campus events. They instituted new policies such as a smoking ban in public halls and rooms of the college in 1904.[13] But reduced involvement during the years from 1870 to 1910 in formal religious exercises, athletic supervision, discipline, and library management yielded desired opportunities to focus professional energies on matters related to curriculum, scholarship, and the academic reputation of Wesleyan.

Faculty members administered admissions policy and process throughout the years 1870–1910. During this period Wesleyan moved with other institutions toward uniform regional and national specification of secondary school studies required for admission to college. In 1880 Wesleyan adopted the list of secondary school studies in Latin, Greek, English, and mathematics recommended by the Association of New England Colleges. Six years later the faculty voted to join a dozen of the most prestigious colleges in organizing the Commission of Colleges in New England on Admissions Examinations. The national secondary school curricular standards recommended by the National Education Association's Committee of Ten received general approval from Wesleyan's faculty in 1897.[14]

Examinations for admission, still conducted by the faculty through individual oral exams in 1870, also soon moved well beyond a local orientation. Authorization in 1874 for written admission examinations administered at Methodist academies led five years later to offering such tests (of three hours each in Latin, Greek, and mathematics) in selected major cities and a few public high schools. Examinations first prepared and administered by the new College Entrance Examination Board in 1901 became acceptable for Wesleyan admission when the college joined this organization in 1908. The alternative method of admission by certificate from faculty-approved secondary schools began with Methodist academies in 1887 and Middletown High School in 1889. In 1904 Wesleyan expanded admission by certificate to include all secondary schools approved by the New England College Entrance Certificate Board. Through a host of such decisions and other activities, the Wesleyan faculty stayed fully abreast of professional developments, set high standards, and worked to attract able students.[15]

Honors conferred on students at graduation expressed faculty approbation for high levels of intellectual effort and achievement. Introduced in 1874, the system of graduation honors recognized two types of excellence. High standing for the whole sequence of undergraduate studies yielded honors in general scholarship. Reward for specialized study, however, indicated most clearly the spirit of scholarship faculty wanted to foster. This second type of honors encouraged independent investigation and required a thesis, an essay, or some other appropriate demonstration of research proficiency. In 1888 and 1896 the faculty introduced increasingly elaborate and exacting criteria for both forms of graduation honors.[16]

Higher standards for advanced and honorary degrees received corresponding attention. A rising tide of honorary Ph.D.'s, granted by institutions ranging from Princeton to small western denominational colleges, threatened to devalue the earned doctorate as a new scholarly credential. Wesleyan's faculty took preventive action in 1877, resolving that the honorary Ph.D. degree not be awarded. Concern about more careful scrutiny of candidates for the honorary D.D. degree and some constraints on the number awarded per year also appeared in the 1870s. The practice at most American colleges of giving unearned M.A. degrees was more firmly entrenched. A four-year faculty campaign, however, yielded board action in 1888 that phased out the M.A. degree available since the 1830s for Wesleyan graduates who, three years after receiving the B.A., had "sustained good moral character" and paid the required fee. The last such degrees were dispensed in 1891. With the M.A. to be conferred as an honorary degree "only in rare cases," the M.A. or M.S. would generally be granted for "non-professional post-graduate study, either at Wesleyan or elsewhere," according to rules and regulations developed by the faculty. Aaron L. Treadwell '88 received Wesleyan's first earned graduate degree (a master of science) in 1890.[17]

Consistent with a focus on matters central to an emerging academic profession, the faculty avoided collective involvement in controversial political issues. They defeated a motion to grant Frederick Douglass an LL.D. at the commencement of 1870. In 1895 the faculty declined an invitation to send a representative to a meeting in Chicago of the National Civil Service Reform League. During the highly charged presidential campaign of William Jennings Bryan a year later, they found it "inexpedient in the present political crisis" to grant a request from the student Sound Money Club to use the chapel for a public speech by Senator Joseph R. Hawley. They also found it "inexpedient" to accept an invitation from Washington requesting that a delegation of students participate in the inaugural parade for William McKinley in 1901.[18]

On issues viewed as closely related to their educational enterprise, however, the faculty did speak out. Precedent for such action can be found as early as 1837, when Wesleyan's professors petitioned the Connecticut General Assembly on the issue of public amusements. With the legislature considering repeal of a law banning circuses, plays, and other performances, Wesleyan's faculty urged retention of statewide legal protection against "the licentious cupidity of strolling players and harlequins." From their experience as "the guardians and instructors of a portion of the youth educated in the state," they warned that repeal of the law would produce "an insidious undermining, not only of the public morals, but also of the literary and political institutions of our land." In the late nineteenth century faculty resolutions addressed to the United States Congress urged creation of an educational institution in China for the mutual benefit of Chinese and Americans and supported continued tariff exemptions for books and scientific equipment imported from Europe.[19]

While defining more clearly their spheres of professional expertise, activity, and authority, the faculty sustained a strong interest in building Wesleyan's reputation and making the college's virtues more widely known. Shortly after the popular Cyrus Foss became president in 1875, the faculty appointed a committee to "confer with the President in regard to the question in what ways and to what extent it is expedient to advertise." A quarter century later, general consideration of this issue received less tentative and more pointed expression. Faculty authorized a committee "to make the college better known to the public, with a view to increasing the number of students." The most important of faculty efforts in the area of public relations was publication of the *Wesleyan University Bulletin*, beginning in 1888. With John Van Vleck as acting president, the faculty moved swiftly to establish the biannual *Bulletin* for distribution to Methodist clergy in the patron conferences, alumni, trustees, preparatory schools, newspapers, and friends of the college. This new publication would give extensive coverage to the curriculum and to faculty research.[20] Of the many priorities weighed and weighted by Wesleyan's faculty from 1870 to 1910, these two would give special clarity to a new professional identity. They would also have the greatest import for changes in institutional identity.

Curricular Authority

Curricular issues supplied the major professional challenge to Wesleyan's faculty in the 1870s. Sensing the need for new patterns of undergraduate study to serve enduring liberal arts objectives, the faculty had introduced in 1869 considerable freedom of course selection for juniors and seniors.[21] But rapidly expanding fields of knowledge, particularly in the sciences, sustained unrelenting pressure on a traditional curriculum that emphasized ancient languages and mathematics. Projections of impending enrollment decline added a sense of urgency to planning for the major curriculum revision of 1873.

From within the Methodist ranks in 1872 came a disturbing demographic analysis. Daniel Dorchester n1847, a minister in the Boston area, presented a careful study of enrollment data for students pursuing the B.A. degree at New England colleges. Despite a large increase of population in the region since 1850, he noted, "we find our eyes opened to startling facts." The ratio of B.A. students to total population showed a steady decline in Connecticut and Massachusetts from 1850 to 1870. One reason for this reduced tendency to seek a B.A. was the rising competition from scientific schools such as those recently founded in Boston and Worcester. "What shall be done," Dorchester asked, "in this emergency? Shall the number of technical schools and scientific departments in our colleges be increased? Or shall a larger number of studies in our colleges be made elective?" Wesleyan drew almost half its students from outside New England and had a pattern of steadily increasing enrollments. Yet Wesleyan's faculty, as well as this alumnus, had sufficient indications of future problems to conclude that these questions must be addressed.[22]

Soon after the *Methodist Review* published Dorchester's analysis, Joseph Cummings departed for eight months of travel in Europe. This leave of absence for the 1872/73 academic year followed fourteen strenuous years in the presidency. Under Van Vleck, who was acting president, the faculty made full use of its opportunity to be the sole architects of a new design for Wesleyan's curriculum. One week after Cummings returned in late May, he became a member of a committee "to consider the question of a new course of study." Three weeks later all but the details for a new educational program received faculty approval. At the request of the faculty, Cummings presented this plan to the board as part of his annual report. Citing competition from new institutions such as Syracuse University and Boston University, he told the board that Wesleyan's curriculum must be expanded to "meet the popular demand" for courses many people felt provided "a more practical preparation for the duties of life." Departing from his previous tendency to keep the instructional staff as small as possible, he even recommended an increase in the size of the faculty. Cummings probably had little choice but to move in concert with extensive faculty preparation for change and intensive faculty pressure to act.[23]

The timing was close. New facilities for more courses in science had become available with the completion of Judd Hall two years earlier. Less than three months after the trustees approved the new curriculum and new expenditures to establish it, the panic of 1873 initiated a depression extending almost to the end of the decade. Elective systems would not be introduced until 1876 at Yale, 1878 at Amherst, 1881 at Williams, and 1882 at Dartmouth.[24]

The revised curriculum of 1873/74 expanded opportunities for student course selection in the B.A. program. Although all first-year courses remained totally required and almost fully devoted to Latin, Greek, and mathematics, a reduction in compulsory study of classical languages during the sophomore year permitted students to elect a course in French or German. In the junior year, where required Latin and Greek were dropped in 1869 to make about half the course load elective, the dozen courses available in 1873 provided a greater depth of coverage in each discipline. Seniors gained a single choice in 1869, usually Latin or Hebrew; now about half of their studies were elective.[25]

In addition to less structured requirements for the B.A., Wesleyan also introduced two new degree programs in 1873. A four-year B.S.

course of study replaced the three-year option created during Wesleyan's first decade. French and German composed the language element in this program. A completely new degree, the bachelor of philosophy, recognized four years of study including Latin but not Greek. These opportunities to reduce or avoid classical studies and to expand electives gave Wesleyan's curriculum in 1873 a more practical appearance.[26]

The curriculum revision of 1873 was an important milestone in development of professional judgment and authority. With applause from students and a growing respect from trustees, the faculty made subsequent refinements in the academic program to serve values fostered by scholarly research. In 1886 they moved introductory courses in science closer to the freshman year and created a sequence of courses that gave students opportunities to explore in depth these rapidly expanding bodies of knowledge. Reduction of the time devoted to Latin, Greek, and mathematics in the first year made room for election of French or German. After 1899 Latin, Greek, and mathematics were no longer required beyond the first year, and half of the four-year B.A. curriculum was elective.[27] Freedom to pursue specialized knowledge encountered few constraints.

As professional specialization expanded the range of course choices, the number of departments also grew rapidly. In 1865 the faculty taught with little attention to departmental boundaries or disciplinary expertise. A graduate of that year recalled their broadly conceived roles:

> The Professor of Mathematics was librarian. One Professor was entitled Professor of Natural Science, and taught all that was taught in regard to the material universe excepting that the Professor of Mathematics taught Astronomy and part of the Physics. The Professor of English taught Hebrew. The Professor of Latin taught History. The Professor of Greek taught French and German. The President taught Psychology, Ethics, Evidences of Christianity, Economics, Constitutional Law, and International Law.

Just before the curriculum revision of 1873, Wesleyan had eight departments, each with a single professor. Twenty years later the number of departments had doubled, largely through bifurcation. From natural science, for example, came the chemistry and physics departments. A curriculum previously ordered by the required sequence of courses over four years of study began in the 1884/85 catalogue to list courses by the new basic unit of professional organization, the department.[28]

A more decentralized curriculum serving the values of scholarly specialization spawned a variety of bureaucratic devices to regulate the growing complexity of academic life. Lists of rules governing class attendance, grades, academic standing, and honors became even more lengthy. The three-term calendar used since 1833 began in 1886 a decade-long evolution toward a semester calendar. Half-year courses appeared, permitting somewhat greater depth of study than those of a trimester. A late-September starting date instituted in 1892 increased the summer vacation from eleven to thirteen weeks, providing additional research time to faculty. The credit system, a resort to quantification adopted throughout American higher education in the late nineteenth century, developed at Wesleyan in several stages. With the inauguration of junior-year electives in 1869, the faculty had to specify that at least three daily recitations were required for progress toward a degree. The faculty began in 1886 to designate the number of daily recitations per year for each course. With this device the amount of required study in Greek and Latin could be shaved steadily but almost imperceptibly to make room for other subjects. In 1908 the learning required for a degree was first expressed in the new professional currency of credit hours. The accumulation of sixty credit hours (annual) yielded one bachelor's degree.[29]

Stimulating and shaping this new curricular structure was a shift in emphasis between the two major traditions in liberal arts education.[30] The orator's stress on civic virtue and mental discipline was yielding ground to the philosopher's penchant for seeking new knowledge. The shift was gradual and subtle. Supporters of the philosophical tradition often claimed that mental discipline and civic virtue were well served by their emphasis on research and expertise. Adherents to the oratorical tradition created new frontiers of scholarly investigation in their approach to ancient languages and cultures. Yet the trends from 1870 to 1910 were clear. The allure of the scientific method steadily reduced the curricular prominence of classical languages and mathematics, subjects standing in the oratorical tradition.

Soon after the Civil War, this impending shift in educational values can be seen in events related to construction of Wesleyan's new science building. At the laying of the cornerstone in 1870, speakers were careful to affirm the enduring value of classical studies and religious beliefs. Paying tribute to the mental discipline he received in the 1840s from Wesleyan's classical curriculum, Orange Judd declared that if the building to be named in honor of his gift "would trench upon or lessen the amount of discipline of that character, I should wish to see its walls crumble here and now to the ground." Rather than reducing the amount of beneficial drill in the languages and mathematics, Judd wanted only to see that science was more fully added to the former course of study. And he looked with great distrust on the call for elective studies. At the dedication of Judd Hall in 1871, he again defended required study of Latin and Greek. The main speaker at the occasion, however, predicted that these languages would soon be displaced from their long-established leading role in American higher education. Judd's classmate Alexander Winchell '47, professor of geology, zoology, and botany at the University of Michigan, argued in great detail for the superiority of scientific analysis to other modes of thought and education. A "revolution in higher education," he said, was about to make the sciences at least equals of the classical subjects in a liberal education.[31]

With its laboratories, lecture hall, and seminar-size classrooms, Judd Hall enabled Wesleyan's faculty to employ the new tools of their emerging profession. Enthusiastic students in 1872 responded to the introduction of lab instruction in chemistry by arriving early and leaving late. Use of lectures increased, as professors imparted new research findings not yet included in texts. The method and spirit of the German seminar, introduced to Wesleyan in 1881 through a senior course in British literature, spread rapidly in the early 1890s. By 1892 seminar rooms with small specialized libraries supported research courses in the departments of biology, English language, English literature, Greek, Latin, and philosophy.[32]

These new methods greatly augmented the pursuit of independent thought previously encouraged within the traditional recitation format. The elective system by 1888 offered opportunities for "work in the true scholarly spirit." Notions of mental discipline, public service, and religious faith remained strong, but by 1895 a faculty leader declared that "the atmosphere of the institution is pervaded by the spirit of original investigation and independent thought."[33]

New teaching methods and scholarly esprit created needs for expanded support facilities, particularly the library. Devoting several years after his graduation to installing Wesleyan's collection of about twenty thousand books in the new building donated by Isaac Rich, Caleb Winchester expressed his hope that this facility would become "a storehouse where the student in any department may find the requisite materials to aid him in his investigations." William J. James '83, Wesleyan's librarian in the 1890s, viewed Rich Hall as the study and workshop of both instructors and students, an "essential instrument" for "the largest results in independent scholarship."[34]

Pressures for increased access to this central workshop and for a much larger and well-organized collection grew with each revision of the curriculum. Library hours steadily expanded from five hours per week in the early 1870s to thirty in the mid-1880s, forty in the mid-1890s, and eighty-two in 1898 with the advent of electric lighting. The collection doubled in size from 1870 to 1890 and again in the next two decades to reach almost eighty-two thousand volumes. Smaller than those of Amherst or Williams in 1870, the collection in 1910 was about to become the largest in this group of three colleges. Endowed funds for book purchases, beginning with that established by the alumni in the 1860s and gradually augmented by them over the next several decades, grew substantially after 1900 due to a few large bequests. Increased annual purchases and serious space problems that required storage of some books in the basement of South College led the librarian and the president in 1907 to note the need for a new library building.[35]

Organization and supervision of the growing collection brought Wesleyan into contact with the emerging profession of librarianship. Systems used by the Boston Public Library served as models when Wesleyan began preparing a card catalogue in the late 1860s. Under the dynamic leadership of Justin Winsor, Boston's collection would soon become the nation's largest. When William J. James assumed responsibility for Wesleyan's library on a part-time basis in 1891, he faced a more complex professional decision. The fixed-shelf system of cataloguing had been superseded in the developing profession by two classification systems that worked independent of reference to the particular alcove or range of shelves where a book resided. A mathematician who continued to teach several courses each year, James had no training in the recently established schools of librarianship. He moved without delay, however, to begin reclassification according to the system developed by Charles A. Cutter at the Boston Athenaeum rather than the much more widely adopted decimal approach of Melvil Dewey. Soon after he became Wesleyan's first full-time, long-term librarian (with the status of full professor) in 1895, James requested authorization to hire "a young woman who has been trained in a library school." Funding for this cataloging expertise arrived in 1899, enabling the appointment of Days Elizabeth Diefendorf, a recent graduate of the New York State Library School. Additional help came in 1907 through subscription to a service of the Library of Congress that supplied printed catalogue cards. The scramble for resources sufficient to catch up with cataloguing needs of an ever-expanding collection continued up to 1910.[36] In the twenty years since 1890, however, the library had become a professional operation.

Wesleyan's museum, installed on the top two floors of Judd Hall in 1871, stood alongside the library as a facility supporting the new research-oriented curricular climate. G. Brown Goode '70, who was preparing for a career in museum administration, took prime responsibility in 1871 for organizing and augmenting collections accumulated since 1831. When he left in 1877 to become curator and then director (1887) of the National Museum of the Smithsonian Institution, Wesleyan's collection of animals, plants, minerals, fossils, and ethnographic objects included well over one hundred thousand specimens and was "surpassed . . . by few in American colleges." For Goode and his close associate on the faculty Rice, the museum was "a comprehensive library of reference," supplying "the materials and appliances for original research, which are necessary alike to instructor and student."[37]

From the 1870s through the 1890s, Wesleyan's collection developed principally through exchanges with other museums, some as far afield as Munich. The Smithsonian served as Wesleyan's chief source. Correspondence between Rice and Goode in the 1880s delineated a steady stream of objects from Washington—including Australian mammals, a kayak, and a moose—in return for pottery, minerals, and corals. Other important sources were expeditions by Samuel W. Loper, curator from 1894 to 1910, and contributors from the Middletown area, who gave objects and money for purchases.[38]

By 1900 the collection had grown significantly in size and scope, but the museum's role in science at Wesleyan was waning. As at other colleges, science instruction was shifting from a field and museum approach to a mode of laboratory investigation. Competition for budget allocations and special gifts to science projects came from exciting experimental projects in chemistry, physics, psychology, and biology. Equipment for experiments designed by chemists and physicists to measure the caloric value of food drew national attention in the late 1890s. The cryogenic laboratory for analysis of materials at extremely low temperatures developed expertise by 1906 that produced air liquefiers for use by physicists at Harvard and Yale. As psychology laboratories sprouted in the early 1890s at more than a dozen universities and a few colleges, Wesleyan's facility for experimental work was set up in 1894 in the basement of South College. Under the directorship of a Wesleyan professor, the state bacteriological laboratory occupied space in the old brick chemistry laboratory behind North College. Expanding biology laboratories in Judd Hall put pressure on museum space. When Loper died in 1910, no curator of the museum was hired to replace him. Hopes for use of another building devoted exclusively to the museum found expression as late as 1919, but the museum would remain in Judd Hall until the mid-1950s.[39] Although a useful teaching adjunct and an attraction for visitors to the campus, it had few of the connections with original investigation that were envisioned in the 1870s.

Graduate students were another resource to support faculty pursuit of independent investigation. From 1873 to 1890 an average of three "post-graduate" students per year, almost all of them Wesleyan graduates staying for a fifth year, received largely individualized instruction to learn "the habits of independent research." About a third simultaneously served as assistants in laboratories and the library. During the next two decades, when Wesleyan offered graduate instruction in almost all departments and the possibility of earning a master's degree for one year of study, an average of twelve graduate students per year enrolled. Most studied in the sciences. A handful were graduates of other institutions. An average of three per year received the M.A. or M.S. Between 1886 and 1892 even the possibility of offering doctoral studies received attention. Probably discouraged by the magnitude of expenditures required for equipment and other resources to start and sustain such programs, the faculty produced no proposals, despite much discussion. Talk in 1890 of Wesleyan "steadily growing into a true University" was soon tempered by comparison with well-endowed emerging institutions of this type and by an ability to attract only a very modest level of enrollment at the master's level.[40]

The growing complexities of an elective curriculum, departmental organization, new methods of teaching, support facilities, and a thin layer of graduate instruction enhanced prospects for professional independence. This connection between development of the academic program and greater faculty autonomy is well illustrated by the demise of the outside examining committee in 1893. The system of annual oral comprehensive examinations for members of each of the four classes was communal in emphasis. The teaching of individual faculty members, as reflected in achievement levels of their students, received at least implicit exposure and scrutiny. Examinations were open to the public. Committees reported the results in detail at an assembly in the chapel and reported their general assessments in denominational newspapers.[41]

Rooted in the new spirit of independent investigation, a harbinger of change in this arrangement for public accountability appeared in 1873. The faculty instituted a system of written examinations given by faculty but available for review by the examining committee. In place of the comprehensive oral interrogations, each faculty member would present at least one class to be tested by the examining committee. Even this sampling approach to quality assessment was bound to yield as the curriculum became too diverse and specialized for a committee of "literary gentlemen" to evaluate. By 1889 a young faculty member found the practice to be "quite old fashioned."[42]

Faculty calls for abolition of the traditional system brought trustee action in 1893 that dispensed with examining committees and oral exams. In their place the board established a visiting committee from within its own ranks to make an annual assessment of the academic program and its needs by talking with faculty and attending a few classes once a year. In 1831 the examining committee was "to mark the progress of the students in all the departments and enquire into the mode and extent of the instruction given in order to decide upon the competency and faithfulness of the Instructor." By 1896 the report of the trustee visiting committee gave general praise to classroom instruction, noted that members lacked sufficient time to see any classes in mathematics, recorded extended visits to laboratories, gave an enthusiastic description of exercise classes in the new gymnasium, and found some of the recitation rooms poorly ventilated.[43] Specific assessments of faculty performance were left to the full professors, constituted as the Academic Council.

With newly established professional autonomy and authority, Wesleyan's faculty put its enduring stamp of scholarly specialization upon the curriculum in 1908. The curricular revision that went into effect in 1908/09 required students to complete at least six semester courses in a major study, consisting "wholly of studies in one department, or partly of studies in cognate departments, so chosen as to make a consistent program." In practice, departments tended to require eight such courses for the major and the collegewide minimum soon grew to ten in 1919.[44]

The curriculum revision of 1908 also instituted a system of distribution requirements. Half the credits earned to meet the graduation requirement must be distributed almost equally across three divisions: languages, social studies, sciences. At institutions like Harvard, where students had almost total elective freedom, the move to introduce requirements for breadth was made primarily to curb the student penchant for avoiding areas of the curriculum they found uninteresting, difficult, or both. At Wesleyan, however, the first year of the B.A. program before 1908 continued to require study of Latin, Greek, mathematics, English, and German or French. Requirements in science, social science, philosophy, ethics, and religion were scattered from sophomore through senior year. The new distribution system for Wesleyan students thus became a framework within which their elective choices expanded. For the first time, a Wesleyan B.A. could be obtained without the study of mathematics, and with either Latin or Greek rather than both. Except for the required course in freshman English, a framework for breadth achieved through electives replaced the remnants of a once totally specified course of study.[45]

The issue at Wesleyan in 1908 was insufficient student specialization. Courses offered increased from 43 in 1873/74 to 155 in 1906/07. An elective system gave "to the best students the opportunity to specialize in their chosen departments." Yet the number of students electing study in depth apparently diminished as the elective system grew. Whereas one-third of graduates in the 1880s achieved departmental honors, only 10 percent did so in the late 1890s. Not just the weaker students but also those with strong abilities and motivation seemed to need less freedom and more guidance. The required capstone experience of senior year—once moral philosophy, more recently ethics and evidences of Christianity—would now be the completion of a major. In stating the case for a required major field, the senior member of the faculty in 1905 identified the primary link between development of the academic profession and revision of the curriculum. Students should complete work, he argued, "so advanced as to give them some experience, real, though it may be slight, of the mental attitude involved in original research."[46]

Research Expertise

While establishing prerogatives and priorities for professional roles within the college and constructing a curriculum consistent with new scholarly ideals, the faculty developed a professional commitment to individual research. This commitment found strong expression in the training acquired by Methodist faculty members of the 1870s and in the less Methodist generation of faculty they recruited in the next two decades. A president conversant with contemporary approaches to scholarship took office in 1889. By 1900 the faculty had a record of research and publication that brought new levels of security, opportunity, control, and prestige to individual professional lives.

Almost two-thirds of Wesleyan's faculty in 1881 had advanced training at German or American universities. The percentage with earned doctorates was about equal to that of the much larger faculty at Harvard, both approaching 30 percent. Along with colleges such as Amherst and Williams, Wesleyan began in the 1860s and 1870s to hire faculty who, though often alumni and members of the sponsoring denomination, had imbibed the spirit of scholarly adventure. They would, in turn, set higher scholarly standards for faculty recruited after 1880. To fill new positions in the 1880s, Wesleyan continued to draw from the pool of young scholars who had studied abroad, particularly those who came home with doctorates. Wesleyan also tapped a steadily increasing supply of Ph.D.'s emerging from the new American university founded by Johns Hopkins. Only four of Wesleyan's faculty attaining the rank of full professor from 1890 to 1910 lacked the Ph.D.[47]

The transition to a faculty with specialized training and research commitments in an academic discipline began to produce tensions in the 1880s. Change that increased the scholarly strength of Wesleyan's faculty threatened to diminish Methodist piety and hegemony. An early indication of concern with this issue emerged in 1880 during the consideration of Morris B. Crawford '74 for appointment as instructor in physics. When he was a graduate student in Germany the year before, Crawford confronted "questions . . . about the difficulties of belief." He requested that his preacher's license be canceled. Despite knowledge that Crawford's Methodist faith included "certain *unorthodox* speculative opinions," Wesleyan hired him. An argument in favor of this decision, made by a trustee who would become Crawford's father-in-law a few years later, maintained that the young physicist could be trusted to refrain from bringing up his religious views either in or beyond the classroom.[48]

Consideration of non-Methodists for long-term appointments became an issue in 1885. The first person to join Wesleyan's faculty after completing graduate studies at Johns Hopkins was Herbert William Conn, a biologist. He arrived in 1884 with both the doctorate and the desired denominational affiliation. The two Hopkins-trained men called to Wesleyan's attention the next year, however, were of a different religious persuasion. An alumnus recommended one of them, a promising young philosopher from Vermont. John Dewey, he noted, "belongs to the Congregational Church, which will of course prevent his ever becoming permanent at Wesleyan, but perhaps you can get him for a few years as instructor." The position in philosophy was filled (with a Methodist) by the time this suggestion arrived, but the faculty did recommend that spring the hiring of another Hopkins-trained Congregationalist, Charles H. Levermore, to teach history and political economy.[49]

Levermore's candidacy contrasted with that of his rival for the position, Abram W. Harris '80. Like George L. Westgate '65, a Methodist minister who had held the appointment from 1880 until his health failed, Harris offered the desirable denominational background but lacked graduate training in the discipline he would teach. He had studied mathematics for a year in Germany. Levermore (Yale '79), the son of a Congregational minister, would become a Unitarian and the founding president of Adelphi College. He had completed two years of graduate study in history and political economy at Johns Hopkins and would obtain his Ph.D. in 1886. When John W. Beach disregarded the faculty's nomination of the appropriately trained Levermore and led the trustees to appoint the denominationally preferable Harris, a serious quarrel began between faculty and president that would contribute to Beach's departure two years later.[50]

Controversy over appointments reappeared in the spring of 1886. The faculty refused to nominate Harris for a second year and asked the president to communicate their reasons to the trustees. Undaunted, Beach obtained trustee approval for reappointment of Harris and worked to thwart the faculty nomination for another position. This time the choice was between a Methodist who did not show signs of becoming a committed scholar in his field and a promising young scholar who would soon move from the Methodist to the Episcopal denomination. The position in Latin was open due to the death of Calvin Harrington, a Methodist minister who served on the Wesleyan faculty for a quarter century. The faculty requested that Beach take to the board the nomination of Elmer T. Merrill '81 to be Harrington's successor. As a tutor at Wesleyan for three years and a graduate student at Yale, Merrill had evidently given early indications of a career that would yield many publications and culminate in an appointment at the University of Chicago. Beach pressured the faculty into concurring with his nomination of Alfred C. True '73, also a tutor at Wesleyan, who would soon become an important administrator in the United States Department of Agriculture. The *Argus* noted Beach's "contempt for the opinions of his colleagues."[51] The faculty soon prevailed. After Beach was forced out a year later, faculty prerogative to make and reject nominations was rein-

John Monroe Van Vleck '50, professor of
mathematics and astronomy, 1853–1904,
and acting president, 1872–73, 1887–89,
1896–97

Woodrow Wilson, professor of history
and political economy, 1888–90

vigorated (particularly with establishment of the Academic Council in
1892). Merrill returned to Wesleyan in 1888. Harris was succeeded that
year by a Presbyterian with a Ph.D. from Johns Hopkins.

Beach's departure in 1887 left John Van Vleck with many opportunities as acting president. The fifty-four-year-old mathematician and his
faculty colleagues were ready to make the most of a two-year interreg-
num. Van Vleck brought to his assignment prior administrative experience as acting president in 1872/73, devout denominational loyalty, close
study of the universities of Europe during a leave of absence in 1878/79,
and a reputation of having done much to mold the character of Wesleyan.
He would go on to earn acclaim as "the dominant influence in shaping
the policy of the college." Using his annual report in 1888 to articulate a
vision for Wesleyan's development, Van Vleck asserted that "Methodism cannot afford to be content with anything less than a college equal
in all respects to the best of which our country can boast." In particular,
he suggested, Methodism needed "an institution developed along the
line of the so-called 'philosophical' faculty of the German University
—that is, in the direction of extended opportunity for instruction, and
no less for research, in the departments of philosophy, literature, and
the sciences." Wesleyan, he noted a year later, would seek "nothing short
of the superiority which befits the prominence of our denomination."
Van Vleck and his colleagues used the new *Bulletin* to document prog-

ress toward such superiority through "increase of students, expansion of curriculum, and increase of original research." The acting president's most enduring achievement was to set scholarly criteria above denominational membership in the recruitment of faculty. "There was no occurrence during the two years . . . which gave me so much gratification," he recalled, as securing two promising scholars (who happened to be Presbyterians): Andrew C. Armstrong and Woodrow Wilson.[52]

Wilson exemplified the new breed of academic professional Wesleyan recruited from major graduate schools in America and Europe during the next two decades. Several of his contemporaries in the doctoral program at Johns Hopkins were candidates for the appointment he accepted. Van Vleck first offered the position in history and political economy to Albert Shaw, who declined and went on to a distinguished career as editor and publisher of the American *Review of Reviews*. J. Franklin Jameson, who would become a leader of the historical profession in the early twentieth century, decided he would accept if asked. An offer came from Brown, however, to rescue him from what he viewed as "the poor fun [of] teaching scrubby Methodist undergraduates." Moving on to yet another non-Methodist, Van Vleck found Wilson attracted by Wesleyan's very competitive salary (better than Brown's), teaching load of eight hours per week, and provision for an annual leave of absence for six weeks in February and March so he could continue giving a lecture course at Johns Hopkins. Wilson was ready to leave Bryn Mawr, his first teaching position, where he felt overworked, underpaid, and much less than enthusiastic about the higher education of women.[53] He arrived at Wesleyan in September 1888 with the new credentials that served as a standard for subsequent appointments. Wesleyan's era of hiring studious Methodist ministers had ended.

As a Presbyterian and graduate of Princeton, Wilson came at the beginning of a movement away from Wesleyan's all-Methodist, mostly alumni faculty of the mid-1880s. Soon after settling into a house on High Street rented from Wesleyan, Wilson and his wife transferred membership from the Presbyterian church in Bryn Mawr to the oldest Congregational church in Middletown. Over the next dozen years, 60 percent of Wesleyan's new faculty recruits would come from outside the Methodist denomination. The representation of alumni among full-time faculty at the rank of instructor or above would drop from 60 percent in 1887 to 32 percent in 1900.[54]

As a published scholar, Wilson came to Wesleyan just a few years before a dramatic increase in the percentage of faculty engaged in pursuing and reporting research. His first book, *Congressional Government* (1885), had achieved high praise and wide usage at Harvard and other institutions. While at Wesleyan he completed a textbook, *The State* (1889), and accepted an invitation to write a brief survey of United States history, 1829–89, as a volume in Albert Bushnell Hart's "Epochs of American History." Several essays and a major critical review of James Bryce's *The American Commonwealth* also came from his Caligraph typewriter. Wilson's scholarship was less than Germanic in its depth and accuracy, but it started placing Wesleyan on the map of institutions known for faculty research. Others would carry the work forward in the early 1890s to the point where professors regularly reporting research results quickly rose from about 25 percent of the faculty in 1888 to 75 percent by the mid-1890s. The "modern college professor," according to an 1899 *Wesleyan University Bulletin* article, "is expected to produce original work of some sort." By demonstrating ways to integrate his teaching and research, Wilson helped to develop this expectation at Wesleyan.[55]

As an energetic young professor in his early thirties, Wilson enlarged the scope of faculty-student rapport. From the start he was very popular due to his polished classroom presentations, "enlivened with wit and humor" and embellished with "a grace of diction that held us enthralled at times." Few students faulted his "very opinionated" approach or his low tolerance for dissenting student views. His major initiative outside the classroom came in early 1889 when he stimulated students to organize opportunity for debate through a House of Commons similar to the one he had started at Johns Hopkins in 1884. Wilson's football knowledge and enthusiasm, developed during undergraduate days at Princeton, led him to help the team plan game strategies at evening meetings held in his classroom. A quarter-century later, an alumnus remembered Wilson as "a tall, thin man running up and down these very side-lines during the afternoon's football practice, waving his closed umbrella in the air and cheering encouragement at the top of his lungs to the team on almost every play."[56]

As a person of talent, accomplishment, driving ambition, and cosmopolitan contacts, Wilson represented a type of appointment risk Wesleyan was willing to take. Even before arriving and finding Wesleyan students "very inferior in point of preparatory culture," he was positioning himself for an appointment at Princeton. He kept many contacts through correspondence and travel to give lectures that enhanced professional reputation and options. During his second year at Wesleyan he received overtures regarding appointment to a new chair at Williams. When the anticipated Princeton offer came in February, Wilson hesitated only long enough to bargain for a higher salary.[57]

Yet Wilson was genuinely sorry to leave friends and colleagues at Wesleyan, and he served as a strong advocate for the college in helping to recruit a replacement. He first approached Frederick Jackson Turner, who was not yet assured that the University of Wisconsin would promote him to a permanent appointment. Wilson told Turner that "the conditions of instruction here . . . are in every way agreeable and advantageous." Turner showed interest, but Wesleyan was unwilling to appoint "so young a man" (Turner was twenty-eight) as full professor. Wilson then helped Wesleyan make a second approach to his friend, Albert Shaw. Two years earlier, Shaw had been assured by another Wesleyan professor who knew him from graduate school days that Wesleyan "had an eager desire for an increase in the literary and scientific work . . . of our faculty," gave every encouragement to such endeavors, and would sustain the "spirit of research" they had shared at Johns Hopkins. Wilson added to this testimonial, noting the advantages of a reasonable teaching load and small classes. "If one's class work lies within the field in which one wants to write," he concluded, "original work for publication is not at all difficult." Hoping for an appointment at Cornell, Shaw declined, but not before Wilson told him, as he had others, that Wesleyan's "liberal and progressive" faculty and trustees were on the verge of major developments in resources and reputation.[58]

To serve as president during this surge of professional and institutional development the faculty needed a person who understood and supported new trends in scholarly growth. They also needed someone who respected their professional prerogatives and exhibited a generous, kindly spirit in personal relations. Due to the rending departure of Beach, another desideratum was the temperament and vision to heal relations among denominational supporters, alumni, and trustees.

The seven prominent members of the denomination who constituted the trustee search committee took almost nineteen months before presenting a recommendation. Their thoughts first turned to Rev. Albert S. Hunt '51, widely read secretary of the American Bible Society. Resisting appeals to his denominational loyalty, Hunt wisely counseled that he was too old (sixty-one) and too far behind the times in his scholarship. Six other Methodist ministers with academic credentials and careers received close consideration. The committee sent Van Vleck on a trip to assess one of the six, Bradford Paul Raymond, president of

Lawrence University in Appleton, Wisconsin. Van Vleck was deeply respected by the trustees as well as by his faculty colleagues. He probably evaluated Raymond primarily with reference to faculty aspirations and apparently made an influential positive report. At a meeting of the board 19 November 1888 the committee unanimously recommended Raymond. When asked for his and faculty opinions, Van Vleck gave a balanced evaluation, leaning in favor and "disposed to make the best" of hiring the strongest currently available candidate, Raymond. Despite opposition led by a few Middletown trustees, Raymond received a majority of votes (16–11) on the first ballot.[59]

Raymond was a faculty-oriented president. With the major gift from Daniel Ayres just prior to the new presidency and distributions throughout the 1890s from the windfall bequest of Daniel Fayerweather, Raymond worked to increase the number of full-time faculty positions. Holding the ratio of full-time students to full-time faculty at about eleven to one during a surge of enrollment growth in the late 1880s and early 1890s, he also doubled the roster of departmental assistants. He regularly taught courses in evidences of Christianity and in ethics. His year of study at German universities and earned Ph.D. from Boston University prepared him to understand, support, and praise faculty research. Faculty remembered him as "profoundly in sympathy with the new Wesleyan to whose presidency he was called."[60]

Faculty also remembered Raymond for "his kindly, pleasant smile," "singular purity of character," and "sweetness of spirit." Those who could recall chafing under Cummings and Beach knew Raymond as a friend who would not "say a single malicious or contemptuous word of any man." His genial optimism and talents as a peacemaker were assets in dealing with key constituencies. Trustees viewed him as "a safe and unselfish First Director." Patron conferences received him as a pious and loyal Methodist. Middletown residents found him amiable and unpretentious. It was with the faculty in particular, however, that Raymond developed a bond of affectionate colleagueship.[61]

Raymond's inauguration introduced a president with a reassuring philosophy as well as warm personality. The densely packed audience on that rainy 26 June 1889 saw a forty-three-year-old Connecticut farmer's son of somewhat slight build and small stature. The full beard and mustache of this Civil War veteran extended below a long nose and receding hairline. Observers noted his scholarly manner and heard a "clear, rich, and penetrating voice." With an ease and command reflecting nine years of experience in Methodist pulpits of New England and six years in the presidency of his alma mater, Lawrence University, Raymond presented a philosophy of education rooted in the idealism of nineteenth-century German philosophers.[62] The spacious framework he constructed provided ample room for college and denomination to sustain congenial relations.

Raymond's inaugural message sounded the major themes that would echo through his baccalaureate sermons, public addresses, and writings across almost two decades as Wesleyan's president. A Wesleyan education would go beyond the empiricist limitations of positivism. There "is something in man that cannot be weighed on hayscales." The spiritual dimensions of man must be addressed in order to develop the "whole man" in a manner consistent with "the modern idea of personality." Standing squarely in the thought patterns of liberal Protestantism, Raymond saw the divine hand in human history working with man to realize God's kingdom. Harmonious, mutually reinforcing roles could be outlined for Wesleyan's students, faculty, and denominational supporters. Students would prepare themselves for lives of "manhood" by training all the powers of mind and spirit. Rather than becoming narrow "cranks," they would be "competent to see things in wide relations" and from multiple points of view. Faculty would supply the research and teaching to prepare students for a rationally self-directed life. Scientists would make a particularly important contribution by illuminating the universal laws of nature that lead man to "demand causation beyond physical phenomena" and to "predicate God." Denominational supporters would share Raymond's confidence in these teachers and support a Wesleyan operating "in harmony with nature, with philosophy, and with Christianity."[63]

Within this philosophical context of the Raymond presidency, Wesleyan's faculty further clarified their professional identity during the 1890s. Beginning with the Foss presidency, faculty had defined their role as one of "independent men" who articulated high aspirations for the institution. The president, neither an equal colleague nor a commanding officer, was to respect independence of opinion among the faculty and to support their aspirations. A faculty still functioning "almost like . . . a family" in 1875 could regard him as a wisely tolerant and attentive father or a "beloved brother." By 1889 the relationship was defined in terms of "friendship." The president was enjoined to complete the work already begun by the faculty, working cooperatively with them so that Wesleyan would "become a University."[64]

Senior faculty at the beginning of a new century had a substantial degree of professional independence and influence. The system of five-year terms instituted in 1860 ended in the mid-1870s. By 1890 there was explicit reference to "permanent tenure of office." With successful completion of a three-year probationary period, even associate professors could achieve this status. There were no standards or procedures to protect against arbitrary dismissal, but the job security of tenured professors seemed substantial when contrasted with the rate of forced departures among recent Wesleyan presidents. Through the new Academic Council, presidents routinely sought the advice and concurrence of professors on matters of appointment, promotion, tenure, titles, and endowed chairs.[65]

Faculty colleagueship in 1900 reflected a recent shift in primary focus from broadly conceived local groups to national disciplinary associations. From its inception in 1871 the Middletown Scientific Association had supplied encouragement in scientific study to Wesleyan's faculty and to nearby residents who pursued such investigation on an amateur basis. At monthly meetings of the association most of the papers presented results of faculty research or reports from faculty on recent scholarly literature in the natural sciences. Wives of members soon joined the occasional "field meetings" and excursions. In 1879 the association opened all its meetings to the public. By 1900 the main purpose of these gatherings was education of the community, often through the use of outside lecturers. While Wesleyan's faculty continued to give support to this "vernacular science" organization, their chief source of professional stimulation came from interacting with departmental colleagues, preparing research publications to be read by disciplinary peers at other institutions, and attending the meetings of national associations. Reports from faculty recently returned from these meetings constituted an important item on the agenda of another local group, the Apostles Club. Formed in 1894 by faculty in the humanities and social sciences, this monthly gathering to discuss topics of interest to the members heard papers during its first decade that usually were based on individual research projects. As faculty increasingly came to report their work only to disciplinary peers beyond the bounds of Middletown, the Apostles Club shifted its attention toward current campus events and issues, particularly in the nonscience sector of Wesleyan's curriculum.[66]

Faculty salaries in 1900 rested on a substantial base established in 1871 and reflected the growing stature of a young profession during the 1890s. Laments over low faculty salaries expressed in the national press around 1870 were quickly answered by colleges such as Wesleyan and

Amherst. Salaries for full professors increased by 25 percent in 1871, with both colleges paying $2,500. Almost three decades of no inflation and occasional drops in prices kept senior faculty at strong institutions such as Wesleyan in a comfortable life style, participating fully in the highest local social circles and enjoying a family income in the top 5 percent of all families in the nation. When Wesleyan announced a major fund-raising campaign in 1876, more than half the faculty made $1,000 pledges. During hard times for Wesleyan in 1877/78, 1878/79, and 1884/85, faculty accepted salary reductions of 10 percent. Waiver of tuition and fees at Wesleyan for faculty children became a policy in 1879. Vigorous competition for faculty among new American universities in the 1890s reached the Wesleyan campus in 1891. Caleb Winchester received an offer from William Rainey Harper, founding president of the University of Chicago. As Harper's chair of the department of English language, literature, and rhetoric, Winchester could double his present salary of $2,500. To keep Winchester, Wesleyan's trustees decided to depart from the long-established pay scale determined only by rank. A graduation of salaries within rank was needed to meet "strong financial inducements" that threatened to draw away the "most valued professors." They raised Winchester's salary by $1,000, and he decided to stay. Over the next two decades, other Wesleyan faculty received offers from Princeton, Stanford, Wisconsin, the Carnegie Institution of Washington, and government agencies. Special compensation increases helped to keep about half of them at Wesleyan.[67]

Wesleyan's investment in a high-powered professional faculty brought substantial yield in institutional reputation by 1900. Atwater's work with the respiration calorimeter was achieving international attention. Winchester was coediting with Harvard's George Lyman Kittredge the Athenaeum Press series of masterpieces in English literature. Rice had recently revised Dana's famous textbook in geology. Conn had exhibited at the 1893 World's Fair in Chicago his work on bacteria cultures in the dairy process and was gaining recognition that would lead to appointment as state bacteriologist. Edward B. Van Vleck '84, Walter P. Bradley, Francis G. Benedict, and Raymond Dodge were beginning to publish in national journals of their disciplines. Research grants were coming from governmental agencies at the state and national level and from major foundations. Atwater and Edward B. Rosa '86 had just received awards from the Franklin Institute of Philadelphia.[68]

Faculty scholarship had also proved valuable in a time of threats to Wesleyan's reputation. A typhoid epidemic involving twenty-three students hit the campus in late October 1894. The first of four student deaths from the disease occurred in early November. When a junior, the son of a Methodist minister in Brooklyn, died four days later, news of a "dreadful epidemic" appeared in hometown newspapers. The *Brooklyn Eagle* repeated rumors of a contaminated college well, and editorial allegations of administrative carelessness appeared in a New York paper. The health tragedy became a public relations nightmare. A team of faculty scientists, led by Conn, the Johns Hopkins-trained bacteriologist, began an investigation on 4 November. Chemical analysis and bacteriological studies eliminated the well water as a possible cause. A sophisticated and precise epidemiological analysis yielded a conclusive report within a week. The typhoid infection had come from contaminated raw oysters purchased near New Haven and consumed at the initiation suppers on 12 October at three fraternities. Wesleyan enrollments continued their steady increase the next fall, and there was one more reason to respect the faculty's scholarly accomplishments so clearly evident by 1900.[69]

Almost all the accouterments of the modern academic profession were in place at turn-of-the-century Wesleyan. The typical faculty member had a disciplinary identity characterized by specialized training, research activity, and membership in national associations. His institutional career followed a clear pathway for promotion and de facto tenure. His career beyond the campus included publications, public lectures, opportunities for interinstitutional mobility, and possibilities for sharing expertise through public service. Personal offices for all faculty would become available with the completion of Fisk Hall and Scott Laboratory in 1904. Only a program of sabbatical leaves was lacking. The trustees considered developing a policy for leaves in the late 1890s but decided to continue the practice of granting leaves on an ad hoc basis, usually without salary. From 1880 to 1910 about a dozen faculty obtained such leaves for further study and research.[70]

Study of a photograph of the faculty in 1900 indicates the extent to which a new generation of academic professionals had established itself. Gone were important members of the second faculty generation appointed soon after mid-century. Rev. Calvin S. Harrington, author of articles for the *Methodist Review* and primarily a leader of "others into a deeper spiritual life," had died in 1886. In the picture is his successor, Merrill, a prolific scholar in the discipline. Rev. George Prentice, professor of modern languages, biographer of Methodist leaders, and a man of "simple, trustful piety," had died in 1893. In the picture is his

Wesleyan's faculty in 1872 seated on the porch of the president's house. *Top row, from left,* Johnston, President Cummings, Van Benschoten; *middle row,* Prentice, Van Vleck, Hibbard; *bottom row,* Rice, Winchester. Absent from this picture is Harrington.

Wesleyan's faculty in 1900 assembled on the chapel portico includes: *row 2,* Van Vleck, President Raymond, and Van Benschoten (5th, 6th, and 7th from left); *row 3,* Merrill (2nd from left); *row 4,* Faust and Farrand (2nd and 6th from left).

successor, Albert B. Faust, who obtained his Ph.D. from Johns Hopkins and went on to teach at Wisconsin and Cornell. Van Vleck and Van Benschoten, pious Methodist patriarchs flanking President Raymond in the center of the photo, are just a few years from the ends of their careers. Another visual indication of changing times came from Van Vleck's congenial relationship with members of the new generation like Max Farrand, the urbane historian with properly tailored and creased attire. They had been recently seen leaving morning chapel together, "Uncle Johnny trying to match his steps with the long graceful strides of his young friend, Uncle Johnny's stove-pipe pants flapping in the breeze in contrast to the rigidity of Max's trousers." A more important departure in dress would occur at the commencement of 1903, when the faculty appeared for the first time in the academic regalia appropriate to their professional achievements.[71]

Drifting Apart
From within the denomination, voices of encouragement for faculty scholarship continued from the 1860s through the 1890s. "Draughts of sanctified learning from fountains of her own" institutions, some argued, would enable the Methodist church to champion a true faith in the arena of modern religious controversy. As part of his plan in 1881 for Methodist colleges to attract much larger numbers of the denomination's youth, Bishop Edward Andrews called for Wesleyan's faculty to "become as conspicuous in the fields of investigation and authorship as they have been faithful and useful in the classroom and in personal intercourse with the students." When faculty members built a tradition of research and achieved wider recognition for their accomplishments in the 1880s, the denominational press applauded. Amid articles in the 1890s praising "the Wesleyan spirit . . . of thoroughness and . . . scholarly research," editorial commentary in 1893 concluded that "everything at Wesleyan is alive, modern, progressive."[72]

Along with such praise, faculty received frequent reminders that being progressive should not preclude being pious. The *Christian Advocate* cautioned faculty in 1895 to keep steadily in view the historical imperative that Wesleyan "exists beyond all else for the promotion of pure and intelligent piety." Reports over the next decade reinforced faculty pursuit of this goal and reassured the denomination that modern thought at Wesleyan entered student minds only after faculty made it "pass through the sieve of judicious criticism." Faculty "coworkers . . . with God" would make sure that scientific skepticism on matters of faith was properly combatted and that students would "never fail to conquer doubt and keep their faith at last."[73]

Wesleyan's faculty sustained high levels of regard and confidence within the denomination because of the way they approached new knowledge. Like some of their mentors and colleagues at Yale until at least 1890, Wesleyan professors combined "*new* ideas of scholarliness and the scholarly vocation with *inherited* religious faith." Wesleyan's late nineteenth-century dedication to "the strenuous search after truth and virtue" remained compatible with denominational goals. Faculty members who increasingly attached themselves to the ideals of the philosopher in pursuit of new truth could also serve the ideals of the orator giving primacy to virtue. New facts simply testified to divine truths and took their place in "an all-embracing divine world of meaning." Van Vleck advised his students in astronomy that study of the nocturnal sky would produce "a deeper conviction that the Heavens declare the glory of God." Conn's research on the typhoid epidemic added a scientific explanation to the providential one traditionally invoked when students died. Yet this Methodist biologist also affirmed that the final outcome of scientific advances would be "a greater faith in God and a greater reverence for his works." In his research on Dante's *Divine Comedy*, Oscar Kuhns '85 found high religious ideals and "a deep and all-pervading spirituality." To Methodists worried that "enlarged thought and widened range of investigations will relax moral discipline and cool religious fervor," both the older and younger generations of faculty, as the century drew to a close, gave reason to view new knowledge as a wellspring for piety and right conduct.[74]

Potential for turbulence between college and denomination, however, lay just beneath this calm surface. Faculty professionalism developed during the 1890s to a point where individuals used their extensive experience or expertise to engage controversial issues. Meanwhile within Methodist ranks resistance to some of the modernist aspects of liberal Protestantism began to stir. A letter to the *Methodist Review* in 1897 challenged Conn's message that "scientists and Christians are joining hands." How could one believe in evolution, the writer asked, without casting doubts on Bible statements? Conn may have provided an artful argument, but did it not devalue "the supernatural origin of man, as recorded in Genesis?" Three faculty members with decades of loyalty to Methodism and service to professional advancement were about to encounter difficulties with the denomination between 1898 and 1902.[75]

Caleb Thomas Winchester, son of a Methodist minister in the Provi-

Caleb Thomas Winchester '69, librarian, 1869–73, and professor of English literature, 1873–1920

dence Conference, grew up on a farm in Middleboro, Massachusetts. While a student at Wesleyan Academy, he used the library to develop a taste for belles lettres. Appointed librarian upon his graduation from the college in 1869, he had ample opportunity during the next four years to read widely. At age twenty-six he became Olin Professor of Rhetoric and English Literature and served on the Wesleyan faculty from 1873 until his death in 1920.[76]

Winchester became known by the late 1870s as "one of the finest rising scholars of the Church." He was also one of a small group of trailblazing scholars in his discipline, including Francis J. Child at Harvard and Thomas R. Lounsbury and Henry A. Beers of Yale, who introduced the study of English literature into the American college curriculum. In 1879 the Wesleyan trustees decided to fund Winchester's first opportunity for graduate training. He spent the 1880/81 academic year studying at Leipzig and traveling in Europe.[77]

During the 1880s Winchester began to build his reputation as a polished public lecturer and an intellectually stimulating teacher. Plain in appearance and restrained in delivery, he engaged listeners with a gentle dignity and a speaking style "so quiet yet so compelling" due to the eloquence of his carefully prepared insights into British prose and poetry. Amid a profusion of muttonchop whiskers, a whimsical half-smile accompanied frequent brief expressions of his genial sense of humor. Cultured, courtly, urbane, Winchester taught with a "scholarly force" that emphasized "the rigorous discipline of . . . mind" and "the joy of elevated thought."[78]

Audiences and classes heard Winchester present great works of literature in a manner that served Christian culture. He seldom moralized, and he avoided dogma, but his outlook was thoroughly theistic. "To know this great and varied world . . . as it stands revealed in literature," he asserted in 1890, "is to see how in all this goodly frame of outward things beauty and charm are but the expression of His divine thought; and how through all the tangled web of human action runs His divine law." Given this merger of matters secular and religious, Winchester found that "it is not a whit more a religious duty for me to take part in a prayer meeting than it is for me to lecture to my college classes."[79]

In the spring of 1898 Winchester expressed concern that his denomination was lacking a similarly flexible approach to changing times. He spoke as an active and devout Methodist. His contributions to Methodist hymnody, *Zion's Herald*, and the *Methodist Review* were substantial. He spoke as a well-established scholar. In addition to coediting the Athenaeum Press series in British literature and receiving a highly publicized offer from the University of Chicago, he had given lectures at Johns Hopkins that were a brilliant academic and popular success. Woodrow Wilson found him to be "the best professor of English Literature in the country." A reviewer of his soon-to-be-published textbook, *Some Principles of Literary Criticism* (1899), would recommend it as "the best [brief] résumé of modern theories of literary aesthetics . . . that we have in English." Finally, he spoke as an academic professional, drawing on three decades of experience with college-level youth.[80]

Methodism was losing young people of culture and education to other denominations, Winchester told an audience of ministers and laymen gathered at the April meeting of the Boston Methodist Social Union. Too narrow an emphasis on evangelism left too little support for education and for the "catholicity and breadth of view" exhibited by John Wesley. Prohibitions against amusements such as theater, dancing, and card playing alienated sons and daughters of Methodist parentage. Winchester concluded with a plea for "a broader, more inclusive idea of the Christian life."[81]

When printed in *Zion's Herald*, Winchester's address was accompanied by a stinging editorial rebuttal from Charles Parkhurst. Although this

Dartmouth graduate was sympathetic to modern scholarship, he thought Winchester violated boundaries of good judgment for a scholar in the church. Intending not only "to deprecate, but to ridicule, the work of evangelism," Winchester and others of his kind would "chill the ardor of our evangelistic spirit." The successful and widely respected editor of *Zion's Herald* found the proposal to eliminate Methodism's prohibition of amusements as indicative of how "the scholar in the church gets away in his secluded realm and loses sight of the status of the average mind and heart in the church." Parkhurst concluded that "the Professor does not understand his own church." Winchester wrote no reply.[82]

Wilbur Olin Atwater, son of a Methodist minister with ties to the Troy and Vermont conferences, grew up on a farm near Burlington, Vermont. He began his college studies at the University of Vermont. In accord with his father's desire that he obtain his upper-level education in a Methodist college, Atwater spent his junior and senior years at Wesleyan, graduating in 1865. After three years as a high school principal and a year of study in agricultural chemistry under Samuel W. Johnson, he obtained one of the first sixteen Ph.D.'s granted at Yale. Two years of study at Leipzig and Berlin and two years of college teaching preceded his appointment in 1873 as instructor at Wesleyan.[83]

Atwater immediately began building his career in Middletown with a high level of energy and entrepreneurial talent. He joined Orange Judd, editor of the *American Agriculturalist*, and Johnson of Yale in lobbying for state funding of an experiment station similar to those he had seen in Europe. Responding to an offer of $1,000 from Judd and free use of a chemical laboratory in Judd Hall, the Connecticut legislature granted a two-year appropriation to establish at Wesleyan in 1875 the nation's first state agricultural experiment station. Yale's influence with the legislature effected relocation of the enterprise to New Haven in 1877, but Atwater soon persuaded the Smithsonian Institution to assume support of his research on nutrition. By cultivating individuals and state agencies who viewed poor nutrition as a source of social problems, he obtained new funds in the mid-1880s. Combining laboratory research on food values with dietary surveys conducted among lower-class families in such locations as Chicago, New York, and rural Alabama, Atwater and other conservative reformers concluded that "problems of poverty and labor unrest could be solved by teaching the masses to shop and to cook economically." Additional resources came as a result of efforts by Atwater and other educators to gain passage of the Hatch Act in 1887. This federal support for experiment stations in each state was allocated

Wilbur Olin Atwater '65, professor of
chemistry, 1873–1907

in Connecticut so as to include funding of basic research at Wesleyan.
While retaining his professorship, Atwater served from 1887 to 1891 as
director of the national Office of Experimental Stations.[84]

The capstone of Atwater's career came with his use of the respiration
calorimeter to study human metabolism. Designed and constructed in
the basement of Judd Hall from 1892 to 1896 with important help from
Edward Rosa, Atwater's colleague in physics, and Olin S. Blakeslee, a
mechanic in the physics department, the respiration calorimeter was a
chamber with chair, table, and bed in which a man spent four or five
days per experiment. By precise measurement of income and outgo of
both matter and energy for the subject during this period, Atwater and
his colleagues demonstrated that the law of the conservation of energy
applied to the human organism as well as to inert matter. They also
used a bomb calorimeter to determine the caloric value of various foods,
initially ranging from beef and bread to milk and ginger snaps.[85]

When his experiments turned from ginger snaps to gin in the late
1890s, however, Atwater incurred a deluge of denominational disdain.
He reported that alcohol had nutritional value. He also argued that
claims to the contrary by the Methodist-backed temperance movement
lacked scientific validity. Atwater spoke as a scientist whose previous
work had elicited expressions of denominational pride in his achieve-

ments. Bearing the names of Willbur Fisk and Stephen Olin, he spoke as a lifelong Methodist and supporter of temperance. His father had served in the 1870s as the zealous secretary and agent of the temperance society in Vermont and as publisher of a temperance newspaper. The loyal and scholarly son now wanted the movement to succeed on the basis of arguments consistent with scientific truth.[86]

A decade earlier he had reported in *Century Magazine* on experiments in Europe indicating that the "fuel value" of alcoholic beverages "appears to be considerable." No flap ensued. By the late 1890s circumstances were more combustible. The Woman's Christian Temperance Union was at the peak of its success in obtaining laws to require throughout the nation's schools instruction from textbooks asserting that alcohol was a poison, not a food. A clear threat to that success now came from a chemist reporting results of his own experiments conducted at a Methodist college, from a researcher of international repute in scholarly circles, and from "perhaps the most widely known American scientist of his day."[87]

It all began in Middletown on the evening of 13 June 1899. Scheduled for one of the presentations he and other Wesleyan faculty regularly made to the Middletown Scientific Association, Atwater decided to share early results from experiments he was conducting for the Committee of Fifty to Investigate the Liquor Problem. The committee was a self-appointed group, including leaders in all areas of American life, formed in 1893 to promote objective study of many issues related to use of alcoholic beverages and to foster rational solutions to a complex social problem. Atwater was serving on the committee and using his calorimeter to prepare a major chapter for the final two-volume report published in 1903.[88]

Atwater probably entered the meeting in his usual buoyant manner. The short, stout scientist in his mid-fifties was "a man of exhaustless enthusiasm and tireless energy." Always courteous and genial, his smile seemed omnipresent. He held the firm conviction that the church and social reform movements had nothing to fear from the discovery of scientific truths. His annual "alcohol lecture" to Wesleyan students, aimed at scientific distortions and inaccuracies in temperance textbooks, was remembered for its peroration: "Almighty God does not need to combat truth with falsehood!" He had already reported, briefly and quietly in the *Wesleyan University Bulletin* of June 1898, that calorimeter tests were showing alcohol to have nutritional value. He spoke that evening in 1899 to friends and colleagues who could understand his carefully qualified conclusions and his strong support for rational temperance reform.[89]

The meeting was open to the public, however, and was covered by an Associated Press correspondent who had used an advance summary of the talk, supplied by Atwater, to alert the daily press in New York City. The next morning Atwater appeared, in name and picture, on page one of metropolitan newspapers. "Alcohol Does Work of Starchy Foods" announced the *Herald*. "Says Alcohol Is Nutritious" reported the *Times*. His colleagues rushed explanatory remarks to the denominational press, but liquor dealers already had copy for their advertisements and temperance leaders had fuel for their indignation.[90]

Methodists stood at the center of church and other temperance groups arrayed against Atwater. Mobilized at a meeting that August in Northfield, Massachusetts, this alliance was ready for battle when Atwater first published some of his results in November. In early January 1900 the alliance issued a pamphlet that used testimony from physicians to question the adequacy of Atwater's experiments and the validity of his conclusions. Among the endorsers of this pamphlet was the Permanent Committee on Temperance of the Methodist General Conference. Methodists backing the pamphlet did so on the basis of a denominational prohibition, adopted in 1872, against members "buying or selling or using intoxicating liquors as a beverage." Methodists were the largest source of membership and leadership for a key organization in the alliance, the Woman's Christian Temperance Union. Given Methodist support for the WCTU (1874), for the Prohibition party (1869), and for its powerful successor, the Anti-Saloon League (1895), the denomination had earned Frances E. Willard's commendation in 1895 as "really the bone and sinew of the temperance movement in this country." The sting was palpable when a brewers and distillers' newsletter noted the irony "that an institution supported by the Methodist church, which has among its members the most rabid cranks on the subject of alcohol, must furnish the evidence dispelling the lies and misrepresentations that form the stock-in-trade of the whole fanatical temperance brood."[91]

The debate dragged on for four years. Much was at stake for all participants. His reputation as a scientist challenged, Atwater defended his position in speeches, articles, correspondence, and public debate. Still recovering from a controversy in 1898 over some alumni drinking wine at the annual banquet of the New York alumni club, Wesleyan encountered "serious misapprehension" of Atwater's experiments among Methodists who might give to the college through the denomination's

Twentieth Century Thank Offering. Opposition to the political power of the WCTU in pedagogical matters was building among teachers, school officials, and others. Royalties paid by publishers to the WCTU were in jeopardy. Mary H. Hunt, leader of the WCTU campaign to discredit Atwater, increased her efforts. If only "the scientific forces and the religious forces are solidly united" to support abstinence, the *Methodist Review* wistfully observed in 1899, nothing could withstand such a union and its potential for making America a truly Christian nation. The deepest of denominational desires was clashing with expertise derived from experimental science.[92]

Atwater received strong support from the president, faculty, and students at Wesleyan, but the controversy with his own denomination probably took a heavy toll. He and Wesleyan were severely denounced at the weekly meeting of the Methodist preachers in New York City on 20 October 1902. (Bradford Raymond visited this influential group a few weeks later and tried to calm the waters.) Soon after the Committee of Fifty's final report appeared in mid-1903, the WCTU issued a twenty-six-page reply, including an attack on Atwater's "shifty suppositions." While dealing with this new phase of the controversy in 1904, Atwater also received sharp criticism from a member of the men's forum at his Methodist church in Middletown. The controversy ended abruptly when Atwater, at age sixty, suffered a stroke in late November 1904. He was totally disabled until his death in 1907.[93]

William North Rice, son of a Methodist minister in the New England Conference, prepared for Wesleyan at the high school in Springfield, Massachusetts. At age nineteen he graduated from Wesleyan as valedictorian of the class of 1865. Licensed to preach while an undergraduate, Rice filled a Methodist pulpit in Boston for a few months before entering graduate studies at Yale under the theistic geologist, James Dwight Dana. In 1867 he earned the twelfth Ph.D. awarded by Yale and obtained an appointment to the Wesleyan faculty. A year's leave of absence gave him time not only to study at the University of Berlin but also to reach age twenty-three before beginning his college teaching career. From 1868 to 1884 he taught botany, zoology, physiology, and mineralogy. Then he served as Seney Professor of Geology until his retirement in 1918.[94]

Dana was a role model for Rice's career as a scientist of deep religious faith. Rice admired his mentor's "profound sense of the sacredness of truth." He remembered the frankness with which his revered teacher changed opinions when evidence and careful study pointed to new truth.

William North Rice '65, professor of
geology, 1867–1918

Like Dana and most other American scientists, Rice initially found Darwin's *Origin of Species* (1859) to be scientifically untenable. His doctoral research was a critique of Darwin. By the mid-1870s, however, Dana, Rice, and most other scientists professing Christian faith adopted the evolutionary model (without random natural selection) as a powerful scientific truth and one that could be squared with Christian doctrine. Creation by "secondary causation" merely required a less literal reading of Genesis. With firm belief that "this world of nature was always God's world" and therefore scientific discovery would always be compatible with religious faith, Rice shared Dana's view that "disloyalty to truth was infidelity to God."[95]

At the turn of the century Rice had very substantial status as a scientist, teacher, and Methodist. Although his research publications in zoology, mineralogy, and geology were modest in number, he had been selected to prepare the fifth edition of Dana's *Revised Text-Book of Geology* (1897). He was a founding member and first president of the American Society of Naturalists. In 1903 he would begin thirteen years of service as superintendent of the Connecticut Geological and Natural History Survey. Two years later he would receive recognition as vice-president of the American Association for the Advancement of Science. Rice viewed his teaching as a divine call and constantly pursued the "pastoral opportunity" he espoused for college professors. By precept and example he communicated to his students a passion for clear, precise thinking. They respected him for his meticulous manner, prodigious memory, and energetic leadership of field trips. An active member of the New York East Conference since 1869, Rice began in 1896 a thirty-year stint as chair of its board of examiners. His spiritual pilgrimage lacked a dramatic moment of conversion, but his deep piety was readily apparent to his denominational colleagues.[96]

Rice saw his primary contribution to Wesleyan students and the church in terms of a "mediatorial ministry" between science and the Christian faith. Building on his many previous efforts to help students through crises of faith during the college years, Rice began teaching an upper-level elective course, "Relations of Science and Religion," in the spring of 1896. In this class the short, wiry, intense scientist with the neatly trimmed beard and engaging smile tackled all the controversial issues. The message of his lecture "Genesis and Geology" before the Middletown Scientific Association in 1892 was no doubt given to successive classes in the late 1890s. "A reconciliation between Genesis and modern science," he argued, "is as unnecessary as it is impossible." Much of the Bible could not and should not be read as literal truth. By 1902 a book manuscript evolved out of this teaching. The devout scientist in his late fifties was in the prime of his professional life when he decided to test his mediatorial skills with reference to his denomination's tolerance for modern science.[97]

The Methodist Book Concern invited Rice in early 1902 to prepare a book on evolution. When he told the editors about his existing manuscript for a larger book designed to effect a reconciliation between science and religion, they said it could serve as a substitute for the text first requested. Rice sought advice from family and colleagues while considering his responsibilities as a scholar and a Methodist. Since the Book Concern had "published mighty little of scholarly value," he wrote, a book from this source had slim chances of gaining professional regard sufficient for making a contribution to the discourse of philosophers and theologians. But if his denomination's press "really wants to get out some good scholarly books on live questions," he thought, "it is rather mean for a Methodist who is asked to help in the business to stand aloof from it."[98]

Rice sent his manuscript to the Book Concern with the awareness it contained "some things . . . that would make somewhat of a howl in some sections of the Methodist Church." After several decades in which the development of modernist thought proceeded almost unopposed within the ranks of Methodist and other Protestant denominations, a conservative reaction was beginning to brew by the turn of the century. Heresy accusations made in 1895 and 1900 against Hinckley G. Mitchell '73, professor of Hebrew and Old Testament at Boston University, signaled that some Methodists thought the scholarship of biblical criticism had gone too far. The issue touched Wesleyan's campus in 1901 when the faculty's recommendation of an honorary degree for Mitchell received board approval only after expression of strong opposition. While Methodists continued to debate whether Mitchell should be permitted to teach at Boston University, formal charges of similar heresies would be brought against his colleague Borden P. Bowne in 1904. Probably foremost in Rice's mind was the current case of Charles W. Pearson, professor of English at Northwestern. In January 1902 the *Evanston Press* had published an article by Pearson that made sweeping observations about the prevalence of inaccuracies and myths in the Bible. The *Christian Advocate* quickly denounced Pearson and demanded that Northwestern's trustees fire him. Even thirty years of service could "constitute no reason for permitting him to turn the guns of the fort against those who erected it, their sons and daughters." The executive committee of Northwestern's board summoned Pearson to a meeting and received his resignation in return for a year's salary as severance pay. In this climate of protofundamentalist protestation against liberal Protestant thought, Rice thought that publication of his manuscript by the Book Concern would be "a tremendous victory for free thought within the church."[99]

With "a keen sense of regret and humiliation," the Book Concern asked Rice in late July 1902 to "release us from accepting the book in its present form." The letter and an anguished covering note came from George P. Mains '70, agent for the publishers, who was one of Rice's first students at Wesleyan. Mains cited the Mitchell and Pearson cases along with other evidence of "a super-sensitive feeling abroad in our Church with reference to all questions pertaining to Biblical criticism." He noted that the manuscript had been reviewed by William V. Kelley '65, editor of the *Methodist Review* and a college classmate of Rice. Kelley, in turn, had consulted with Bishop Andrews, a fellow trustee and alumnus of Wesleyan. These longtime friends, church colleagues, and sons of Wesleyan told Rice that it would be "inexpedient" to publish a manuscript that "denies the historicity of the first eleven chapters of Genesis" and otherwise "propounds a theory of the inspiration and authority of the Bible which is much removed from the view found in the standards of the Church." Rice sent his manuscript to a commercial publisher.[100]

"Billy," "Bobbie," and "Winch,"—as they were known to their students—continued to be loyal Methodists. Rice remained active in the New York East Conference and submitted articles to Methodist publications. Atwater sustained his active role in the local church for the brief time that health permitted. Winchester served as a delegate to the Methodist General Conference of 1904 in Los Angeles. Leaders in the denomination continued to take pride in the scholarly achievements of Wesleyan's faculty. The liberal majority in church councils sustained its hegemony well beyond this brief burst of controversy and the subsequent fundamentalist movement that emerged more clearly around 1910.[101] By 1905, however, all parties concerned could sense a gap opening between professional values held by Wesleyan's faculty and beliefs held within the Methodist denomination.

6 The Metropolitan Milieu

*D*espite the surge of financial support from wealthy metropolitan Methodists in the 1870s and 1880s, followed by a peak of faculty professional achievement in the 1890s, Wesleyan at the turn of the century found itself in a precarious position. Pressing financial problems persisted. Currents of change were strong and unsettling. Denominational reference points were yielding to those adopted by alumni in New York, Boston, and other urban settings. Notions of the successful gentleman, exemplified by Stephen Henry Olin '66, suggested new dimensions of institutional identity. Urban interests, enthusiasms, tastes, and values infused Wesleyan's athletic endeavors, campus development, and student activities. Metropolitan ties would soon shape the search for a new president, the demise of coeducation, and the drive for recognition as a traditional male New England liberal arts college of high repute. Once a satellite of New York City Methodism, Wesleyan by 1910 traveled in an orbit plotted according to broader cultural and financial forces of the metropolis.

Hard Times

"The last four years . . . have gone heavily against us," Bradford Raymond reported in 1903. Expenses had exceeded revenues in each of those years by more than 10 percent. Annual deficits could no longer be covered by passing the hat and singing the doxology at trustee meetings. The wealthiest trustee, John Andrus, was no longer willing to supplement insufficient revenues with personal interest-free loans and with leadership in the annual trustee subscriptions to balance the budget. He resigned as treasurer of the board in 1902. Contributions from Methodists barely met the need for two new buildings. Raymond sought to create "a league of alumni and friends" whose contributions would balance the budget.[1]

These strained efforts just to "sustain the work we are now doing" stood in stark contrast to the "sanguine expectations" of the 1890s, when Wesleyan talked of becoming "a true University." The major gifts from Ayres and Fayerweather plus a surge of undergraduate enrollment, from 224 in 1890 to 324 in 1899, permitted growth in faculty and staff positions from twenty-three in 1890 to thirty-five in 1899. Corresponding expansion occurred in the number of courses offered. In the fall of 1897 Wesleyan's entering class reached one hundred, surpassing those at Amherst and Williams.[2]

By the fall of 1903, however, the tuition-revenue outlook held little promise for helping to achieve a balanced budget. Whereas Amherst had 122 freshmen and Williams 142, Wesleyan's entering class numbered 99. Zero growth over six years was all the more discouraging with reference to comparative rates of tuition: Amherst $110; Williams $105; Wesleyan $75. The college was beginning to cut back on the practice of waiving tuition for a very large majority of students, but net tuition revenue did not yet provide for even 10 percent of annual expenditures.[3]

Endowment income, which supplied 60–80 percent of Wesleyan's revenue throughout the late nineteenth century, declined in the years from 1898 to 1903, a time of shrinking interest rates. Wesleyan's endowment in 1896 almost equalled that of Amherst and far exceeded that of Williams. The next seven years of only minor additions beyond that from the Fayerweather estate, however, left Wesleyan well under Amherst and also below Williams.[4] After fourteen years as president, Bradford Raymond had cause to be concerned about Wesleyan's financial future.

Wesleyan trustees had corresponding reason for concern about fund-raising and enrollment-building aspects of an otherwise effective presidency. It is unlikely that Raymond was hired on the basis of his abilities or inclination to increase Wesleyan's financial resources. His prior presidency of six years at Lawrence University earned credit for modestly increasing the number of undergraduates and for cultivating a Milwaukee businessman to fund about half the cost of a women's dormitory. But he found the task of raising money tedious. And lack of significant growth in endowment funds created a pattern of budget deficits. Praise for his presidency at Lawrence was usually limited to his abilities as a teacher, scholar, and administrator. When he left for Wesleyan, Lawrence's endowment had not yet reached $100,000.[5]

Even Raymond's reputation as a respected churchman in the 1890s could not be weighed as a major asset by 1900. At his inauguration the trustees stated their expectation that he make himself "an influence" for the advancement of Wesleyan. Raymond did speak in his quietly dignified manner at national and regional conventions of administrators, schoolteachers, and YMCA workers in the early years of his presidency, but it was primarily within the denomination that he built a reputation for sound commentary on educational and ethical questions. The Methodist denomination's record for supplying students to its colleges in the 1890s, however, was not impressive. Although enrollments at the nation's liberal arts colleges increased by 86 percent in the 1890s, those at Methodist colleges went up by only 35 percent.[6]

Comparison with leadership and prosperity levels at other New England colleges in the earliest years of the new century made calls for more students and a larger endowment at Wesleyan all the more urgent. Not only Amherst and Williams but also Brown and Dartmouth were enjoying vigorous presidencies and surges of growth in students and resources. The most notable growth at Wesleyan was in terms of accumulated debt, almost $27,000 in 1903. Faculty began talking privately in 1901 about "a change of administrative team." Alumni concerned about "the apparent falling off at Middletown" would soon speak quietly of the need for "a more executive and aggressive leader." Approaching age sixty, Raymond had insufficient stamina and drive to pursue the enrollment and endowment objectives he set in 1903.[7]

An Urban Orientation

The principal field of action for meeting the needs articulated by Raymond was metropolitan rather than denominational. By the early years of the twentieth century urban centers exerted powerful influence on the financial destiny and campus values of colleges such as Wesleyan. Williams had reoriented itself from rural to urban ties soon after the Civil War. Harvard and the urban elite of Boston forged close connections through most of the nineteenth century. Major gifts from alumni and parents in Boston, New York, and Philadelphia brought new levels of prosperity to Amherst in the 1880s. Dartmouth's growing metropolitan orientation, with particular reference to Boston and New York, was apparent by 1881.[8]

Although Wesleyan had important links with Boston and Philadelphia, the cosmopolitan influences of New York City were most immediate and extensive. First noted by the Bureau of the Census as a metropolitan district in 1880, New York expanded its political boundaries in 1898 through annexation of Brooklyn, the Bronx, Queens, and Staten Island. The new urban unit by 1900 included more than three million people. Opening of a direct railroad link in 1870 between Middletown and this burgeoning metropolis eighty-eight miles to the southwest signaled a new era in Wesleyan's urban connections. Later in the decade, the new line facilitated frequent trips by Cyrus Foss to cultivate support for Wesleyan and to supplement his presidential salary by preaching in metropolitan churches. A businessman such as Orange Judd could even conduct his New York-based publishing enterprise from a residence in Middletown. Reporting in 1875 that he was only three and one-half hours from New York by express train, Judd found "the three daily mails and double telegraph give me constant communication with my city business." Foss advertised Middletown in 1876 as "near enough to feel the movements of thought and opinion in the large cities" yet "removed from the noise and unwholesome excitement of city life." By the early 1890s Wesleyan had a telephone line connecting the president's office to urban centers (1888), travel time to New York reduced to less than three hours (1891), and speedy access to Boston as well as New York, with Middletown the only stop on the fastest Air Line express (six hours) between the two cities.[9]

Trains brought metropolitan newspapers in timely fashion to stock the much-used reading room in North College. Students began to serve as agents assigned to supply stories to newspapers in northeastern cities. Improved communications and growing public interest in college life made collegiate news a regular feature of metropolitan dailies such as the *New York World* by the 1880s. Hazing incidents received scandal status. The railroad also brought prominent speakers to address national issues. John Fiske, the popular philosopher and historian, spoke in 1888. Russell Conwell gave his "Acres of Diamonds" exhortation in 1889. A current and a former member of Congress debated the protective tariff in 1895. Using an urban-oriented metaphor, a New York alumnus praised the improved tone of intellectual life at Wesleyan, by stating that "the University had been keyed up much nearer to concert pitch" and would soon produce "a much higher class of music."[10]

"Sixty or seventy percent of our alumni and the alumni of all colleges," Raymond noted in 1894, "go into . . . cities." The movement of graduates to major cities and their suburbs brought the percentage located in or near New York, Boston, Philadelphia, and Washington, D.C., from 25 percent in 1893 to 30 percent in 1903. By 1909 almost 15 percent of Wesleyan graduates lived in the New York City boroughs of Manhattan and Brooklyn. A steadily increasing number went to begin business careers. About 11 percent of male graduates from the early 1880s became businessmen. By 1910 this occupation usually attracted more than 40 percent. (Those entering the ministry declined from 29 to 10 percent.) And 12 percent of all living graduates were lawyers, with almost three dozen graduates pursuing legal careers in Manhattan or Brooklyn by 1903. "It is to New York," one of them observed in 1904, "that most young men from college naturally turn, and it is there that the first skirmish of life's battle begins."[11]

Alumni clubs in this urban field of competition offered a "common tie," a group adept at "helping fellows recently graduated to find themselves, as it were, when they first come to the city." The New York Wesleyan alumni club (1869), although preceded by an association started in Boston two years earlier, was the largest and most influential of these Wesleyan outposts. Groups organized in Chicago (1871), Washington, D.C. (1881), and Philadelphia (1881) were followed over the next several decades by a dozen regional alumni clubs and even by "young alumni" clubs in New York (1894–1910) and Boston (1897–1914). Annual meetings of the Alumni Association in Middletown continued to serve as a limited forum for opinions on college issues and as a vehicle for electing alumni trustees. The most vital ties between alumni and the interests of the college, however, resided in discourse at meetings of urban associations.[12]

These clubs provided an education in the ways of urban gentility. "There the younger graduates, full of ambition to be and to do," it was observed in 1882, "meet the elder alumni who represent their Alma Mater in important positions of professional or business life." The primary figure in the ensuing tutelage was the toastmaster. He served as an exemplar of quick wit and other social graces. Despite the prevalence of ministers among alumni, polish was expected to predominate over piety. The New York club, organized "with dignity at a dinner at Delmonico's," stipulated that the toastmaster chosen each year must be a layman. Reports of the meetings noted the content of remarks made by those called upon for toasts, or short after-dinner speeches, on topics such as "muscular Christianity," the practice of law, and scholarly achievements of the faculty. Wesleyan's president almost always attended and delivered appropriate remarks. Singing of college songs was a regular feature. Distinguished guests such as Nicholas Murray Butler, president of Columbia University, and Seth Low, mayor-elect, might attend. But special attention and praise were most often reserved for the urbane toastmaster. [13]

Looking at Wesleyan from perspectives increasingly shaped by metropolitan experiences and values, alumni used their clubs and college publications to address major issues. From 1880 to 1910 alumni developed strong and influential opinions on Wesleyan's position in the competitive world of higher education with regard to enrollment, endowment, athletics, public image, and leadership. Visiting committees sent to the campus by clubs in New York and Boston during the 1890s returned with reports that contributed to the process of constructive criticism. Calls for an alumni periodical in 1903 led to the creation a year later of an alumni section in the *Wesleyan Literary Monthly*. Going beyond the columns in the *Argus* that had since the 1870s carried alumni personals and brief accounts of club gatherings, the *Monthly* offered "a place for views . . . a free forum for the expression of graduate opinion." A call from the Philadelphia club in 1907 for an alumni senate to receive grievances and suggestions and to draw up recommendations that express "an authoritative alumni sentiment" stimulated plans for centralizing alumni interests in a more active, campus-based alumni association. The Alumni Council, with a paid secretary, would not be established until 1911. This organization would not publish an alumni magazine until 1916. By then, however, alumni had decades of experience in critiquing and shaping the policy of the college. [14]

Alumni assessed Wesleyan's progress within a context of intercollegiate competition for students, resources, and reputation. They worried about whether Wesleyan had "kept pace with some of her sister New England colleges." They feared that Wesleyan might fall "hopelessly behind in the small college race." Those in an urban setting could readily verify an observation made in 1882: "Not only the question, 'Have you a degree?' but also the question, 'Where did you get it?' has to be answered now-a-days; and the degrees from first-class colleges are most in demand." Augustus F. Nightingale '66 helped to initiate this era of comparison and competition by publishing in 1878 what may be the first systematic and selective guidebook to American colleges. He did not attempt to rank the forty-four institutions featured in his slim volume, but readers on the Wesleyan campus quickly noted that "the relative standing of the colleges, with reference to their requirements, can be easily determined." Some of the comparative assessments in the 1890s still used the context of other Methodist-related colleges and universities. And the Wesley Bicentennial celebration in 1903 drew acclaim as "the best advertisement the college has ever had" for the purpose of increasing enrollment. But alumni knew that praise from the president of Stanford that same year contributed a more important long-term advantage. They could also rejoice in the impressive showing attained by Wesleyan faculty in the first edition of Cattell's *American Men of Science* (1906), testimony to Wesleyan's academic quality in a national context. As the scramble for status in American higher education became ever more intense, urban alumni found a great deal at stake for themselves and their alma mater.[15]

Static enrollments in a range between 290 and 315 from 1901 to 1908 had alumni searching for explanations and solutions. President Raymond told them in 1901 that a drop of 25 percent in the entering class probably derived from denial of scholarships to fifteen or twenty applicants and to lack of exciting news from Wesleyan during the year that class was recruited. But alumni worried about the disturbing enrollment outlook, despite their recruiting efforts and those of undergraduates, in comparison with Amherst and Williams. (See appendix 3.) Looking for larger causes, alumni analysts cited two. Wesleyan "cannot make its appeal to prospective students as an undenominational institution," they found, yet "as a Methodist institution it must divide patronage with altogether too large a number of institutions founded and maintained by that church." The presence of Syracuse University and Boston University in two of Wesleyan's prime recruiting states significantly limited the benefits of denominational affiliation. The second and more important reason presented for "falling behind in . . . ratio of increase as compared with that of other colleges" was coeducation. In its troubled state at Wesleyan, the education of women had an even larger cost-benefit imbalance in admissions than that of Methodist identity.[16] Not until the upswing in enrollments beginning in 1909 would the alumni become less anxious about the student body size.

Endowment growth relative to other eastern colleges became a concern of alumni as they expanded their analysis of Wesleyan's fitness for the rigors of competition in a new century. (See accompanying graph.) Analysis led to action in 1902, with a pledge by the Alumni Association to raise $100,000. The goal was doubled in 1905, but receipts by 1910 were about $89,000. As during the financial pinch of the late 1870s, alumni were asked to make annual contributions, this time by reassign-

ENDOWMENT FUNDS

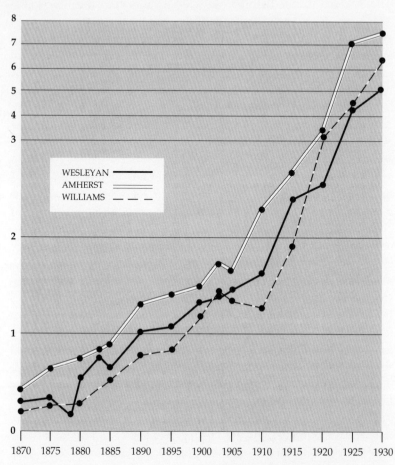

Endowment funds at Wesleyan, Amherst, and Williams, 1870–1930 (in millions of dollars). The data graphed are compiled from financial exhibits, audits, treasurer reports, and annual totals supplied by financial and archival staffs at Amherst and Williams.

ing their endowment fund subscription payments to meet current deficits. Such gifts over the next five years would help sustain the college's level of annual expenditures. Talk of a permanent annual alumni fund drive appeared at the Alumni Association meeting in 1907 and continued through 1910. The Wesleyan Alumni Fund did not launch its first campaign until 1914, but by 1910 it was clear that annual gift revenues and endowment increases had become a large responsibility for the alumni.[17]

Public awareness and perceptions of Wesleyan became major issues for alumni in the years from 1880 to 1910. Recent graduates worried in 1890 that Wesleyan was "failing to avail itself of the opportunities now offered by the leading metropolitan journals to keep itself before the public." The Alumni Association urged the trustees to employ a landscape architect and initiate planning for a more attractive campus. The Boston Wesleyan young alumni club prepared ideas in 1905 for "advertising Wesleyan."[18]

Definition of a public image, however, created considerable controversy. Some alumni in the 1880s agreed with a strategy to "boom" Wesleyan as "*the* college of the Methodist church" and viewed the advertising task as one of distinguishing Wesleyan from other Methodist institutions of higher education. "Why should we be ashamed," asked a Brooklyn minister as late as 1905, "of our Methodist inheritance and tradition?" Others in the 1880s were uncomfortable with the public perception of Wesleyan as a "Methodist minister shop" and with the tendency of sports writers to describe its football players as "the embryo ministers." Growing disappointment with the level of financial support from denominational sources led to an awareness by 1905 that "we are in the sorry position of being dominated by Methodism without possessing the reasonable support of Methodism." Stated more bluntly that year was the conclusion that "Wesleyan's ultra-Methodistic atmosphere is calculated to repel more possible students than it attracts." And Methodist identity was particularly likely to repel "those for whom social prestige is attractive."[19]

A change of name, many alumni and students argued, might soften the sectarian image that embarrassed them. Debate on this issue stretched from 1871 to 1891. Lawyers complained of being asked to explain why they had attended a theological school. Ministers chafed at the confusion of Wesleyan with so many "lesser lights" in higher education also bearing that institutional name. A real estate broker wrote on behalf of alumni assembled in Chicago, informing trustees in 1874 that Middletown College would be an acceptable alternative. A few alumni used the issue to blast Wesleyan's Methodist ties. A handful of staunch Methodists stood firm for retaining the name as an appropriate recognition of denominational affiliation. Most alumni, however, looked for a name that would bring greater public esteem without severing denominational connections.[20]

After extended consideration by a committee of the Alumni Association during the 1879/80 academic year and by a trustee committee appointed in 1887, the name-change controversy reached its nineteenth-century conclusion in 1891. As Joseph Cummings had observed in 1874, it was difficult to produce a new name that would generate approval of sufficient strength to justify making a change. By 1891 there were at least sixteen Middletowns in various states. Even the possibility of using Willbur Fisk's name was precluded after 1866 by the university in Nashville named for another Fisk. A canvass of alumni opinion in 1890/91 brought responses from almost two-thirds of the living graduates. Just over 50 percent favored a change, but this was offset by a clear majority of undergraduates opposing change. Little more than a quarter of the alumni polled could agree on a new name, with Middletown College or University achieving this plurality. Lacking a popular solution, the trustees and the Alumni Association voted unanimously against any change.[21]

With a sense that Wesleyan could prosper despite its name, alumni turned to other means for building a less sectarian identity. Athletics received increasing attention. The Alumni Association campaigned through most of the 1890s for new sports facilities. The graduate advisory committee began annual solicitations in 1891 to help meet expenses of teams in intercollegiate competition. A system of alumni coaching in football evolved two years later. By 1904 the Alumni Athletic Association regularly covered expenses of professional coaching in football. Successful competition with Amherst and Williams had greater potential to reshape Wesleyan's image than a mere change of institutional name. "To the great public mind of today," said a young alumnus in 1908, "a college is . . . known by the football team it keeps."[22]

Probably of greatest concern to alumni at the dawn of a new century was the leadership of Wesleyan. A close look at the Raymond presidency after more than a decade yielded disappointing assessments of results in enrollment and endowment. Henry I. Harriman '95 took the initiative in 1901 to collect and present to the Boston Wesleyan young alumni club statistics on the growth of sixteen leading eastern colleges during the 1890s. From these data alumni learned of Wesleyan's "general falling behind in its ratio of increase as compared with that of other colleges." The New York Wesleyan young alumni club heard a speaker in 1904 who found Wesleyan continuing "through mere inertia to drift on amiably and aimlessly." Given the widely held affection and respect for Raymond and the signs that his health was deteriorating rapidly, alumni critics avoided direct attacks on the president. But within months of his resignation, alumni were calling for "a young president who shall be up-to-date, progressive, and endowed with the ability to obtain financial support for the institution."[23]

Criticism of trustee leadership was more direct. Echoing sentiments present in alumni clubs for several years, an alumnus writing from New York in 1907 found the board "composed for the most part of men who are not in sympathy with modern times." Its membership included too many ministers, he argued, and not enough "men of worldly affairs —men who are up-to-date and stand for progress." The importance of alumni opinion and support had been recognized by trustees in the mid-1890s. A suggestion in 1894 to increase the number of Methodist conferences serving as patrons of Wesleyan was transformed during board discussion into appointment of a committee to consider not only "such enlargement of our legitimate territory" but also "putting the University in more intimate touch with our Alumni." That year also marked the first of several annual joint meetings of the trustees and the Alumni Association for about an hour during commencement week to discuss suggestions for improving Wesleyan. And 1894 was the first year when alumni not present for the annual meeting of the association could cast ballots by mail for the election of alumni trustees. Such trustees would carry a much larger popular mandate in representing alumni views.[24]

Within the gradually changing board, alumni organizations had influential allies. Although some alumni in 1901 thought the board had too many ministers and too few "able business men . . . capable of conducting the College in accordance with the most advanced business methods of the time," the ten alumni-elected trustees had been bringing more modern and diverse metropolitan perspectives to trustee deliberations since the mid-1890s. In 1890 almost 91 percent of the board was Methodist. Two years later ministerial presence on the board reached an all-time high of 50 percent. The year 1893, however, also brought election of William C. Wallace '76 by alumni and an impending tip point in board demography. Replacing Bishop Edward Andrews, Wallace brought the number of non-Methodist alumni trustees to five. Darius Baker '70 would soon create a non-Methodist majority among alumni trustees by completing his transition from the Methodist to the Episcopal church in early 1895. A lawyer from Brooklyn, Wallace also increased the number of lawyers among alumni trustees to six (along with three businessmen) and the number from metropolitan New York to six (along with two from Washington, D.C.). Within the total board, the number of businessmen, lawyers, and non-Methodists would steadily increase over the next two decades. More important, the newly established general executive committee in 1893 had three alumni trustees among the six nonlocal members. One of the three was George Reynolds, an alumni-elected trustee since 1870, who had become president of the board in 1887.[25]

Alumni trustees probably supplied substantial initiative and support for building by 1910 a board membership increasingly infused with men of metropolitan success in business and law. An initial effort in this direction came in 1879, when enlargement of the board to fifty-five not only brought five new alumni-elected trustees but also created ten new positions to be filled by trustee election. The board quickly selected ten wealthy Methodist businessmen, including six from New York City. This hastily cast net brought in one major donor, Charles Scott, two who declined to serve, one who would soon become an Episcopalian and resign, and another whom the board did not reelect in 1882 when he was expelled from the New York Stock Exchange for defrauding a client of about $1 million. In the 1890s the board itself began adding a few non-Methodists to those elected by alumni and to the one or two from Middletown serving as ties to local constituencies. By 1910 five Episcopalians, five Congregationalists, one Presbyterian, and two members with no denominational tie composed almost one-fourth of the board. Six of these non-Methodists were lawyers.[26]

A reorientation in cultural reference points for a growing number of board members derived from the interaction of social, economic, and religious changes. Through business and professional connections, marriage, and increased wealth, some trustees moved from Methodist family backgrounds into the Episcopal church. If lawyers are included in what E. Digby Baltzell terms "the Episcopalianization of the American business aristocracy," Wesleyan's board provides several interesting examples from the early stages of this trend. For John C. Rand '63, whose father published *Zion's Herald*, the first sign of a switch in denomination came with his daughter's confirmation in an Episcopal church in 1888. William Wallace moved to the Episcopal church in the 1880s along with his father, who had been a prominent member of Summerfield Methodist Church. Darius Baker, a Newport, Rhode Island, lawyer and judge, made the transition from Methodism to Episcopalianism as a result of his second marriage. Among those who remained Methodist, a few such as Henry C. M. Ingraham '64 and Joseph S. Stout were active not only in denominational affairs but also in metropolitan club circles.[27] For them, as well as for many of those outside the Methodist fold, the world of metropolitan men's clubs would begin to rival the Methodist church in shaping trustee views of Wesleyan's identity and destiny.

Club life flourished in New York City after the Civil War. Providing "the amenities of stylish living," a large variety of clubs in the 1870s chiefly attracted "men of extensive financial transactions and responsibilities." Many held membership in several clubs as a means of "reference or passport to higher social circles." Those of a "clubbable disposition" gathered in elegant quarters for meals, conversation, and reading. An observer in 1890 found each club containing a homogeneous social set and providing a meeting place where "men who love their kind may sometimes escape the general rush and swirl of the human tide outside." Once inside a retreat such as the University Club on Madison Avenue, they could be assured that "its Burgundy is always at the proper temperature."[28]

A Metropolitan Trustee

In the metropolitan milieu of men's clubs, alumni clubs, and Wesleyan alumni concerned about building institutional leadership, resources, and reputation, one person stood out as both agent and symbol of gradual changes in Wesleyan's identity from 1880 to 1910. Stephen Henry Olin was a club man devoted to promoting Wesleyan's welfare. Like his father, the college's third president, Olin was tall, erect, and commanding in general presence. He was well read and had a fine command of language. His wavy hair and mustache began to take on a dignified silver hue in his mid-forties. "Ever graceful and stimulating in public address," Olin employed a keen wit and "magnetic quality of . . . voice" to charm his audiences. Unlike his father, this prominent metropolitan attorney spoke at the bar and from the toastmaster's rostrum rather than the pulpit. Whereas Rev. Stephen Olin in the 1840s joined the Evangelical Alliance, Stephen Henry Olin, Esq., qualified by membership to sip burgundy in the 1890s at the University Club.[29]

From his early childhood on the Wesleyan campus, Olin traveled a clear pathway toward adult years of culture and refinement. His father's death when he was four left full parental responsibility with his mother,

Stephen Henry Olin '66, New York City
attorney and trustee of Wesleyan
(1880–1925), worked to achieve broader
fame for his alma mater

Julia M. Olin. A wellborn, gracious woman of letters, she raised her only surviving son in New York City and at Glenburn, her family's summer estate on the Hudson. The ebullient, voluble young boy was quick to learn and seemed to remember everything he read or heard. During winters in New York City he met his mother's many associates in church and other charitable enterprises. At age fifteen Olin entered Wesleyan, where he excelled in debate and oratory, played baseball, and enjoyed a very active social life with some of the best families in town. Toward the end of his junior year he wrote home for a new pair of gloves to replace a pair that had lost "their unsullied appearance and perfect fit." The hue, he told his mother, must be "light enough for a party and yet with color enough for a morning visit."[30]

Olin held a highly generalized religious outlook. His mother, a leading churchwoman in metropolitan Methodism, sent him to a Long Island preparatory school headed by a Presbyterian. While at Wesleyan, he showed a mild interest in Episcopal and Methodist church services. A watchful friend from undergraduate days through all the adult years, however, probably best described the extent of Olin's Christian beliefs. He found Olin to be "not very wide-awake on the subject of religion" as a freshman and to have only a "respect for religion" toward the end of his life. Olin's marital and social ties were consistently Episcopalian. Both of his marriages were to women from wealthy Episcopal families. Both of his daughters were married by Episcopal ministers. His funeral service was conducted at St. Thomas Church on Fifth Avenue. Probably never a communicant, Olin was nonetheless far closer to Episcopalianism than to the Methodist denomination of his parents.[31]

Olin's law career reflected a well-charted route to eminence. After graduating from Wesleyan, he obtained his LL.B. from Albany Law School in one year. Travel in Europe with his mother preceded his admission to the bar and start of a metropolitan law practice near Wall Street in 1869. He formed a series of partnerships with highly capable attorneys. One soon became a judge; another subsequently served as corporation counsel of New York City and chaired Columbia's board of trustees. Olin quickly became an authority in copyright and trademark law, serving as counsel for the Metropolitan Opera Company and for leading publishers such as Scribner's and Harper & Brothers. In 1898 his peers elected him vice-president of the New York City Bar Association. At the time of his death, Olin was widely respected and recognized as one of the New York bar's foremost members.[32]

Closely related to Olin's legal talents and achievements were his activities to secure urban order and to build metropolitan culture. He joined the New York National Guard as judge advocate in 1882. In 1898 he attained the rank of colonel and began five years of service as chief of staff to the general who commanded New York's troops. While still a major, Olin published *Suggestions Upon the Strategy of Street Fighting* (1886), the text of an address to field and staff officers on "operations to be undertaken by troops acting against riotous assemblages in cities." This task, he said, was "likely to be the most important service" of the metropolitan Guard. From the history of popular uprisings in Paris, 1830–71, he developed a strategy for combating widespread disorder in New York City. Olin's interests in promoting as well as protecting urban culture and institutions made him a logical choice to serve from 1888 to 1895 as a trustee of the Astor Library. He took an active part in the consolidation of that library with two others to form the New York Public Library in 1895. As a trustee of the new entity over the next three decades, Olin served on a board of wealth and social prestige.[33]

Olin's most important involvement in the development of metropolitan institutions came during the mid-1890s. He worked closely with his good friend Nicholas Murray Butler in organizing the movement that brought centralized administration to the schools of New York City. Articles by Olin argued the case for a modern, efficient, rational, and professional system to replace the ward-based, patronage-driven, Tammany Hall-dominated arrangement. For eight years Olin played almost as important a role as Butler in building the coalition of economic, social, and cultural elites that won this political victory in 1896. After supporting the mayoral campaigns of Columbia's president, Seth Low, Olin shifted his civic interests to the social settlement movement. He served as president of the University Settlement Society from 1902 to 1906.[34]

"In the life of modern man," Olin noted in 1889, "the club counts for much." He spoke as a founder of one club and a member of at least five others. Olin's clubs tended to choose members according to their devotion to culture more than their wealth or ancestry. He was, for example, an "eager and earnest" member of the Round Table Club, a charter member of the Players, and a half-century member of the Century Association. A "prince of conversationalists" with "manliness and good looks," Olin was not only a club man but also a prominent figure in the society life of the metropolis. He appeared in 1892 among the "400" on Ward McAllister's elite invitation list, "the *beau monde* of New York today."[35]

Fellow members of the New York Wesleyan alumni club articulated clearly the major objective of Olin's many activities as a Wesleyan alumnus and trustee. Memorializing his life, they noted that he worked "to put the college he loved in a position of commanding dignity among the colleges represented by alumni in the great Metropolitan center where he had his home." Many friends saw the roots of this devotion to Wesleyan's progress in Olin's reverence for the memory of his famous father. In 1923 Olin retold the well-known story of 1851 when he, as a four-year-old, received a solemn benediction at his father's deathbed. Now, listening to friends celebrate eight decades of the Olin tradition at Wesleyan and "link my name with his," the urbane attorney was deeply moved to hear "that I am a not unprofitable servant of the college that he served!" Always attentive to projects that would bring "broader fame" to Wesleyan, Olin was an advocate for his alma mater "in the drawing rooms, the clubs, and the courts of his long life." In 1919 he assessed the results of steps he and others had taken over four decades to create a Wesleyan suited to "the temper of the times." During those years, he remarked, "we have watched the value of our diplomas . . . rising toward par. Now we claim to stand in the front rank of the colleges with which we may justly be compared."[36]

Alumni, trustees, and students frequently expressed their pride in Olin's achievements and their appreciation for his service to Wesleyan. His forty-five years as an alumni-elected trustee began at age thirty-three, and he was reelected every five years by huge majorities. Regarded as "that prince of toastmasters," he was often selected for this role at annual alumni banquets in New York and on campus. Olin soon became an influential trustee, gaining appointment to special committees such as that on a change of name and to standing committees such as that on faculty appointments. He was an original member of the general executive committee established in 1893. Students followed with great interest Olin's career as successful metropolitan professional, public-spirited citizen, and holder of "enviable" social rank. An alumnus recalled in 1925: "He was a living example of what we all wanted to be—an exemplification of culture."[37]

The life and shaping influence of Stephen Henry Olin connected with every important change at Wesleyan from 1880 to 1910. He held "a place in the consciousness of the University" through those years and beyond. A poem he composed as an undergraduate even provided the metaphor others would use to represent these connections. He wrote of the "Goddess fair" weaving "life-threads" into the pattern of human history. One of his memorialists in 1925 used this literary device in going immediately to the main point: "There has seldom been an alumnus whose life is so woven into the fabric of his Alma Mater as is that of Stephen Henry Olin."[38]

Intercollegiate Athletics

Olin loved sports. As a young alumnus living in New York, he was in close proximity to the evolution of modern spectator sports. His interest in athletic events evolved along with the development of organized and commercialized competition in urban settings, particularly Manhattan and Brooklyn. One of the earliest sports to attract large crowds in New York was professional rowing. This sport grew rapidly from 1855 to 1865. Through great attention from the metropolitan press, the crew contagion spread to college campuses, where it reached a peak in popularity during the 1870s.[39] Olin's enthusiasm for crew waxed correspondingly.

Wesleyan students received applause and support from Olin and other urban alumni when crew competition moved from the intramural contests of the late 1850s to the intercollegiate regattas of the early 1870s. After the first major college regatta, held in 1871 on the Connecticut River near Springfield, Massachusetts, a recent graduate wrote to the *Argus* from his residence "under the shadow of 'Fair Harvard.'" He urged Wesleyan to "keep abreast of its rivals" in athletic pursuits. A crew representing Wesleyan responded to this challenge by winning the freshman competition at Springfield in 1872. Olin joined the thousands traveling to Springfield by train from Boston and New York in 1873. With great pleasure he watched Wesleyan finish the varsity race only two seconds behind the winning Yale crew. A New York reporter might sneer at the "strange and weird crew from that nurse of Methodism," but the metropolitan press recorded on page one Wesleyan's finish ahead of Harvard, Columbia, Cornell, and six other colleges. Olin became a regular contributor to the Wesleyan University Rowing Association. Watson C. Squire '59 led donors from Manhattan and Brooklyn with a gift of $2,000 toward expenses of sending Wesleyan's crew to the new regatta site at Saratoga in 1874. By then, a Brooklyn alumnus reported, Olin and a few other urban alumni had advanced cases of "boat club on the brain."[40]

Continued reason for excitement attended the change of venue in annual regattas of the Rowing Association of American Colleges. Already a well-known summer resort, Saratoga had used horse racing for a

Intercollegiate regatta of 1874. A
fashionable crowd at Saratoga Lake
watched Columbia's crew cross the finish
line, with Wesleyan second and Harvard
third.

decade to lure increasing patronage from the wealthy and fashionable of
New York City. The regatta of 1874, in which Wesleyan finished second
to Columbia, was a mid-July event that drew tens of thousands from the
metropolis and smaller nearby cities. In the month-long press coverage
preceding the 1875 race, Wesleyan received much attention as "a country
crew whose strength is greater than their skill." Noting that city boys
rowing for Columbia, Harvard, and Yale learned their techniques at "the
center of boating ideas," the *New York Tribune* said this race would decide "whether the natural country physique can put forth more strength
in a three-mile race than the artificial product of the city gymnasium."
Equipment problems, however, complicated this neat formulation. A
loosened rudder wire greatly hampered the Wesleyan crew's effort, and
they finished fifth. Rowing declined in popularity among college students and the public over the next few years as Yale and Harvard, tired
of losing to less prestigious schools, pulled out of the association.
Wesleyan capped its decade of rowing enthusiasm in 1882 with a victory
over Princeton and two noncollege crews at the Harlem River regatta.
Olin celebrated this achievement by entertaining the crew that evening.[41]

Crew racing elicited criticism as well as cheers. Methodist editors in the 1870s worried about the impact of metropolitan aquatic sports on morals and scholarship at Wesleyan. "Our colleges," Daniel Curry thundered in the *Christian Advocate*, were not designed "to make gladiators or athletes." He printed and endorsed the complaints of an ardent Methodist who was "deeply pained . . . that students from a Methodist University were so prominent in the regatta" at Springfield, where gambling was rampant and where those of "Christian nobility" joined with "the fashion and elites of the city" to rub elbows with "the filthy scum of society." The lengthy lamentation of this correspondent scaled the peaks of pious sarcasm: "Sporting journals took up the report and announced that students of *Wesleyan* University won the freshman race. O shades of the church fathers, how can you sleep? A Wesleyan crew gambled over by the outscourings of humanity! Write the sacred name next over theatre doors; engrave it on billiard cues; . . . cut it into the corner-stones of brothels." The editor of *Zion's Herald* decried overemphasis on athletics and the meal of "sherry and eggs which it seems our Wesleyan boys had prescribed for them" before the race. "If sherry is a necessary article of diet for young boatmen," he asked, "who will assure us that an appetite will not be engendered that will clamor for wine and something stronger after the regatta is passed?" A letter to *Zion's Herald* expressed agreement, noting that Methodists founded Wesleyan in order that "our sons would be preserved from contamination by the low vulgar associations of city fast young men."[42]

These critics questioned whether "our colleges need popularity in order to make them serviceable" and whether regattas were "the best means for advertising the college" and recruiting students. Alumni and students responded to this critical question with a resounding affirmation of athletic success as a "shrewd and politic" device for attracting more students to Wesleyan. "The heroic effort of six stalwart representatives," they observed, "has written the name of 'Wesleyan' between that of Yale and Harvard on the pages of every newspaper in the land, and in the memory of thousands." Even within the denominational context of stiff competition with Syracuse University and Boston University for "Methodist prodigy," they argued, Wesleyan "needs the reputation which boating gives her." Challenging the assumption of denominational critics that aquatic amusements were sinful, students and alumni aligned regattas with popular notions of muscular Christianity. Methodist fears quickly faded; metropolitan tastes prevailed.[43]

Football superseded boating in cities and on campuses of the 1880s.

The first intercollegiate game occurred in 1869, when Princeton and Rutgers engaged in a contest resembling rugby. Wesleyan began such competition with a twenty-per-side game against Yale in 1875. Colleges soon learned that urban spectators, accustomed to paying admission for entertainments, could be charged an entrance fee to cover costs of this sport. The Yale-Princeton game of 1876 took place at St. George's Cricket Club, Hoboken, New Jersey, initiating the practice of scheduling important college games at metropolitan sites. By 1881 games had moved to the Polo Grounds on upper Fifth Avenue, where a large crowd attended the Thanksgiving Day contest.[44]

Wesleyan's initial football game in New York City came during the third season of regularly scheduled games. This loss to Princeton in 1883 was the first of many plucky efforts and honorable defeats during the next decade in metropolitan contests with major college teams. Lop-sided losses at this level of competition were partially offset by occasional wins against the University of Pennsylvania and by single victories over: Michigan (1883), Harvard (1884), Columbia (1890), and Cornell (1890). According to Olin and other alumni spectators, Wesleyan players deserved considerable credit even after a 61–0 defeat by Yale in 1885 on Thanksgiving Day at the Polo Grounds. Olin felt it was "a great honor for Wesleyan to even have the *opportunity* of playing this game" against the second-ranking team in the nation.[45]

Enjoying much greater football success against Amherst, Williams, and Trinity in the 1880s, Wesleyan nonetheless clung to membership in the "big league" of Yale, Princeton, Harvard, and Pennsylvania. Much public attention could be gained from play in the Intercollegiate Football Association beside the largest colleges in the East. Early in the decade, the urban press humorously depicted a Wesleyan game against Amherst in Springfield as "a sort of denominational struggle in the hinterland." A decade later, however, Wesleyan was part of the metropolitan football frenzy that attracted tens of thousands in New York to a Princeton-Yale game on Thanksgiving Day and five thousand to a Wesleyan-Pennsylvania game in Philadelphia. Spectators in Brooklyn at Wesleyan's game with Pennsylvania in 1890 intently recorded touchdown plays on scorecards assigning a number to each player. A large "bulletin board" at one end of the field showed the numbers for players deserving special credit. Perhaps with spectators in mind, Wesleyan had painted its athletic future in bold colors. In 1884 a unanimous undergraduate vote changed the college color from lavender, regarded as insufficiently striking, to the more rich and "brilliant" red and black.[46]

Student cartoon depicting Wesleyan's
marginal membership in the Intercollegiate Football Association,
dominated during the 1880s by Yale
and Princeton

Play in the big league, however, began in the 1890s to yield more
bruises than benefits. The game during the 1880s had exchanged "its
free and open character for a deadly combination of mass and wedge
plays." Players drawn from the much larger student enrollments at other
institutions in the league greatly outweighed those on Wesleyan's team.
As honorable losses became literally crushing defeats, students and
alumni began to question the wisdom of continuing to use football as a
means of raising Wesleyan "to a position of honor among the few leading colleges in the country." When Wesleyan's line was routinely forced
back by the brute strength of teams with much larger players, newspaper accounts turned from respect to ridicule. After considerable debate
about leaving the league to form an association with Williams and other
comparable colleges, matters came to a head in 1893. Battered by a
76–0 loss in New York against a much heavier Princeton squad,
Wesleyan was unable to field a team for the next scheduled game against
Yale. Wesleyan immediately resigned from the league.[47]

The new football schedule for 1894 included Amherst, Dartmouth,
Trinity, and Union. This winless season marked the nadir of football
fortunes for Wesleyan and concluded with a Thanksgiving Day loss to

Union before about two thousand spectators in Albany. Harvard and Yale returned to the schedule in 1896, the year when annual play against Williams began. A New York paper announced in 1898 that Wesleyan had "forged to the front rank of minor football this season." From this position of strength during a time of considerable maneuvering for athletic alliances among New England colleges, Wesleyan joined Amherst and Williams in early 1899 to form a new Triangular League. Football, baseball, and track competition in this league was something of a trial run for later contests in a wide range of sports under the rubric "Little Three." Wesleyan's *Argus* stated its approval of this alliance among "institutions of equally high standing in athletics and in scholarship." Remembering the days of dignity in the big league, an alumnus hailed Wesleyan for having "at length won anew the recognition of the college world."[48]

Alumni athletic supporters vowed to "work enthusiastically to place the red and black in the forefront of the colleges of her own class." Their assistance in the 1890s took the form of coaching, financial contributions, and collaboration in the management of Wesleyan's athletic enterprise. Collegiate coaching responsibilities initially resided in the elected student captain. Wesleyan enlisted occasional outside help during the 1880s. Walter Camp, who had six years of experience playing for the Yale varsity, visited from New Haven in 1883 to spend an afternoon coaching team. Former Wesleyan players made similar brief visits. By 1890 the captain received support from an advisory committee of one faculty member and one alumnus. Two years later a recent Yale graduate and star fullback was employed as coach throughout the season. The alumni system of coaching prevailed, however, from 1893 to 1903. Recently graduated players established a schedule in which each would return for a few days or longer to help the team. Long-standing calls for a full-time paid coach brought results in 1905, with the hiring of a former star player at Princeton, Howard R. "Bosey" Reiter, as director of the gymnasium and football coach.[49]

Alumni contributions paid the coaching portion of Reiter's salary. Students found the funding of intercollegiate competition in football, baseball, and then track increasingly difficult by 1890. Meager gate receipts and uncertain undergraduate and faculty donations left a major role for alumni in financing and managing Wesleyan's athletic program. The collaborative governance system for athletics adopted in 1891 provided for a joint athletic committee composed of representatives from student associations (formed in the 1890s to administer and support each of the three sports) and of five alumni (elected by students) who constituted the graduate advisory committee. This system of a joint committee (chaired by an alumnus), and its student and alumni sub-groups was modeled after that at Princeton. The graduate advisory committee led fund-raising efforts among alumni, and the athletic associations solicited voluntary annual dues from students. A stronger role for alumni and faculty developed in 1903, with adoption of a more centralized system like that of Harvard. The Athletic Council, composed of three alumni, three faculty, and three students, elected by their peers, would manage Wesleyan's athletic interests. The new Alumni Athletic Association (1904) would elect its three representatives on the council and raise money for the coaching fund.[50]

Beyond its days of metropolitan glory but with a well-organized base of urban alumni support, Wesleyan football in 1906 stood in the forefront of national developments. When the issue of brutality in football reached fever pitch in 1905 and resulted in calls for abolition of the sport, Wesleyan was a leader of the colleges advocating major reforms. When many major institutions held back, Wesleyan was a member of the small band that established the National Collegiate Athletic Association in 1906. When rules adopted in 1906 to open up the game and reduce brutal play included introduction of the forward pass, a Wesleyan quarterback made one of the earliest completed spiral overhead throws in a regular season game between major colleges.[51]

Baseball's popularity at Wesleyan in the 1890s built on organizational initiatives taken by Olin and his fellow undergraduates in the mid-1860s. Just as it was appropriate for Williams, one of the first colleges to be well connected with New York City, to play the nation's first intercollegiate baseball game (against Amherst in 1859), it was fitting that a city boy named Olin help to establish baseball at Wesleyan in 1864. From its beginnings as an organized sport in the 1840s, baseball was an "urban product." New York City and Brooklyn virtually dominated its evolution from variations of the British game of rounders to the nine-inning "New York-style game" that became standard in the early 1860s. As president of the newly organized baseball club in the fall of 1864, Olin could measure off a diamond on the Washington Street green and have bats turned locally, but baseballs had to be obtained from New York. Wearing blue caps, the team first represented Wesleyan the next spring in a game against Hartford's Charter Oaks on a field in that city.[52]

Urban alumni followed the team closely, often with an eye to its value for advertising Wesleyan. "It is a shame you have not sent your nine around more," a Boston alumnus had commented in 1871. "Do you know that the Harvard, Yale, and Brown nines have done more to attract young students to their Universities than all the D.D.'s in their Directory?" Interest in crew and then football, however, kept baseball activity at the level of a few games each year until 1888. A schedule of eight games that spring included one against Columbia at the Polo Grounds. Strong records and important victories in the 1890s brought praise from metropolitan alumni. The Wesleyan nine played two games at the Chicago World's Fair invitation tournament in 1893. After decades of defeat by Yale in baseball as well as football, three runs in the ninth inning brought a 4–2 victory over the visitors from New Haven that same spring. "The whole college turned out and paraded the town, singing, yelling, and blowing horns. The cannon was fired, the chapel bell rung, and fireworks were shot off until all ordinary 4th of July celebrations were outdone." A telegram of congratulations from Olin took memories back to the initial 39–13 loss to Yale in 1865. "Tho we've waited long," he said, "revenge is sweet."[53]

Along with moments of great joy, the city sport also brought hazards of professionalism. From baseball's earliest years at Wesleyan, students saw the need to reassure denominational objectors that the "immoral conduct" of gamblers and urban "roughs" associated with professional teams in the city would not infiltrate collegiate contests. Harvard's president tried without success in 1882 to halt the frequent games between college and city teams. Others tried to block the contagion of manners and morals that might come from employment of professional athletes to give occasional instruction or coaching to college teams. In a few instances Wesleyan crossed the most tightly drawn lines. The team hired a National League pitcher in 1892 to spend several days with its players. Occasional games between Wesleyan and city teams with paid players continued until 1908. On the key issue of using players who had received payment for their sports skills, however, eligibility rules adopted by Wesleyan's faculty in 1898 clearly affirmed the ideal of amateurism. In the late 1890s an article in *Harper's Weekly* applauded Wesleyan's "glorious battle for honest sport," and students asserted that Wesleyan had "never . . . been stained with the blot of professionalism."[54]

Particularly troublesome was the lack of regional or national rules on the eligibility of students who had received compensation for playing during the summer on teams representing clubs, resorts, towns, or cities. This issue achieved an intensity at the turn of the century second only to that of brutality in football. The University of Pennsylvania faculty had taken a strong stand against "summer ball" in 1896. But Brown and many other colleges were lenient. With the eligibility of a star pitcher at stake, Harvard vacillated from 1901 to 1904. Mutual support in drawing this eligibility line could only come from small alliances among like-minded colleges.[55]

For reasons of prestige as well as principle, Wesleyan began in the mid-1880s to seek and consider various possibilities for a baseball league. The most desirable opportunity did not develop until 1898, when Dartmouth expressed disdain for the stature of her companions in the original Triangular League. Amherst and Williams reacted by withdrawing and inviting Wesleyan to join them in a new Triangular League. Wesleyan quickly accepted in January 1899. Championship competition began in baseball and track that spring and in football that fall. Standards of eligibility promised to be clear and strong.[56]

Cordial relations and consistent standards prevailed in the new league for little more than two years. The issue of summer ball arose in the spring of 1901, with charges made against one player on each team. Wesleyan's faculty, the only one with a rule against any hint of professionalism, took swift action to remove eligibility from the star pitcher, George B. Lufkin '02, for playing as a professional during the two previous summers. Williams disqualified its shortstop a few weeks later. Amherst prohibited a pitcher who had played for money during several summer seasons from competing in league games. Among some members of the Amherst community, however, the issue was not settled. Faculty on that campus had little influence on an athletic system dominated by alumni and student zeal for winning games. In the spring of 1902 Amherst was unwilling to declare ineligible a student who had pitched on a town team in Maine while receiving full-time pay as a clerk in a summer job requiring few if any hours of work. A league committee investigated and found, by majority vote, that an eligibility rule had been broken. Students at Amherst and Wesleyan voted to sever athletic relations. The Triangular League ended that spring.[57]

Wesleyan continued to hold the belief that a permissive policy on summer ball, such as the one at Brown, was an "entering wedge" in decline toward "rank professionalism." Athletic relations with Trinity were suspended from 1905 to 1908 due to Wesleyan's perception that eligibility rules had not been vigorously enforced. In a new triangular agreement made in June 1902 with Williams and Dartmouth, Wesleyan found compatible emphasis on "purity" in intercollegiate athletics. Eligibility rules on each campus provided virtually ironclad protection against professionalism. Some alumni opposed this stance against summer ball, and a majority of students voting in 1908 agreed with them. But Dean Frank W. Nicolson and his faculty colleagues would keep baseball free from any trace of metropolitan vice.[58]

"Perhaps we give athletics too much prominence," a student said in 1895, "but it is the fault of the age. The end of the century is an era of rampant athleticism." Intercollegiate and recreational sports in the 1890s had the full support of Wesleyan's president, who found that "athletics in our colleges are doing a great deal for the development of physical men who must be able to stand the stress of hard business life, and of professional life, and to carry on with success the enterprises which they take hold of." Even his social reform message incorporated sports, asserting that "the man who goes on the football field is the man who learns to develop the right kind of courage to meet the difficulties of great cities." With this enthusiastic backing, Wesleyan's intercollegiate sports program expanded from 1890 to 1910. By 1910 football and baseball had track, tennis, and basketball as well-developed companions in intercollegiate competition.[59]

The gymnasium (1894) and athletic field (1898) emanated from metropolitan zeal for manly sport. As voluntary athletic associations in cities constructed gymnasiums for their clubs during the 1880s, it seemed appropriate for urban alumni to expect and to help fund such facilities for their alma maters. A wave of modern gymnasium-building moved across the New England collegiate landscape: Hemenway at Harvard (1878), Pratt at Amherst (1884), Lasell at Williams (1886), Lyman at Brown (1891), and the new facility costing more than $200,000 at Yale (1892).[60] Olin and other urban alumni began a concerted effort in 1889 to place Wesleyan in such company.

As chair of a gymnasium committee established by the Alumni Association in June 1889, Olin convened the group at his New York office that October to plan a fund-raising campaign. "If the new President wants to immortalize himself," a friend of Wesleyan had advised that spring, "let him build a gymnasium." Bradford Raymond had recently responded with an enthusiastic personal pledge of $100 to initiate the solicitation of student and faculty donations. When the work of Raymond and of Olin's committee yielded no major donors during the campaign's first year, however, alumni turned to the prospect of allocating $50,000 from the recent unrestricted bequest of Daniel Fayerweather. Olin's motion to this effect, supported by the Alumni Association, won board approval in June 1891. The board appointed Olin to chair a committee to raise another $10,000, obtain plans, and supervise construction. Gifts from a few urban alumni quickly surpassed this amount and encouraged an upward revision of the goal to $25,000. Delay in receipt of the Fayerweather bequest slowed the move toward construction for a while, but the building committee led by Olin went ahead with borrowed funds to break ground in 1893. The new facility opened a year later. Grateful students correctly identified Olin as "the most instrumental of any of our alumni in securing for us the new gymnasium."[61]

"Here will be formed ideals of manliness and sportsmanship," Olin said at the groundbreaking ceremonies. After decades of associating baseball and football with manliness, students and alumni in the audience well understood the connection between their new gymnasium and this pervasive metropolitan ideal. Often expressed in terms of muscular Christianity, the values of courage, muscular strength, and self-discipline elicited strong support from alumni who applauded "a renewal of manliness in the colleges and universities of both England and America" in the 1880s. Finding Christianity and manliness fully compatible, *Zion's Herald* argued that there is nothing "cringing or crawling" about a true Christian: "He stands up straight. He has plenty of backbone." At the dedication of Fayerweather Gymnasium in 1894, Rev. Elisha B. Andrews, the tall, muscular president of Brown University, advocated regular exercise in gymnastics and defended intercollegiate football. "If a game develops courage at the risk of limb and even of life," he said "let that game be encouraged. . . . Football makes men manly."[62]

Less than two years after representing the building committee in presenting the new gym to Wesleyan's trustees, Olin led the alumni movement for a new athletic field. He served with John Andrus, who provided the necessary $5,700, on the trustee committee appointed "to fit up the rear campus as an athletic field." Work began during the summer of 1897 under the direction of Doc Raymond to turn "a swamp . . . into a fine athletic field" that would be "worthy of Wesleyan's growing athletic prominence." On 14 May 1898 Andrus Field opened with a baseball game against the University of Virginia. An oval quarter-mile running track was installed that summer, and a grandstand seating 350 was built in 1902.[63]

If Olin paused in 1910 to assess the results of his support over four decades for Wesleyan's intercollegiate teams and athletic facilities, he had ample reason to be pleased. He could begin by acknowledging the role of other urban alumni and trustees, such as Andrus, who joined him in the enterprise. He could note the benefits for student health derived from required gymnasium classes instituted in 1894. Annual interclass competition in gymnastics for the silver cup Olin donated in 1895 continued to be an important campus event. Faculty supervision of admissions and eligibility standards for athletes remained rigorous. Wesleyan was still a leader among colleges demanding radical reforms to address the excesses of football. Olin might share some alumni disappointment over a string of losing records in football and baseball from 1902 to 1909, but he could clearly see the benefits of schedules including many New England colleges of high academic prestige. Finally, he could appreciate the role of athletics in making Wesleyan a more cosmopolitan college. From the time he used the baseball team's trip to Yale in 1865 as an opportunity to see that campus, Olin was aware of sports as a means for students to offset the seclusion of solitary study on a small campus. Intercollegiate athletics, he said, "ended our isolation and gave us glimpses of the great world." Sports and the new gymnasium also marked "a new era" for the college, giving the metropolitan world more frequent glimpses of Wesleyan. Olin's pleasure can only be imagined when a sketch of Fayerweather Gymnasium appeared prominently in the *New York Tribune*.[64]

A New England Campus

Olin devoted much of his trustee service to improving Wesleyan's campus. His work on the planning committee and the building committee for Fayerweather Gymnasium helped to inaugurate an era of Wesleyan buildings designed by major architects from New York City. When the trustees established the committee on buildings and grounds in 1912, Olin was their logical choice to serve as chair. From 1891 to 1907 he saw the campus develop from little more than a brownstone row, started by Middletown and completed by Methodists, to a configuration of nine new or recently acquired buildings and an athletic field encircling the central row with metropolitan tastes and values.[65] (See map, p. 198.)

Fayerweather Gymnasium (1894) introduced Romanesque architecture to Wesleyan's campus through the design of J. C. Cady, head of Cady, Berg & See. Cady had become prominent as architect for the Metropolitan Opera House (1883) and the south wing of the American Museum of Natural History (1892–98). Wesleyan's new gymnasium bore a strong stylistic resemblance to the latter and to many of the castellated urban armories with which Olin was familiar. The firm's recent work in Middletown on the First Methodist Church (1886) and Wesleyan's boiler plant (1891) built its local reputation. Cady drew

American Museum of Natural History, New York City, designed by J. C. Cady. The center portion of this wing on 77th Street opened in 1892.

specifically on his experience in designing a gymnasium for Williams, and he joined the building committee in studying such facilities at Harvard, Yale, Brown, and Amherst. His interest in collegiate architecture would find fullest expression in the design of fifteen buildings at Yale (1871–1903). Students, faculty, and alumni took pride in having this "well-known architect of New York" inaugurate the expansion of campus facilities.[66]

Choice of a site for the new gymnasium prompted thoughts about larger plans for campus development. One observer saw Fayerweather as "prophetic of the quadrangle yet to be" behind College Row. Commitment of that space to an athletic field a few years later reduced this idea by 1902 to one of several options. Another was to have a row of buildings on each side of High Street. This proposal and one to locate new buildings along the southern boundary of the front campus raised the issue of where new fraternity buildings might find sites. The Alumni Association asked the trustees in 1902 to prepare a comprehensive plan for development of Wesleyan's buildings and grounds, but the board did not move in this direction until 1913.[67]

Meanwhile, incremental steps proceeded during the years 1880–1910 to create a campus with aesthetic appeal. Purchase of a few remaining lots completed formation of a square campus in 1908. Land acquired on the periphery of this square provided additional options for building sites. A property purchased in 1890 at the north corner of High and College streets supplied the location for a new classroom building com-

Fayerweather Gymnasium, designed by
J. C. Cady. Construction began in the
summer of 1893; the building opened
5 October 1894.

pleted in 1904. Concern over unsightly structures across from campus
on the adjacent corner had found frequent expression in the 1880s. Although a vacant shanty once occupied by "Black Maria," a washer-
woman, mysteriously burned down in 1882, the site continued to offend
campus sensibilities with a large billboard advertising events at the Middlesex Opera House. Consumed by fire almost on an annual basis (probably due to student incendiaries), a new billboard rose each time from
the ashes until Psi Upsilon purchased the property in 1888 as the site
for its new chapter house. Farther south on High Street, the death of
Willbur Fisk's widow in 1884 and removal of the dilapidated house she
occupied for forty-five years after her husband's death "permitted the
opening up of the whole front grounds into one magnificent campus."
Thanks to a lawn mower acquired in 1876 and to the maturing of trees
planted from the early 1840s through the early 1880s, Wesleyan's front
campus had made the transition from "a ragged pasture into a velvety
lawn," well shaded and free of eyesores.[68]

Willbur Fisk Hall was one of two new academic buildings completed in
1904 that helped to draw a circle around the lawn and venerable brown-

Bryant Park Studio Building, New York City, designed by Charles A. Rich. This facility for artists opened in 1901.

stone row. Olin served on the building committee for this "chaste" Romanesque brownstone structure designed by Cady, Berg & See. With comprehensive systems for heating, lighting, ventilation, and drainage, Fisk Hall brought new levels of comfort and convenience to faculty and students.[69]

The John Bell Scott Memorial joined Fisk Hall in relieving a pressing need for classroom, laboratory, and faculty office space noted since the early 1890s. Charles A. Rich of New York City served as architect, working with the same building committee that supervised construction of Fisk. Rich brought Beaux Arts classicism to the Wesleyan campus in a physics laboratory that resembled his Bryant Park Studio Building (1901) at the corner of Sixth Avenue and Fortieth Street, behind the New York Public Library. Although he designed metropolitan buildings, including theaters, Rich was best known in the field of collegiate architecture. Around 1904 he submitted a master plan for enlarging the Barnard campus, and he was architect for some twenty buildings at Dartmouth (1893–1909), as well as others at Williams, Amherst, and Smith. Located not far from the southern end of College Row, Scott Laboratory's ornate facade of Harvard brick and Indiana limestone created a vivid contrast with its brownstone predecessors.[70]

Scott Laboratory, dedicated 7 December
1904. This building designed by Charles
A. Rich provided first-rate facilities for
instruction and research in physics.

Fraternity chapter houses filled in around the southern and eastern
borders of campus between Scott and Fisk during the years 1893–1907.
A shortage of dormitory space in the 1890s forced more than half the
students to live off campus. An additional dormitory was low on the
college's priority list for new buildings. Alumni attuned to the world of
urban men's clubs and to the residential fraternity movement on other
campuses provided a solution. They incorporated as alumni members
of particular fraternities, raised funds for new chapter houses, and held
the property for principal use by undergraduate members. The portion
of undergraduates housed by fraternities went from just under 15 percent in 1884/85 to 50 percent in 1907/08. Spared the expense of building additional dormitories, Wesleyan had good reason to welcome these
new accommodations.[71]

Psi Upsilon (1893) initiated the new generation of chapter houses that
replaced those of the 1870s and 1880s with major facilities for room and
board. Carrère and Hastings, the firm that would soon be selected to
design the New York Public Library (1897–1911), submitted a plan in
1890. But an alumnus from London who made a substantial pledge

Eclectic House, designed by Henry Bacon and completed in 1907. The central portion of this building anticipates the Lincoln Memorial, for which Bacon received the Gold Medal of the American Institute of Architects in 1923.

toward construction successfully advocated a young British architect and friend, Colin C. Wilson, who had recently moved to the United States. This decision placed a neo–Dutch Renaissance style, expressed in yellow Perth Amboy brick and red sandstone trim, facing College Row from across High Street. Providing suites for eighteen residents, a dining hall seating forty-eight to seventy-two, reception room, parlor, and lounging room, Psi Upsilon claimed to have "the model college fraternity club house."[72]

Chi Psi Lodge (1904) brought to Wesleyan the work of Raymond F. Almirall, a prominent metropolitan architect whose works would include the Brooklyn Public Library (1908) and the Emigrant Savings Bank (1910). Located on the south side of campus just below Scott, Chi Psi reflected an English colonial style done in brick and stained shingles. It supplied suites for sixteen residents and had a dining room, library, music room, and main hall on the first floor.[73]

Alpha Delta Phi replaced its deteriorating frame building in 1905 with one designed by Charles Rich. As with Scott Laboratory, he used brick. Within the colonial-style structure members enjoyed ground-floor rooms finished in Flemish oak and upper-floor suites accommodating fourteen residents. Along with its next-door neighbor, Chi Psi, this fraternity house gave the south side of campus an architectural echo of the eating clubs constructed on Prospect Avenue at Princeton during the preceding decade.[74]

Eclectic House (1907) initiated a relationship sustained for two decades between Wesleyan and a New York City architect of national repute, Henry Bacon. Olin made this match in 1903 as a member of the building committee for his fraternity. From his friend Stanford White, Olin sought the name of a young architect "whose triumphs are still before him." White recommended Bacon, who had worked for McKim, Mead & White from the mid-1880s to 1897. This devoted student of Greek architecture was in his late thirties and had recently begun practice under his own name. He would be selected in the spring of 1912 to design the Lincoln Memorial and retained that fall as advisory architect to Wesleyan's new committee on buildings and grounds. Bacon's plans of 1905–06 for Phi Nu Theta, the local fraternity usually known as Eclectic, included an imposing Greek portico supported by four Doric columns. Olin donated large oil paintings and two classical busts, and his wife, Emeline, contributed furniture for the thirty-five-by-thirty-eight-foot living room of this "club house."[75]

A new president's house, acquired in 1904, virtually closed the northern arc of campus development around College Row. Built in 1856 just north of the original president's house, this spacious Italian villa stood in as sharp contrast to the modest proportions and simple lines of its predecessor as Scott Laboratory did to the brownstone row completed in 1871. Metropolitan trustees and alumni entertained at presidents' receptions could now sense an affinity with settings they knew in New York or Newport.[76]

Amid all the architectural activity of 1890–1910, College Row was not neglected. Students of the early 1890s from well-appointed homes or schools found little attraction in the austerity of North College (1825), the main dormitory. A total remodeling during the summer of 1893 was funded by John Andrus. The "prison-like appearance of its bare, . . . dingy rooms" yielded to the "home-like appearance" of hardwood floors, polished ash paneling, and other improvements done in "a substantial and even elegant manner." Renovation of the second-floor worship room in Memorial Chapel during the early months of 1898 included a new pipe organ and new pews with velvet cushions.[77]

Photogravure of the Wesleyan campus,
1908, made from a watercolor painting
by Richard Rummell

Destruction of North College by fire 1 March 1906 prompted two major decisions. As the embers cooled, Bradford Raymond declared that a new dormitory would rise on the same site. Board authorization for this expenditure came a few weeks later. The board also endorsed his recommendation that South College be remodeled at once to provide for the administrative offices, including the president's office, previously located in North College. From May through December work on South College created a new raised entrance and a two-story, "elegantly furnished" room to serve as general office of the college and as site for faculty and trustee meetings. First used in January 1907, these new quarters were "in keeping with the dignity of the institution." North College's new walls rose that spring according to plans drawn by Harrie T. Lindeberg, a young architect in New York trained by McKim, Mead & White. Olin played a major role on the building committee. Although of greater height, the new building substantially reproduced the form of its predecessor. "The unpretentious dignity of the old building, with its rubble walls" of brownstone, however, yielded to "the richer effect of cut stone with elaborate portico and cornice."[78]

North College reappeared just in time for a significant pictorial moment in Wesleyan's history. Sensing the increased inclination of colleges toward self-promotion and the growing alumni market, a small New

York art publisher commissioned a series of watercolor paintings of well-known educational institutions. Photogravures of these campus panoramas, printed from copper plates in brown ink, reached a large market. Most of the paintings represented in the photogravures were the work of Richard Rummell, a Brooklyn artist. As in his published and framed scenes of New York City, Rummell rendered the Wesleyan campus of 1908 from a "bird's-eye view." Work over the preceding two decades by Olin and others to create a campus worthy of metropolitan aesthetic values enabled Rummell to present a substantial array of buildings, an athletic field, and a well-shaded campus. Wesleyan ordered copies of this print for placement in preparatory schools and for sale to alumni. A smaller version appeared as a photograph and then as a foldout page in annual catalogues from 1908 to 1920. Seeing Wesleyan join the Ivy League universities and top liberal arts colleges in this artistic series, Olin probably found the visual result of his labors to be that of a prestigious New England institution.[79]

Student Life

Olin's alumni activities marked him as "one of the most enthusiastic members of his fraternity." He also supported the elaborate array of other student activities that by the 1890s extended far beyond those once attracting much of his attention as an undergraduate in the 1860s. Adjustments to "the temper of the times," Olin understood, involved more than athletics and campus facilities. Important changes in characteristics of entering students yielded new emphasis on fraternal life and on other extracurricular enterprises that interested the growing segment of undergraduates preparing themselves for metropolitan lives and careers.[80]

Students in the 1880s tended to come from families of farmers, ministers, tradesmen, and educators. By 1910 the presence of such students had decreased from more than 60 percent of each entering class to about 40 percent. During these same decades the segment of new students from families headed by businessmen, lawyers, and physicians increased from about 20 percent to almost 40 percent. The portion of students enrolling from Methodist preparatory schools dropped from half to less than a fifth of entering classes; the portion from the burgeoning public high schools rose correspondingly, from about one-fifth in 1885 to two-thirds in 1910. As the age and grade educational ladder of public schools established itself, the average age of first-year students decreased from twenty to nineteen. Fewer students came from northern New England; more came from New Jersey and Pennsylvania. These changes were

CAMPUS DEVELOPMENT, 1891-1907

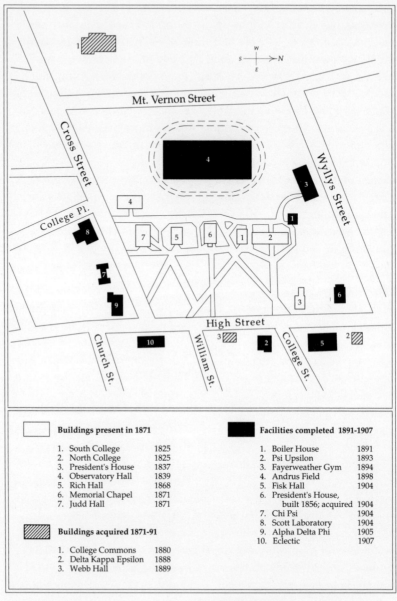

Buildings present in 1871

1.	South College	1825
2.	North College	1825
3.	President's House	1837
4.	Observatory Hall	1839
5.	Rich Hall	1868
6.	Memorial Chapel	1871
7.	Judd Hall	1871

Buildings acquired 1871-91

1.	College Commons	1880
2.	Delta Kappa Epsilon	1888
3.	Webb Hall	1889

Facilities completed 1891-1907

1.	Boiler House	1891
2.	Psi Upsilon	1893
3.	Fayerweather Gym	1894
4.	Andrus Field	1898
5.	Fisk Hall	1904
6.	President's House, built 1856; acquired	1904
7.	Chi Psi	1904
8.	Scott Laboratory	1904
9.	Alpha Delta Phi	1905
10.	Eclectic	1907

Campus map showing buildings constructed and acquired between 1871 and 1907. All the buildings completed after 1871, except the new home of Psi Upsilon, were designed by architects from New York City.

gradual, but the entering classes from 1890 to 1910 showed steadily increasing percentages of students from families of middle-class means who prepared for Wesleyan at public high schools in urban and suburban areas from Boston to Philadelphia.[81]

When they arrived at Wesleyan in the 1890s, students from solidly middle-class homes entered a fraternity system becoming ever more comfortable and commodious. The Alpha Delta Phi house had "woodwork, furniture, and objects of art which would be in no wise out of place in the most attractive of modern city homes." By 1905 the second-generation chapter houses at Wesleyan were usually referred to as club houses rather than homes. Their ground-floor accommodations included libraries and other rooms for lounging, where members and guests could gather for male-oriented events such as "smokers."[82]

Fraternities were a place to prepare for membership in urban men's clubs. Major national fraternities even sponsored such clubs for their alumni in large cities. Like their metropolitan counterparts, campus fraternities were "islands of untainted masculinity" amid concerns about the perceived feminization of American young men. Fraternities at Wesleyan fostered "the development of true manhood," as each member learned "to know men better, to cultivate the man within himself." And they were often helpful to young men after graduation, providing associations that put them on the road to successful urban careers.[83]

Issues of choosing a fraternity and being chosen confronted freshmen from their first day on campus. Only after an intensive rushing period of a week or two did each entering class "settle down in the societies" and begin the routine of college work. Competing for the attention of freshmen by 1902 were the venerable local, Eclectic; four national fraternity chapters established prior to 1870; and two founded more recently, Beta Theta Pi (1890) and Delta Tau Delta (started as Phi Rho, 1893–1902). The cultivation period offered glimpses of the daily pleasures acquired with membership, especially at dinnertime:

> Everybody is in his best mood. The jokes and puns are more than usually frequent and atrocious, and merriment runs high. After supper the parlors are filled with groups of fellows; one group here in animated discussion—there, one with knotted brows studying the perilous position of the chess king. A few are watching the flying fingers of the pianist, . . . until some familiar chords quickly draw all about the piano, and in a moment the whole house rings with the vociferous chorus of some rollicking college

song. A new-comer thus surrounded by the refining influence of his club-house, and by fellows of his own choice, always ready to aid and sympathize, cannot get homesick, and every day his love for the society is strengthened.

About 90 percent of Wesleyan's male undergraduates entered this fraternal world.[84]

Those who declined or lacked an invitation used the College Commons (opened in 1899 at the Foss House) for meals, literary programs, and social activities. By 1902 these students were organized as the Commons Club. Membership in this "democratic club" grew from forty-six in 1902 to fifty-five in 1910. The college upgraded accommodations at Foss House in 1902, and a few faculty members began to join the organization in 1904. The Commons Club soon affiliated with a federation that included similar clubs at Union, Norwich, Middlebury, and Tufts. Professing to be "in no sense anti-fraternity," the club offered a low-cost alternative to membership in a fraternity.[85]

The fraternity system received almost total approbation as a staple of student life. There were some moments of tension whenever fraternity feeling seemed to undermine college spirit, or when fraternities asked Phi Beta Kappa to reschedule its annual oration so it would not draw alumni away from annual fraternity meetings. Articles in the denominational press, however, were usually supportive. "What would the hardworking heroes of the simple, poverty-stricken past say," one writer asked, "to the luxury of the modern college club-house?" He reassuringly answered that the Methodist forefathers would probably take kindly to the new ways. Another writer found fraternities to be one of the best features of Wesleyan. There was ample evidence to support the observation made in 1911 that American college fraternities were "recognized and patronized by the authorities." Wesleyan's faculty and trustees served as fraternal alumni, advisors, incorporators, and trustees. Frank Nicolson, secretary of the faculty, noted with approval that "the hard-working man of slender means is to be found in every fraternity." Bradford Raymond viewed fraternities as serving "the best interests, social, intellectual, moral, and religious." He also reported that they provided housing for Wesleyan students equivalent to $200,000 worth of dormitory construction.[86]

Complementing the lessons of fraternity life were those from many other collegiate activities. Students formed friendships and gained new experiences through athletics and a burgeoning array of extracurricular organizations. Glee club, drama, debate, student publications, campus YMCA, student government, and honor system joined fraternities and intercollegiate teams in helping to "knock off the rough corners and give symmetry and finish to the whole man."[87]

Singing at Wesleyan had deep roots in the denomination of Charles Wesley. The "good old Methodist thunder," so vividly described by Henry Ward Beecher in 1857, provided glee clubs with experienced and zealous singers. Almost all of the ten juniors and seniors who went on a singing tour in northern New England during the early summer of 1862 were from Methodist families.[88]

Glee club tours in the late 1880s began attracting large metropolitan audiences. After two decades of occasional organization under various names, the club began continuous existence in 1882. Two years later the dozen singers representing Wesleyan appeared in Bridgeport under the auspices of P. T. Barnum. The concert given in 1886 by sixteen young men wearing formal swallow-tail jackets at "New York's most aristocratic hall" received favorable review in the *New York Tribune*. The Metropolitan Opera House concert of 1888 drew a standing-room-only audience of six thousand, including New York City's wealthiest Methodists and leading ministers of the denomination. After delighting an audience of almost three thousand in Chicago two years later, the club sang into a recording phonograph at the request of Thomas Edison's local agent. Annual tours along the eastern seaboard from Boston to Washington, D.C., during the next two decades established Wesleyan's reputation as a "singing college."[89]

Songs composed by undergraduates and alumni in the 1880s and 1890s created a college scene of mostly carefree years just prior to the time when students would enter the world and "cease to be boys." Praise of alma mater was effusive. Pledges of ever loyal sons to protect and to honor "our mother benign" were frequent. "The magic power of song" both created and expressed enduring bonds with "Wesleyan our queen."[90]

Pride in Wesleyan and her singing prompted frequent calls for a greater number of distinctive Wesleyan songs, for one that would serve as the alma mater, and for a song book. Eighteen of the songs produced by undergraduates and alumni from 1862 to 1890 appeared in the yearbook of 1891. "Come Raise the Song" was probably written in late 1894 and first performed in early 1895, about a dozen years prior to being designated as Wesleyan's alma mater. *The Wesleyan Song Book* (1901), although somewhat late in joining the genre, was of sufficient substance to stand alongside contemporary editions of books first published at Yale (1853), Williams (1859), and Amherst (1860). Weekly sings organized each spring on the chapel steps began in 1901. New editions of the song book appeared in 1903 and 1906 to meet increased demand. Wesleyan's songs had become "part and parcel of her college life."[91]

Drama at Wesleyan survived a sputtering start in the 1890s and established a continuous presence on campus with founding of the dramatic club in 1904. Performances in the early years came to the stage of the Middlesex Opera House with the assistance of a "theatrical coach" from Boston. Males played the female roles. This was also the case when the glee club and dramatic club combined talents to produce "The Girl and the Graduate," a comic opera written by Kenneth M. Goode '04 and William B. Davis '94. First performed locally in 1907, this farce filled with "college hits and jokes" elicited many laughs and much applause a year later from a standing-room-only audience at the Berkeley Theatre in New York.[92]

Debate acquired a new emphasis and role after 1890. Urban reform issues stimulated a civic movement in colleges. A revival of public debate at Wesleyan, once pursued in literary societies and more recently in the House of Commons conducted by Woodrow Wilson in 1889, occurred under auspices of the citizenship club. Founded in 1894 "to secure addresses by prominent public men" on "modern day problems," the club also assumed responsibility for preparing an intercollegiate debate team ready to address issues in American politics. Four years after Harvard and Yale held America's first intercollegiate debate, Wesleyan's team made its debut against Boston University. In this losing effort of 4 March 1896, Wesleyan's three debaters supported a resolution that "the United States should own and control the Nicaragua Canal." Contests against Williams began in 1900 and addressed issues such as a federal income tax and tactics of labor unions. The role of debate in positioning Wesleyan with a particular type of college became clear a few years later. Formation of the Triangular Debating League with Amherst and Williams in 1906 placed Wesleyan comfortably within a New England context. Dropping Syracuse and adding Bowdoin to the schedule in 1908 completed this reorientation.[93]

Student publications in the 1890s devoted increased attention to campus issues. The *Olla Podrida*, published by a board of editors from the junior class, went beyond the usual yearbook role as a book of record. The decade began with an editorial campaign for a new gymnasium and ended with hostility toward coeducation. The *Wesleyan Argus* gave more space to issues and events of intercollegiate athletics in the 1890s than to any other topic. Published every ten days until 1894 and weekly thereafter, this well-written newspaper had "no apology to make for the amount of space it is devoting to football." Later in the decade editorials found coeducation "a menace to the welfare of the college." Exchanges with newspapers of other colleges kept Wesleyan students informed on changes and controversies among their peers in higher education throughout the nation. Special letters circulated campus news among newspapers at Wesleyan, Amherst, and Williams. In the fall of 1909, the editors dropped "the magazine tone" and began semi-weekly editions in a full-size newspaper format with advertisements filling most of its columns. The *Wesleyan Literary Monthly* appeared in June 1892 as a journal of literature and opinion. An artist from New York City designed the cover first used in January 1894.[94] Along with short stories, poetry, and literary criticism, the *Monthly* offered spicy editorials and alumni columns addressing the twin concerns of athletic success and coeducation.

The campus YMCA reached a peak of popularity in the 1890s. Levels of affiliation ranged from 70 to 90 percent of male undergraduates. Striving to "make the religious life of Wesleyan as earnest and vigorous as her intellectual or athletic" activities, this organization took responsibility for campus evangelical activity. It sponsored weekly prayer meetings, Bible study classes, visits from revivalists, and efforts to support foreign missions. "Battling evil in all its forms," members engaged in neighborhood work to help the less fortunate. They sent used clothing to the poor in New York City. In 1908 they established an Italian Mission at Middletown's Methodist church. Competition with other extracurricular activities, such as fraternities, constrained some aspirations. Sufficient funds could not be found for a YMCA building like those found at Yale and almost twenty other colleges by 1900. But when the trustees authorized employment of an administrator in 1910 to supervise this student activity, they clearly recognized the campus Y as central to religious life at Wesleyan.[95]

Compulsory daily chapel and required attendance at a Sunday worship service in town formed a rigid backdrop by the 1890s to the voluntary Bible study, prayer meetings, and social justice projects sponsored by the student YMCA. Most students seemed to grant the legitimacy of daily morning prayers (at 7:50 A.M.) "in a family school like ours." Participation in a Sunday church service, however, became increasingly perfunctory and rebellious. Pressure mounted to abolish mandatory attendance. In 1903 the faculty asked the board to drop required Sunday church attendance. A compromise reached in 1904 retained the usual brief compulsory morning chapel on Sundays and rescinded the rule that students must also attend a Sunday morning church service in Middletown. This faculty action apparently disturbed some Methodist leaders on the board, whose efforts to restore a Sunday worship service requirement resulted in a return of the required Sunday afternoon vesper service last offered in 1883. Faculty reluctance to conduct such services and student preferences for visiting preachers yielded vesper services beginning fall term 1909 in which "distinguished speakers representing different denominations" occupied the pulpit. The faculty also provided, effective that fall, a 50-percent increase in the maximum number of chapel cuts a student might take per term. Religious life at Wesleyan was shifting gradually away from denominational emphasis and toward the encouragement of "voluntary religious acts."[96]

Student participation in governance came more swiftly than the changes in worship service regulations so closely scrutinized by denominational supporters. A few years after the paternalistic mode of the 1880s yielded to the new presidency of Bradford Raymond, Wesleyan's faculty granted student requests for a voice in campus governance. Their rapid positive response to an able campaign led by Ashley H. Thorndike '93, editor of the *Argus*, supports the report that faculty had been predisposed in this direction for several years. Established in 1893, the joint advisory committee consisted of ten students, three faculty, and the president. Experiments in student government started a decade earlier at Amherst and Bowdoin served as stimuli for student proposals at Wesleyan. But the joint advisory committee was to range far beyond the specific judiciary functions assigned to the college senate at Amherst or the college jury at Bowdoin. Its broad purpose was to "consider and discuss all questions affecting the relations of faculty and undergraduates." Lacking legislative or executive powers, the group was sometimes called the conference committee, a term used at Harvard. The faculty conferred with the joint advisory committee only occasionally, however, during the 1890s. Student desire for meaningful self-governance, faculty needs for help with a spate of hazing cases, and "an alarming lack of college spirit" led to the establishment of a successor group, the college body, and its executive council, the college senate, in 1904. Primary responsibility for fostering order among the undergraduates now rested squarely with students.[97]

The honor system for conduct of examinations was closely related to student government in function and purpose. Rapidly introduced in 1893, two months prior to creation of the joint advisory committee, the honor system was a copy of that approved by the faculty at Princeton a few weeks earlier. Wesleyan was the first New England college to adopt such a system. Williams followed suit in 1896 and Amherst in 1905. Supervision of the honor system was a chief task of organizations for student government. Self-governance and the pledge appended to all examination papers ("I hereby certify on honor that in this examination I have neither received nor given any assistance whatever") shared a common objective: to foster "that sense of dignity and honor which marks the true gentleman."[98]

Student recruitment in the 1890s began to include references to the full range of collegiate activities conducive to gentlemanly success. As in publications of the 1880s directed toward secondary-school students and their parents, the twenty-four-page pamphlet of 1895 portrayed Wesleyan's curriculum as a means to "prominent positions in the learned professions and the world of letters." This pamphlet, however, went far beyond the academic aspects of Wesleyan. Prospective students learned that they could anticipate rooming and eating in "a fraternity house occupied by thirty good fellows of congenial tastes and dispositions." Activities such as the glee club, sports, and student publications provided other "ties which bind Wesleyan men to one another." There was a "broad opportunity for religious culture" through programs of the YMCA. The "large and elegant" new gymnasium, renovated dormitory "finished in hard woods," and campus located "in one of the most beautiful cities of New England" provided additional inducements to choose a Wesleyan that was no longer the rough-hewn Methodist college of the 1870s.[99]

Students selecting Wesleyan in the mid-1890s most often cited the scholarly reputation of the faculty as the prime reason for their decision. But the fraternity system ranked second and athletics third. Methodist influences played a lesser role, even though the percentage of students from Methodist families, down from 80 percent in the 1880s to about 67 percent by 1901, was still high. Faculty, students, trustees, and alumni were very attentive and active in the "missionary work" of recruiting new students. A campus visit, particularly for the celebration of Washington's birthday, proved highly influential. The annual Washington's birthday banquet, first held in 1891, brought Wesleyan's constituencies together in "a blending of love for country with love for *Alma Mater*." Replete with witty toasts and spirited song, this event soon became a major device for recruiting "sub-freshmen" invited from secondary schools. Such a visit gave prospective students intensive exposure to Wesleyan's collegiate culture. [100]

That student culture was staunchly Republican in politics and increasingly suited to young men who would enter the business world. The six-to-one ratio of Republicans to Democrats among Wesleyan students of the mid-1880s increased to almost ten-to-one by 1904. The campaign and election in 1896 of William McKinley, Republican and Methodist, gave special impetus to this trend. The number of graduates who became businessmen increased gradually in the 1890s but lagged behind counts taken at Williams and Amherst. Only 20 percent of Wesleyan's graduates in the mid-1890s pursued business careers, as compared to 36 percent of their peers at Amherst. Within the next ten years, however, the proportion of Wesleyan seniors choosing to enter business moved up to about one-third. By 1909 a senior faculty member worried about the increasing numbers of American college students oriented toward "the variety of pursuits embraced under the general name of business." Instead of engaging in serious study, he observed, these students devoted themselves to "the avocations of student life —athletics, social events, amusements, college politics."[101]

Wesleyan students of 1890 to 1910 sustained a tradition of earnestness, but they extended its range far beyond the classroom and library. Intellectual and moral earnestness continued with a significant segment of students who, like Edward Lee Thorndike '95, pursued careers of scholarship and teaching or, like Joseph Beech '99, became ministers and missionaries. The campus rejoiced when Paul Nixon '04 won appointment as Connecticut's first Rhodes scholar, topping four contenders from Yale. Much energy and enthusiasm, however, flowed toward nonacademic events. Freshman-sophomore rivalry evolved into a highly competitive spectator sport at annual contests such as the venerable Douglas Cannon scrap and the flag rush instituted in 1906. Patriotism flowed freely in late April 1898 as sixty-five students conducted military drills in preparation for possible enlistment in the "splendid little war" with Spain. Athletic zeal led to calls for more successful teams, even if it meant admitting "a larger number of men who are strong athletes and only fair students," and for better organized cheering through the appointment of cheerleaders. "The student life at Middletown," according to an observer in 1894, "may be characterized in one word as earnest. The Middletown boy has pluck and resolution. He is bound that his football team, his glee club, shall be the equal of any in the country. And he carries the same temper through all his work."[102]

With his broadly distributed earnestness, the college man at Wesleyan in 1900 or 1910 avoided the dismally depicted life of a "grind." In poetry and parable, the grind sacrificed health, happiness, and peer approval: "Let others say / That social life is best— / But I'm the grind, / And for my kind / High marks alone are blest." Condemned as "a freak," the grind lacked talents attributed to the "broad man" or the "shark." The broad man was astute at cramming in order to get a passing grade. He might study for the Ph.B., which required no Greek and only a minimum of mathematics, rather than the B.A. or B.S. The shark was adept at bluffing his way through situations that threatened to expose his lack of preparation for classes or exams. Advice to entering students usually paid tribute to Wesleyan's high standard of scholarship, but a countervailing comment became increasingly influential after 1900: "Know that you are not in College to study books merely; you are here to broaden in numberless ways—to become College men in the best sense of the word."[103]

Of the many campus values and activities developed from 1890 to 1910, dancing most directly pitted the growing breadth of collegiate life against Wesleyan's denominational heritage. A dancing school in Middletown began to attract student interest in the 1870s. The first junior promenade took place in 1883 at the Armory Hall in Middletown. By the late 1880s there was substantial student patronage for dance classes in Middletown. Information about a German club for those interested in this type of cotillion dancing appeared in the yearbook of 1893. Objections to lack of college constraint on this amusement prohibited by the Methodist *Discipline* surfaced in 1895. A group of older Methodist trustees tried to initiate an investigation of the junior prom. Frustrated when their attempt lost in a close vote and when the president disavowed all jurisdiction over this off-campus event, six trustees registered a "protest against the said non-action." Use of the college gymnasium for such events, however, was clearly within the range of trustee control and denominational influence. Students started a senior ball in 1900 and a sophomore hop in 1903, but none of the three annual dances, despite repeated undergraduate requests and support from young metropolitan alumni, occurred in the gymnasium until 1913. The only dances on campus prior to that date took place in fraternity houses, beginning around 1903.[104]

Costs for attending Wesleyan grew along with the elaboration of college life. Tuition held at $75 from 1874 to 1906, and it remained possible for an industrious, frugal student to work his or her way through, particularly with help from partial or full tuition waiver and from scholarship awards. By the mid-1890s, however, the provision of steam heat and room care in North College initiated modest increases in total basic costs. Room and board in the new fraternity houses contributed to this trend. While most students kept close to the average of $350 to $400 for a year of collegiate life, some spent in excess of $1,000. A student happily noted in 1901 that Wesleyan had enough of these "sports" to "leaven the whole lump." The first advertisement for Brooks Brothers clothing appeared in the *Argus* of 1891, and by 1910 student consumers could consider the allures of fraternity jewelry and stationery from Tiffany, custom tailoring in Hartford, hotels in Boston and New York, Fatima Turkish cigarettes, and local billiard parlors. Wesleyan's financial exhibits from 1895 to 1910 show a clear trend toward more students paying more of their own way. James Bryce, an astute British observer of America's polity and people, noted in 1911 the rapid increase since 1890 of "the number of persons with incomes large enough to make it easy for them to send sons and daughters to college." Wesleyan and this expanding middle class were finding one another.[105]

Investment in a Wesleyan education at the turn of a new century yielded subtle benefits appropriate to the metropolitan era. The instructor in declamation and elocution gave additional advice on correct walking. The professor of literature served as an example of "cultural grace." The faculty secretary operated a "bureau of vacant positions," replacing the prior Methodist school and pulpit network with placement services suited to a student body that typically came from and returned to urban areas. Students learned to set themselves apart as a group destined for professional success in upper ranges of the middle class. They announced their new identity as college graduates, beginning in the 1890s, by wearing caps and gowns at commencement. They learned to gather for good fellowship in college smokers, where they entertained one another with music, comedy, sketches, and short talks. They proclaimed "the glory of Wesleyan's manhood."[106]

Left on the periphery of Wesleyan's college life were students whom the white, Anglo-Saxon, male, Protestant majority found unsuitable for close fellowship due to ethnicity, religion, race, or gender. Constantine M. Panunzio '11, a recent Italian immigrant enrolling from Maine, lived in the most shabby dormitory, Observatory Hall, and then alone in the isolated two-person room in South College. He belonged to the Commons Club, a group outside the mainstream of fraternity life. Only a few Jewish students, probably all of them women from cities near Middletown, attended prior to 1910. A survey of religious preference among Wesleyan students in 1907 found none of the Jewish faith.[107]

Eight African-American students attending Wesleyan between 1902 and 1911 presented the greatest test of attitudes toward those on the periphery of college life. James A. Wilson '06, the first of this group, had only two predecessors in the prior four decades. Isaac N. Cardozo n1879 had enrolled for a year in the mid-1870s, and William L. Bulkley n1888 had stayed for only a month or two a decade later. Five of the seven who followed Wilson graduated, two in 1908, one in 1910, and two in 1911. John D. Smith n1907 transferred to Boston University for his senior year and B.A. degree. Augustus G. Purvis n1908 transferred to the University of Michigan for his senior year, B.A., and M.D. All either lived alone in rooms normally used as doubles or roomed with another of the group. Several joined the Commons Club, but that was the closest any came to membership in the world of fraternities.[108]

Only guesses can be made regarding the reasons for the arrival of these young men at Wesleyan at this time. Wilson may have gained attention as an orator at Plattsburgh State Normal and Training School, where he graduated in 1902. In his commencement oration, "Struggling Up From the Depths," he cited evidence from his home state of Alabama in praising the work of Booker T. Washington. Smith, the ward of a minister, and Thomas J. Taylor '08, the son of a coachman, prepared at Congregational schools but lived only about thirty miles from Wesleyan. Purvis came from South Carolina but prepared at Mount Hermon School, where Wesleyan had regularly recruited students since the mid-1890s. James S. Thomas '08, Perry D. G. Pennington '10, John W. E. Bowen, Jr., '11, and David D. Jones '11 probably came as a result of Methodist connections. Thomas, son of a Methodist minister in Baltimore, prepared at Wesleyan Academy. Bowen, also son of a Methodist minister who had once preached in Baltimore, and Pennington, whose father was a butler in the same city, prepared at Phillips Exeter Academy. Prior to entering Wesleyan, Jones, son of a Methodist minister in New Orleans, graduated from New Orleans University, founded by the Methodist Freedman's Aid Society.[109]

Bradford Raymond may have played a major role in making Wesleyan receptive to enrollment of African-Americans. Booker T. Washington spoke at Wesleyan 4 April 1895 in a lecture sponsored by the citizenship club. This talk in the chapel on "The Negro and the South" preceded by less than six months the Atlanta Exposition address that established Washington's national reputation as a black leader. Raymond visited the Exposition, praised Washington, and wrote an article filled with optimism about the influence of industrialism, schools, and churches in producing "the new Negro," particularly in the South. "That the schools of our Church are to play a most important part in this development," he noted, "is already very evident. They are to furnish leaders for the new age." He primarily referred to southern schools, but Wesleyan could make a contribution. All but two African-Americans enrolled during Raymond's presidency became educators or clergy in communities from Baltimore to New Orleans. And Purvis established his medical practice in South Carolina. Throughout his presidency Raymond sustained and made public his interest in Methodist-sponsored schools for blacks.[110]

As Booker T. Washington made clear, however, a modest amount of educational and economic opportunity was one thing, political and social opportunities another. Investigating race relations in the North as well as the South at the turn of the century, a journalist reported "growing prejudices" against African-Americans. Southern states used legislative and other means to construct a system of segregation. Northern churches were notably silent on issues of racial justice. Wesleyan students had reported with approval in the 1880s the achievements of black students at other colleges. A *Literary Monthly* article in 1902 praised the poetry of Paul Laurence Dunbar. James Wilson won the Rich Prize for the best commencement oration in 1906, speaking on "Shall the Negro Have a Share in American Politics?" Announcement of his victory brought enthusiastic applause. But stereotyped caricatures of blacks had begun to appear in yearbook humor several years earlier. In 1906 African-Americans ceased to be members of the Commons Club, and after 1907 they no longer appeared in class pictures taken for the yearbook.[111]

Wesleyan's white male students drew the color line on campus at this time. The precipitating incident and the connection with increasing racism in American culture came through baseball. In 1905 and 1906 Princeton's baseball team refused to play the visiting Wesleyan squad unless any black players were removed from the previously announced starting lineup. On both occasions the Wesleyan captain acquiesced, using a substitute catcher for Thomas Taylor and in 1905 persuading the Princetonians that John Smith, whose skin was of lighter color, was Armenian. African-Americans had long been denied admission to Princeton and had been forced out of the nation's organized professional

CLARK   COACH MACKEY   TAYLOR
MORGAN   BRISTOL
         HALEY   MONROE (CAPT.)   HANCOCK   DAY
S. F. HANCOCK (MAN.)   CAMPAIGNE   ANDERSON   SMITH   CLEMENTS (ASST. MAN.)

Wesleyan University baseball team, 1905.
Smith (second row, third from left) was
an infielder and Taylor (top row, far right)
usually played catcher.

baseball teams in 1898. A similarly prejudiced step was now taken at Wesleyan in response to the Princeton incident and to the possibility of a third black player in 1905. At a college body meeting in the early fall of 1905, a student vote prohibited blacks from participation in intercollegiate athletics. Perhaps through some special provision in that vote, Taylor played early in the 1906 season, until shortly after the second Princeton incident. Smith rejoined the team in early May and played in several games but was then excluded from the lineup through a combination of fraternity and race-conscious politics. No African-Americans entered Wesleyan that fall. Two entered in 1907 and one in 1908 as the Raymond presidency reached its conclusion, but the next would not arrive until 1918. Only five more would enroll before 1930.[112]

Movement toward white, male, middle-class homogeneity at Wesleyan was close to completion by 1908. Students had created a college life that conformed to metropolitan definitions of a prestigious New England liberal arts college. Through athletics, fraternities, glee club, drama, debate, and other student activities, prospects for institutional and individual success went hand-in-hand. Wesleyan would benefit from the

Women students at Wesleyan, 1891/92

prosperity of alumni in business and law. They constituted one-third of the graduates in the 1880s and were rapidly approaching one-half of those receiving degrees from 1902 to 1911. The gentlemanly, athletic, earnest, well-spoken, civic-minded, Anglo-Saxon Protestant graduating from Wesleyan's extracurriculum was well prepared for such careers in urban settings. Olin could feel comfortable hiring able Wesleyan men for his law firm.[113]

Dropping Coeducation

Olin favored the abolition of coeducation at Wesleyan. After supporting a proposal in 1900 to replace coeducation with a separate women's department, Olin no doubt voted in 1909 to abandon entirely Wesleyan's education of women undergraduates unless a coordinate college could be funded. His position on this issue can be related to his attitudes toward women expressed at a later date. In 1915 Olin told a group of women that he would vote against the women's suffrage amendment proposal for the New York state constitution. Extending a right to vote to "the weaker sex," he predicted, would diminish the quality and stability of state government. Endorsing a "division of labor . . . in political as well as industrial activity," he argued that strong and experienced males would be ever "anxious for your welfare" and best represent the political and economic interests of women. Olin urged the women in his audience to persuade "every man of your acquaintance for your sake to vote NO" on an amendment that would "disturb the foundations of that social structure which shelters . . . the hopes of your children."[114] The extended root system for Olin's positions on feminism and coeducation included metropolitan male-oriented athleticism, values embodied in club and fraternity life, and related elements of Wesleyan's campus culture that predominated from 1890 to 1910.

Consistent with national trends and with tendencies at other coeducational campuses in New England, increasingly separate spheres for men and women developed at Wesleyan in the 1890s. The immediate stimulus came in the fall of 1892, when the number of women in the entering class doubled. Subsequent increases carried the number of first-year women from seven (10 percent of all full-time class members) in 1891 to twenty-four (23 percent) in 1898. The "increasing proportion of 'co-eds' who are flocking here," according to male students, represented a threat to the reputation and survival of Wesleyan. Most directly threatened were those who advocated a strategy combining athletic victories and success of alumni in secular pursuits to "make old Wesleyan the pride of New England, not of the New England Methodist Conference." For those most alarmed about an increasingly feminine Wesleyan, it was clear that coeducation must be contained, isolated, and eliminated.[115]

Attacks on coeducation by male undergraduates intensified from 1893 to 1900. A sophomore called for "a more stringent set of 'game laws'" to limit the number of "quails." A group of athletes and fraternity members from all four classes formed the mostly mythical and transitory but clearly hostile PDQ Society, whose motto was "press the damsels quietly." Pressure from a variety of male sources took many forms. A visitor to campus in 1893 noted "the half-contemptuous way in which the men speak of the women students." The practice of electing a woman to serve as vice-president for each class ended in the mid-1890s. Exclusion from participation in class day exercises closely followed exclusion from service as a class officer. Participation by women in student publications faded away as the decade progressed. Access to the new gymnasium was denied, even though women had contributed toward its construction. Foundations were in place by 1898 for the social boycott that sustained gender segregation until 1912.[116]

Alumni opposition to coeducation closely interacted with the hostility of male students. Startled by the growing number of women at Wesleyan in 1894, an alumnus worried that his alma mater might become "a namby pamby college" and "a nonentity among our fellow institutions." Wesleyan's "pride and boast," he asserted, "has been masculine strength and virility. If we can survey other Methodist institutions from above, it is from this very vantage point." Particularly vocal among the alumni was the New York Wesleyan young alumni club. All those present at the organizational meeting in January 1894 were graduates of the last ten years and members of fraternities. Many had an association with football at Wesleyan as former players or managers. This group began with a focus on athletics but soon added coeducation to its concerns. Edwin O. Smith '93, member of Psi Upsilon and former captain of the football and baseball teams, expressed sentiments of the association on several occasions from 1896 through 1898. He argued that coeducation hurt recruitment of students by "turning good men away from the college." He also questioned "whether Methodist lines ought to be drawn so closely at Wesleyan." Fear of Wesleyan becoming feminized like Boston University (where women in the 1880s had become a large majority of the undergraduates) fueled his argument to the point where withdrawal of alumni support became a thinly veiled threat. Both Smith and the *Argus* felt authorized to speak in 1898 for a powerful alliance of "undergraduate men and very clear-headed alumni, a body of men who have no trivial part in making Wesleyan, **W**esleyan." Thus partially italicized, the college name began with a varsity letter.[117]

Amid this rising din of opposition, women at Wesleyan created a campus life for themselves within the separate sphere assigned to them. Webb Hall provided a center for women's activities, particularly after it was renovated and refurnished in 1892. Facing College Row from a site on High Street at the corner of William, this Greek Revival building accommodated about two dozen students and supplied space for meetings and social events. Receptions for alumnae in the 1890s helped to sustain ties with an important support group. The women's literary society, Phi Sigma (1893), and the two sororities of this decade, Delta Delta Delta (1895) and Zeta Epsilon (which evolved in late 1895 from Alpha Kappa Upsilon, started as a literary society in 1893), probably used Webb Hall for meetings. By the late 1890s women had a substantial array of literary and social enterprises, including their own class day observances during commencement week.[118]

Two developments in 1898 revealed the flaws of any separate-spheres solutions for the issue of coeducation. There could be only one yearbook, and it was controlled by men. Hostility expressed toward women in the 1897 annual incited a protest. Toleration for the traditional exclusion of women from class pictures might continue, but the joking reference to torching Webb Hall and the announcement of "a crusade against the Quails" by junior class males responsible for producing the *Olla Podrida* could not go unchallenged. In the fall of 1897 the fourteen women of the junior class told their male classmates who constituted the editorial board for next spring's yearbook that they would refuse to pay the class tax helping to fund the publication unless "proof sheets were previously submitted to their inspection or to that of a third party." After defending their position in a spirited class meeting on 30 April 1898, the junior women accepted a concession from the yearbook board. Women would not be required to pay the class tax until publication; they would then pay only if nothing objectionable was found by a third party. Backlash from the protest prompted a policy of excluding women's names and organizations from the *Olla Podrida* after 1898.[119]

The second development was an increase of fifteen in female enrollment and a decrease of fifteen in male enrollment for the fall term of 1898. Provision of housing for women became a pressing problem just when Wesleyan needed more facilities for instruction. Neither the national financial picture nor the fiscal health of Wesleyan was robust. Debate over coeducation rose to new levels of emotional intensity that fall. Proper institutional reference points for Wesleyan, according to students opposing coeducation, were that "well-defined distinctive . . . class of small New England colleges," not coeducational Methodist universities in Boston, Syracuse, or Chicago. Only at great peril to Wesleyan, they warned the trustees, could policies on coeducation be pursued with disregard for the opinions of "our increasing body of younger alumni" and "practically the entire [male] undergraduate body." With acrimonious arguments spreading into the metropolitan press and alumni clubs, the faculty and President Raymond saw it was time to appoint a committee.[120]

Trustees agreed. They established in March 1899 a committee "on the relation of Wesleyan University to the higher education of women." Three of the four trustees elected to this committee by the board (Andrus, Foss, and Joseph E. King '47) probably held views favorable to coeducation, while Olin was more likely to represent the negative viewpoint of many New York City alumni. This distribution counterbalanced the two members elected by the Alumni Association; Herbert Welch '87 and Seward V. Coffin '89 were closely aligned with those who supported athletics and opposed coeducation. The faculty elected John Van Vleck, the most influential proponent of coeducation, and Caleb Winchester, a weighty opponent. The committee deliberated from July 1899 to March 1900 and received a recommendation from only one group, the New York Wesleyan young alumni club. Concerned that "the masculine character of the college shall be changed to feminine," the young alumni urged that Wesleyan become more like Brown by establishing "a women's college organized within the university." The joint committee recommended this solution to the board in March 1900.[121]

The board postponed action until June and invited opinions on the proposed change. The Alumni Association registered its opposition by a vote of 107 to 37 endorsing an alternate proposal. This plan merely formalized a separate sphere of collegiate life for women undergraduates, without founding a new college, and limited their number to 15 percent of the student body. Alumnae organized and stated their opposition to a women's college by petitioning for continued coeducation, although they conceded the wisdom of "some definite limitation of numbers, provided the limit be large enough to permit the maintenance of a healthy community life among the women." One alumna had already argued that an annex or coordinate college would only raise the costs for all students, including the large group of women who attend because "life at Wesleyan is cheaper than at any college for women of the first rank." Male undergraduates memorialized the trustees to end the admission of women. They noted that "the establishment of a women's college would take away funds from the college sorely needed for other purposes," and cited the futility of resisting "the general sentiment in the East against co-education." A majority of the faculty probably supported continuation of coeducation. Even the board's joint committee was now split into three factions, with two of them questioning the current feasibility of funding a bona fide women's college.[122]

A beleaguered board voted to remain near the status quo. As of fall 1900 there would be a 20-percent quota for admitting women. A separate category for women would be created in publications, public events, and election to honors. The collegiate life of women would be separately administered. Meanwhile, Wesleyan would "maintain standards of admission, educational methods, curriculum, and community life primarily adapted to men."[123]

Anticoeducationalists were more angered than appeased by this stance. But they agreed to a temporary truce and hoped for an upturn in Wesleyan's enrollment and endowment. With Wesleyan devoting special efforts to raise funds from Methodists for buildings and endowment, students sensed that continued agitation would be detrimental to the college. The Argus supported "a dignified silence upon the subject of co-education until the 20 per cent compromise has a fair trial." Faculty worked to implement the board decision. They notified women applicants that admissions would become competitive if the number of qualified female candidates threatened the 20-percent barrier. They arranged for the catalogue to list the women apart from the men of each class. On the page where previous catalogues stated that "women are admitted to equal privileges in the University with men," the faculty substituted a summary of the trustee action. Women would now be seated at commencement off to one side from other seniors and receive degrees after the men. Reports in the denominational press expressed hope that the new arrangements would settle matters for a while.[124]

Women students adapted to these constraints without further overt protest, thus tacitly endorsing the period of "dignified silence." The number of women entering the first year of studies dropped from an average of sixteen during the years 1892–99 to almost half that number for the years 1900–08. The loss was largely in students from out of state. After 1900 about 84 percent of entering women were Connecticut residents, with almost 60 percent coming from Middletown and environs. They resigned themselves to a difficult tradeoff. Access at low cost to nearby, first-rate academic resources came at the price of social ostracism by most male undergraduates.[125]

The widespread practice of men ignoring women students after 1900 proved to be only a prelude to more direct forms of harassment. By 1902 men were shouting offensive language outside Webb Hall in the early morning hours. In 1903 they painted hostile messages on or near the building and distributed posters that ridiculed women who entered that fall. For the first time, women in 1903 were not invited to the opening reception for entering students sponsored by the campus YMCA. A clear sign that the truce within student and alumni ranks no longer prevailed came at the annual dinner of New York alumni in December 1903. Speaking for the undergraduates, Paul Nixon said he found "that two facts are incontestable: First we as a college fail yearly to enroll men because we have coeducation. Secondly, the discreditable parody of co-education practiced at Wesleyan . . . makes Wesleyan notorious." Alumni opponents of coeducation soon resumed hostilities toward "the disagreeable custom of admitting women to Wesleyan." Their renewed efforts to revise "the blunder of 1872" intensified after *Collier's* published a list that compared enrollments at forty-seven colleges in 1898 with those for 1908. Whereas Amherst, Williams, Trinity, Dartmouth, and Yale showed healthy increases, Wesleyan stood with a handful of colleges where enrollments over the decade decreased. To the issue of feminization, alumni now added the related question of survival as a college of high reputation.[126]

Facing this intense pressure, coeducation at Wesleyan had few remaining influential allies by 1908, even within its most important original source of support, the denomination. Orange Judd, author of Methodist Sunday school texts and of the motion to admit women, died in 1892. His grandson Kenneth Goode '04 argued in 1908 as a young metropolitan alumnus that coeducation was not only an anachronism but also "a drag on the finances that the college cannot long endure." John Van Vleck had retired in 1904. Bradford Raymond, a steady advocate of coeducation and larger opportunities for women within the church, was in poor health and about to leave office. William North Rice waged a lonely struggle for coeducation, finding little support within his denomination. Writing to Rice in late 1907, a discouraged Raymond observed that "the whole movement for women's emancipation has had a definite setback in the Methodist Episcopal Church, if not in the whole country."[127]

Last-ditch efforts to sustain Wesleyan's engagement in the education of women undergraduates focused on the only politically viable solution consistent with this aim. Those who originally supported coeducation began in 1907 to seek funding for a coordinate women's college. Raymond approached the General Education Board, established in 1902 by John D. Rockefeller. Citing the women's college at Brown as a model, Raymond requested a grant of $500,000 for the land and new buildings to create a campus for women a few blocks to the south of Wesleyan's campus. He suggested that Wesleyan would be willing to raise a matching amount "for the general development of the university." The General Education Board declined to make a grant of this magnitude. On the eve of the trustee vote to drop coeducation, president-elect William Arnold Shanklin made a final check with John Andrus, Wesleyan's wealthiest trustee, to see if he might be interested in funding the continuation of women's education at Wesleyan. His daughter had graduated in 1897, and he could have solved Wesleyan's problem with a single sheet from his checkbook. Although Andrus opposed the abolition of coeducation, he was too alienated by the college's string of unbalanced budgets to invest in any Wesleyan enterprise at that time. And Shanklin's visit was probably more an attempt to begin a promising relationship than to rescue women's education at Wesleyan.[128]

Without an eleventh-hour influx of resources to create a coordinate-college solution, it became ever more clear that Wesleyan was caught in a self-perpetuating dilemma. The chilly climate male students and alumni created for women students kept female enrollment to a minimum. The presence of women students limited the growth of male enrollment. In the fall of 1907 only eighty-eight first-year students (including twelve women) entered, a drop of 11 percent from the previous year. Senior faculty saw a need to get the issue of women's education back on the trustee agenda. They did so with a resolution that "the early establishment of a Separate Women's College is the wisest solution of the problem of the coeducation of women at Wesleyan." The trustees established a committee of five trustees and five faculty (elected by the faculty) to study the feasibility and desirability of a coordinate college. Before the committee had prepared its report, however, Charles Scott, Jr., '86 made a motion at the annual meeting of 1908 that no women be admitted after the fall of 1909 and that the trustees pledge "to establish a coordinate college . . . as soon as the necessary funds are available." A Philadelphia businessman whose contributions were helping to build the new Wesleyan, Scott saw the need for prompt action.[129]

The trustees postponed final action on Scott's first proposal until the mid-year meeting, giving full notice to board members and all interested parties. The end was in sight. Even coeducation's most persistent proponent, Rice, saw the necessity for "compromise." The New York Wesleyan young alumni club urged the trustees "to take appropriate action to prevent the admission of women undergraduates at the earliest date possible." Noting the "Teddy-bearish attitude" toward coeducation and the social boycott of women by male undergraduates, journalists assumed that coeducation would be abandoned. On 26 February 1909 the board voted to cease admitting women after the fall of 1909. They also approved Scott's second motion, pledging to establish a separate college for women "as soon as the necessary funds are provided."[130]

Reactions to this decision revealed little dissent. The *Argus* applauded with a banner headline: "Co-Education Abolished!" The *Literary Monthly* expressed its pleasure: "The Barnacle is at last to be scraped from the keel of the good ship Wesleyan!" The *Olla Podrida* editor exclaimed: "Here's to a Segregated Wesleyan!" The *Christian Advocate* urged approval of the trustee decision. The *New York Times* concluded that "Wesleyan authorities have acted wisely." Other metropolitan papers reported the action without comment. Only the *Independent*, a crusading weekly, denounced "the shame of Wesleyan" in yielding to "sex prejudice."[131]

After the trustee vote William North Rice led the efforts to found a coordinate women's college. "We do not covet the position in history," he wrote, "of being the only college in the civilized world that ever excluded women after having once received them." He was certainly aware of the models of Barnard (1889) and Radcliffe (1894) as well as arrangements that evolved from 1891 to 1896 for the Women's College in Brown University (renamed Pembroke College in 1928). He saw an important trend in the movement from coeducation toward coordinate college at Middlebury (1902), Colby (1905), and Tufts (Jackson, 1910). But the minimum of $400,000 needed to set up a women's college at Wesleyan was a daunting amount. Trustee action in June 1909 made it clear that raising endowment for Wesleyan's current programs would take priority over raising funds for the facilities and endowment of a coordinate college. Rice attempted to enlist the support of women's groups in Connecticut currently considering alternatives for the higher education of women in the state. The group taking strongest initiative by mid-1910, however, was looking beyond Middletown. Led by Elizabeth C. Wright '97, college and university alumnae who formed the Hartford College Club considered only "definite offers." When citizens in the New London area made a very attractive bid of land, buildings, and endowment, the founding group obtained a charter in 1911 for Connecticut College for Women. A decade before the new college opened in 1915, Olin's two daughters had married into wealthy families and charted lives without higher education.[132]

Selecting a President

Olin's efforts to reshape Wesleyan faltered briefly in the search for a new president. While wrestling with difficult issues regarding women's education, Wesleyan's trustees also searched for new leadership. In June 1907 Bradford Raymond submitted his resignation, mainly because of failing health. He received a leave of absence for fall and winter terms and a release from his duties effective June 1908. William North Rice served as acting president during Raymond's leave and the 1908/09 academic year, a time of prolonged presidential search and transition. The choice of a new president in November 1908 prompted Olin to resign from the board. Writing the day after Shanklin's election, Olin said his resignation was to take effect immediately. He asked that his name be deleted from the list of trustees in the catalogue copy that would soon go to the printer.[133]

The search committee appointed from the board in June 1907 had faced the task of finding leadership for a financially strained institution reorienting itself in a highly competitive environment. New buildings and the destruction of North College put great pressure on annual budgets. An endowment fund drive faltered. With annual deficits exceeding 10 percent of the operating budget, institutional debt accumulated rapidly. Faculty salaries remained unchanged while the cost of living from 1900 to 1909 grew by almost 50 percent. To keep up with Amherst and Williams, Wesleyan needed to increase its endowment by $1 million and its enrollment by one hundred students.[134]

Advice to the committee came in abundance from concerned alumni. After the presidency of Raymond, "a courtly gentleman of the old school," young alumni in New York City called for a man of "personal magnetism, . . . vigor, ability to grasp the drift of modern education . . . a businessman rather than a clergyman." He should be "at once a scholar, an educator, and a money-raising manager." Alumni in upstate New York even proposed that the right nonministerial president need not necessarily be a Methodist. The original committee of seven Methodist trustees did expand its membership to include two somewhat younger trustees from outside the denominational fold, but most members were men in their mid-sixties or older who were ministerial and lay leaders of the denomination. Selection of a non-Methodist or even a Methodist layman at a time of delicate transition in constituencies was highly improbable. Advice about finding someone who would have "a definite aggressive policy" and be "a man of all men," however, was likely to be well received.[135]

A major metropolitan minister of enormous physical and intellectual vitality was the committee's first choice. S. Parkes Cadman, forty-four-year-old pastor of the Central Congregational Church in Brooklyn, was a lifelong Methodist. His successor as pastor of Methodist churches in Yonkers and Manhattan in the 1890s caught the eye of the ecumenically minded search committee at Central. While in his eighth year at Central, Cadman received Wesleyan's offer. In an embarrassingly public manner, he considered and then declined. Continuing his pastorate at Central until his death in 1936, Cadman published more than a dozen books, wrote a widely syndicated newspaper column for the *New York Herald Tribune*, and gained a national reputation as one of the first radio preachers.[136]

Frederick M. Davenport '89, who like Cadman had held a Methodist pastorate in Yonkers in the mid-1890s, received close consideration as a candidate with considerable alumni support and unanimous sub-rosa faculty endorsement. Three handicaps to Davenport's candidacy precluded an offer. He had left the Methodist ministry in 1901 to obtain a

Ph.D. from Columbia and become a professor of law and political science at Hamilton College. He had married a daughter of John Andrus, a man many Wesleyan alumni had come to resent because he gave so little of his great wealth to his alma mater. Davenport's interests had migrated from church to education to politics. In early 1908 he became a candidate for the New York State Senate. After his brief brush with a possible Wesleyan presidency, Davenport became increasingly active in New York politics and left Hamilton in 1925 to serve four terms as a Republican member of the United States House of Representatives. He later gained national prominence in the field of federal personnel administration and civil service.[137]

William Arnold Shanklin, president of Upper Iowa University, was elected to serve as Wesleyan's ninth president on 13 November 1908. With the search well into its second year, the committee and the board probably concluded that "there was no man within reach whose name would have inspired unanimous and hearty confidence among our constituency." By a split vote, the search committee decided in late October to recommend Shanklin, whose candidacy earlier in the search had generated scant enthusiasm. Giving little more than a week's notice, Henry Ingraham, president of the board and chair of the search committee, announced a trustee meeting. Less than half the board attended. Perhaps out of surprise or anger, five of the twenty-three present cast no vote. Three voted against Shanklin, leaving a less-than-two-thirds majority of those present and little more than a quarter of the board voting for him. Without hesitation, Shanklin accepted.[138]

Shanklin's leading supporters were probably William Kelley, chair of the subcommittee that did much of the search committee's work, George S. Bennett '64, and James Buckley. Kelley, editor of the *Methodist Review* since 1893, had a reputation for paternal solicitude toward "my boys," those he considered to be promising and pious young members of the denomination. The smooth-cheeked Shanklin, a devout Methodist minister with youthful enthusiasm, had all the attributes needed to attract Kelley's patronage. Kelley's close friend and fraternity brother, Bennett, a businessman from Wilkes Barre, Pennsylvania, served for forty-two years as superintendent of a model Sunday school at First Methodist Church. A man of tireless activity and "buoyancy of spirit," Bennett might have responded favorably to Shanklin's reputation as "a hustler, who brings things to pass." This characteristic impressed Buckley, editor of the *Christian Advocate* since 1880, when he visited Upper Iowa in June 1908 to give the commencement address.[139]

William Arnold Shanklin, president of
Wesleyan, 1909–23

Opposition to Shanklin probably came from Olin and a few others who found no credentials or other clues in Shanklin's biography that suggested a person of the stature they expected for Wesleyan. Whereas Raymond held a Ph.D., Shanklin lacked even an earned B.A. Despite frequent claims to have graduated in 1883 from Hamilton College, Shanklin had attended for only his freshman year. In 1893 he obtained, probably through close connections with the Root family, a B.A. *ex gratia* from Hamilton. Claiming to have a B.A., he obtained a B.D. degree from Garrett Biblical Institute in 1891 after about two years' residence in a three-year program. He sometimes reported this as a S.T.B. degree. He listed as his earliest honorary doctorate a D.D. from the University of Washington in 1895 that did not appear in records of the university. Shanklin's career route was barely recognizable to eastern eyes. After a sophomore year at the University of Missouri, he probably returned to Carrollton, his home town. He moved to Chetopa, Kansas, in 1884 and became co-owner of a drug store. A call to the ministry in 1887 took the young licensed preacher sixty miles west to Peru, where he conducted a "gracious revival" and raised funds to build a church. Ordained in 1889, he held successive pastorates in Fort Scott, and then Spokane and Seattle, Washington, and Dubuque, Iowa. Five years at a church in Reading, Pennsylvania, preceded Shanklin's election to the presidency of Upper Iowa University in 1905. This Methodist institution, largely dedicated to secondary and vocational training, had about one hundred twenty-five students in the regular college course. One of Shanklin's major tasks was to achieve full accreditation for the university. Ever eager to excel, the new president wrote a brief letter to President Arthur T. Hadley of Yale, requesting a list of the best recent books on higher education.[140]

Shanklin could hardly qualify as even a much-reduced version of Columbia's Nicholas Murray Butler, Olin's model for a college president. Yet Olin kept the faith with Wesleyan, quickly withdrawing his resignation and agreeing to serve as chair of the committee planning Shanklin's inauguration. And Shanklin did bring to Wesleyan attributes Olin could find desirable. Colleagues in Iowa viewed him as a man of "aggressive and active leadership." Enrollments grew during his presidency there, and he knew the Midwest, a region from which Wesleyan hoped to draw more students. With a matching grant from Andrew Carnegie, Shanklin raised $150,000 in subscriptions for Upper Iowa's endowment. He was a member of Sigma Phi and a supporter of fraternities. He "did not believe in coeducation anywhere and under any circumstances in colleges." He was well connected to the Republican party. Above all he had a magnetic personality based on "passionate earnestness." It was hard to dislike William Arnold Shanklin.[141]

Shanklin proved his potential for popularity on his first campus visit as president-elect. Anxieties and hopes were high. Although faculty realized Wesleyan had not obtained someone "who would rank with the leaders in educational movements," they eagerly expected a fund-raiser of "great executive force." Students anticipated a "congenial . . . energetic and forceful spirit," a friend and confidant "thoroughly in sympathy with student life, entering into it and enjoying it as much as the students do." Young metropolitan alumni sensed he would be decisive in eliminating coeducation, effective in recruiting a male student body of five hundred, adept at raising money for buildings and endowment, and ready to improve the record of athletic teams. Denominational supporters foresaw a Wesleyan presidency that would "energize the situation." During his three-day visit in February 1908, Shanklin captivated the campus with his winning personality. He visited each fraternity house and each faculty member. Addressing the faculty and students at morning chapel, the slender forty-five-year-old with a youthful appearance said he felt as if he were "still a college man." He pledged to maintain personal contact with every student organization, from the football team to the dramatic association, and to help bring the team "up to par." His peroration was worthy of a revival or a political nominating convention: "All I have in heart, in mind, and in strength—myself—I give to this work to which God has called me. Will you help me, men? My colleagues will you help me? In the name of the college we love, I greet you." This prompted a demonstration lasting several minutes that had "never been equalled in the college chapel."[142]

Shanklin's inaugural address placed heavy emphasis on personality. Speaking earnestly from a text considerably more coherent than his usual awkward, gushing, and murky prose, Shanklin put faculty at the center of the collegiate enterprise. Through a faculty with "power in personality," more than through books or curriculum, he argued, a college should produce students with "the will and determination to be of service." Faculties of "scholarly and courageous and believing personalities" would enable colleges to "instill a deeper discipline, a higher manhood, and a more intelligent patriotism than we have at present." The speech made appropriate gestures to all the other constituencies and particularly reassured those who supported the deepening and broadening influences that carried Wesleyan beyond narrow sectarianism. Quotations from more than a dozen sources provided a scholarly patina. Immediate and long-term memories of the event appropriately yielded vivid impressions of the personality rather than the ideas of this bespectacled minister. A trustee recalled almost two decades later the contagious enthusiasm of the new president, "his whole frame responding to the fire that burned within him . . . his voice vibrant with his ambition for Wesleyan."[143]

Personalities attending the inauguration on a warm, sunny day in early November 1909 gave the event its larger meaning. President William Howard Taft, Vice-President James S. Sherman, and Senator Elihu Root were the featured guests. Their speeches and presence yielded praise for Shanklin and endorsement of Wesleyan as an important college in New England. Shanklin and Wesleyan were clearly connected to a Republican establishment fresh from its fourth consecutive victory in presidential politics. Republicans had close ties with the financial and business communities of the East to which Wesleyan would increasingly turn for students and support.[144]

With what special efforts and effect did Shanklin assemble this roster of Republican power and respectability? He met Taft en route to Minneapolis during the campaign of 1908, when he was invited to travel in the presidential candidate's private car. Taft took a liking to Shanklin, whose brother served the Republican administration as a diplomat in Central America. A few weeks after the trustees elected Shanklin, he informed Taft of his coming inauguration, saying, "I covet beyond expression an address from you on that occasion." Taft declined, but Shanklin persisted until shifts of date from June to October to November yielded a time convenient for Taft's schedule. After being greeted with a gala parade in Middletown, Taft offered remarks before the installation audience of more than one thousand alumni, trustees, students, faculty, and invited guests packing the Middlesex Opera House. He congratulated Wesleyan for acquiring a president who had both pedagogical understanding and executive ability. Sherman and Root joined Melancthon W. Stryker, president of Hamilton College, in attesting to the status of their fraternity brother as the worthy "son" of a venerable eastern college. Loyally and discreetly declining to separate fact from fiction, they told Wesleyan what it needed to believe.[145]

As Wesleyan's glorious inaugural festivities ended shortly before midnight with undergraduates giving a silver loving cup to Shanklin, Olin was able to count many benefits for Wesleyan. Chosen to speak for the

Taft button commemorating William
Howard Taft's visit to Wesleyan for the
inauguration of William A. Shanklin

alumni that morning, Olin used the occasion to hail the evolution of a
Wesleyan "grown stronger, richer, less austere, more tolerant, broader in
aim and sympathy." He then heard the new president echo those sentiments. Olin also had early indications that Shanklin's background and
personality would enable Wesleyan to reap whatever remained of Methodist support while nurturing new connections to the Republican circles of middle-class America. Urged by the chair of the search
committee and the board to stage an inauguration that would announce
Wesleyan's "new era—one of growth and glory," Olin's planning committee spared no expense. In return, Wesleyan reaped enormous benefits in terms of a bright new public image widely disseminated.
Articles in the metropolitan press from Philadelphia to Boston proclaimed a new era for Wesleyan.[146]

Securing Foundation Recognition

Olin knew, as he basked in the inaugural glow produced by fellow Republicans, that Wesleyan needed one more form of recognition to confirm a new identity. Efforts had begun three years earlier to have Wesleyan's stature enhanced by grants from the new philanthropic foundations that were rapidly becoming arbiters of collegiate prosperity and respectability.[147] Only the imprimaturs of Carnegie and Rockefeller would bring fast-moving developments in Middletown to a fully successful conclusion.

The Carnegie Foundation for the Advancement of Teaching, established in 1905, received credit from Olin for "furnishing an occasion" to review and revise Wesleyan's charter amendment of 1870. Andrew Carnegie set up his foundation with initial funding of $10 million to provide pensions for college professors, "the least rewarded of all professions." He excluded from participation in the foundation's retirement system, however, private institutions that were "under control of a sect," or required "Trustees (or a majority thereof), Officers, Faculty, or Students to belong to any specified sect." Since Wesleyan's charter stipulated that the president and a majority of trustees and faculty must be Methodist, there was no chance of joining the select group of fifty American colleges and universities admitted, as of October 1906, to Carnegie membership. Additional criteria imposed by the Carnegie board to promote standards of quality in American higher education gave the group considerable prestige. Members were generally the nation's stronger institutions, particularly those located in the Northeast. Wesleyan's continued absence would be conspicuous.[148]

Potential loss of prestige was one of five major reasons for Wesleyan to initiate charter revision in 1906. For two years the deficit-ridden budget had carried pension payments to the recently retired Van Vleck and the permanently disabled Atwater. Bradford Raymond's declining health indicated he might soon join the list of institutional responsibilities. Carnegie membership could stop the growth of this new budget item. The anticipated search for a new president would be limited by the denominational restriction. Recruitment of faculty during the 1906/07 academic year faced similar constraints; non-Methodist faculty had reached a level just one position below the less-than-fifty-percent limit.[149] Most important, the development of metropolitan values and corresponding changes in campus life had prepared alumni for initiatives to de-emphasize the denominational element of institutional identity.

Whereas the Wesley Bicentennial in 1903 was a bow to denominational heritage, the seventy-fifth anniversary celebration in 1906 was a tribute to Wesleyan alumni. All but one of the speakers were graduates. More than three-fourths of the twenty-one honorary degrees went to alumni. Over five hundred alumni and alumnae attended. Plans for the event included organizing a system of class secretaries and raising an alumni fund of $200,000. It was a time for alumni to "hold undisputed sway." Sports, fraternities, and singing had prominent places on the program. In this five-day celebration the episode of greatest significance for Wesleyan's future occurred at the Alumni Association meeting. Alumni on the faculty, through printed page and public address, had recently been drawing a contrast between the liberality of Wesleyan's 1831 charter and the "backward steps" into sectarianism taken with the charter revision of 1870. Roswell S. Douglass '61, a Boston manufacturer and active Methodist layman, moved that the Alumni Association ask the trustees "to petition the Legislature to amend the charter of the University so as no longer to require membership in the Methodist Episcopal Church as a qualification for holding a position as Trustee, President of the University, or member of the Faculty." Soon after a minister from New Jersey raised the single voice of opposition, saying he "did not think it was wise or expedient to draw away from the church which had founded and fostered the institution," alumni opinion in favor of the charter change filled Memorial Chapel "with a thunder of 'ayes.'"[150]

Wesleyan's trustees integrated the alumni request into deliberations begun two years earlier on several unrelated charter revisions. In consultation with Henry S. Pritchett, president of the Carnegie Foundation for the Advancement of Teaching, a trustee committee removed the Methodist membership stipulation of 1870 regarding the president and a majority of trustees and faculty; restricted the Methodist-conference-elected trustees to no more than a fourth of the board; and added a statement forbidding any denominational test in selection of trustees, officers, teachers, or students. The newly revised charter of 1907 met little discernible opposition. The text secured approval by the board and the legislature during a two-week period in June. There were some sensitivities to be soothed and a stir of dissent in the denomination, but the major problem following charter revision was with the Carnegie board, not the Methodists.[151]

When Wesleyan applied for Carnegie membership in November 1907, foundation trustees were learning with some embarrassment the difference between de jure and de facto in the relationship between colleges and denominations. Another Methodist institution, Randolph-Macon

Woman's College of Lynchburg, Virginia, had been admitted in March after its president persuaded Pritchett that the college's self-perpetuating board was legally free of church control and ready to make a declaration of this freedom to the Virginia Methodist Conference. A stormy reaction in the conference that fall encouraged denominational opposition that finally forced Randolph-Macon's trustees to relinquish their independence and Carnegie membership in 1909. Early in the course of this unpleasant episode the Carnegie trustees became wary of any institutional ties to a denomination, even if there were no legal stipulations of church control. They responded to Wesleyan's application by notifying Bradford Raymond in late December that election of thirteen trustees by Methodist conferences, although not constituting denominational control, "conveys to the public mind the impression of denominational control." Admission to Carnegie membership would not be granted until Wesleyan's trustees found it "desirable to discontinue this formal denominational connection."[152]

Unprepared to make a full and final break with the denomination, Wesleyan's trustees began to assess long-term damage that would accrue from the Carnegie rejection. Raymond reported in April that he encountered "serious embarrassment" in faculty recruitment. In June the board resolved to develop its own system for faculty pensions. The blow to Wesleyan's prestige was hardest of all. All the leading colleges of New England except Brown held positions on the accepted list. Carnegie's board was fast becoming "the national unofficial accrediting agency for colleges and universities." It was time for Wesleyan's most prestige-minded trustee to enter the fray.[153]

Olin began a correspondence with Pritchett in early October 1908, writing as a Wesleyan graduate and trustee holding "deep interest in the result of your action." He pointed out that rejection of Wesleyan came from a board whose "decisions determine public opinion almost without appeal." Lack of Carnegie membership would leave Wesleyan "isolated, its prestige injured, its progress checked, and its influence impaired." Olin's polite, lawyerly argument in this letter and four subsequent responses to Pritchett's replies kept the focus on Wesleyan having met Carnegie's original published criteria. He slowly but surely backed the foundation president into an untenable position. Pritchett was a man much like Olin: son of a Methodist minister-educator, tall, handsome, gentlemanly, member of elite clubs. He surely sensed his predicament when Olin, informed that Carnegie action in Wesleyan's case would not come for at least a year, published the correspondence.[154]

While Olin suspended his efforts to "weary" Pritchett "by continual troubling" and to set him up for "crushing retort," Wesleyan received in early 1910 the promise of a matching grant from John D. Rockefeller's General Education Board. Provided by Rockefeller with a permanent endowment of $10 million in 1905, the board supplied generous aid to denominational colleges of high quality as well as to those on the Carnegie list. Additional Rockefeller gifts of $42 million by 1909 enabled the board to appropriate, as of 1914, more than $10 million in grants to about one hundred colleges and universities. They included Harvard, Yale, Brown, Amherst, Williams, and Bowdoin. Wesleyan joined this list when Shanklin, following up on earlier attempts by Raymond, obtained a promise of $100,000 if Wesleyan raised $900,000 to increase its endowment.[155]

Encouraging news from Pritchett came just a week before learning about success with the General Education Board. He informed Shanklin that the Carnegie executive committee was ready to consider applications from colleges where denominational bodies appointed a minority of trustees. Shanklin immediately filed a new application. On 5 May 1910 the Carnegie trustees, on grounds that Wesleyan was "a college of educationally high type" with a board of "high-minded men" who could be trusted to honor the pledge to "undenominational administration" found in the charter of 1907, voted to admit Wesleyan to the privileges of the foundation. As soon as the meeting adjourned, Nicholas Murray Butler telephoned word of this "invaluable recognition" to his friend Olin.[156]

Along the trail of many decades in Olin's ambitions for Wesleyan, Butler's call signaled a shining moment in a landmark year. Alumni still had a link in 1910 to Wesleyan's founding decade through Rev. Bostwick Hawley '38, the last living graduate with a diploma signed by Willbur Fisk. Yet Olin could see the new Wesleyan represented in a particularly appropriate toast, at the Washington's birthday celebration of 1910, to alumni in the "Metropolis." He was also aware that well over a hundred alumni were listed in *Who's Who in America*. Faculty had a link to the days of Olin's father through a masterful teacher, John Van Vleck, now emeritus. Yet Olin could use evidence from the first edition of Cattell's *American Men of Science* to applaud the substantial scholarly tradition sustained by the faculty of 1910. Student demography reflected a departure from earlier decades, with an all-male entering class in 1909/10 that was more than 15 percent larger than any previously admitted. Olin would soon see this nascent growth spurt carry Wesleyan enrollments to the level of Amherst in 1914 and almost to that of Williams a year later. And he probably voted affirmatively in the trustee decision of late 1910 to reposition Wesleyan through a tuition increase from $125 to the $140 charge just set at Amherst and sustained at Williams since 1904. Trustees had a tie to the Fisk years through George G. Reynolds '41, but Olin's law partner, John C. Clark '86, became a member of the board in April 1910 and would be elected to lead this body two years later. The days of Daniel Curry, when Methodists could claim Wesleyan as "the crown and glory of our Church," were gone. At their annual meeting in June 1910, Olin's fellow trustees recorded their appreciation for his successful work in placing Wesleyan on Carnegie's list of accepted institutions. For this most recent contribution toward reshaping Wesleyan into a traditional male New England liberal arts college of high reputation, Stephen Henry Olin's colleagues gave him a warm and enthusiastic rising vote of thanks.[157]

An Act to incorporate the Wesleyan University

Sec. 1. Be it enacted by the Senate and House of Representatives in General Assembly convened, That Laban Clark, Thomas Birch, Heman Bangs, Isaac Kellogg, Aaron Sanford, Jr., James L. Phelps, John L. Smith, Willbur Fisk, Joseph A. Merrill, Abel Bliss, Abraham Avery, John W. Hardy, Isaiah Fisk, William R. Shafter, George W. Stanley, Elijah Hubbard, Henry L. Dekoven, Jonathan Barnes, Wm. L. Storrs, Samuel D. Hubbard, and Isaac Webb, and their successors in office, forever be, and they are hereby incorporated, and made, created, and constituted a corporation, and body politic, by the name and style of "The Wesleyan University," for the sole and exclusive purpose of establishing, organizing, maintaining and conducting a university or collegiate Institution, in the city of Middletown, of as high an order as the said corporation shall deem fit and proper; and by that name shall be, and are hereby, made capable in law to purchase, have, hold, receive, possess and enjoy estate, real, personal and mixed, of every kind, and nature whatsoever, to an amount not exceeding 200,000 dollars, exclusive of the collegiate buildings, libraries and apparatus, and the same to sell, grant, convey, alien, demise, manage, and dispose of at pleasure; to sue and be sued, plead and be impleaded, defend and be defended, in any and all courts; and also to make, have and use, a common seal, and the same to alter, break and renew at pleasure; to ordain, establish and execute such by-laws, ordinances, rules and regulations, as shall to them seem necessary, expedient or convenient, for the wise ordering and conducting the affairs and government of said corporation, not being contrary to the laws of the United States, or of this State; and generally to do and execute all, and singular the acts, matters

The Public Statute Laws of . . . Connecticut . . . 1831 (Hartford: Charles Babcock, 1831), 346–49.

and things, and to transact all business which to them shall, or may appertain, tending to promote the usefulness and prosperity of said institution, subject and according to the rules, limitations, conditions and restrictions, herein after provided.

Provided, That no by-law or ordinances, shall be established by said corporation, which shall make the religious tenets of any person, a condition of admission to any privilege in said university; and that no president, professor or other officer shall be made ineligible for, or by reason of any religious tenets, that he may profess, nor be compelled by any by-laws or otherwise, to subscribe to any religious test whatever.

Sec. 2. All the estate and property of the said corporation, shall be managed for, and on behalf of, the New York annual conference, the New England annual conference, [and] the New Hampshire and Vermont annual conference, of the Methodist Episcopal Church, in the United States of America, or for and on behalf of the above named conferences, and such other annual conferences, as the conferences aforesaid may associate with them, or with the consent and agreement of the three annual conferences, first above mentioned, for and in behalf of the general conference of the said Methodist Episcopal Church, by the persons aforesaid, and such others as shall or may in pursuance of the provisions of this act, be added to their number, and their successors forever, who are hereby constituted a board of trustees for the purposes aforesaid.

Sec. 3. Nine members of said board of trustees, shall constitute a quorum for the transaction of business, except for the disposal of real estate, or for the election of trustees, for either of which purposes, there shall be at least a majority of the whole number of trustees; and such majority shall have power, at any legal meeting, by a major vote of those present, to fill any vacancy or vacancies in the board, or increase the number thereof, provided the whole number of said board, shall not at any time exceed thirty nine; and also by a vote of two thirds of those present, to remove any member of said board, whom they shall judge to be deficient in competency and faithfulness, in the discharge of his official duty, or in moral character.

Sec. 4. The three annual conferences first specified in the second section of this act; or they together with such other annual conferences as shall be associated with them in pursuance of the provisions of said second section; or the said general conferences of the Methodist Episcopal Church, with the consent and agreement of the said three conferences first above mentioned, may elect, in such manner, at such times, for such periods, and in such proportions as shall by them be mutually agreed upon, a board of Visitors not exceeding in number the board of trustees, who shall with said board of trustees constitute a joint board, to which said joint board it shall appertain, and power and authority is hereby conferred and granted to elect, by a majority of the votes of those convened, the president and faculty of the said university, or institution; to frame, ordain and enact by-laws, ordinances, rules and regulations; to prescribe the course of study in said university, or institution; to direct and act in all other matters that relate to the proper regulation, government, discipline and instruction of the students, and to manage all the affairs of the said corporation, and to execute all the powers, and privileges given by this charter, and not vested in the said board of trustees: Provided that a majority of the said joint board, shall in all cases be necessary to constitute a board for the transaction of business.

Sec. 5. The president for the time being, of the said university and institution, shall have power to confer degrees, and grant diplomas, in such form and for such persons, as may be approved, by a majority of the faculty, and a majority of the joint board of trustees, and visitors; which diplomas shall entitle their possessors respectively, to all the immunities and privileges, which, either by usage or by statute, are allowed to possessors of similar diplomas, from any other university, college, or seminary of learning.

Sec. 6. This act is hereby declared to be a public act, and shall be construed liberally, for every beneficial purpose hereby intended; and no omission to use any of the privileges hereby granted, shall cause a forfeiture of the same; nor shall any gift, grant, conveyances or devise, to or for the benefit of the corporation, be defeated or prejudiced, by any misnomer, misdescription, or informality whatever, provided the intention of the parties can be shown or ascertained, beyond reasonable doubt.

Sec. 7. And be it further enacted, That the funds which may, at any time, belong to the institution, now incorporated, shall enjoy the like exemption from taxation, and the institution itself, and its officers and students, shall enjoy the same privileges, and exemptions, as having already been granted to Yale College, its officers, and its funds. Provided, however, That the corporation shall never hold in this State, real estate free from taxation, affording an annual income of more than six thousand dollars; and provided also, that the private property of the officers of the institution, shall not be exempt from taxation.

Sec. 8. The Reverend Laban Clark is hereby authorized to fix the

time, and place, and give the notice, for the first meeting of said board
of trustees, and of said joint board of trustees and visitors.

Martin Welles

Speaker of the House of Representatives

Robert Fairchild

President of the Senate, pro tem.

May 26th, 1831—Approved.

John S. Peters.

President	Elected	Assumed Duties	Presidency Ended
Fisk	24 Aug. 1830	Dec. 1830	22 Feb. 1839
Bangs	20 Jan. 1841	Feb. 1841	2 Aug. 1842
Olin[a]	2 Aug. 1842	Sept. 1842	16 Aug. 1851
Smith	3 Aug. 1852	Aug. 1852	5 Aug. 1857
Cummings	5 Aug. 1857	Mar. 1858	22 June 1875
Foss	28 July 1875	Sept. 1875	22 June 1880
Beach	22 June 1880	July 1880	30 June 1887
Raymond	19 Nov. 1888	June 1889	24 June 1908
Shanklin	13 Nov. 1908	June 1909	7 Sept. 1923
McConaughy	18 Oct. 1924	Feb. 1925	12 Apr. 1943
Butterfield[b]	15 Sept. 1943	Sept. 1943	30 June 1967
Etherington	30 June 1966	July 1967	7 Feb. 1970
Campbell	19 Oct. 1970	Oct. 1970	31 July 1988
Chace	23 July 1988	Oct. 1988	

[a] Olin was president-elect from November 1839 to January 1841, but illness prevented him from assuming duties of the office.

[b] Butterfield served as acting president from September 1942 to September 1943.

Appendix 3.
Enrollments at
Wesleyan, Amherst,
and Williams,
1831–1990

	Wesleyan		Amherst		Williams	
Fall	Total	First-year	Total	First-year	Total	First-year
1831	48	NA	195	60	120	34
1832	60	NA	227	72	128	39
1833	70	NA	239	85	126	20
1834	95	NA	243	70	119	33
1835	111	NA	252	76	121	31
1836	120	34	259	76	119	26
1837	135	36	206	50	120	25
1838	152	49	189	37	135	29
1839	147	24	169	38	129	34
1840	133	23	157	52	143	49
1841	123	24	142	44	144	34
1842	112	31	129	32	150	30
1843	110	19	124	32	146	35
1844	105	25	121	34	155	38
1845	119	28	118	34	168	43
1846	125	29	120	35	176	35
1847	118	26	150	50	177	42
1848	124	29	166	52	179	44
1849	102	21	176	53	163	27
1850	116	33	182	40	179	42
1851	117	28	190	63	208	59
1852	103	23	195	57	203	41

Fall	Wesleyan		Amherst		Williams	
	Total	First-year	Total	First-year	Total	First-year
1853	117	31	201	56	231	62
1854	123	37	237	66	231	58
1855	116	31	218	54	224	57
1856	151	54	229	64	225	51
1857	149	31	221	66	212	50
1858	148	24	235	74	229	71
1859	138	39	242	67	240	56
1860	135	39	220	53	233	56
1861	150	52	235	78	212	53
1862	150	33	220	60	169	35
1863	132	36	202	50	182	40
1864	112	30	212	45	187	43
1865	121	43	203	54	177	31
1866	131	45	225	70	186	50
1867	138	33	244	73	182	57
1868	148	41	251	65	173	46
1869	153	51	255	75	159	35
1870	163	49	261	71	141	32
1871	153	47	244	62	119	23
1872	189	55	268	82	119	44
1873	189	47	303	94	136	41
1874	180	48	325	108	160	52
1875	176	62	335	84	170	43
1876	184	50	320	75	191	56
1877	172	46	325	85	204	67
1878	163	45	333	92	208	62
1879	164	46	345	111	206	67
1880	163	51	337	82	227	72
1881	184	61	343	96	253	88
1882	191	62	352	82	249	69
1883	201	54	321	71	274	85
1884	202	51	334	103	252	58
1885	193	55	352	100	255	66
1886	194	60	330	68	289	95
1887	190	54	348	93	281	73
1888	218	66	355	93	282	77
1889	230	57	343	103	311	86

	Wesleyan		Amherst		Williams	
Fall	Total	First- year	Total	First- year	Total	First- year
1890	250	74	347	73	308	80
1891	266	70	330	85	351	115
1892	271	89	355	123	336	100
1893	273	74	403	134	317	96
1894	288	91	414	100	300	81
1895	301	87	419	118	307	112
1896	307	90	403	101	328	98
1897	327	100	369	98	324	92
1898	331	104	376	122	341	87
1899	339	99	364	102	326	89
1900	350	103	393	124	326	104
1901	320	76	399	116	322	86
1902	322	103	385	109	347	113
1903	332	99	408	122	384	142
1904	305	90	406	129	396	124
1905	338	99	455	172	418	134
1906	328	99	469	177	446	160
1907	316	88	508	197	452	156
1908	322	102	524	172	454	162
1909	340	119	527	174	506	195
1910	367	133	494	144	534	225
1911	377	111	462	137	530	197
1912	393	119	422	112	517	171
1913	407	140	416	134	491	160
1914	433	174	411	120	495	182
1915	473	167	391	119	508	185
1916	468	154	480	167	549	186
1917	376	163	364	124	432	180
1918	387	171	374	132	480	199
1919	552	198	493	146	554	184
1920	538	183	497	169	577	222
1921	532	201	519	170	583	213
1922	520	204	523	179	630	240
1923	541	223	547	168	690	252
1924	584	237	599	211	744	277
1925	593	214	677	233	757	283
1926	599	204	699	234	774	266

Fall	Wesleyan Total	First-year	Amherst Total	First-year	Williams Total	First-year
1927	599	211	748	232	812	273
1928	603	201	723	197	798	233
1929	575	199	684	201	814	225
1930	583	198	672	209	802	230
1931	595	202	638	191	800	225
1932	601	215	686	201	764	222
1933	612	204	754	239	743	195
1934	616	201	778	229	789	253
1935	645	216	838	243	822	257
1936	654	224	837	225	819	252
1937	674	231	837	232	822	229
1938	737	244	872	240	818	248
1939	731	217	846	241	825	248
1940	737	209	850	241	837	264
1941	717	218	870	273	869	285
1942	635	216	799	252	831	264
1943	Academic programs and calendars altered to meet wartime					
1944	needs; enrollments by term too varied to yield meaningful					
1945	annual totals.					
1946	833	251	1154	430	1059	390
1947	909	231	1161	254	1223	277
1948	901	200	1202	275	1126	274
1949	855	220	1189	265	1127	282
1950	831	236	1051	267	1017	290
1951	757	204	1047	299	1045	311
1952	734	208	1022	263	1046	272
1953	733	198	1047	272	1058	278
1954	739	203	1056	254	1061	280
1955	760	206	1055	307	1042	290
1956	720	185	1058	280	1049	287
1957	742	226	1044	255	1069	289
1958	746	228	1025	259	1103	302
1959	792	249	987	260	1105	289
1960	874	264	1003	271	1127	288
1961	950	293	1025	273	1122	287
1962	987	294	1029	274	1137	304
1963	1043	307	1072	302	1160	302

	Wesleyan		Amherst		Williams	
Fall	Total	First-year	Total	First-year	Total	First-year
1964	1122	346	1162	312	1176	323
1965	1223	385	1201	305	1229	323
1966	1296	357	1214	318	1225	320
1967	1367	361	1210	304	1226	334
1968	1367	333	1224	309	1245	339
1969	1327	331	1208	313	1275	334
1970	1393	382	1204	319	1322	342
1971	1480	432	1206	325	1534	473
1972	1547	442	1226	312	1667	482
1973	1810	564	1272	340	1763	473
1974	1947	546	1277	308	1834	478
1975	2182	582	1292	292	1861	483
1976	2239	569	1468	425	1913	499
1977	2390	610	1496	386	1895	481
1978	2428	575	1452	379	1947	501
1979	2453	598	1517	395	1969	491
1980	2585	644	1545	405	1991	506
1981	2619	642	1541	391	2009	510
1982	2701	646	1521	366	2005	500
1983	2749	656	1508	390	2057	513
1984	2767	652	1520	427	2030	510
1985	2794	680	1525	431	2037	508
1986	2804	683	1550	408	2047	510
1987	2789	645	1601	443	2036	507
1988	2843	676	1581	368	2061	544
1989	2873	684	1558	421	2063	520
1990	2821	666	1587	407	1960	507

Note: These data for full-time undergraduate students are drawn from annual catalogue summaries reporting fall enrollment for the year indicated. First-year enrollment numbers indicate students listed as fully qualified for the "freshman class," and they include students who enrolled a year earlier but are not yet qualified for sophomore standing. Total enrollment numbers do not include graduate students, special students (usually part time) or those "provisionally enrolled."

Archivists at Amherst and Williams assisted in the collection and verification of data.

Abbreviations
Used in Notes

MG	*Middlesex Gazette*, Middletown, Conn.
MH	*Methodist History*
MNEC	*Minutes of the New England Conference*
MNYC	*Minutes of the New York Conference*
MNYEC	*Minutes of the New York East Conference*
MP	*Middletown Press*, Middletown, Conn. (1884–1918 as the *Penny Press*)
MR	*Methodist Review* (title varies), New York
MTyC	*Minutes of the Troy Conference*
MVtC	*Minutes of the Vermont Conference*
MYB	*Methodist Yearbook* (published prior to 1880 as the *Methodist Almanac*)
NAW	*Notable American Women*, ed. Edward T. James, 3 vols. (Cambridge: Harvard University Press, 1971)
NCAB	*National Cyclopedia of American Biography*, 76 vols. (New York: James T. White, 1892–1984)
NYH	*New York Herald*
NYT	*New York Times*
NYTr	*New York Tribune*
OP	*Olla Podrida*. Due to irregularities in year listed on title page and in dates of publication, citations refer to the graduation year of the seniors in a particular volume (e.g., '87) and to the volume and page (e.g., 29:14).
PWW	*The Papers of Woodrow Wilson*, ed. Arthur S. Link, 64 vols. (Princeton: Princeton University Press, 1966–91)
SAC	*Special Acts of the Connecticut General Assembly, 1789–1909*, 15 vols. Almost all citations for actions of the Connecticut legislature are to this series of multiyear, cumulative volumes. In the case of a resolution not included in this series, citation is to the annual publication of legislative acts, giving year and page.
WA	*Wesleyan Argus* (1868–87 as the *College Argus*)
WAR	*Wesleyan Alumni Record*
WLM	*Wesleyan Literary Monthly*
WOR	*Wesleyan Obituary Record*
WUA	*Wesleyan University Alumnus*
WUB	*Wesleyan University Bulletin*
WUC	*Wesleyan University Catalogue*
WWA	*Who's Who in America*
WWAM	*Who's Who in American Methodism*, comp. and ed. Carl F. Price (New York: E. B. Treat, 1916)
ZH	*Zion's Herald* (title varies), Boston

Manuscript Sources

AAM	Alumni Association Minutes, 1836–1916
APP	Alden Partridge Papers, Manuscript Division, Library of Congress
ARL	Annual Report of the Librarian
ARP	Annual Report of the President

Note: To achieve maximum economy in references to this frequently used source, it is cited, even for the years when it is in manuscript (1832–75), with punctuation normally used for periodical publications. In published form it is sometimes a pamphlet addressed to the trustees and sometimes a circular addressed to the Methodist conferences.

ASP	Augustus Smith Papers, Special Collections and Archives, Olin Library, Wesleyan University
AWP	Alexander Winchell Papers, Michigan Historical Collections, University of Michigan
AWSP	Augustus William Smith Papers, Special Collections, John Hay Library, Brown University
BTM	Board of Trustees Minutes

From 1890 to 1914 minutes of the trustees were published, but information on salaries and a few other confidential matters was not included in the published version.

CDFP	Cyrus D. Foss Papers
CF	Coeducation File
CFATR	Carnegie Foundation for the Advancement of Teaching Records, Rare Book and Manuscript Library, Columbia University
CRMG	Chronological Record of Major Gifts made to Wesleyan, 1831–1981, compiled by David B. Potts and Anne-Michele Mortimer
CTWP	Caleb T. Winchester Papers
EXCM	Executive Committee Minutes, 1871–1909
FM	Faculty Minutes
GEBF	General Education Board Files, Rockefeller Archives Center, North Tarrytown, New York
JBM	Joint Board Minutes
JCP	Joseph Cummings Papers
MLR	Middletown Land Records, City Hall
MSA	Middletown Scientific Association Papers
NCAR	Nineteenth Century Administrative Records
NEMHS	New England Methodist Historical Society Collection, School of Theology Library, Boston University
NMBP	Nicholas Murray Butler Papers, Rare Book and Manuscript Library, Columbia University
OFP	Olin Family Papers

PCM	Prudential Committee Minutes
PFMD	Papers of Frederick M. Davenport, RG4 Maxwell School, Syracuse University Archives
RAC	Records of the Academic Council (after 1910, Records of the Advisory Committee)
RAM	Record of the Acts of Middletown, City Hall
REC	Reports of the Examining Committees (NCAR, Box 12)
RSC-GA	Records of the State of Connecticut—General Assembly, Connecticut State Library Archives
R1939	Recollections solicited by the Alumni Council in 1939
TDB	Trustee Data Base, a collection of biographical information on the 535 trustees serving on Wesleyan's board during the years 1831–1991, comp. David B. Potts and Deirdre C. Stiles
UMA	United Methodist Archives and History Center, Drew University
VF	Vertical Files of documents on an individual, organization, building, or topic
WFP	Willbur Fisk Papers
WNRD	William North Rice Diary
WNRP	William North Rice Papers
WOAP	Wilbur Olin Atwater Papers

Names Frequently Used

ALS&MA	American Literary, Scientific, and Military Academy
BPR	Bradford P. Raymond
CDF	Cyrus D. Foss
CFAT	Carnegie Foundation for the Advancement of Teaching
CTW	Caleb T. Winchester
SHO	Stephen Henry Olin
SO	Stephen Olin
WAS	William Arnold Shanklin
WF	Willbur Fisk
WNR	William North Rice
WOA	Wilbur O. Atwater
WW	Woodrow Wilson

Notes

All unpublished materials, unless otherwise noted, can be found in the Wesleyan University Archives.

Graduates of Wesleyan are identified in the text by an apostrophe and the last two digits of the class year (e.g., '40 = 1840). Those who attended but did not graduate are identified by *n* and the full class year (e.g. n1840).

Notes

See Index of First Citations in Notes for location of full references.

Introduction

1. Hugh Hawkins, *Between Harvard and America: The Educational Leadership of Charles W. Eliot* (New York: Oxford University Press, 1972); Ronald Story, *The Forging of an Aristocracy: Harvard and the Boston Upper Class, 1800–1870* (Middletown: Wesleyan University Press, 1980); Marilyn Tobias, *Old Dartmouth on Trial: The Transformation of the Academic Community in Nineteenth-Century America* (New York: New York University Press, 1982); Louise L. Stevenson, *Scholarly Means to Evangelical Ends: The New Haven Scholars and the Transformation of Higher Learning in America, 1830–1890* (Baltimore: Johns Hopkins University Press, 1986); Mark A. Noll, *Princeton and the Republic, 1768–1822: The Search for a Christian Enlightenment in the Era of Samuel Stanhope Smith* (Princeton: Princeton University Press, 1989).

2. David Stameshkin, *The Town's College: Middlebury College, 1800–1915* (Middlebury, Vt.: Middlebury College Press, 1985). For a comprehensive survey of 210 works on American colleges and universities, see L. F. Goodchild and I. F. Huk, "The American College History: A Survey of Its Historiographic Schools and Analytic Approaches from the Mid-Nineteenth Century to the Present," in *Higher Education: Handbook of Theory and Research*, ed. John C. Smart, vol. 6 (New York: Agathon Press, 1990), 201–90.

Chapter 1 An Enterprising Spirit

1. Peter [D.] Hall, *Middletown: Streets, Commerce, and People, 1650–1981* (Middletown: Wesleyan University, 1981), 7–21; Margaret E. Martin, *Merchants and Traders of the Connecticut River Valley, 1750–1820* (Northampton, Mass.: Smith College, 1939), 55–57, 11; *Heads of Families at the First Census of the United States, Taken in the Year 1790: Connecticut* (Washington, D.C.: GPO, 1908), 9. During slow times after the War of 1812 a member of the Alsop family, in which earlier generations had prospered through trade with the West Indies, went to Philadelphia to make his fortune. Samuel Russell left for Canton, China, in 1819, with similar results, before returning to Middletown in 1831. See William Kerr and Nancy Campbell, "Notes" in Philip Trager, *Wesleyan Photographs* (Middletown: Wesleyan University Press, 1982), 28.

2. Karl P. Harrington, *The Background of Wesleyan: A Study of Local Conditions about the Time the College Was Founded* (Middletown: Wesleyan University, 1942), 1–6; Martin, *Merchants*, 208.

3. Glenn Weaver, *The History of Trinity College*, vol. 1 (Hartford, Conn.: Trinity College Press, 1967), chaps. 1–2; *SAC* 1:470; *AS* 13, 6 Aug. 1823. See also similar appeals in *MG* 24, 31 Mar. 1824. Special town meetings of 30 Mar., 21 Apr. 1824, RAM; *MG* 12 May 1824. This was not the first loss of a possible college. Middletown was briefly considered for the location of Yale in 1717. See Edwin Oviatt, *The Beginnings of Yale, 1701–1726* (New Haven: Yale University Press, 1916), 338–43.

4. William A. Ellis, comp. and ed., *Norwich University, 1819–1911*, vol. 1: *General History, 1819–1911* (Montpelier, Vt.: Grenville M. Dodge, 1911), 60; Steven E. Ambrose, *Duty, Honor, and Country: A History of West Point* (Baltimore: Johns Hopkins University Press, 1966), 44–61; Weaver, *History*, 53; Dean Paul Baker, "The Partridge Connection: Alden Partridge and Southern Military Education" (Ph.D. diss., University of North Carolina, Chapel Hill, 1986), 200; *AS* 12 May 1824.

5. *AS* 23 June, 14, 21 July 1824.

6. *AS* 13 Aug. 1823; special town meeting, 2 Aug. 1824, RAM.

7. Account book of the ALS&MA, 1824–33, Middlesex County Historical Society, Middletown, Conn.; *AS* 1 Sept. 1824; George Stanley to William Lyman, 28 Aug. 1824, with share subscription certificate, VF for ALS&MA; MLR 54:57–59. By late August 1825 acquisition of an additional 1.25 acres created a campus of thirteen acres owned by the newly incorporated proprietors of the academy (MLR 54:59–63). *AS* 8 Sept., 27 Oct. 1824.

8. The petition accompanying the proposed charter is dated 28 Apr. 1825 and is document 1 in folder labeled "Petitions and Resolves," box 6, RG2 RSC-GA. For the charter, granted 18 May 1825, see RSC-GA 15:195–97. MLR 54:62–63; *AS* 14 Sept. 1825; ALS&MA, *Catalogue* 1825/26, 4–12, 16–17; student register, APP.

9. George Ticknor to Alden Partridge, 1 Aug. 1826, VF for ALS&MA; Alden Partridge to General H. A. S. Dearborn, 12 Mar. 1827, Autograph File, Houghton Library, Harvard University; Harrington, *Background*, 34–51.

10. ALS&MA, *Catalogue* 1826/27, 13, 1827/28, 12; *To the Senate and House of Representatives of the United States* (single printed sheet signed by George W. Stanley, dated 9 Jan. 1826) plus letters to Alden Partridge from Stephen Van Rensselaer (20 Jan. 1826), George E. Whales (20 Jan. 1826), James Hamilton (25 Feb. 1826), Alden Partridge Papers, Norwich University Library; documents 10–18, folder 16, box 6, Rejected bills, 1825–26, and documents 12–16, folder 24, box 7, Rejected bills, 1827–29, RG2 RSC-GA. Lotteries sanctioned by a legislature were a common form of state aid in the antebellum years. For a discussion of this practice in Massachusetts, see Oscar Handlin and Mary Flug Handlin, *Commonwealth, A Study of the Role of*

Government in the American Economy: Massachusetts, 1774–1861, rev. ed. (Cambridge: Harvard University Press, 1969), 68–69. Various documents from the subscription drive of August 1827, VF for ALS&MA; Baker, "Partridge," 265–90, 311, 164, 166; *AS* 25 July 1827; Anne Royall, *The Black Book; or A Continuation of Travels in the United States* . . . , vol. 2 (Washington: printed for the author, 1828), 77–79. Comments by a British visitor in October 1827 were almost as caustic. See Basil Hall, *Travels in North America in the Years 1827 and 1828*, vol. 2 (London: Simpkin and Marshall, 1829), 197–200; ALS&MA, *Catalogue* 1827/28, 13, 38.

11. By mid-May 1828 one of Partridge's chief supporters in New York City had made plans for his grandson to transfer to another academy. The academy in Middletown, he observed a month later, "declines weekly." See *Letters from John Pintard to His Daughter* . . . , *1816–1833*, vol. 3 (New York: New-York Historical Society, 1941), 32–34, 89. *MG* 18 June, 22 Oct. 1828, 25 Mar. 1829; David Gould to WF, 11 Apr. 1829, WFP, box 3; *AS* 24 Sept., 26 Nov. 1828; correspondence for December 1828–June 1829, APP; Ellis, *Norwich*, 69–72.

12. Royall, *Black Book*, 75; *MG* 4 Aug. 1830; J. G. Woodward, "Currency and Banking in Connecticut," *The New England States*, vol. 2 (Boston: D. H. Hurd, 1897), 652, 657; *MG* 25 June 1828; town meeting of 27 Oct. 1828, RAM; Harrington, *Background*, 4; *MG* 30 Apr., 25 June, 3 Sept. 1828; letters to Samuel D. Hubbard from Samuel Russell (29 Jan., 13 Dec. 1828), Ithiel Town (6 Sept. 1828), David Hoadley (20 Oct. 1828), VF for Russell House; *MG* 24 Dec. 1828.

13. Edwin Gaustad, *Historical Atlas of Religion in America* (New York: Harper & Row, 1962), 52; Winthrop S. Hudson, "The Methodist Age in America," *MH* 12(April 1974): 11; Sydney A. Ahlstrom, *A Religious History of the American People* (New Haven: Yale University Press, 1972), 373.

14. Sylvanus M. Duvall, *The Methodist Episcopal Church and Education up to 1869* (New York: Teachers College, Columbia University, 1928), 17, 21; *Journals of the General Conference of the Methodist Episcopal Church, 1796–1836*, vol. 1 (New York: Carlton Phillips, 1855), 207–8; Donald M. Scott, *From Office to Profession: the New England Ministry, 1750–1850* (Philadelphia: University of Pennsylvania Press, 1978), chap. 4; James W. Fraser, "Randolph-Macon College, Wesleyan University—Methodist Schools: A Case Study in the Founding of Antebellum Colleges" (Paper presented at the annual meeting of the Society for Historians of the Early American Republic, Waltham, Mass., July 1983), 15–16.

15. Willbur Fisk's name is spelled in some publications (and even on his tombstone) as "Wilbur" Fisk. The name *Willbur* was the family name of his maternal grandmother. He was named for her (Holdich, *Life*, p. 19). *Journals of the General Conference* 1:356; *CA* 13 June 1828; Joseph Holdich, *The Life of Willbur Fisk, D.D., First President of the Wesleyan University* (New York:

Harper, 1842), chaps. 1–10. Regarding Fisk's election to the position at Wesleyan Academy 28 Sept. 1825 and his part-time pursuit of duties there until spring 1826, see David Sherman, *History of the Wesleyan Academy at Wilbraham, Mass., 1817–1890* (Boston: McDonald and Gill, 1893), 88–105. Donald G. Tewksbury, *The Founding of American Colleges and Universities Before the Civil War* (New York: Teachers College, Columbia University, 1932), 104. For an analysis of the motives for this activity, see Duvall, *Methodist*, 80–83.

16. Hudson, "Methodist Age," 14.

17. Laban Clark, untitled and undated account of the founding of Wesleyan University, 1, Laban Clark Papers, box 1; Edwin Warriner, *Old Sands Street Methodist Episcopal Church, of Brooklyn, N.Y. . . . Biographical* (New York: Phillips and Hunt, 1885), 232–36; *MG* 5 Nov. 1828; *The Autobiography and Journal of Rev. Heman Bangs*, ed. by his daughters (New York: N. Tibbals, 1872), 303; MLR 65:225.

18. *M* 24 Nov. 1860; *Autobiography of Bangs*, 163–67, 301–3; *To the Public* (single printed sheet signed by Heman Bangs et al., dated 4 Feb. 1828), Records of the First Methodist Church, storage room, First United Methodist Church, Middletown; *The First Methodist Church, Middletown, Connecticut . . . , 1791–1966* (n.p., 1966), 8–9. Bangs's forceful preaching style is described in *CM*, 85.

19. Sherman, *History*, 131–34, 139–40; *ZH* 31 Aug. 1892; Clark, untitled account, 1; *CA* 16 Jan. 1829.

20. David D. Field, *Centennial Address* (Middletown: W. B. Casey, 1853), 158; Martin, *Merchants*, 179–81; *Commemorative Biographical Record of Middlesex County, Connecticut* (Chicago: J. H. Beers, 1903), 21; *AS* 13 Aug. 1823; special town meeting of 2 Aug. 1824, town meeting of 5 Oct. 1829, RAM; *AS* 17 Aug. 1825; *MC* 17 Apr. 1844, 22 Nov. 1845; Betsy H. Potts, "'A Flourishing College Will . . . Build Up a Town': The Twelve Local Trustees of Wesleyan University, 1830–1840" (Paper written for Social Studies 637, Wesleyan University, 1986), app. A; *WAR* (1883), 347, 87. For additional information on the six Yale graduates, see chap. 3 n36.

21. Testimony to initiative taken by Middletown residents and to their provision of indispensable initial funding for the founding of Wesleyan can be found in writings of the three Methodists closest to the process: Clark, untitled account, 1; *Autobiography of Bangs*, 301–3; Willbur Fisk, *Wesleyan University*, one folded sheet, two leaves (Birmingham, Eng.: Richard Peart, 1836), 1 (in Fisk file, UMA). See also the informative letter written from Middletown by David Gould, a Boston lawyer and boyhood friend of Fisk, 11 Apr. 1829, WFP, box 3. Towns played an important role in the founding and early development of antebellum colleges. For an analysis of this role at another New England institution, see Stameshkin, *Town's College*.

22. Clark, untitled account, 1–3; Journals of the New York Annual Con-

ference 13:162, Methodist Episcopal Church Records, Rare Books and Manuscripts Division, New York Public Library; *CA* 1 Jan. 1830; A Journal of the New England Conferences, Commencing June 29 AD 1822[–1835], Daniel Fillmore, secretary, entry for 16 June 1829, UMA; WF to Laban Clark, 12 Sept. 1829, rpt. in Frederick A. Norwood, "More Letters to Laban Clark," *MH* 11(October 1972): 31–32; *Autobiography of Bangs*, 304; report of the joint committee to the conferences, 12 May 1830, NCAR, box 1, folder 2.

23. Clark, untitled account, 2; *Autobiography of Bangs*, 303–4.

24. *MG* 15 July 1829; *Autobiography of Bangs*, 303–4; Norwood, "More Letters," 31–32; minutes of a meeting of the ALS&MA proprietors, 17 July 1829, Papers of Elijah Kent Hubbard (1812–1839), Norwich University Library; Henry DeKoven to the joint committee, 20 July 1829, NCAR, box 1, folder 3; Harrington, *Background*, 60–62; Susan Brewer to Ruth Fisk, 29 Sept. 1829, WFP, box 1; Henry DeKoven to the joint committee, 1 Dec. 1829, NCAR, box 1, folder 3; town meetings of 5, 16 Oct. 1829, RAM; Thomas Burch to Laban Clark, 3 Nov. 1829, Laban Clark Papers, box 2.

25. Clark, untitled account, 3–4; draft of the joint committee report on recommendations adopted 3 Dec. 1829, WFP, box 9; Henry DeKoven to the joint committee, 15 Dec. 1829, NCAR, box 1, folder 3; report of the joint committee, 12 May 1830, NCAR, box 1, folder 2; T. B. Ransom to Alden Partridge, 20 Mar. 1830, APP; Journals of the New York Conference 14:16, 28; A Journal of the New England Conferences, entry for 25 May 1825; report of the New Hampshire and Vermont Conferences, 29 June 1830, NCAR, box 1, folder 2; Elijah Hubbard to Alden Partridge, 13 May 1830, APP.

26. Report of the joint committee; *Articles Agreed Upon by the . . . Conferences* (single sheet, ca. July 1830), NCAR, box 1, folder 1; *CA* 11 June 1830.

27. *MG* 15 July 1829; Samuel Eliot Morison, *Three Centuries of Harvard, 1636–1936* (Cambridge: Harvard University Press, 1936), 167; Brooks Mather Kelley, *Yale: A History* (New Haven: Yale University Press, 1974), 241–42, 275; Walter C. Bronson, *The History of Brown University, 1764–1914* (Providence: Brown University, 1914), 155–58; John C. French, *A History of the University Founded by Johns Hopkins* (Baltimore: Johns Hopkins University Press, 1946), 4; draft of the joint committee report; Tewksbury, *Founding*, 32–54. *The* was capitalized in the charters of Wesleyan and Johns Hopkins.

28. Report of the joint committee; *Articles Agreed*; F[itch] Reed, *Wesleyan University* (single sheet [1833]); Frederick Rudolph, *The American College and University: A History* (New York: Knopf, 1962), 190–92.

29. Bronson, *History of Brown*, 500–507; Jurgen Herbst, *From Crisis to Crisis: American College Government, 1636–1819* (Cambridge: Harvard University Press, 1982), esp. 48.

30. *Articles Agreed*. The original manuscript charter, officially signed into law by Governor Peters 26 May 1831, is document 54, folder labeled "1831,

Public Acts, Resolves, Petitions Granted," box 14, RG2 RSC-GA. The first published text is in *The Public Statute Laws of . . . Connecticut . . . , 1831* (Hartford: Charles Babcock, 1831), 346–49. The charter was accepted by the trustees 20 Sept. 1831 and by the Joint Board 10 Oct. 1832. Trustee membership grew to an antebellum high of 35 in 1860.

31. Conference committee reports regarding the election of trustees and visitors, NCAR, box 1, folder 2; JBM 24–26 Aug. 1830.

32. JBM 24–26 Aug. 1830; Potts, "Flourishing College," app. A.

33. JBM 24–26 Aug. 1830; petition for the charter of 1831. This petition accompanying the proposed charter is dated 9 May 1831 and is document 34, folder labeled "Petitions Granted," box 14 RG2 RSC-GA. *MG* 25 May 1831; *Public Statute Laws*, 349; Tewksbury, *Founding*, 32–39; Colin B. Burke, *American Collegiate Populations: A Test of the Traditional View* (New York: New York University Press, 1982), 18. A high rate of college founding resumed in 1870 and continued to 1900 (Burke, *American*, 223).

34. Herbst, *Crisis*, 241; Burke, *American*, 18; David B. Potts, "American Colleges in the Nineteenth Century: From Localism to Denominationalism," *HEQ* 11(Winter 1971): 363–80 and "'College Enthusiasm!' as Public Response, 1800–1860," *Harvard Educational Review* 47(February 1977): 28–42.

35. Saul Sack, *History of Higher Education in Pennsylvania*, vol. 1 (Harrisburg: Pennsylvania Historical and Museum Commission, 1963), 158–61; Ernest A. Smith, *Allegheny: A Century of Education, 1815–1915* (Meadville, Pa.: Allegheny College History Company, 1916), 69–72; John D. Wright, Jr., *Transylvania: Tutor to the West* (Lexington, Ky.: Transylvania University, 1975), 160; Walter B. Posey, "La Grange, Alabama's Earliest College," *Wesleyan Quarterly Review* 1(1964): 3–24; Burke, *American*, 25.

36. For various views on the presence of sectarianism at antebellum colleges, see the general comments of Richard Hofstadter and the charter-related interpretations of Walter Metzger in *The Development of Academic Freedom in the United States* (New York: Columbia University Press, 1955), chap. 5, 293–303; David B. Potts, *Baptist Colleges in the Development of American Society, 1812–1861* (New York: Garland, 1988); Robert E. Engel, "Non-Sectarianism and the Relationship of the Methodist Church in Iowa to Upper Iowa College and Iowa Wesleyan College" (Ph.D. diss., University of Iowa, 1969); Potts, "American Colleges," 363–69; James Findlay, "Agency, Denominations, and the Western Colleges, 1830–1860: Some Connections between Evangelicalism and American Higher Education," *Church History* 50(March 1981): 64–81. Wesleyan's charter (1831), section 1, follows very closely the wording in the Washington (now Trinity) College charter (1823), section 7 (*SAC* 1:469–71). On Randolph-Macon, see Roberta D. Cornelius, *The History of Randolph-Macon Women's College* (Chapel Hill: University of North Carolina Press, 1951), 11; James E. Scanlon, *Randolph-Macon College: A Southern History, 1825–1967* (Charlottesville: University Press of Virginia, 1983), 31.

37. Willbur Fisk, *The Science of Education: An Inaugural Address, Delivered at the Opening of the Wesleyan University, in Middletown, Connecticut, September 21, 1831* (New York: M'Elrath and Bangs, 1832), 3; *CA* 30 September 1831. On the popularity and influence of public addresses, see Donald M. Scott, "The Popular Lecture and the Creation of a Public Mind in Mid-Nineteenth-Century America," *Journal of American History* 66(March 1980): 805–6. Frederick Rudolph, *Curriculum: A History of the American Undergraduate Course of Study since 1636* (San Francisco: Jossey-Bass, 1977), 76–84; *An Exposition of the System of Instruction and Discipline Pursued in the University of Vermont*, 2d ed. (Burlington, Vt.: Chauncey Goodrich, 1831), 3–27; Gabriel P. Disosway to WF, 22 Sept. 1830, WFP, box 2; Theodore Dwight Woolsey to WF [ca. 5 Nov. 1831], WFP, box 6; Holdich, *Life*, 235. Holdich is almost certainly incorrect regarding Fisk probably lacking awareness of ideas discussed at the Convention of Scientific Gentlemen held in New York City in October 1830. Fisk visited New York several times in late fall and winter 1830–31 and was in contact with his friend Disosway, who was deeply involved in the convention (Gabriel P. Disosway to WF, 22 Sept., 7 Nov. 1830, 25 Jan. 1831, WFP, box 2). Also, a lengthy review of the *Proceedings* in New York City appeared in the *MR* 13(April 1831): 160–89. John Emory, editor of the *Review*, participated in the convention from the start (Norwood, "More Letters," 32–33) and was in frequent contact with Fisk on a variety of matters in the early 1830s.

38. Rudolph, *Curriculum*, 76; Codman Hislop, *Eliphalet Nott* (Middletown: Wesleyan University Press, 1971), 209–33; Eliphalet Nott, *Counsels to Young Men . . . Union College* (New York: Harper, 1840), 278, 292, 309, 277; WF to Ruth Fisk, 21 Apr. 1828, WFP, box 7.

39. Fisk, *Science*, 6; Willbur Fisk, *Introductory Address, Delivered at the Opening of the Wesleyan Academy, in Wilbraham, Mass., November 8, 1825*, 2d ed. (Boston: T. R. Marvin, 1826), 5, 7, 21; Walter B. Kolesnik, *Mental Discipline in Modern Education* (Madison: University of Wisconsin Press, 1958), 11; Rudolph, *Curriculum*, 68.

40. *Reports on the Course of Instruction in Yale College; by a Committee of the Corporation and the Academical Faculty* (New Haven, Conn.: Hezekiah Howe, 1828), 6, 31, 15, 33, 34.

41. *MG* 28 Jan. 1829; Potts, "Flourishing College," app. A; Bryant Franklin Tolles, Jr., "College Architecture in New England before 1860 in Printed and Sketched Views," *Antiques* (March 1973), 504–7; Paul V. Turner, *Campus: An American Planning Tradition* (Cambridge: MIT Press, 1985), 38–42; *CA* 12 Feb. 1830; *Articles Agreed; CA* 29 July 1869; James Mudge, *History of the New England Conference of the Methodist Episcopal Church, 1796–1910* (Boston: New England Conference, 1910), 77.

42. WF to Marcia Knowlton, 31 Dec. 1830, WF to Susan Brewer 10 Aug. 1831, WFP, box 7.

43. Bruce A. Kimball, *Orators and Philosophers: A History of the Idea of Liberal Education* (New York: Teachers College Press, 1986), chaps. 1–5; Fisk, *Science*, 11. Fisk was using the concept of benevolence just a few years before doubts developed regarding its theological viability. See Perry Miller, *The Life of the Mind in America: From the Revolution to the Civil War* (New York: Harcourt, Brace, 1965), 78–84.

44. Joseph Holdich, *The Wesleyan Student; or Memoirs of Aaron Haynes Hurd, Late a Member of The Wesleyan University, Middletown, Conn.* (Middletown: E. Hunt, 1839), 151; Samuel A. Seaman, *Annals of New York Methodism . . . to AD 1890* (New York: Hunt and Eaton, 1892), 254; Fisk, *Science*, 6; Holdich, *Life*, 38–42; Douglas Williamson, "The Rise of the New England Temperance Movement, 1823–1836," *MH* 21(October 1982): 17–28; Douglas Williamson, "Willbur Fisk and African Colonization: A Painful Portion of American Methodist History," *MH* 23(Jan. 1985):79–98.

45. Fisk, *Science*, 9–11, 16–18. The theological positions advanced by Jacobus Arminius of Holland during the Reformation and the terms using his name to identify these positions were often employed by such Methodists as Fisk in their debates with the New England Calvinists on the role of moral agency and the larger complex issue of free will versus predestination. On Fisk's religious Arminianism see "Rev. Willbur Fisk, D.D." *MR* 64(January 1882): 203–4; George Prentice, *Wilbur Fisk* (Boston: Houghton, Mifflin, 1890), chap. 6. Fisk even speculated that heaven would be "a place of enterprise," where the "enterprising spirit is excited and exercised only with joyous wonder and ecstatic praise" (WF to Ruth Fisk, 14 Jan. 1831, WFP, box 7).

46. Fisk advocated classifying students by levels of achievement rather than by years in college, and he suggested granting degrees (other than the B.A.) to students successfully completing a nontraditional course of study (Fisk, *Science*, 19–22, 12–15).

47. For a somewhat different perspective on the "adroit" aspects of Fisk's inaugural address, see George Matthew Dutcher, *An Historical and Critical Survey of the Curriculum of Wesleyan University and Related Subjects* (Middletown: Wesleyan University, 1948), 10. *CA* 30 Sept. 1831; Fisk, *Science*, 24; David H. Markle, "Willbur Fisk, Pioneer Methodist Educator" (Ph.D. diss., Yale University, 1935), 77–78, 250; *CA* 14 Jan. 1831, 21 June 1839, 15 Jan. 1852; *MG* 28 Sept. 1831; Holdich, *Life*, 193–94; Mudge, *History*, 334.

48. *MR* 13(October 1831): 419–41; *CA* 28 Oct. 1831; PCM 20 Dec. 1831.

Chapter 2 An Earnest Education

1. Fisk, *Science*, 5–6, 8. For an exploration of similar efforts at other antebellum colleges, see James Findlay, "Agency," 64–80, esp. 78.

2. Fisk, *Science*, 4; Holdich, *Life*, 392–93; Robert T. Handy, *A Christian America: Protestant Hopes and Historical Realities*, 2d ed. (New York: Oxford

University Press, 1984), 27–28; Prentice, *Wilbur Fisk*, 244–46.

3. Holdich, *Life*, 45–46; *CA* 21 June 1839; Fisk, *Science*, 24.

4. Fisk, *Science*, 6–7; Joseph C. Burke, "Annals of Wesleyan University," in *WAR* (1883), lxxxiv; FM 25 Aug. 1836; Missionary Lyceum, records, 1834–71; *CA* 28 Mar. 1834, 24 Feb. 1837; Holdich, *Life*, 321.

5. *WUC* 1833/34, 17, 1835/36, 19; D. H. Meyer, *The Instructed Conscience: The Shaping of the American National Ethic* (Philadelphia: University of Pennsylvania Press, 1972), 7, 14–15.

6. PCM 28 Feb. 1839; JBM 6 Aug. 1839; *The Life and Letters of Stephen Olin, D.D. LL.D., Late President of the Wesleyan University*, vol. 1 (New York: Harper, 1853), 358–59; so to Laban Clark, 11 Nov. 1839, rpt. in Norwood, "More Letters," 37–39; JBM 20 Jan. 1841; Nathan Bangs, "Inaugural Address," *Classic* 2(December 1841): 1. Nathan's younger brother Heman was pastor of Middletown's Methodist church, 1827–29.

7. Abel Stevens, *Life and Times of Nathan Bangs, D.D.* (New York: Carlton and Porter, 1863), esp. 423; *ZH* 5 Jan. 1842; *CA* 19 May 1841; series of articles by Bangs in *CA* 7 Apr.–19 May 1841. A leader in early efforts to shape a more socially respectable Methodist denomination, Bangs "relentlessly advanced the cause of higher intellectual standards for the church." See Nathan O. Hatch, *The Democratization of American Christianity* (New Haven: Yale University Press, 1989), 201–4.

8. Bangs, "Inaugural," 2, 12; JBM 20 Jan., 3 Aug. 1841; *CA* 19 May 1841.

9. Assessment by Joseph Holdich in *Life of Olin*, 2:76–77; Stevens, *Life of Bangs*, 334; E. Stevens to Nathaniel C. Lewis (9 Apr. 1841), E. Otis Haven to Nathaniel C. Lewis (4 Apr. 1841), VF for Lewis '40. For a suggestion of some faculty discontent, see D. M. Reese to so, 9 Aug. 1842, OFP, box 1. Charles F. Stockwell to B. R. Hoyt, 12 July 1842, Nathan Bangs Papers; *ZH* 26 May 1841; Seymour Landon to so, 20 June 1842, OFP, box 1; MC 22 June 1842; JBM 2 Aug. 1842. Bangs also experienced the first deterioration of his health during his presidency and noted that his troubles in the spring and summer of 1842 "well nigh killed me" (*Life of Olin*, 2:43; Nathan Bangs to so, 20 Aug. 1842, OFP, box 1). After leaving the Wesleyan presidency, Bangs served as a pastor and then presiding elder in the New York City area. During ten years of retirement he also served as a trustee of Wesleyan. He died in 1862.

10. John Quincy Adams, *Diary*, 1 Jan. 1845–10 Aug. 1846, Microfilms of the Adams Papers, pt. 1, reel 48 (Boston: Massachusetts Historical Society, 1954), 5 Jan. 1845. This quotation is made by permission of the Society. For a description of Olin's preaching that tells more about "his fervid spiritual enthusiasm" and "heat of spiritual feeling," see *ZH* 16 Dec. 1896. *WA* 4 Mar. 1881; *ZH* 1 Oct. 1851; *The Works of Stephen Olin, D.D., LL.D., Late President of the Wesleyan University*, vol. 2 (New York: Harper, 1852), 125, 200, 240–53; *CA* 8 Jan. 1845.

11. The best sources of biographical data on Olin are *Life of Olin*, 2 vols.; *Works of Olin*, 2 vols.; and John McClintock, "Stephen Olin," *MR* 36(January 1854): 9–33. Scanlon, *Randolph-Macon*, 51–57; *CA* 24 July 1841; JBM 2 Aug. 1842; *CA* 11 Dec. 1851; *Works of Olin*, 2:106.

12. *Life of Olin*, 1:314, chap. 8; *Works of Olin*, 2:466–75; *ZH* 15 Feb. 1843, 25 July 1894, 8 Aug. 1849, 20 Aug., 24 Sept. 1851.

13. Lawrence Cremin, *American Education: The National Experience, 1783–1876* (New York: Harper & Row, 1980), 67–69, 383–84; Handy, *Christian America*, 42–56.

14. JBM 16 Oct. 1851; *DAB* 6:589; G. R. Crooks, *Life and Letters of the Rev. John McClintock, D.D., LL.D., Late President of Drew Theological Seminary* (New York: Nelson and Phillips, 1876), chap. 6; Caleb T. Winchester, "Wesleyan's Third President," *WUA* 3(October 1918): 13. For additional information on the candidacies of McClintock, Smith, and Holdich, see letters to McClintock from James Floy (16 Oct. 1851), John Johnston and all Wesleyan students (17 Oct. 1851), John M. Reid (20 Oct. 1851), and Harvey B. Lane (21 Oct. 1851), John McClintock Papers, Special Collections Department, Robert W. Woodruff Library, Emory University; Ruben H. Loomis to John Johnston 10, 21 Oct., 4 Dec. 1851, John Johnston Papers; *CA* 4 Dec. 1851. John McClintock to James Floy, 24 Nov. 1851, VF for Floy '35. On McClintock's health and his editorship of *MR*, see Charles D. Cashdollar, *The Transformation of Theology, 1830–1890: Positivism and Protestant Thought in Britain and America* (Princeton: Princeton University Press, 1989), 124–25.

15. JBM 3 Aug. 1852. A mathematics teacher at Adrian College wrote to Smith in 1884 (he died in 1866) asking for help with a problem in Smith's textbook (G. B. McElroy to A. W. Smith, 27 Feb. 1884, AWSP).

16. *ZH* 2 May 1866. Smith often worried about his health (A. W. Smith to Louisa Meacham, 6 Mar. 1847, AWSP). *MR* 49(January 1867): 101; *CA* 12 Aug. 1846; *ZH* 11 Aug. 1852; *MR* 49(January 1867): 100; *CA* 3 May 1866; Winchester "Wesleyan's Third," 12–13; *CA* 30 Sept. 1852; *ZH* 8 Aug. 1855.

17. For evidence that Smith's lack of clerical status was an issue when he was selected and when he was dismissed, see J. Floy to A. W. Smith (12 Sept. 1851), D. W. Clark to A. W. Smith (9 Aug. 1856), AWSP; Perry C. Smith to Catherine Smith, 21 Oct. 1851, ASP; "Lay Educators," *Litchfield Journal* 26 Aug. 1857, clipping in AWSP. *MR* 49(January 1867): 101; H. Bannister "Augustus W. Smith, LL.D." *Northwestern Christian Advocate* 18 Apr. 1866; *CA* 19 Aug. 1852; JBM 3 Aug. 1852.

18. *ZH* 23 July 1868; *JGC* (1852), 166; *ZH* 3 May 1854, 10 Aug. 1853; *CA* 19 Feb. 1857; JBM 6 Aug. 1856; A. W. Smith to Anna Smith, 19 Sept. 1857; AWSP; To the Joint Board of Trustees and Visitors, petition signed by sixty-two students and presented 4 Aug. 1857, ASP; *ZH* 12 Aug. 1857. Although opposition to Smith seemed to appear suddenly in late spring

1857, rumor of a change in the presidency was present several months before (E. O. Haven to Alexander Winchell, 1 Mar. 1857, AWP). For descriptions of Smith's strenuous efforts to raise funds, see A. W. Smith to Catherine Smith, 30 June 1853, AWSP. Smith taught at the United States Naval Academy from 1859 until his death in 1866.

19. JBM 5 Aug. 1857; *DAB* 2:596; *ZH* 31 Mar. 1858.

20. *ZH* 31 Mar. 1858, 14 May 1890; George Prentice, "Joseph Cummings," *WOR* (June 1890), 7; *ZH* 2 Dec. 1863; WNRD 8 Sept. 1861; *DAB* 2:596.

21. *"Faithful unto Death": Addresses in Memory of Joseph Cummings, D.D., LL.D., President of Northwestern University* (Evanston, Ill: n.p. [ca. 1890]), 27, 29; *CA* 19 Aug. 1858. For other comments on Cummings's preaching style, see *M* 26 July 1862, 29 July 1865; WNRD 22 June 1861; *CA* 27 July 1865; *MR* 76(November 1894): 851; *ZH* 14 May 1890; *CA* 28 July 1870.

22. WNRD 2 Aug. 1864; *CA* 23 July 1868; Joseph Cummings, "Introduction," in M. L. Scudder, *American Methodism* (Hartford, Conn.: S. S. Scranton, 1867), viii; Stevenson, *Scholarly Means*, 9, chap. 4; Thomas Le Duc, *Piety and Intellect at Amherst College, 1865–1912* (New York: Columbia University Press, 1946), 27–34; Frederick Rudolph, *Mark Hopkins and the Log: Williams College, 1836–1872* (New Haven: Yale University Press, 1956), chap. 5; Joseph Cummings, *The Object of Life . . . , 1846* (Poughkeepsie, N.Y.: Journal and Eagle, 1846), 6; Joseph Cummings, "The True Dignity of Human Nature, and the Evidences of Man's Progress Towards It," *Southern Repertory and College Review* 1(December 1851): 148, 153. Cummings used Joseph Butler's *Analogy of Religion*, a classic reconciliation of reason and faith, in his course for seniors. He edited a version published in 1875 that was designed to make Butler more easily read and understood by students. WNRD 2 Aug. 1864; *ZH* 23 July 1868; *CA* 23 July 1868. Cummings continued his interest in social issues long after leaving Wesleyan. See, e.g., Joseph Cummings, "Capitalists and Laborers," *Proceedings of the American Association for the Advancement of Science . . . , 1886* (Salem, Mass.: Published by the Permanent Secretary, 1887), 339–53.

23. *"Faithful Unto Death,"* 9; Cummings, *Object,* 6, 20; Joseph Cummings, *Believers Partakers of the Cup and the Baptism of Jesus Christ . . . April 16, 1854* (Boston: George C. Rand, 1854), 27; *ZH* 29 June 1859; Joseph Cummings, "Address," *Addresses at the Inauguration of Rev. Cyrus D. Foss, D.D. . . . , October 26, 1875* (Middletown: Pelton and King, 1876), 11; Joseph Cummings, "The Reign of God a Source of Joy," in Davis W. Clark, comp., *The Methodist Episcopal Pulpit . . . Church* (New York: Lane and Scott, 1848), 322–25; *ZH* 14 May 1890.

24. Fisk, *Science,* 9, 11; "Collegiana," *CL* 2(August 1841): 94–95; *Works of Olin,* 2:189; Joseph Cummings, "On Endowment of Our Educational Institutions," in *Methodist Centenary Convention . . . Boston, June 5–7, 1866* (Boston: B. B. Russell, 1866), 52.

25. Fisk, *Science*, 12–13; Bangs, "Inaugural," 2; *Works of Olin*, 2:314; *ZH* 27 Aug. 1851; *Life of Olin*, 2:445.

26. G. P. Disosway, "The Wesleyan University—Dr. A. W. Smith," *MR* 49(January, 1867): 101; Augustus W. Smith, *An Elementary Treatise on Mechanics* . . . (New York: Harper, 1849), i; M. Eugene Culver '75, 1939; WNR to William Rice, 26 Jan. 1862, WNRP; Caleb T. Winchester, undated text of a talk on Joseph Cummings, 3, JCP; "*Faithful Unto Death*," 22, 33; *CA* 28 July 1870; *M* 14 May 1870. Stevenson finds that the New Haven scholars rejected the "old-time college of mental discipline and religious revival" (*Scholarly Means*, 5). A continuing allegiance to mental discipline at Wesleyan to 1870 stands in contrast to her findings for antebellum Yale.

27. David Allmendinger, *Paupers and Scholars: The Transformation of Student Life in Nineteenth-Century New England* (New York: St. Martin's Press, 1975), chap. 7.

28. Bronson, *History of Brown*, 182–92; Fisk, *Science*, 19; *Works of Olin*, 2:289–93. For evidence that even Olin could be viewed on occasion by some students as "the old Autocrat" and as heavy-handed in discipline, see diary of Alexander Winchell, 31 May 1847, AWP.

29. Nathan Bangs, *A Discourse on* . . . *Wilbur Fisk* . . . , *29th of March, 1839* (New York: T. Mason and G. Lane, 1839), 23; "Collegiana," *CL* 2(July 1841): 46; Erastus O. Haven, *Autobiography of Erastus O. Haven, D.D., LL.D., One of the Bishops of the Methodist Episcopal Church*, ed. C. C. Stratton (New York: Phillips and Hunt, 1883), 60–63; E. O. Haven, "Reminiscences of 1838–42," *WA* 18 Dec. 1879; Charles F. Stockwell to B. R. Hoyt, 12 July 1842, typescript, VH for Stockwell '43; FM 24, 26, 31 May, 11, 15, 16, 17 June 1842; MC 2 June 1842; Seymour Landon to SO, 20 June 1842, OFP, box 1. Another perspective on disciplinary disorders in spring 1842 can be found in Asa Kent to Nathan Bangs, 13 May 1842, Nathan Bangs Papers. William J. Foss, valedictory address, 7 Aug. 1856, CFP, box 9; Carl F. Price, *Wesleyan's First Century* (Middletown: Wesleyan University, 1932), 97. For an indication of student interest in the campaign, see Young Men's Republican Club of Wesleyan, Record Book, 1855–56; diary of James O. Longstreet '57, 27 Oct., 3 Nov. 1856. FM 8, 22, 24 Sept. 1856, 3, 6 Apr. 1857; Longstreet diary, 6, 22 Sept. 1856; Robert L. Mathison, undated note probably written about ten years after his graduation, VF for Mathison '60; Charles C. Adams, "Wesleyan When Young," *MP* 25 Mar. 1925; To the President [August 1856], AWSP; To the Joint Board. Almost three-fourths of the petitioners belonged to the Young Men's Republican Club; a little less than two-thirds of the student body were club members.

30. *ZH* 31 Mar. 1858; WNR to E. H. Rice, 18 June 1864, WNR to William Rice, 3, 5, 6 June 1865, WNRP; WNRD 31 May, 1, 7, 8 June 1865; SHO to Julia M. Olin, 20, 22 June 1865, OFP, box 6; JBM 18, 19 July 1865; *ZH* 12, 26 July 1865; *CA* 27 July 1865; *ZH* 14 May 1890. For student reminiscences on the

impact of Cummings as a disciplinarian, see Winchester, undated text on
Cummings, 4; Charles Bennett in *Faithful Unto Death*, 13.

31. Fisk, *Science*, 9.

32. Fisk, *Science*, 16: Le Duc, *Piety*, 8; Rudolph, *Hopkins*, 127–28;
Stameshkin, *Town's College*, 112–13; FM 10 Sept. 1835; *WAR* (1883), xxix,
entry for Jacob Huber; Charles C. Sellers, *Dickinson College: A History*
(Middletown: Wesleyan University Press, 1973), 176; George M. Dutcher,
"William Magoun . . ." (Unpublished paper, 1948), 4, 10, George Dutcher
Papers; Robert A. McCaughey, "The Transformation of American Aca-
demic Life: Harvard University, 1821–1892," *Perspectives in American History*
8(1974): 329; *CA* 27 Dec. 1839; Cummings, "Endowment," 52; Caleb T.
Winchester, manuscript tribute to Calvin S. Harrington, ca. 1886, VF for
Harrington '52; "James Cooke Van Benschoten," *WA* 22 Jan. 1902; *Tributes to
Professor William North Rice* (n.p.: Wesleyan Alumni Council [ca. 1915]), 40.

33. Le Duc, *Piety*, 49; Rudolph, *Hopkins*, 53; Stameshkin, *Town's College*,
146–47. Omitted from this account is yet another alumnus, A. C. Foss '52,
who taught Latin and Hebrew, 1860–63.

34. *WAR* (1883), 8; *Tributes to Rice*, 22; Burke, "Annals," lxxxiv; *ZH* 11
Aug., 10 Nov. 1858, 2 Dec. 1863; ARP (1857):141–42; *CA* 18 Aug. 1847; *ZH*
27 Aug. 1851.

35. Draft of articles of organization for Wesleyan, ca. 1830, NCAR, box 1,
folder 4; "Laws and Rules . . . ," chap. 5, section 3, JBM 21 June 1859; WNR
to William Rice, 6 June 1863, WNRP; Augustus Smith et al., To the Trustees
of Wesleyan University, 5 Aug. 1845, ASP; FM 24 July 1854; JBM 1 Aug.
1854; FM 18 July 1855; ARP (1855):108; JBM 31 July 1855; *ZH* 25 July 1866;
PCM 16 Dec. 1836; *FEx* 1857–72; Claude M. Fuess, *Amherst: The Story of
a New England College* (Boston: Little, Brown, 1935), 80, 94, 210n; W. S.
Tyler, *History of Amherst College . . . , 1821–1871* (Springfield, Mass.:
Clark W. Bryon, 1873), 626; Rudolph, *Hopkins*, 11, 224; Stameshkin,
Town's College, 113, 158; Kelley, *Yale*, 143, 192–93, 242. Wesleyan faculty salaries were $800 to $1,000 in the mid-1830s, $1,000 to $1,400 in the
mid-1850s, $2,000 in 1866/67, and $2,500 in 1871/72. Presidents were
generally paid $500 more than professors (and had use of the president's
house) and less than half of what top lawyers and physicians earned in the
1850s (Burke, *American*, 270n60). Faculty recruitment and activity at
Wesleyan from 1831 to 1870 tend to support the view that the second and
third quarters of the nineteenth century constitute an early era for establishing an academic profession in America. For a statement of this position,
see Martin Finkelstein, "From Tutor to Specialized Scholar: Academic
Professionalization in Eighteenth- and Nineteenth-Century America,"
History of Higher Education Annual 3(1983): 99–121. For a discussion of
the emerging concept of career and its academic version in 1870, see Burton
J. Bledstein, *The Culture of Professionalism: The Middle Class and the Develop-*

ment of Higher Education in America (New York: W. W. Norton, 1976), 170–72.

36. For bibliographical data on the works referred to in this and the next paragraph, see *WAR* (1883), 529–668. Eugene Exman, *The Brothers Harper* . . . (New York: Harper & Row, 1965), 104, but cf. J. Henry Harper, *The House of Harper* . . . (New York: Harper, 1912), 69–70. The four Harper brothers were strong Methodists (*CM*, 428–30). They published works of and about Olin, Smith's textbook, and Harrington's text of three comedies by Plautus. Fisk's *Travels* (1838) had, by spring 1842, run through seven printings, with sales of more than eight thousand copies (Holdich, *Life*, 403). On the Olin versus Edward Robinson controversy, see *North American Review* 57(October 1843): 491–95 and 58(January 1844): 253–56; folder of correspondence concerning the controversy, OFP, box 2. On Johnston and Smith, see Stanley M. Guralnick, *Science and the Antebellum American College* (Philadelphia: American Philosophical Society, 1975), 104n39, 196–97, 212. In letters written throughout his career at Wesleyan, Smith contributed astronomical observations and thoughts on other matters to work done by scientists and mathematicians of national repute. See letters to Smith from Charles H. Davis, Joseph Henry, Benjamin Pierce, and others in AWSP.

37. WNRD 15 Sept. 1861, 12 Feb. 1864.

38. Morison, *Three Centuries*, 224–38; Kelley, *Yale*, 173; Le Duc, *Piety*, 14; Rudolph, *Hopkins*, 128; WNR to William Rice, 1 June 1863, WNRP; [William Henry Van Benschoten] *Concerning the Van Benschoten or Van Benschoten Family in America: A Genealogy and Brief History* (n.p., 1907), 145; SHO to Julia M. Olin, 14 Sept. 1863, OFP, box 6; WNRD 12 Apr. 1864; *ZH* 2 Dec. 1863; WNR to William Rice, 8 Feb. 1864, WNRP; William N. Rice, ed., *Personal History of the Class of 1865* (Brooklyn, N.Y.: E. B. Spooner, 1867), 20; *WAR* (1883), 210, 77.

39. "Van Benschoten"; "Personals," *WA* 24 Apr. 1883; Burton H. Camp, "Billy Rice" (Talk given at the Eclectic Fraternity, June 1953), VF for WNR; Winchester, "Wesleyan's Third," 12.

40. For the full range of this editorial campaign, see issues of *M* 10 Sept. 1864–7 Jan. 1865, particularly 22 Oct., 5 Nov. 3, 10, 31 Dec. 1864, and 7 Jan. 1865; *New England Methodist Centenary Convention* . . . *Held in Boston, June 5–7, 1866* (Boston: B. B. Russell, 1866), 61–62, 84.

41. On the harmonious relation between science and religion in these years, see Theodore Dwight Bozeman, *Protestants in the Age of Science: The Baconian Ideal and Antebellum Religious Thought* (Chapel Hill: University of North Carolina Press, 1977). For Dana, see Stevenson, *Scholarly Means*, chap. 5. John Johnston, "Dana's Manual of Geology," *MR* 47(July 1865): 385; *Tributes to Rice*, 11; D. D. Whedon, "Inaugural Address," *MR* 16(January 1834): 19; Plautus, *Captivi, Trinummus, et Rudens*, ed. C. S. Harrington

(New York: Harper, 1870), iii; C. S. Harrington, "Our Colleges," *MR* 61(October 1879): 633.

42. Holdich, *Wesleyan Student*, 148; B[enjamin] H. Hall, *A Collection of College Words and Customs*, rev. and enlarged ed. (Cambridge, Mass.: John Bartlett, 1856), 202–3, 434; WNRD 5 Jan. 1864. Yale in the 1820s had more tutors than professors (Cremin, *National*, 404). Wesleyan usually had one tutor and occasionally two during its first two decades. They assisted only with freshman-level courses (Dutcher, *Historical*, 13). Among those who find the recitation method a major defect in nineteenth-century higher education are Kimball, *Orators*, 250; Rudolph, *Curriculum*, 69, 94, 146–47, 232–33; Stameshkin, *Town's College*, 71, 169; and Le Duc, *Piety*, 55, 119–20. Possibilities of an alternative interpretation are suggested in Kelley, *Yale*, 158–61, and Guralnick, *Science*, 74–75.

43. Holdich, *Life*, 321–22; *Works of Olin*, 2:283; *Life of Olin*, 1:189–90; *CA* 9 Aug. 1848. For a similar report, see *CA* 22 Aug. 1850. For a report on Cummings's use of the recitation method in the late 1860s, with its stress not on recall but as an "exercise in close thinking," see the address of Caleb T. Winchester in *Wesleyan University New York Alumni Association, Annual Banquet, January 10th, 1913* (n.p., 1913), 5–6. For a description of the use of examining committees, see text at chap. 2 n54.

44. Dutcher, *Historical*, 11; Thornton Page, *The Fisk Telescope* (n.p., 1968). The committee included graduates of Columbia, Amherst, and Bowdoin (*CA* 13 Aug. 1845). For a description of the use of examining committees, see text at chap. 2 n54. Wesleyan's curriculum embraced the standard subjects for American colleges of this period. See Douglas Sloan, "Harmony, Chaos, and Consensus: The American College Curriculum," *Teachers College Record* 73(December 1971): 232–47.

45. JBM 11 Oct. 1832, 27 Aug. 1833; PCM 9 Oct. 1833, 2 Oct. 1834; JBM 20 Jan. 1841, 3 Aug. 1841; Scanlon, *Randolph-Macon*, 60–61; Duvall, *Methodist*, 47–51; Dutcher, *Historical*, 14; FM 6 Mar., 17, 18 July 1855; ZH 11 Aug., 10 Nov. 1858, 2 Dec. 1863. Annual catalogues provide much of the information for this and subsequent paragraphs on the curriculum.

46. Fisk, *Science*, 15; Dutcher, *Historical*, 14; WAR (1883), 304–11.

47. *CA* 25 July 1850.

48. Morison, *Three Centuries*, 306; Rudolph, *Curriculum*, 135, 195; WA 15 July, 13 Oct. 1869; report of the examining committee [18 July 1866], NCAR, box 1, folder 9; JBM 18 July 1866; REC 1866; *CM*, 232; FM 10 June 1867, 8, 23 June 1868, 19 Mar., 8, 14 June 1869; JBM 15 July 1868, 13 July 1869; report of the committee on the course of study, 13 July 1869, NCAR, box 1, folder 9; ARP (1868):282; G. H. Palmer, "Possible Limitations on the Elective System," *Andover Review* 6(December 1886): 581; Stameshkin, *Town's College*, 201–2; George E. Peterson, *The New England College in the Age of the University* (Amherst, Mass.: Amherst College, 1964), 54, 56.

49. Interpretive issues regarding the role of student societies at antebellum colleges are illustrated by James McLachlan, "The Choice of Hercules: American Student Societies in the Early Nineteenth Century," in *The University in Society*, ed. Lawrence Stone, vol. 2 (Princeton: Princeton University Press, 1974), 449–94; Lowell Simpson, "The Development and Scope of Undergraduate Literary Society Libraries at Columbia, Dartmouth, Princeton, and Yale, 1783–1830," *Journal of Library History* 12(Summer 1977): 209–21; Rita S. Saslaw, "Student Societies in Nineteenth-Century Ohio: Misconceptions and Realities," *Ohio History* 88(Summer 1979): 192–210. Rudolph, *Hopkins*, 74, 102; Fuess, *Amherst*, 116; Le Duc, *Piety*, 119–20. Record books and catalogues of the literary societies at Wesleyan provide a wealth of information on their activities from 1831 to the late 1860s. FM 22 June 1847; PCM 14 Aug. 1839, 13 May 1841.

50. WNRD 15 Sept. 1861; so to Theodore Dwight Woolsey, 12 July 1850, Manuscript Collection of the Beinecke Library, Yale University; *CA* 28 Apr. 1841; *OP* '69, 10:4; Burke, "Annals," xcix; Thomas S. Harding, *College Literary Societies: Their Contribution to Higher Education in the United States, 1815–1876* (New York: Pageant Press, 1971), 262–73; Stameshkin, *Town's College*, 317n22; diary of Dexter Wright '45, 7 June 1843; "Opening of the Philorhetorian Society This Term," *CL* 1(November 1840): 196–97.

51. Frederick M. Davenport, *Address at the One Hundredth Anniversary of the Eclectic Society . . . , 1937* (n.p., n.d.), 2, 9; WNR to William Rice, 7 Sept. 1861, WNRP; Carl F. Price, *The Mystical Seven, Wesleyan University, 1837–1937* (Middletown: (n.p., n.d.), 12, 16, 22, 36; *OP* '66, 7:12; Karl P. Harrington, *A History of the Xi Chapter of the Psi Upsilon Fraternity* (Middletown: Xi Corporation, 1935), 11–12; Oscar M. Voorhees, *The History of Phi Beta Kappa* (New York: Crown, 1945), 357; Phi Beta Kappa, Gamma of Connecticut, minutes, 1845–1956; Natural History Society–Cuvierian Society, records, 1836–46; Missionary Lyceum, minutes, 1834–70, 8 June 1858; *CA* 25 July 1850.

52. "College Papers," *WA* 16 Mar. 1870; "Ourselves," *WA* 11 June 1868.

53. See appropriate archival boxes for programs of exhibitions and commencements. *CA* 29 Nov. 1839; *ZH* 26 May 1841, 29 June 1859.

54. For the view that public examinations at the typical antebellum college were largely "gestures in public relations," see Rudolph, *Curriculum*, 145–47. WUC 1836/37, 20; Jacob Huber, draft of an undated invitation letter, NCAR, box 1, folder 17; *ZH* 13 Aug. 1851. Disosway, a dry goods merchant in New York City, helped in the founding of Randolph-Macon College (*CM*, 974). Jeremiah Day to WF, 18, 29 July 1835, WFP, box 2; Benjamin Silliman, to WF, 6 July 1835, WFP, box 6; *ZH* 27 June 1860, 4 Sept. 1850; WNRD 29 July 1862; WNR to William Rice, 10 July 1863, WNRP; REC 1856, 1857, 1866, 1844; *CA* 27 July 1865, 22 Aug. 1850; REC 1860, 1864, 1859, 1869; *CA* 9 Aug. 1848. For a more skeptical assessment, see William

P. Lyon, journal of a trip to Middletown, Connecticut, summer, 1841, photostat, 19, 46–47.

55. *CL* 1(September 1840): 97–98; W[illbur Fisk], "The Wesleyan University," *Youth's Magazine* 1(January 1839): 297; *CA* 8 Jan. 1845. "Wesleyan in the Fifties," *OP* '92, 34:119. An exception would be Stephen Henry Olin, who "chartered a darkey" to clean his room (SHO to Julia M. Olin, 23 Jan. 1865, OFP, box 6). Wesleyan probably had fewer urban students than Harvard, Yale, Brown, and Trinity (Burke, *American*, 111–12). Holdich, *Life*, 395; *CA* 17 July 1840; *ZH* 19 Sept. 1838; Allmendinger, *Paupers*, 9; Frank W. Nicolson, "Age of Graduation, and Birthplaces, of Wesleyan University Graduates, 1831–1931," *WUA* 17(October 1932): 45. Fourteen was the minimum age for admission stated in the catalogue, and a few such as J. C. Keener '35 were admitted at an even younger age. Allmendinger, *Paupers*, chap. 1, 134–36, 138; Burke, *American*, chap. 3, 102. Compilations made from data in "Statistics Regarding the Alumni," *WUB* (June 1922): 30, were compared with those provided by Allmendinger, *Paupers*, 134–35. In the 1850s, 44.6 percent of Wesleyan's graduates were more than twenty-four years old.

56. Burke, *American*, 7; "Statistics Regarding the Alumni," *WUB* (December 1922):20. Yale and Trinity were also major importers of students from New York (Burke, *American*, 65, 78, 113). *CA* 21 Apr. 1841; *ZH* 25 Nov. 1863. For a similar first reaction on arrival to enter Wesleyan, see Alexander Winchell's letter to his brother, 9 Sept. 1844, AWP. [John Emery], "Education," *MR* 13(April 1831): 187–88; Burke, *American*, 57–60; Bledstein, *Culture*, 205–8.

57. "Wesleyan in the Fifties," 118–19; William Fairfield Warren, "Seventy Years Ago: A Picture of Wesleyan Life in 1852," *WA* 20, 23 Mar. 1922; REC 1865, 1869; *CA* 2 Dec. 1863, 20 Apr. 1854; *ZH* 11 Aug. 1858, 2 Dec. 1863. School teaching in the 1840s paid $5 per week and in the 1850s up to $15 per week (E. O. Haven, *Autobiography*, 68–69; Wright diary, 15 Oct. 1843; Alexander Winchell to Davis W. Clark, 1 Oct. 1844, AWP; Longstreet diary, 31 Dec. 1856; Allmendinger, *Paupers*, 91).

58. *OP* '69, 10:11–17; James E. Stiles, ed., *Seventy-Five Years of Gamma Phi* (Rockville Center, N.Y.: Review-Starr, 1942), 12–14; *OP* '61, 3:2.

59. Burke, "Annals," lxxxiv; WNR to Edward Rice, 13 Apr. 1862, WNRP; Daniel H. Chase to Morris B. Crawford, 6 May 1904, VF for Chase '33; SHO to Julia M. Olin, 20 Feb. 1864, OFP, box 6; Guy Lewis, "The Beginnings of Organized Collegiate Sport," *American Quarterly* 22(Summer 1970): 224; *OP* '58, 1:4, '61 3:4; WNRD 4, 7 Feb. 1864. Similar structures appeared at Williams in 1851 and Amherst in 1860 (Rudolph, *Hopkins*, 159; Fuess, *Amherst*, 197).

60. Frank W. Nicolson, ed., *Athletics at Wesleyan* (Middletown: Wesleyan University Alumni Council, 1938), 7; Rudolph *Hopkins*, 164; *OP* '61, 3:4;

"Base Ball," *WA* 11 June 1868; Agallian Base Ball Club, Middletown, Conn., scorebook, 1865–69, entry for 30 Sept. 1865; sho to Julia M. Olin, 3 May 1864, 27 Sept., 7 Nov. 1865, 5 June 1866, ofp, box 6.

61. For examples of discipline cases, see fm 9 July 1836, 25, 31 Oct. 1837, 15, 28 Apr. 1846, 29 Apr. 1851. Allmendinger, *Paupers*, chap. 7. Stameshkin finds a similarly quiet and serious student scene at Middlebury (*Town's College*, 98, 107–8, 181). For the student role in presidential departures, see text at chap. 2 n29. *ZH* 6 Oct. 1897; *CM*, 770; *DAB* 8:253–54; Richard S. Rust, comp., *Freedom's Gift; or, Sentiments of the Free* (Hartford, Conn.: S. S. Cowles, 1840). Another Wesleyan student of the 1840s who supported abolition was Gilbert Haven '46. For information on Haven's activities, see David E. Swift, "To Create an American Conscience," *WUA* 58(Fall 1973): 18–19; William B. Gravely, *Gilbert Haven, Methodist Abolitionist: A Study in Race, Religion, and Reform, 1850–1880* (Nashville, Tenn.: Abingdon Press, 1973), 21–26. For the intensity of student interest in the campaign of 1856, see text at chap. 2 n29. *ZH* 6 Oct. 1897.

62. "War Times at Wesleyan," *WA* 15 Mar. 1880; S. P. Hatfield, "Company G," in *Hartford of the First Connecticut Artillery . . . , 1862–1865* (Hartford, Conn.: Press of the Case, Lockwood and Brainard, 1893), 216–17; Samuel P. Hatfield, First Connecticut Artillery—Photographs, album covering 1861–65; [Fales G.] Newhall, "Wesleyan University in the War for the Union," *The Centennial, 1766–1866* (n.p., n.d.), 3; *ZH* 17 Oct. 1867. For data on other New England colleges, see Fuess, *Amherst*, 187–88; Rudolph, *Hopkins*, 216; Kelley, *Yale*, 198; Peter D. Hall, *The Organization of American Culture, 1700–1900: Private Institutions, Elites, and the Origins of American Nationality* (New York: New York University Press, 1982), 223–24. Section 7 in Wesleyan's charter of 1831 granted students "the same privileges and exemptions as have already been granted to Yale College." Since Yale's charter of 1745 "freed and exempted" students from military service, Wesleyan's undergraduates were not subject to the draft (*SAC* 1:472, 477). *ZH* 13 Aug. 1862; James M. McPherson, *Battle Cry of Freedom: The Civil War Era* (New York: Oxford University Press, 1988), 492–93. A carefully compiled roster of Wesleyan men in the Civil War lists 298 participants, ranging from the class of 1835 to that of 1877. See Lesley J. Gordon, "Roster of Wesleyan's Civil War Participants" (Unpublished MS, 1988). Two dozen of these Wesleyan men served in the Confederate Army. On Wesleyan's extensive ties with the antebellum South, see George F. Mellen, "Wesleyan University in the South," *MR* 85(July 1903): 593–605.

63. Charles Warren, "An Inquiry Concerning the Vital Statistics of College Graduates," in U.S. Bureau of Education, *Circular of Information for March, 1872* (Washington, D.C.: GPO, 1872), 19; *WAR* (1883), 385; David E. Swift, "Sense of Mission, White and Black, in the Jacksonian Era: Willbur Fisk and Charles Ray," (Unpublished MS, 1978), chap. 2; David E.

Swift, "O! This Heartless Prejudice," *WUA* 67(Spring 1984): 13–17; Jeffrey
H. Liss, "Attitudes toward Blacks and Immigrants at Wesleyan University,
1831–1920" (Honors thesis, Wesleyan University, 1986), app. 2; *ZH* 27 June
1860. Charles Henry Gardner, who entered in 1855, left during his senior
year (see *WAR* [1883], 437). Thomas Francis Barnswell '62, who entered in
1859, was variously described as "coloured" (Lee Claflin's Sunday journal,
20 July 1862, William and Mary Claflin Collection, Rutherford B. Hayes
Library, Fremont, Ohio), as "of African descent" (*ZH* 23 July 1862), and as
"mulatto" (U.S. Census for 1870). For the census notation, see *Population
Schedules of the Ninth Census of the United States, 1870* (Washington, D.C.: National Archives and Records Service, 1965), microfilm roll 114, Connecticut, vol. 9 (437–859) New London County, Stonington Borough, p. 31, line
39. Amos Beman, whose education was constrained by racism at Wesleyan
in 1833 (see text at chap. 3 n10), visited Barnswell in his dormitory room a
month before commencement in 1862. He viewed Barnswell as "another
star . . . of our race" (letter from Beman, probably to the *Weekly Anglo-
African*, 4 June 1862, clipping in the Amos Beman scrapbook 2:80, James
Weldon Johnson Memorial Collection, Beinecke Rare Book and Manuscript
Library, Yale University). WNR to Edward Rice, 7 Sept. 1861, 2 June 1862,
and WNR to William Rice, 12 Jan. 1862, WNRP; *ZH* 12 July 1865; *WAR*
(1881), 459. A similarly low level of diversity existed at Middlebury
(Stameshkin, *Town's College*, 108, 179–80). Edward Otheman, *The Christian
Student: Memoir of Isaac Jennison, Jr., . . . Letters* (New York: G. Lane and
P. P. Sanford, 1843), 39; *CA* 28 Apr. 1841; Field, *Centennial*, 181; Charles
Buck, *A Theological Dictionary* (Philadelphia: Joseph J. Woodward, 1831),
494; *CA* 12 Aug. 1846; *ZH* 1 Apr. 1846, 27 Sept. 1848; W. S. Tyler, *Prayer
for Colleges: A Premium Essay* (New York: M. W. Dodd, 1855), 136; *WA* 14
June 1871; Joseph Cummings to Albert S. Hunt, 20 Jan. 1862, letters to
Rev. Albert S. Hunt '51 on the subject of religion in colleges; *ZH* 27 Feb.
1867. For data on revivals at New England Colleges, see Allmendinger, *Paupers*, 119. Revivals involving Wesleyan students are reported for the years
1834, 1837, 1839, 1840, 1843, 1846, 1849, 1850, 1851, 1857, 1860, 1866,
and 1870. See Andrew A. Bushko, "Religious Revivals at American
Colleges, 1783–1860: An Exploratory Study" (Ed.D. diss., Teachers
College, Columbia University, 1974), 32; *CR* 1(March 1870): 107.

64. Karl P. Harrington, "The Singing College" (typescript, 10 Jan. 1935),
1–4, Harrington Papers; SHO to Julia M. Olin, 5 July 1863, 28 Feb. 1864,
OFP, box 6; *WA* 13 Oct. 1869; "Wesleyan University," *CR* 1(May 1870); *OP*
'91 33:80–83; class of 1859, class song for junior exhibition [1858],
exhibition programs; AAM 23 Aug. 1836; *WUC* 1864/65, 35; *ZH* 17 Oct.
1867; *CA* 11 Mar. 1869; *WA* 1 July 1869; "Wesleyan in the Fifties," 118.

65. Fisk, *Science*, 10; *ZH* 19 Sept. 1838; *Works of Olin*, 2:106; Holdich,
Wesleyan Student, 194; PCM 23 Aug. 1833, 26 Mar., 22 Apr. 1834, 5 Mar.

1835, 16 Oct. 1837, 16 July 1839; JBM 27 Aug. 1833; *WUC* 1835/36, 24, 1836/37, 23. Similarly brief experiences with the manual labor system can be found at Allegheny (Smith, *Allegheny*, 85, 90–92, 98–99, 133), Dickinson (Sellers, *Dickinson*, 216, 449), most Baptist colleges in the 1830s (Potts, *Baptist Colleges*, 216–24), and on quite a few other campuses (Rudolph, *American*, 217–18).

66. "Scenes In and About the Wesleyan University," *CL* 1(January 1841): 296. Data on careers of Wesleyan graduates are compiled from "Statistics Regarding the Alumni," *WUB* 16(June 1922): 26, and Frank W. Nicolson, "Occupations of Wesleyan University Graduates, 1831–1931," *WUA* 17(January 1933): 91. [Emory], "Education," 187–88; *Works of Olin*, 2:243; *CA* 18 Aug. 1847; *ZH* 19 Sept. 1838; Fisk, *Science*, 7–8.

67. For comparative data suggesting Wesleyan's distinctively high level of graduates who became either ministers or educators, see Burke, *American*, 61, 140–41, 143, 189; Stameshkin, *Town's College*, 169. Comparative data on Amherst are drawn from Tyler, *History of Amherst*, 643–44.

68. AAM 20 June 1860; *WUC* 1860/61, 31 and subsequent years; *WAR* (1869), 4.

Chapter 3 Entrepreneurial Strategy

1. David W. Engstrom, "A Tale of Two Cities: The Development of Industry in Middletown and Meriden, Connecticut, 1810–1860" (Honors thesis, Wesleyan University, 1980), 63–64, 74, 86–87, 100–103; Martin J. Waters, "To Gain a Railroad: Nineteenth-Century Efforts to Build a Major Rail Line through Middletown, Connecticut" (M.A. thesis, Wesleyan University, 1987), 1, 10, 100–102. For a less comparative approach with somewhat different emphasis, see Hall, *Middletown*, 25–27. *Fifth Census of the United States, 1830* (Washington, D.C.: Duff Green, 1832), 26–28; *U.S. Census Office. Ninth Census, 1870* (Washington, D.C.: GPO, 1872), 93–95.

2. Waters, "To Gain," 28–29, 5, 39–52, 55; Franklin L. Green, "Sibling Rivalry: A Study of Civic Competition in Nineteenth-Century Connecticut" (Honors thesis, Wesleyan University, 1965), chaps. 2–3. Edward C. Kirkland, *Men, Cities, and Transportation: A Study in New England History* (Cambridge: Harvard University Press, 1948), 233–37, 258–60.

3. Engstrom "Tale," 54–56; Waters "To Gain," 55, 4, chaps. 3–5; Green, "Sibling Rivalry," chaps. 4–9; Karl P. Harrington, *Karl Pomeroy Harrington: The Autobiography of a Versatile and Vigorous Professor*, ed. Mabel Harrington Potter (Boston: Thomas Todd, 1975), chap. 11.

4. Waters, "To Gain," 4, 71–72; Green, "Sibling Rivalry," 111–15.

5. The travel time from Boston to Middletown in 1850 was reported in *ZH* 24 July 1850; that from New York to Middletown is an estimate based on information in Kent T. Healy, "Development of Transportation in Southern New England," in *Annual Report* of the Connecticut Society of Civil En-

gineers (New Haven: Tuttle, Morehouse, and Taylor, 1934), 114; Lyon, journal, 8–10. Travel time from New York City to Middletown in the early 1830s is reported in "Wesleyan University, Middletown, Conn.," *Family Magazine* 2(1834–35): 372; that from Boston to Middletown is an estimate based on information in Haven, *Autobiography*, 55. For an interesting account of the three days of travel from upstate New York by a student enrolling in September 1831, see *WA* 2 Nov. 1893. "Desperate for a railroad," Middletown by the mid-1870s had subscribed $887,000 to the Air Line enterprise (Kirkland, *Men*, 83–84, 311).

6. *CA* 10 Feb. 1837; Samuel Rezneck, "The Social History of an American Depression, 1837–1843," *American Historical Review* 40(July 1935): 662–64; *CA* 5 May 1837; ARP (1837):74; WF to Daniel Brayton (10 Jan. 1838), WF to Ruth Fisk (10 Feb. 1838), WFP, box 7; Markle, "Willbur Fisk," 164. Wesleyan's enrollments dropped by a third during the depression and Amherst's by half, while Williams and Yale showed little or no decline (Stameshkin, *Town's College*, 138).

7. Walter B. Smith and Arthur H. Cole, *Fluctuations in American Business, 1790–1860* (Cambridge: Harvard University Press, 1935), 60,94; ARP (1840):9–10, (1847):51–52, (1850):65.

8. Smith, *Fluctuations*, 94; ARP (1855):119–20; James L. Huston, *The Panic of 1857 and the Coming of the Civil War* (Baton Rouge: Louisiana State University Press, 1987), 13–34; Joseph Cummings, *Wesleyan University* (single sheet dated 13 Jan. 1860); ARP (1860):214–15, (1861):261, (1862):276, (1865):330–32, (1868):373; Clara Van Vleck, *A Historical Sketch of the Endowment of Wesleyan University*, (Middletown: Pelton and King, 1904), 23. The land was given to Wesleyan as payment on a few individual subscriptions made in the 1840s and 1850s.

9. Swift, "Sense," chaps. 2, 4–5, 7; Swift, "Heartless," 13–14, 16–17. David E. Swift, *Black Prophets of Justice: Activist Clergy before the Civil War* (Baton Rouge: Louisiana State University Press, 1989), 78–90, 113–45, 155–61, 3; Raymond A. Mohl, *Poverty in New York, 1783–1825* (New York: Oxford University Press, 1971), 20–21, 26–27. Swift's extensive research led me to many of the sources cited for the next several paragraphs.

10. Swift, "Heartless," 14; *The Liberator* 12 Jan. 1833; JBM 10 Oct. 1832; *The Liberator* 2 Nov. 1833; *Frederick Douglass' Paper* 13 Oct. 1854; Horatio T. Strother, *The Underground Railroad in Connecticut* (Middletown: Wesleyan University Press, 1962), 154–55. Beman was twenty-one years old and pursuing a course of self-education. JBM 25 Aug. 1835.

11. *The Liberator* 12, 26 Jan. 1833; *The Emancipator* 15 Dec. 1836; John Gove to WF, 12 Dec. 1837, WFP, box 3.

12. John Gove to WF, 19 Jan. 1838, WFP, box 3. For general and detailed accounts of Fisk's role in the colonization versus abolition controversy, see Williamson, "Willbur Fisk"; Swift, "Sense," chap. 6; Donald G. Mathews,

Slavery and Methodism: A Chapter in American Morality, 1780–1845 (Princeton: Princeton University Press, 1965), chaps. 4–7. *CA* 9 Feb. 1838. Fisk's scathing tone of attack on Methodist abolitionists in New England was present from the early days of the controversy (e.g., *CA* 4 Sept. 1835). *The Liberator* 28 February 1835. For Fisk's reply to Garrison, see *ZH* 1 Apr. 1835. Twelve of the one hundred eleven students listed in Wesleyan's catalogue for 1835/36 came from below the Mason-Dixon line. *ZH* 1 July 1835; *Zion's Watchman* 3 Mar. 1838. Fisk's spirited rejoinder said there was no evidence for a claim that Wesleyan promoted an antiabolition viewpoint or discriminated against students who were abolitionists (*CA* 23 Mar. 1838).

13. Fisk supported the Whig party and found Andrew Jackson and the Democratic party to be "a curse . . . to our country!" (WF to Isaiah and Hannah Fisk, 20 Oct. 1832, WF to Franklin Deming, 15 Mar., 25 Apr. 1834, WFP, box 7). McClintock, "Stephen Olin," 29–33. Fisk quoted Olin for support of his antiabolitionist arguments (*ZH* 23 Sept. 1835). John R. Bodo, *The Protestant Clergy and Public Issues, 1812–1848* (Princeton: Princeton University Press, 1954), 141; Swift, "Sense," 66–72; Lawrence J. Friedman, *Inventors of the Promised Land* (New York: Knopf, 1975), 268–82. For the fullest account of Prudence Crandall's school in Canterbury, see Susan Strane, *A Whole-Souled Woman: Prudence Crandall and the Education of Black Women* (New York: W. W. Norton, 1990), chaps. 1–14. Strother, *Underground*, 35, 156–57; *MC* 3 June 1879.

14. Graduates of Wesleyan are identified by an apostrophe and the last two digits of the class year (e.g., '40 = 1840). Those who attended but did not graduate are identified by *n* and the full class year (e.g., n1840). *WUC* 1855/56, 14; *WUC* 1856/57, 15; *WAR* (1883), 437, 169; *ZH* 27 June 1860. For additional information on Barnswell, see chap. 2 n63. Charles S. Johnson, *The Negro College Graduate* (Chapel Hill: University of North Carolina Press, 1938), 7; *DANB*, 613, 617, 50, 364. Washington (later Trinity) awarded an honorary M.A. to Edward Jones (Amherst '26) in 1830 but has no records or research results to indicate that there were any black graduates before 1860. The first black graduate of Yale earned his degree in 1874.

15. Charles E. Rosenberg, *The Cholera Years: The United States in 1832, 1849, and 1866* (Chicago: University of Chicago Press, 1962), 25–39; *CA* 21 Sept. 1832; *To the General Assembly of the State of Connecticut, at Their Session in May, 1834* (single sheet signed by Willbur Fisk et al. dated 7 May 1834).

16. Holdich, *Life*, 338–39, 344–87, 403; *CA* 26 Oct. 1832; ARP (1837):61–62; Wesley C. Mitchell, *Business Cycles: The Problem and Its Setting* (New York: National Bureau of Economic Research, 1927), 387; *Life of Olin*, 2:381; ARP (1849):61, (1850):63.

17. *CA* 13 Dec., 18 Oct. 1833; *ZH* 27 Jan. 1836, 5 Nov. 1845; ARP (1849):59– 60; Schuyler Seager to SO, 6 Aug. 1845, 2 Mar. 1847, 28 July 1851, OFP, box 1; Genesee College was chartered 27 Feb. 1849, and instruc-

tion began in 1850. See Nancy E. Beadie, "Defining the Public: Congregation, Commerce, and Social Economy in the Formation of the Educational
System, 1790–1840" (Ph.D. diss., Syracuse University, 1989), chap. 7; Arthur J. May, *A History of the University of Rochester, 1850–1962*, ed. and abr.
Lawrence E. Klein (Rochester, N.Y.: University of Rochester, 1977), 9–17.

18. Jacob Sleeper to so, 4 Aug. 1845, OFP, box 1; *CA* 6 Apr. 1854; *ZH* 3
May 1854, 13 Aug. 1856; ARP (1859):190–91; *CA* 6, 20 Apr. 1854; *M* 20, 27
Dec. 1862, 10 Dec. 1864. For a later assessment, see *CA* 26 Sept. 1867.

19. Donald B. Marti, "Laymen Bring Your Money: Lee Claflin, Methodist Philanthropist, 1791–1871," *MH* 14(April 1976): 176–77; *WA* 15 Apr.
1869; *CM*, 125; William F. Galpin, *Syracuse University*, vol. 1 (Syracuse: Syracuse University Press, 1952), 33; Marti, "Laymen," 178; *DAB* 8:548, 9:208.
In terms of endowment-fund dollars per student, Wesleyan's ratio in 1870
equaled Yale's. Rich's legacy of $700,000 would have tripled the Wesleyan
endowment. See George W. Pierson, *Yale College: An Educational History,
1871–1921*, vol. 1 (New Haven: Yale University Press, 1952), 705; *FEx*
1871; *WAR* (1883), cx. Isaac Rich's will was made 7 Aug. 1869, just a few
months after Boston University obtained its charter (26 May 1869). For
more on Rich's bequest, see text at chap. 4 nn1, 2.

20. For details on the terms for various discounts, see text at chap. 1 n28.
CA 3 Feb. 1837, 3 Feb. 1847; Van Vleck, *Historical Sketch*, 5–6; ARP
(1839):3, (1840):16, (1845):45, (1847):55, (1858):155–57; *ZH* 22 Dec. 1858;
ARP (1860):215–16, 246, (1856):124–26; *FEx* 1861–70.

21. Van Vleck, *Historical Sketch*, 7, 11; *FEx* 1860, 1870. Endowment
funds at Amherst and Williams also increased rapidly in the 1850s and
1860s. In 1870 Amherst's was about $500,000, Williams's about $200,000
(Tyler, *History of Amherst*, 610–13; Rudolph, *Hopkins*, 190).

22. The analysis of deficits is based on information from the following:
ARP (1833):6, (1835):19, (1837):59, (1838):75, (1839):2, (1845):45; *ZH* 21
June 1843, 10 Apr. 1844, 10 June 1846, 9 Aug. 1848, 13 Aug. 1851; *FEx*
1857–70; Abstract of the Financial Report of the Wesleyan University for
the Year Ending July 20, 1849, John Johnston Papers. Figures on indebtedness are drawn from: ARP (1836):53–56; *ZH* 21 June 1843, 10 Apr. 1844;
CA 3 Feb. 1847; Abstract of the Financial Report . . . , 1849; *FEx* 1869.
Interest on indebtedness was about equal to one-ninth of the annual salary
budget for 1849 (Abstract of the Financial Report . . . , 1849), approached
one-fifth for 1859 (*FEx* 1859), and came close to one-seventh in 1869
(*FEx* 1869).

23. *ZH* 10 Sept. 1851; ARP (1859):188, (1861):257; Van Vleck, *Historical
Sketch*, 14–16; Clifford Browder, *The Money Game in Old New York: Daniel
Drew and His Times* (Lexington: University Press of Kentucky, 1986), chaps.
22–23; BTM 27 June 1877. Even Wesleyan's first life annuity arrangement,
with Eleanor Trafton of Boston, resulted in a long-term loss. She made a

gift of $1,000 in 1853 in return for annual payments to her at 6 percent. She lived another forty-seven years (NCAR, box 6; Van Vleck, *Historical Sketch*, 9; *ZH* 4 July 1900).

24. Royall, *Black Book*, 78–79; Ruth Fisk, notes and anecdotes, WFP, box 12; PCM 20 June 1831, 9 Oct. 1833; *CA* 26 Oct. 1832; ARP (1853):79; *ZH* 24 Dec. 1856; ARP (1858):159–61, (1859):176–77, 182–83, (1860):259; *FEx* 1857–63.

25. Rudolph, *American*, 46; ARP (1856):129; Tyler, *History of Amherst*, 242; Stameshkin, *Town's College*, 137; Rudolph, *Hopkins*, 215, 232; "Professor Hall's Letters—No. IV," *National Intelligencer* 15 Oct. 1838; Frederick Hall, *Letters from the East and from the West* (Washington, D.C.: F. Taylor and William M. Morrison, 1840), 10–12. For information on Hall, see Wyndham D. Miles, "Frederick Hall, Washington's First Teacher of Mineralogy," *Capital Chemist* 20(April 1970): 77–79. For Anne Royall's visit, see text at chap. 1 n10.

26. *DAB* 3:415–16; John Allen Krout, *The Origins of Prohibition* (New York: Knopf, 1925), 117; Henry Barnard to WF, 15 June 1838, WFP, box 1; Francis Wayland to WF, 15 Oct. 1833, WFP, box 6; McClintock, "Stephen Olin," 21–26; *DAB* 7:14–15; *WAR* (1883), xxvii–xxviii; Holdich, *Life*, 343; Jeremiah Day to SO, 24 Aug. 1845, Stephen Olin Correspondence, Personal Miscellaneous Papers, Rare Books and Manuscript Division, New York Public Library.

27. *ZH* 19 Sept. 1838; *CA* 15 Aug. 1850.

28. Orestes Brownson, *Social Reform: An Address Before the Society of the Mystical Seven* . . . (Boston: Waite, Pierce, 1844); *CA* 14 Aug. 1851; *CA* 13 Aug., 3 Sept. 1845; *MC* 30 July 1845; *Works of Olin*, 2:136–48. Emerson delivered his address, sponsored by the student literary societies, in the late afternoon of 6 Aug. 1845, following commencement exercises. His text, which has not survived, was a revised version of one delivered a few weeks earlier. For the earlier version, see "Discourse Read Before the Philomathesian Society of Middlebury College in Vermont," 22 July 1845, Emerson Papers, microfilm bMS 1280.199 (9) Houghton Library, Harvard University. George Prentice, *The Life of Gilbert Haven, Bishop of the Methodist Episcopal Church* (New York: Phillips and Hunt, 1883), 64–65, 55; SO to Ralph Waldo Emerson, 8 Aug. 1845, Emerson Papers, bMS Am 1280 (2328) Houghton Library, Harvard University. Emerson wrote a gracious and conciliatory reply. He used portions of the text in subsequent books, but this address was not published as such. See Ralph Waldo Emerson to SO, 14 Aug. 1845, Stephen Olin Correspondence, Personal Miscellaneous Papers, Rare Books and Manuscripts Division, New York Public Library; Ralph L. Rusk, ed., *The Letters of Ralph Waldo Emerson*, vol. 3 (New York: Columbia University Press, 1939), 294–96; Benjamin F. Gronewold, "Emerson at Middletown in Connecticut," *Emerson Society Quarterly*, no. 11 (2d

quarter 1958), 55–62; Bledstein, *Culture*, 256–68; *ZH* 13 Aug. 1845. Emerson spoke at Williams in 1854 and 1865 (Rudolph, *Hopkins*, 162–63) and at Amherst in 1855, 1872, and 1879 (Le Duc, *Piety*, 120).

29. For a list of honorary alumni, 1833–70, see *WAR* (1911), 807–38. *CA* 13 Aug. 1845; *ZH* 13 Aug. 1845. Citing a surge of public opinion critical of awarding honorary doctorates, the faculty refrained from recommending such degrees in the mid-1830s. See ARP (1836):51.

30. *OP '58*, 1:2. Burke says that presidents wore cap and gown "from the first" ("Annals," lxxxvii), but *CA* 19 Aug. 1858 also found Cummings's attire noteworthy. ARP (1853):75–80, (1854):102; Van Vleck, *Historical Sketch*, 6–7.

31. *OP '58*, 1:2; *NYTr* 30, 31 Dec. 1859, 9, 10 Jan. 1860; Cummings, *Wesleyan University*; *CA* 26 Jan. 1860; ARP (1862):285–86.

32. ARP (1858):166, (1862):281, 287, 279, (1864):330–31, (1868):373, 371, (1859):194, 203, (1860):233, (1861):266–67; *WA* 8 Dec. 1869.

33. ARP (1859):197–201, (1860):239–41, (1861):264, (1862):282, (1866):360, (1868):380.

34. *Public Statute Laws*, 346–49. Generalizations about the governing boards are based on analysis of membership records printed annually in *WUC* and attendance records kept in the minutes of the joint board.

35. The analysis in these four paragraphs is based on information in *WUC* 1831–71 and in TDB.

36. Six of the seven non-Methodist trustees named in Wesleyan's charter were Yale graduates. Elijah Hubbard (1795) and Isaac Webb (1822) helped draft bylaws for Wesleyan's governing bodies. The prudential committee in the 1830s often met in the downtown office of Samuel D. Hubbard (1819). George Stanley (1793) served until he moved to Ohio in 1837, and Jonathan Barnes (1810) and William Storrs (1814) each served for three decades. Of this group, Samuel D. Hubbard gave the fullest sustained support to Wesleyan, serving on the prudential committee for almost fifteen years. Seven of the twelve original trustees of Williams were Yale graduates (Rudolph, *Hopkins*, 13). For Yale's early influence on Middlebury and Amherst, see Stameshkin, *Town's College*, 69–70; Fuess, *Amherst*, 47, 61. AAM 1836–53, 1 Aug. 1854; ARP (1856):123; report of the committee appointed by the alumni to consider the present state and administration of the faculty of the Wesleyan University [1857], ASP; AAM 6 Aug. 1856; *CA* 14 Aug. 1856. The alumni organization became known as the Alumni Association. By 1916 it had yielded its role to the Alumni Council, organized in 1911.

37. BTM 7 Aug. 1856, 4 Aug. 1857; JBM 5 Aug. 1857; BTM 3 Aug. 1858; *SAC* 6:796, section 4; AAM 20 July 1870; TDB. Alumni gained majority status on the boards at Amherst and Williams in the mid-1860s.

38. AAM 15 July 1863; *ZH* 7 June 1865; AAM 18 July 1866; *WA* 29 Sept. 1869. Harvey B. Lane, professor of Greek, kept full records of degree recipi-

ents (*CA* 14 Aug. 1851). The first publication of this data in a separate pamphlet was *Catalogue of the Wesleyan University* (Hartford, Conn.: Eliher Geer, 1851). AAM 20 June 1860; *ZH* 17 Oct. 1867; *WA* 18 Mar. 1869. Regional alumni groups linking another provincial college to the urban club culture of metropolitan centers such as New York and Boston were initiated by Williams alumni in 1867 (Rudolph, *Hopkins*, 206). ARP (1859):203.

39. Developments at Middlebury College resemble those at Wesleyan in terms of the few alumni on the board until its fourth decade and the movement from local orientation to firmer denominational ties and a more distinct denominational tone after mid-century (Stameshkin, *Town's College*, 69–70, 141, 147, 91, 171). The question of local and denominational roles has not been explored in depth in other histories of New England colleges. On alumni developments, see Rudolph, *Hopkins*, 201, 206; Kelley, *Yale*, 150, 236; Tyler, *History of Amherst*, 260, 632; Fuess, *Amherst*, 71; Morison, *Three Centuries*, 295, 309. On clergy as trustees, see TDB; Rudolph, *Hopkins*, 91,131; Earl J. McGrath, "The Control of Higher Education in America," *Educational Record* 18(April 1936): 264, 261n4.

40. TDB. With clergy comprising more than 40 percent of its board, Amherst also deviated from the general trend (Tyler, *Amherst*, 661; Le Duc, *Piety*, 6). And clergy formed a majority of Yale trustees throughout the nineteenth century (Kelley, *Yale*, 236, 273, 325). TDB; McGrath, "Control," 264.

41. Report of the committee [1857]; ARP (1859):184, 178, (1856):133–34. The numbering practice was last used in *WAR* (1931).

42. In his letter to the joint committee 20 July 1829, Henry DeKoven estimated the value of the academy's land and buildings at $33,333 (NCAR, box 1, folder 3). *CA* 26 Oct. 1832, 29 Nov. 1833; Fisk, *Science*, 23; Fisk, *Wesleyan*. For another contemporary acknowledgment of the "commendable zeal" of Middletown citizens, see "Wesleyan University, Middletown, Conn.," 372.

43. PCM 11 Apr., 9 Oct. 1833; RAM; *AS* 20 Nov. 1833. Working Men's parties in Connecticut have received little attention compared to those in nearby states. Edward Pessen, *Most Uncommon Jacksonians: The Radical Leaders of the Early Labor Movement* (Albany: State University of New York Press, 1967), 9–11, 183–89; *MG* 30 Oct. 1833. The tendency of workers to oppose public funding for higher education and to promote common schools is discussed in Rush Welter, *Popular Education and Democratic Thought in America* (New York: Columbia University Press, 1962), 45–47.

44. Most letters in the debate were published in both Middletown newspapers. A complete set can be found in *AS* 23, 30 Oct. 6, 13, 20 Nov. 1833.

45. Philip A. Grant, Jr., "The Bank Controversy and Connecticut Politics, 1834," CHS*B* 33(July 1968): 90, and "Jacksonian Democracy Triumphs in Connecticut," CHS*B* 33(October 1968): 117–24. The relation between Working Men's party leaders and the Democratic party resides

more in general political orientation than in commonality of specific goals (Pessen, *Most Uncommon*, 23–27). RAM; *AS* 30 Oct., 27 Nov. 1833.

46. ARP (1835):19; *FEx* 1861; PCM 4 Apr. 1832; *CA* 26 Oct. 1832; JBM 27 Aug. 1833; *CA* 29 Nov. 1833; PCM 29 Nov. 1833; MLR 61:204–6; PCM 21 Dec. 1833. Although the academy trustees had accumulated a thirteen-acre plot by 1825, the campus transferred in 1833 was described in the deed as twelve acres. The MLR yield no information to explain this discrepancy.

47. Notices of unpaid loans due, WFP, box 9, folder 23; PCM 5 Mar. 1839; annual report of the prudential committee, 4 Aug. 1846, NCAR, box 1, folder 14.

48. Centum Millia account books, NCAR, box 6; Mudge, *History*, 334; JBM 4–5 Aug. 1857; *The Resignation of Doctor Smith* (single sheet dated 6 August 1857), ASP. Daniel Drew was probably a supporter of Smith (Perry C. Smith to Catherine Smith, 21 Oct. 1851, ASP; Perry C. Smith to A. W. Smith, 24 July 1857, AWSP).

49. Joseph Cummings to Ebenezer Jackson, 5 Aug. 1863, JCP; ARP (1864):314; *M* 20 Dec. 1862. For earlier talk of removal, see *CA* 13 Apr. 1854. *ZH* 24 Jan. 1866; Engstrom, "Tale," 87–88.

50. John S. Whitehead, *The Separation of College and State: Columbia, Dartmouth, Harvard, and Yale, 1776–1876* (New Haven: Yale University Press, 1973), chap. 3, 157, 75–76; Frank W. Blackmar, *The History of Federal and State Aid to Higher Education in the United States* (Washington, D.C.: GPO, 1890), 105–9, 121, 140–41, 147, 156–57. For current interpretation of the Dartmouth College Case, see Herbst, *Crisis*, chap. 17; John S. Whitehead and Jurgen Herbst, "How to Think about the Dartmouth College Case," *HEQ* 26(Fall 1986): 333–49.

51. Kelley, *Yale*, 11, 18, 37; Whitehead, *Separation*, 111; Weaver, *History of Trinity*, 42–43; Rudolph, *Hopkins*, 193; *ZH* 16 Jan., 19 Mar. 1828. Grants to Amherst came later, with $52,500 realized from 1847 to 1863. See Stanley King, *A History of the Endowment of Amherst College* (Amherst, Mass.: Amherst College, 1950), 27–28. Middlebury began receiving state funds in 1888, and annual appropriations increased to the point where one-third of the college's annual income in 1915 came from the state (Stameshkin, *Town's College*, 207, 229, 246–52).

52. PCM 18 Jan. 1833; To the Honorable the General Assembly of the State of Connecticut . . . said State, draft of a petition, ca. 1833, NCAR, box 7, folder 4; *To the General Assembly* . . . . My assessment of strategy is inferred from information in Grant, "Bank Controversy."

53. The legislative trail for 1834 can be traced in Journal of the House of Representatives of the State of Connecticut, 1830–34, RG2.9 RSC-GA, 13, 28, 29, 30 May 1834; Journal of the Senate of the State of Connecticut, 1830–35, RG2.6 RSC-GA, 5 June 1834. For the charters, see An Act to Incorporate the Manufacturers Bank at Farmington, document 34, folder labeled

"1834 Public Acts 1–40," box 20, RG2 RSC-GA; *SAC* 1:104, 141–44, 3:126–27. Wesleyan immediately used the $2,000 from the Middlesex Bank to purchase stock of that bank. See ARP (1852):69.

54. Regarding unsuccessful approaches to the state for grants and loans from 1835 to 1838, see PCM 3 Apr. 1835; ARP (1835):17; PCM 23 Mar., 16 Dec. 1836, 30 Jan. 1837, 23 Apr. 1838. PCM 19 Apr. 1839; [Willbur Fisk], *An Appeal to the Citizens of Connecticut in Behalf of the Wesleyan University* (Middletown: William D. Starr, 1839), 3–4; ARP (1837):59–61, 73–74. Fisk, like many educational leaders of the 1830s, apparently viewed dormitories as a necessity for the paternalistic supervision of students. Francis Wayland, president of Brown, was an early dissenter, presenting in 1842 the case for students rooming with families near campus (Rudolph, *American*, 96; Allmendinger, *Paupers*, 103, 116).

55. [Fisk], *Appeal*, 5–9, 13–16, 9–12; *CA* 17 Aug. 1838, 31 May 1839.

56. The governor's message can be found in M*C* 8 May 1839. Regarding the efforts in 1838, see petition from the prudential committee, 30 Apr. 1838, document 5, folder labeled "Petitions in aid of Wesleyan University," box 27, RG2 RSC-GA; *Journal of the House of Representatives . . . , 1838* (Hartford, Conn.: John B. Eldredge, 1838), 9, 101–2; Jarvis M. Morse, *A Neglected Period of Connecticut's History, 1818–1850* (New Haven: Yale University Press, 1938), 305–6. To trace the legislative history of efforts to aid Wesleyan in 1839, see petition of Samuel D. Hubbard et al., May 1839, document 37, box 30, RG2 RSC-GA; *MC* 8, 15, 22, 29 May 1839; *AS* 8, 15, 22, 29 May, 5 June 1839; *Journal of the House of Representatives . . . , 1839* (Hartford: printed at the *Courant* office, 1839), 7, 14–15, 19, 21–22, 24, 29, 31–32, 38, 46, 63–65; *SAC* (1839), 71. The prudential committee gave Woodward considerable discretion in pursuing "the interests of the University" (PCM 11 May 1839). *ZH* 13 Aug. 1856. Washington (later Trinity) College's petition for $15,000 was unsuccessful (petition of Washington College, document 66, box 30, RG2 RSC-GA).

57. *SAC* (1854), 231–32; *Circular: The Wesleyan University* (single sheet signed by Heman Bangs dated October 1854), NCAR, box 7.

58. *CA* 14 Jan. 1831, 2 Nov. 1832. For similar appeals see *CA* 27 June 1832, 24 Feb. 1837, 17 Aug. 1838; *ZH* 17 Apr. 1844. For the Bangs approach, see *CA* 7 Apr., 12 May, 15, 29 Sept. 1841. *The Board of Trustees and Visitors of the Wesleyan University to . . . Annual Conferences* (single sheet signed by L. Clark et al. dated 1 Sept. 1836), NCAR, box 7. For information on agents, their costs, and meager results, see ARP (1835):18–19; *CA* 6 June 1834, 19 June 1835; Jacob Sleeper to SO, 19 June 1844, 9 June, 8 Nov. 1845, OFP, box 1. Holdich, *Life*, 302, 445. For Olin's efforts and frustrations, see ARP (1843):39–40, (1849):42–44; *ZH* 29 Feb., 2 Aug. 1843, 31 Jan. 1844, 5 Mar., 18 June, 9, 16 July 1845; *CA* 7 Feb., 17 July, 18 Dec. 1844, 8 Jan. 1845, 3 Feb. 1847, 26 Apr. 1848, 2 Aug. 1849. The income-expenses analy-

sis is based on data in ARP (1836):53–56; *CA* 3 Feb. 1837; Abstract of the Financial Report . . . , 1849.

59. James Findlay, "The SPCTEW and Western Colleges: Religion and Higher Education in Mid-Nineteenth-Century America," *HEQ* 17(Spring 1977): 44–46; Samuel C. Pearson, Jr., "From Church to Denomination: American Congregationalism in the Nineteenth Century," *Church History* 38(March 1969): 67–87; Potts, "American Colleges," 369–73; Nolan B. Harmon, *Organization of the Methodist Church: Historical Development and Present Working Structure*, 2d rev. ed. (Nashville, Tenn.: Methodist Publishing House, 1962), 116–19, 228; Ahlstrom, *Religious History*, 847, 859. For the larger context of this topic, see Russell E. Richey, "The Social Sources of Denominationalism: Methodism," in *Denominationalism*, ed. Russell E. Richey (Nashville, Tenn.: Abingdon Press, 1977), 161–79.

60. Joseph Cummings to Ebenezer Jackson, 5 Aug. 1863, JCP; *CA* 13 Apr. 1854; *ZH* 25 Nov. 1863, 23 Aug. 1843; ARP (1855):105, 230, (1865):229. A Methodist removal controversy in the late 1860s involving Genesee College and the founding of Syracuse University had fuller development of denominational and legal arguments (Galpin, *Syracuse*, 4–24; Beadie, "Defining," chap. 7; *CA* 4 June 1868). On college removal controversies in this period, see Potts, "'College Enthusiasm!'" 33–37.

61. *CA* 19 Aug. 1858; 28 Aug. 1862; *ZH* 24 Jan. 1866; *CA* 14 Mar. 1867.

62. A graduate of Dickinson College in 1840, Crooks closed his career as a professor at Drew Theological Seminary (*DAB* 2:564). *M* 20 Dec. 1862, 10, 17 Sept., 1, 8, 22, 29 Oct., 5, 12 Nov., 31 Dec. 1864; *New England*, 87–88; *CA* 27 Oct. 1870; *M* 14 Jan., 10 Dec. 1870; Daniel Calhoun, *The Intelligence of a People* (Princeton: Princeton University Press, 1973), 257–58.

63. Norwood, "More Letters," 40–41. For evidence of Smith's rather distant relationship with Methodist conferences, see H. M. Johnson to A. W. Smith, 3 May 1859, AWSP. For the "general impressions . . . of the Methodist Community" that it was time for a change of president, see E. G. Andrews to A. W. Smith, 15 Sept. 1857, AWSP. Cummings received a D.D. from Harvard in 1861. Fales H. Newhall, journal and commonplace book, 21 May 1864, NEMHS; SHO to Julia M. Olin, 1 June 1864, OFP, box 6; *ZH* 7 Apr. 1858; ARP (1860):217–18, (1858):168, 171. A campus church with regular Sunday preaching was in operation from 1836 (FM 25 Aug. 1836) to the mid-1840s (SO to Charles K. True, 13 Mar. 1843, OFP, box 1). ARP (1859):179, (1860):235–36, (1859):190–92, 194, (1865):335; *Methodist Centenary Convention . . . Boston, June 5–7, 1866* (Boston: B. B. Russell, 1866), 51–59; ARP (1860):241–42, (1863):299, (1865):333, (1868):380, (1863):301, (1868):377–78. For an extended statement of his denominationally oriented educational philosophy, see Joseph Cummings, "Educational Work and Spirit of Methodism," in *Proceedings . . . of the Centennial Methodist Conference . . . , 1884* (New York: Phillips and Hunt, 1885), 391–95.

64. William North Rice, "Claims of the Educational Institutions of Methodism," in *Report of the Proceedings of the Methodist Convention of the State of Connecticut . . . , 1869* (New Haven: College Courant Print., 1870), 21–23; *Methodist Centenary . . . , 1866*, 58; *ZH* 28 Mar. 1866; Cummings, *Wesleyan University*; *ZH* 9 Aug. 1865; *M* 6 Oct. 1866; Joseph Cummings, "How to Save Our Young People in the Church," in *Report of the Methodist Convention . . . , 1869*, 47; *ZH* 7 Mar. 1866; ARP (1868):367, (1869):392.

65. The assessment in this paragraph is based on data in ARP (1836):53–56; Abstract of the Financial Report . . . , 1849; ARP (1853):76; *ZH* 13 Aug. 1856; ARP (1866):355; New York East Conference Centenary Committee, *Statistical Report, April, 1868* (n.p., 1868); Van Vleck, *Historical Sketch*, 1–18.

66. Walter W. Benjamin, "The Methodist Episcopal Church in the Postwar Era," in *HAM* 2:316–22, 335–36; BTM 1845–70; *ZH* 8 Aug. 1855; *OP* '68, 9:5; ARP (1865):334, (1868):380, (1863):296; WNR to William Rice, 6 Mar. 1865, WNRP; Mudge, *History*, 245–46; Nolan B. Harmon, "Structural and Administrative Changes," in *HAM* 3:51–56; Marti, "Laymen," 183–85. Jacob Sleeper served as president of the trustees from 1869 to 1871, and C. C. North served from 1871 to 1877. W. Bruce Leslie, "Localism, Denominationalism, and Institutional Strategies in Urban America: Three Pennsylvania Colleges, 1870–1915," *HEQ* 17(Fall 1977):250–51.

67. Account book of Jacob Sleeper, 1844–54, NEMHS; *DAB* 9:208; Abner Forbes and J. W. Green, *The Rich Men of Massachusetts* (Boston: W. V. Spencer, 1851), 58–59; Mudge, *History*, 265; William F. Warren, "Jacob Sleeper: A Founder of Boston University," *MR* 71(September 1889): 694–95; Jacob Sleeper to SO, 7 Jan., 4 Aug., 8 Nov. 1845, OFP, box 1.

68. *DAB* 7:548; *WA* 31 Jan. 1872; "The Late Isaac Rich," *Harper's Weekly* 16(17 Feb. 1872): 148; CRMG; Mudge, *History*, 264.

69. *ZH* 2 Mar. 1871; Marti "Laymen," 169–83.

70. BTM; Browder, *Money Game*, 31, 119, 121–22; *DAB* 3:451; Van Vleck, *Historical Sketch*, 15–16; *FEx* 1857–76. Drew contributed to Wesleyan as early as 1844, with a gift of $500 (*ZH* 31 Jan. 1844).

71. New Rochelle *Pioneer* 21 Feb. 1885; *M* 25 July 1863; ARP (1863):393; *FEx* 1864–75. The arrangement with Cutts led to John M. Van Vleck being named Cutts Professor of Mathematics and Astronomy, 1863/64–1875/76. Creighton Lacy, *Frank Mason North: His Social and Ecumenical Mission* (New York: Abingdon Press, 1967), 25; Centum Millia account books, chapel subscription book, NCAR, box 6; ARP (1868):370; *CA* 26 Sept., 3 Oct. 1867; *M* 27 Nov. 1869.

72. *CA* 1 Dec. 1853; ARP (1856):123; *ZH* 22 July 1863, 3 Aug. 1864; *CA* 27 July 1865. Last-minute help from a wealthy layman and a minister who were not alumni guaranteed the final few thousand to meet Rich's challenge.

73. *CA* 4 Nov. 1869; *WAR* (1869), 4; *CA* 29 July 1869; Anne M. Boylan, *Sunday School: The Formation of an American Institution, 1790–1880* (New Haven: Yale University Press, 1988), 150; *WAR* (1883), 592, 82; *DAB* 5:231; Van Vleck, *Historical Sketch*, 26–29.

74. *CA* 23 July 1868, 3 Feb. 1870.

75. MLR 60:198, 220, 62:500, 63:7,223, 65:266–67, 67:26, 226; ARP (1868):371. By 1874 Wesleyan owned almost 80 percent of the parallelogram-like plot bounded by High, Cross, Mt. Vernon, and Wyllys streets. See Frederick W. Beers, *County Atlas of Middlesex Connecticut* (New York: F. W. Beers, 1874), 34–36. The last parcel needed for complete ownership of the plot was acquired in 1908. See *WUB* (May 1908):3. The name Foss Hill derives from the residence and property south of the college cemetery purchased in 1860 by Archibald C. Foss '52, brother of Cyrus Foss and professor of Latin and Hebrew, 1860–63. Until the 1870s, this elevation in back of the campus was known as Vernon Hill. As the building on it became known as Foss House (Caroline Foss continued to live there for a decade after Archibald's death in 1870), the usage Foss Hill emerged to replace Vernon Hill. Foss House was purchased by George Seney in 1880 and given to Wesleyan. It was used by Chi Psi (1883–93), Phi Rho (later Delta Tau Delta) (1894–99) and Commons Club 1899–1919. It housed the college infirmary (1918–36), and in 1955 it was demolished by fire to furnish land for the Foss Hill Dormitories. ARP (1838):79; *CL* 1(August 1840): 51–54, 2(August 1841): 95; PCM 15 Mar. 1832; *CL* 2(July 1841): 47; *WA* 4 Mar. 1881; *OP* '58, 1:2; *ZH* 25 Nov. 1863, 8 Aug. 1849; *CR* 1(July 1870): 173; *ZH* 25 Nov. 1863.

76. Harvey B. Lane to A. W. Smith, 14 Dec. 1835, ASP; *CA* 29 July 1836; ARP (1868):371; report to the conferences (1869); *CR* 1(July 1870): 173; ARP (1837):66; *WUC* 1869/70, 33; ARP (1868):372–73. John Johnston "The Early History of the Museum," in *Fifth and Sixth Annual Reports of the Curators of the Museum* . . . (Middletown: Pelton and King, 1877), 15–17.

77. *CA* 11 Nov. 1831. According to *Catalogue of Books in the Cadet's Library* . . . (Middletown: E. and H. Clark, 1827) there were 1,100 volumes in the library of Partridge's academy. *CA* 26 Oct., 24 Feb., 26 Oct. 1832; *ZH* 16 Sept. 1835; ARP (1835):35; *ZH* 3 Feb. 1836; ARP (1836):45; G. Brown Goode, "Wesleyan University," *CR* 2(September 1870):7–8; ARP (1837):61; *Catalogue of the Library of the Wesleyan University* (Middletown: William D. Starr, 1837); copy of Willbur Fisk's will, 8 Feb. 1839, WFP, box 9; "Statistics of Colleges" *American Quarterly Register* 13(August 1840): 111; Goode, "Wesleyan," 8; *M* 25 July 1868; Fremont Rider, "The Growth of American College and University Libraries—and of Wesleyan's," *About Books* 11(September 1940): 3–4.

78. Except for citations supplied in subsequent notes, documentation for information on buildings can be found in the VF for each.

79. ARP(1838):78; Holdich, *Life*, 403; Burke, "Annals," xcvii; ARP (1868):368–69.

80. Amherst built its row between 1820 and 1827 (Tolles, "College Architecture," 505). François Peyre-Ferry, *The Art of Epistolary Composition* . . . (Middletown: E. and H. Clark, 1826), etching facing frontispiece; [Fisk], "The Wesleyan University," 297; JBM 31 July 1855; ARP (1858):168; JBM 4 Aug. 1858.

81. ARP (1835):24–25, (1837):60,68–69, (1859):183; Cummings, *Wesleyan University*; ARP (1858):164, (1860):218, (1863):301, (1868):375,377–78. Similar sentiments were expressed in the report of the examining committee, 1870, NCAR, box 12.

82. Van Vleck, *Historical Sketch*, 17; *Memorial Chapel for the Wesleyan University* (n.p., 1866),1; VF for Civil War; records of the Ladies' Centenary Association . . . 1866, NCAR, box 6; *ZH* 7 Mar., 20 June 1866; *MC* 8 Aug. 1866; *M* 25 July 1868. The association apparently used the name Ladies Memorial Chapel Association in soliciting local gifts from non-Methodists. Women who made substantial gifts to Wesleyan before 1870 include Eleanor Trafton, L. Livingstone, Julia Olin, and Lucretia Van Pelt (copy of annuity agreement with Trafton, NCAR, box 6; Van Vleck, *Historical Sketch*, 9, 12; *FEx* 1857, 1859). *Army and Navy Union of Wesleyan University* (n.p., 1866), 3; George C. Round to "My Dear Prof.," 11 Apr. 1883, VF for Civil War; *CA* 23 July 1868; Gordon, "Roster," 2. There was an awareness of plans at Yale and Harvard for memorial buildings (*ZH* 1 Aug. 1866). *CA* 15 Mar. 1866, 2 Dec. 1869; *WA* 18 May 1870. An important precursor of Judd Hall was Rhode Island Hall (1840) at Brown, designed to accommodate instruction in natural philosophy, chemistry, mineralogy, geology, and natural history (Bronson, *History*, 222–24). Exactly contemporary with Judd Hall among the earliest comprehensive science buildings in the post–Civil War years is Culver Hall, constructed at Dartmouth primarily for use by the New Hampshire College of Agriculture and the Mechanic Arts (later the University of New Hampshire). This building was dedicated 23 June 1871, less than a month prior to similar ceremonies for Judd Hall. See Sally Gregory Kohlstedt, "Museums on Campus: A Tradition of Inquiry and Teaching," in Ronald Rainger, et al., *The American Development of Biology* (Philadelphia: University of Pennsylvania Press, 1988), 34–35; Philip M. Marston, ed., *History of the University of New Hampshire, 1866–1941* Durham: The *Record* Press, 1941), 21–29. Wesleyan's building program was about a decade or so behind two of its older neighbors in Massachusetts. By 1860 Williams had a library (1846), a student-built structure for natural science (1855), and a chapel (1859). Amherst had a library (1853) and several science buildings constructed in the mid-1850s. A college church was completed in 1873. See Leverett W. Spring, *A History of Williams College* (Boston: Houghton Mifflin, 1917), 260–63, 162; Rudolph, *Hopkins*, 147–48; Stanley King, *"The Consecrated Eminence": The Story of the Campus and Buildings of Amherst College* (Am-

herst, Mass.: Amherst College, 1951), 46–47, 74–75, 310–16. Some Methodists were a bit uneasy with the "brownstone palaces" and other signs of collegiate prosperity unbecoming a denomination of humble social origins (*CA* 26 June 1873; *M* 19 July 1873).

83. There was talk in 1860 and 1869 of changing the name of the university, perhaps to Middletown College. The timing of such proposals could not have been worse, and they went nowhere. The proposers wanted Wesleyan to continue attracting some non-Methodist students and to avoid being misperceived as a theological seminary. See ARP (1860):248; *ZH* 25 Feb., 22 July 1869. *SAC* 6:795–96, sections 1, 3–5. By 1860, ten conferences had joined the original three in support of Wesleyan: Troy (1833), Providence (1841), Maine (1842), Black River (1843), Oneida (1843), Vermont (1848), East Maine (1849), New York East (1849), Wyoming (1860), Newark (1860). Genesee was a patron, 1843–50.

84. JBM 14–15 July 1868; report of the committee on charter revision, NCAR, box 1; BTM 14 July 1869; JBM 13–14 July 1869; *SAC* 6:797.

85. For the most comprehensive assessments of Curry, see D. A. Goodsell, "In Memoriam—Daniel Curry," *MR* 69(November 1887): 809–24; *MNYEC* (1888), 61–67. WNR to William Rice, 6 June 1863, WNRP; minutes of the central committee on the Centenary Celebration for 1866, 14 Apr. 1865–18 Sept. 1868, UMA; JBM 18 July 1866; *ZH* 13 Aug. 1845; AAM 3 Aug. 1853, 3 Aug. 1858, 21 June 1859, 20 June 1860; *CA* 27 July 1865, 22 July 1869; *WA* 18 Mar. 1869; *CA* 3 Feb. 1870; George Preston Maines, *James Monroe Buckley* (New York: Methodist Book Concern, 1917), 125; *CA* 25 Aug. 1887, 9 Sept. 1926; *ZH* 24 Aug. 1887. On Curry's brief, stormy presidency at DePauw, 1854–57, see George B. Manhart, *DePauw through the Years*, vol. 1 (Greencastle, Ind.: DePauw University, 1962), 53–57. *CA* 8, 15 Dec. 1864; *CA* 29 July, 28 Dec. 1869, 9 Mar., 1 June, 3 Aug. 1871. Curry advocated reorganization of the board as early as 1860 (JBM 20 June 1860; report of the committee on reorganization of the board [20 June 1860], NCAR, box 1, folder 9). *MC* 4 May 1870; *HC* 28 May 1870; *M* 30 July 1870; *CA* 22 July 1869, 28 July 1870; *ZH* 22 July 1869. Randolph-Macon, founded at the same time as Wesleyan, moved closer to the denomination in the 1860s. See James Monroe Becker, "Was Randolph-Macon Different? Revivalism, Sectionalism, and the Academic Tradition: The Methodist Mission in Higher Education, 1830–1880" (Ph.D. diss., University of North Carolina, Chapel Hill, 1980), 23; Scanlon, *Randolph-Macon*, 141. Syracuse University's charter of 1870 stipulated Methodist control (Galpin, *Syracuse* 1:33). Boston University's charter (1869), however, prohibited any religious test for appointment to the faculty (except in the "Theological Department") and did not stipulate Methodist control. See *Charter, Statutes and By-Laws of the Trustees of Boston University, 1954* (Boston: Boston University, 1954), 8. For increased denominationalism within Congregational ranks, see Stameshkin, *Town's*

College, 171; Ruth E. Ratliff, "The Society for the Promotion of Collegiate and Theological Education at the West: A Congregational Education Society" (Ph.D. diss., University of Iowa, 1988); Potts, "American Colleges," 369–73.

Chapter 4 Denominational Support and Influence

1. *DAB* 8:548; *ZH* 23 July 1868; William Rice to WNR, 17 July 1868, WNRP; Bradford K. Pierce, "In Behalf of the Alumni," in *Addresses at the Inauguration of Rev. Cyrus D. Foss . . . , 1875* (Middletown: Pelton and King, 1876), 21; Prentice, *Life of Gilbert Haven*, 466–67; Fales H. Newhall, journal and commonplace book, 23 Feb. 1854–13 Aug. 1881, NEMHS, entries for 12, 29 Jan. 1872; *Boston Evening Transcript* 27, 29 Jan. 1872; *ZH* 18 Jan., 1 Feb. 1872; *WA* 28 Feb. 1872; *ZH* 18 Feb. 1872. The will is recorded in Suffolk County Registry of Probate, Boston 456:15–22. For more on Rich's will and its potential for Wesleyan, see text at chap. 3 n19.

2. TDB; *WA* 8 Dec. 1869; CRMG. Major donors in Connecticut were J. F. Judd, Hartford; J. H. Sessions, Bristol; C. B. Rogers, Meriden.

3. *CA* 22 Feb. 1872; *WA* 28 Feb. 1872; TDB. Oliver Hoyt, for example, was one of the founders of the *Methodist* (*CM*, 457), a charter member of the denomination's board of education (*JGC of . . . 1872*, 706), and active along with Seney, Judd, and other Wesleyan trustees in the lay representative movement (Proceedings of the Electoral Conferences of Laymen of the New York East Conference, 1872–88, UMA).

4. *MYB* (1871), 32 and (1901), 33; Ben Primer, *Protestants and American Business Methods* (Ann Arbor, Mich.: UMI Research Press, 1979), 30, 37; Benjamin, "Methodist," 316–22; Ellen Weiss, *City in the Woods: The Life and Design of an American Camp Meeting on Martha's Vineyard* (New York: Oxford University Press, 1987), chap. 7. Ocean Grove, the largest of these enterprises, retained a tent section, but the cottages soon outnumbered the tents. See Charles Parker, "Ocean Grove, New Jersey: Queen of the Victorian Methodist Camp Meeting Resorts," *Nineteenth Century* 9 (1984): 19–25. Ensign McChesney, "The Effect of Increased Wealth upon American Methodism," in *The Present State of the Methodist Episcopal Church: A Symposium*, ed. George R. Crooks (Syracuse, N.Y.: Hunt and Eaton, 1891), 53–64.

5. McChesney, "Effect," 57; Benjamin, "Methodist," 329–30; Primer, *Protestants*, chaps. 3–4; *CM*, 125; Galpin, *Syracuse* 2:v; Paul K. Conkin, *Gone with the Ivy: A Biography of Vanderbilt University* (Knoxville: University of Tennessee Press, 1985), 25; Sellers, *Dickinson*, 279; Scanlon, *Randolph-Macon*, chaps. 7–8; *ZH* 30 Aug. 1882; *CA* 1 June 1871.

6. Duvall, *Methodist*, chap. 6; *CA* 29 May 1884; Myron F. Wicke, *A Brief History of the University Senate of the Methodist Church* (Nashville, Tenn.: Board of Education, 1956), 7–12.

7. TDB. Of the sixty-five conference trustees elected from 1870 to 1910, four were laymen. One of the lawyers, Stephen Henry Olin, was an Episcopalian by association, if not membership (see text at chap. 6 n31). Minutes of the central committee on the Centenary Celebration for 1866, 22 Feb. 1865–18 Sept. 1868, UMA; Charles F. Sitterly, *The Building of Drew University* (New York: Methodist Book Concern, 1938), chap. 1; William P. Tolley, ed., *Alumni Record of Drew Theological Seminary . . . , 1867–1925* (New York: Methodist Book Concern, 1926), 9–11; *WAR* (1921), xxviii–xxxii; *Autobiography of Bangs*, 315, 369; *CA* 5 July 1877; *MNYC* (1887), 72.

8. BTM 19 July 1870, 21 Nov. 1877; TDB; *SAC* 8:140, 14:868; BTM 28 June 1892; *WUC* 1892/93, 5, 1893/94, 3–7.

9. Drew declared bankruptcy in 1876 (Browder, *Money Game*, chap. 22). Judd was in a greatly weakened financial state after 1873 (James S. Judd, "His Life History," *Orange Judd Farmer*, 7 Jan. 1893, 9–10). Since payments from all three ceased in 1875, there is a good chance that Cutts, too, lost considerable wealth in the panic and subsequent depression. The faculty recommended that the names of these three be dropped from the professorships they no longer funded (FM 21 Nov. 1876). In addition to evidence for assessments in this paragraph found in *FEx* 1870–79 and BTM 1870–79, see *CA* 6 July 1876; *Wesleyan University* (single sheet dated 4 Apr. 1876); *Wesleyan University* (single sheet dated 10 May 1876); ARP (1874):456–58, 465, 468; EXCM 29 Sept. 1875; *WUC* 1873/74, 34, 1874/75, 34; CDF to Jane Foss, 19 Feb., 16 Mar., 16 Apr. 1876, 28 Jan., 13, 14 Feb., 1 July, 15 Oct. 1877, CDFP, box 1; William Rice to WNR, 1 Jan. 1877, WNRP.

10. *CM*, 457; *NCAB* 33:457; David W. Hoyt, *A Genealogical History of the Hoyt, Haight, and Hight Families* (Boston: Henry Hoyt, 1871), 461–62; *NYT* 6, 8, 10 May 1887; Estelle F. Feinstein, *Stamford in the Gilded Age: The Political Life of a Connecticut Town, 1868–1893* (Stamford, Conn.: Stamford Historical Society, 1973), 87,92; *FEx* 1870–1903; [Harvey C. Williams], "Wesleyan University," *Harper's Weekly* 33(28 Dec. 1889): 1044.

11. Seman, *Annals*, 326; *CA* 13 Sept. 1883; *M* 17 Feb. 1877; Browder, *Money Game*, 225; CDF to Jane C. Foss, 12 Apr. 1876, CDFP, box 1; *CM*, 836; *CA* 13 Sept. 1883.

12. *FEx* 1879–81; Van Vleck, *Historical Sketch*, 34–35; *DAB* 8:583–84; *CA* 13 Apr. 1893; Henry Clews, *Twenty-Eight Years in Wall Street* (New York: Irving, 1887), 162–67; *NYT* 8 Apr. 1893; John F. Stover, *The Railroads of the South, 1865–1900: A Study in Finance and Control* (Chapel Hill: University of North Carolina Press, 1955), xv, 201, 242–43; Maury Klein, *The Great Richmond Terminal: A Study in Businessmen and Business Strategy* (Charlottesville: University Press of Virginia, 1970), 48–49, chap. 5; John F. Stover, *American Railroads* (Chicago: University of Chicago Press, 1961), 115; Maury Klein, *The Life and Legend of Jay Gould* (Baltimore: Johns Hopkins University Press, 1986), 299; Clews, *Twenty-Eight*, 361–62; Taylor Hampton, *The Nickel*

Plate Road: The History of a Great Railroad (New York: World, 1947), chaps. 3, 10–11; Henry M. Bullock, *A History of Emory University* (Nashville, Tenn.: Parthenon Press, 1936), 171–73.

13. *CA* 22 Dec. 1881, 3 July 1884; *ZH* 9 July 1884. Beginning as early as 1871, when he funded the steeple for the chapel, Seney also gave about $50,000 for special projects. During most of the years from 1882 to 1893, he also paid annual interest on about $100,000 to fund Seney scholarships (Williams, "Wesleyan," 1044); *MP* 30 Dec. 1889). Clews, *Twenty-Eight*, 166; Robert Sobel, *Panic on Wall Street: A History of America's Financial Disasters* (New York: Macmillan, 1968), chap. 6; *DAB* 8:584; *CA* 13 Apr. 1893; *NYTr* 8 Apr. 1893; *FEx* 1870–85.

14. *CA* 3 July 1884; *ZH* 9 July 1884; BTM 24 June 1884, 20 Jan., 22 June 1886, 29 June 1887, 26 June 1888; Sobel, *Panic*, chap. 7; *FEx* 1893–97.

15. Van Vleck, *Historical Sketch*, 36–37; *NYTr* 20 Oct. 1889; Williams, "Wesleyan," 1044; *CA* 23 May 1889, 28 Jan. 1892; *WUB* (May 1892):15–16; Howard A. Kelly and Walter L. Burrage, *American Medical Biographies* (Baltimore: Norman Remington, 1920), 49–50; *Brooklyn Daily Eagle* 18 Jan. 1892; *FEx* 1890.

16. *Boston Journal* 9 Dec. 1890; *FEx* 1892–93, 1895, 1898, 1900, 1905, 1906; *CA* 18 Dec. 1890; *DAB* 3:306; *NYTr* 9 Dec. 1890; "The Late Daniel B. Fayerweather," *Harper's Weekly* 34(20 Dec. 1890): 996, 999. For a good summary of the Fayerweather bequest story, see "College Notes," *Bachelor of Arts* 4(February 1897): 111–15. New England institutions receiving funds from the Fayerweather estate were Amherst, Bowdoin, Dartmouth, Wesleyan, Williams, and Yale (*NYT* 29 Nov. 1904; *NCAB* 33:457). Fayerweather augmented the profits received from his leather business through investments in railroad securities. See Charles H. McDermott, ed., *A History of the Shoe and Leather Industries of the United States* (Boston: John W. Denehy, 1918), 334.

17. Williams, "Wesleyan," 1044; *FEx* 1894–98; BTM 23 June 1891.

18. George P. Morrill, *The Multimillionaire Straphanger: A Life of John Emory Andrus* (Middletown: Wesleyan University Press, 1971), 25, 31, 91, 45, 48–54, 56–68, 37, 69–70, 185, 64, 175, 166, 179, chaps. 9–10; *FEx* 1894–1911.

19. *CA* 1, 8, 15 Dec. 1904; H. C. M. Ingraham, "Address," in *Celebration of the Seventy-Fifth Anniversary of the Founding of Wesleyan University* (Middletown: Wesleyan University, 1907), 204–205; *CM*, 789; *FEx* 1878–1910.

20. For biographical information on Reynolds, see *NCAB* 9:421; *CA* 13, 30 Jan. 1913. Most of his gifts are recorded in *FEx* 1876–1910 and Socratic Literary Society, treasurer's account, 27 June 1893–8 June 1915, 190–243, 174–82, Eclectic Papers. The other four were Henry J. Baker (*CM*, 77), Joseph S. Spinney (*CA* 11 May 1893), William E. Sessions (*NCAB* 18:421), and Frank S. Jones (*NCAB* 25:149). CRMG; BTM 30 Mar. 1899; *WUB* (June

1899):4; ARP (1899):1, 4; *WUB* (November 1899):2, 7; *FEx* 1900–1904; *WUB* (November 1904):2, 9, (May 1905):5.

21. Except where otherwise noted, information for generalizations in this paragraph is drawn from biographical sources previously cited for these individuals. Scott made his fortune in the Philadelphia area; Sessions in Bristol, Connecticut. Those not active in Methodist denominational affairs were Ayres, Fayerweather, and Jones. *CA* 19 Mar. 1885; Edwin S. Spinning, "History of the Mountain Colony" (undated typescript in the Bernardsville, N.J., Public Library), 1–2.

22. *DAB* 2:596; Mudge, *History*, 334. At the peak of his presidency in 1871, Cummings and his wife received a free-will offering of more than $1,000 collected by Orange Judd and his wife during commencement week (*CA* 27 July 1871). Six months later the publicly reported bequest of $10,000 to Cummings from Isaac Rich stood in stark and awkward contrast to the absence of any provision for Wesleyan (except as a contingent legatee if Boston University failed to prosper) in Rich's will. See "The Late Isaac Rich," *Harper's Weekly* 16(17 Feb. 1872): 148.

23. *WA* 15 Jan. 1873; Newhall, journal and commonplace book, 30 Apr. 1864, 19, 22 Mar. 1869; Joseph E. King, "Fisk, Olin, Cummings," *CA* 18 Nov. 1909; WNR to Daniel A. Whedon, 14 Feb. 1874, VF for Whedon '45; ARP (1873):436–38, (1874):463–66; WNR to Daniel A. Whedon, 19 Jan., 14 Feb. 1874, VF for Whedon '45; Daniel A. Whedon to WNR, 31 Jan., 3 Mar. 1874, WNRP; Edward H. Rice to WNR, two undated letters ca. 1874, WNRP. Cummings's caution in curricular expansion may have derived principally from his sense of Wesleyan's financial constraints in the mid-1870s. During his subsequent successful presidency at Northwestern University, 1881–90, he was at least moderately expansionist in curricular matters. See Harold F. Williamson and Payson S. Weld, *Northwestern University: A History, 1850–1975* (Evanston, Ill.: Northwestern University, 1976), 53, 56–57, 64. Cummings's difficulties of 1874–75 were somewhat compounded by seniors cutting his classes (*WA* 3 Dec. 1873, 30 Sept. 1874, 28 Oct. 1874) and by other student discipline problems (*WA* 11 Nov. 1874, 26 May 1875; WNR to Daniel A. Whedon, 14 Feb. 1874, VF for Whedon '45; CDF to Jane C. Foss, 18 Sept. 1875, CDFP, box 1).

24. BTM 22 Jan., 23–24 June 1874; WNR to Daniel A. Whedon, 14 Feb. 1874, VF for Whedon '45; J. C. Rand to WNR, 3 Mar. 1874, WNRP; *M* 24 Apr., 1 May 1875; *FEx* 1871–75; Frank Mason North, "Cyrus David Foss," *MR* 94(March 1912): 186–87; King, "Fisk," 11; BTM 22 June, 28 July 1875. To ease the departure of Cummings from the presidency, faculty members proposed that he stay on as Hedding Professor of Mental Philosophy and Political Economy. He did so until leaving Middletown on 18 Dec. 1877 for a pastorate in Malden, Massachusetts. (WNR to Daniel A. Whedon, 19 Jan. 1874, VF for Whedon '45; CDF to Jane C. Foss, 18 Dec. 1877, CDFP, box 1).

Less than two months after Foss became president, the board set a goal of $500,000 for the Centennial (of American independence) campaign (BTM 26 Oct. 1875). This was part of a national campaign and observance sponsored by the denomination (*CM*, 179–81).

25. *ZH* 4 Nov. 1875; *CA* 1 July 1880, 24 Dec. 1908; "Bishop Foss: A Memorial Minute," (typescript of a text adopted by the managers of the board of foreign missions of the Methodist church, 15 Mar. 1910), 1, CDFP, box 3; *CA* 3, 10 Feb. 1910; *Central Christian Advocate* 2 Feb. 1910 and *NYH* 1 May 1871, clippings in CDFP, boxes 9, 7; *ZH* 25 July 1872, 5 July 1877; North, "Cyrus Foss," 185; *ZH* 26 July 1865; *CA* 13 Sept. 1883; John W. Maynard, ed. and comp., *History of the Hanson Place . . . Church* (New York: Willis Mc-Donald, 1891), 91. For examples of Foss's writings on Methodist faith and practice, see "The Vital Forces of Methodism," *Ladies' Repository* 27(March 1867): 129–33; "Wesley and Personal Religious Experience," in *The Wesley Memorial Volume*, ed. James O. A. Clark (New York: Phillips and Hunt, 1881), 128–48. BTM 28 July 1875; *CA* 4 Nov. 1875; CDF to Jane C. Foss, 9 Aug. 1875, CDFP, box 1; *CA* 10 Feb. 1910. Foss's salary at St. Paul's in 1874 was $5,000. See Wilson Lee Cannon, Jr., "Our History—IV," *Communicant* 1(May 1903): 23. At Wesleyan, he was paid $3,000 *FEx* 1875–80. He supplemented this salary by preaching in the metropolis, particularly during summer. "I love to preach," he told his mother, and it was a rare Sunday when he was not in the pulpit (CDF to Jane C. Foss, 27 Apr., 9 Sept. 1878, 18 Dec. 1877, CDFP, box 1).

26. Bangs gave his inaugural address as part of the commencement exercises in 1841 (*ZH* 18 Aug. 1841); none was given by Olin, Smith, or Cummings. BTM 26 Oct. 1875; *M* 1 May 1875; *ZH* 4 Nov. 1875; *CA* 4 Nov. 1875; *Address . . . Foss*, 5, 16, 11, 18, 13. Although Foss's address was less than half as long as that given four years earlier at Yale by Noah Porter, there were many similarities between the two ceremonies. See *Addresses at the Inauguration of Professor Noah Porter as President of Yale College . . . , 1871* (New York: Charles Scribner, 1871).

27. *ZH* 4 Nov. 1875; *DAB* 3:540. *Addresses . . . Foss*, 23, 29, 23, 29. For a discussion of the "whole man" concept used by Foss's contemporaries, see Peterson, *New England*, chap. 2. *Addresses . . . Foss*, 29, 31, 26, 27, 31–35; *CA* 4 Nov. 1875.

28. CDF to Amelia Foss, 26 Aug. 1876, 15, 24 Apr. 1879, CDFP, box 1; CDF to Jane C. Foss, 18 Dec. 1877, 21 Mar. 1878, 13 Feb., 28 Jan. 1877, 16 Apr. 1876, 14 Feb. 1877, 24 Dec. 1875, 1 July 1877, 15 Oct., 13 Feb. 1877, 6 Dec. 1879, CDFP, box 1; *WA* 15 Oct. 1879; CDF to Jane C. Foss, 11 Feb. 1880, CDFP, box 1. During his first year as president, Foss provided a timeless description of the job: "Such a multitude of diverse duties. Not a steady pull but a succession of jerks." See CDF to Jane C. Foss, 18 Jan. 1876, CDFP, box 1.

29. *CA* 9 Jan. 1902; *WAR* (1883), 66; *CA* 9 Jan. 1902; BTM 22 June 1880.

30. *CA* 9 Jan. 1902; B. M. Adams, "Rev. John Wesley Beach," in *MNYEC* (1902), 117–19; *CA* 24 Dec. 1908, 1 July 1880.

31. *MTyC* (1884), 68; *MNYEC* (1881–86); Edward H. Rice to WNR, 29 Jan. 1888, WNRP; *ZH* 4 Jan. 1882, 16 Jan. 1884; *CA* 6 July 1882; *ZH* 9 July 1884, 30 July 1885; *CA* 14 July 1887, 9 July, 12 Mar. 1885.

32. *WA* 29 Nov. 1881; FM 2 Nov. 1881; Harrington, *Autobiography*, 29; *WLM* 15(February 1907): 204–5; *OP* '82, 24:78; *WA* 24 Apr. 1883; *ZH* 9 July 1884; *OP* '85, 27:5; *WA* 14 June 1883; *MP* 21 Sept. 1885; *WA* 5, 17 Mar. 1887; *MP* 24, 28 Feb., 1, 2, 8, 10 Mar. 1887; *To the Honorable Board of Trustees of Wesleyan University* (folded sheet, 3 pp., ca. 5 May 1887, bearing the name of Walter R. Breed and thirty-one other members of the class of 1887).

33. *To the Honorable Board*, 1–2; BTM 28 June 1887, 24 June 1884, 23 June 1885, 20 Jan. 1886; *FEx* 1884–87. Even the *WA* (23 Feb. 1887) noted "a stagnation of enterprise." W. E. Woodruff '87, R1939; AAM 29 June 1887; BTM 28 June 1887; CDF to Amelia Foss, 27–30 June, 1 July 1887, CDFP, box 2; *WAR* (1911), 66; *WA* 7 Apr. 1888; *MNYEC* (1888), 9. For reports on these events in the Methodist press, see *ZH* 6 July 1887; *CA* 7 July 1887.

34. For a collection of articles on this topic published from 1868 to 1872, see James Orton, ed., *The Liberal Education of Women . . . in America and England* (New York: A. S. Barnes, 1873). Barbara Miller Solomon, *In the Company of Educated Women: A History of Women and Higher Education in America* (New Haven: Yale University Press, 1985), 45. About 8 percent of the white male population died in the conflict. See Maris A. Vinovskis, "Have Social Historians Lost the Civil War? Some Preliminary Demographic Speculations" *Journal of American History* 76(June 1989): 38. For recent scholarship with a focus on the early years of coeducation, see Carol Lasser, ed., *Educating Men and Women Together: Coeducation in a Changing World* (Urbana: University of Illinois Press, 1987), 49–90; Rosalind Rosenberg, "The Limits of Access: The History of Coeducation in America," in *Women and Higher Education in American History . . . Symposia*, ed. John M. Faragher and Florence Howe (New York: W. W. Norton, 1988), 107–29.

35. Solomon, *In the Company*, 47; Ronald W. Hogeland, "Coeducation of the Sexes at Oberlin College: A Study of Social Ideas in Mid-Nineteenth-Century America," *Journal of Social History* 6(Winter 1972–73): 160–76; James H. Fairchild, "Coeducation of the Sexes," *American Journal of Education* 17(January 1868): 385, 390, 387, 393; Solomon, *In the Company*, 50–58.

36. JBM 17 July 1867.

37. *Catalogue of Bates College . . . , 1863* (Lewiston, Maine: *Daily Journal* Office, 1863), 9; Alfred W. Anthony, *Bates College and Its Background: A Review of Origins and Causes* (Philadelphia: Judson Press, 1936), 274; Hawkins, *Between*, 193–97; Patricia M. King, "The Campaign for Higher

Education for Women in Nineteenth-Century Boston," *Proceedings of the Massachusetts Historical Society* 93(1982): 65–76. At Bowdoin the only mention located in college records is passing reference, in an inaugural address, to the injustice of excluding women from full access to institutions of higher education. See Joshua L. Chamberlain, "The New Education" (Typescript of inaugural address delivered in 1872, Joshua L. Chamberlain Papers, Special Collections, Bowdoin College Library, Brunswick, Maine), 4, 8–9. At Dartmouth the trustees appointed a committee on "the question of admitting females to the privileges of the College," but there is no record of this committee meeting or presenting a report. See minutes of the trustees of Dartmouth College, 26 June 1872, Dartmouth College Archives; John King Lord, *A History of Dartmouth College, 1815–1909* (Concord, N.H.: Rumford Press, 1913), 391; Leon B. Richardson, *History of Dartmouth College*, vol. 2 (Hanover, N.H.: Dartmouth College, 1932), 552. No mention of coeducation has been found in the records of Trinity or Yale (conversations with institutional historians and archivists of these two institutions). Because of the emphasis on military training at Norwich University and the Catholic tradition of male education at Holy Cross, the absence of coeducation as an issue at these institutions is not surprising.

38. Women applying for admission raised the issue at Amherst a year earlier (*Amherst Student* 12 Feb. 1870), and discussion of coeducation had begun at Brown and the University of Vermont in 1870 (see sources on these institutions cited below). "The Sexes in College," *Nation* 3 Mar. 1870; *WA* 17 Jan. 1872; Ellen C. DuBois, *Feminism and Suffrage: The Emergence of an Independent Women's Movement in America, 1848–1869* (Ithaca, N.Y.: Cornell University Press, 1978), 199–200; Eleanor Flexner, *Century of Struggle: The Woman's Rights Movement in the United States*, rev. ed. (Cambridge: Harvard University Press, 1975), 156–58; Elizabeth Cady Stanton et al., eds., *History of Woman Suffrage*, vol. 2 (New York: Fowler and Wells, 1882), 445. Phebe Stone, one of Wesleyan's first four women students, was the niece of Lucy Stone, a leader in the suffrage movement (*WA* 6 Nov. 1872). In a letter to Lucy Stone during the fall of junior year, Phebe reported that Joseph Cummings had agreed to add the *Woman's Journal*, her aunt's weekly newspaper, to subscriptions supplying the reading room in North College (Phebe Stone to Lucy Stone, 8 Nov. 1874, Blackwell Family Papers, Manuscript Division, Library of Congress). Society of Alumni minutes, 28 June 1871, 26 June 1872, 1 July 1873, Williams College Archives; minutes of the trustees of Amherst College, 10 July, 21 Nov. 1871, Amherst College Archives; minutes of the trustees of Middlebury College, 9 Aug. 1870, 8 Aug. 1871, Middlebury College Archives; Stameshkin, *Town's College*, 200–204, 321n22; Bronson, *History of Brown*, 450–54; Linda M. Eisenmann, "Women at Brown, 1891–1930: 'Academically Identical, But Socially Quite Distinct'" (Ed.D. diss., Harvard University, 1987), 26; minutes of the trustees of

Colby College, 1 Aug. 1871, Colby College Archives; Edwin C. Whittemore, *Colby College, 1820–1925: An Account of Its Beginnings, Progress and Service* (Waterville, Maine: Colby College, 1927), 100–101; Julian I. Lindsay, *Tradition Looks Forward: The University of Vermont, A History, 1791–1909* (Burlington: University of Vermont, 1954), 229, 234. Outside the ranks of established liberal arts institutions in New England, coeducation first appeared at the University of Maine. An act approved by the state legislature on 23 Feb. 1872 provided for admission of women to the Maine State College of Agriculture and the Mechanic Arts. This institution (which became the University of Maine in 1897) had opened in 1868. The first woman enrolled 29 Aug. 1872. See Merritt C. Fernald, *History of the Maine State College and the University of Maine* (Orono: University of Maine, 1916), 244–46; David C. Smith, *The First Century: A History of the University of Maine, 1865–1965* (Orono: University of Maine at Orono Press, 1979), 11, 52–54, 38–39. The number of woman undergraduates in fall 1872 at institutions of higher education in New England was fifteen (eight at Vermont, four at Wesleyan, and one each at Bates, Colby, and Maine).

39. JBM 1867–70.

40. BTM 19 July 1871; *M* 29 July 1871; ARP (1871):413.

41. Colby College, *Catalogue*, 1859–71; University of Vermont, *Catalogue*, 1861–71; *WUC*, 1860–71; ARP (1871):414; *M* 29 July 1871; TDB. Calef had four sons and no daughters. See *WAR* (1881), 109.

42. The other largest benefactor, Isaac Rich, also favored coeducation (*NCAB* 10:176). *CR* 1(May 1870): 38. Sarah Judd, age sixteen, did not become a student at Wesleyan. AAM 19 July 1871; *WA* 20 July 1871, 10 Nov. 1869, 29 Nov. 1871; Cummings, "Educational Work," 393; BTM 14 July 1868; Gravely, *Gilbert Haven*, 158, 48, 254. John Van Vleck and William North Rice probably led the faculty on this issue. Van Vleck, the most respected member of the faculty in 1870, had daughters aged fourteen, eleven, and six, who would become graduates. Rice, a highly able and energetic young geologist, had a fourteen-year-old sister who would, like the three Van Vleck sisters, not only graduate but also earn election to Phi Beta Kappa.

43. Janet S. Everhart, "Maggie Newton Van Cott," in Rosemary Skinner Keller et al., *Women in New Worlds: Historical Perspectives on the Wesleyan Tradition*, vol. 1 (Nashville, Tenn.: Abingdon Press [ca. 1982]), 303–309; Kenneth E. Rowe, "The Ordination of Women: Round One; Anna Oliver and the General Conference of 1880," *MH* 12(April 1974): 60–72.

44. *ZH* 14 Apr. 1870; *M* 9 Aug. 1873. The Wesleyan Seminary (1819) in New York City included a Female Department. See *MR* 2(August 1819): 299. *MYB* (1870), 33; *Report of the Commissioner of Education . . . for 1870 . . . Papers* (Washington, D.C.: GPO, 1870): 506–17. An early guide to American colleges listed forty-four of the leading institutions. Of the twelve that

were coeducational and not under state control, eight were affiliated with the Methodists. See A[ugustus] F. Nightingale, *Handbook of Requirements for Admission to Colleges of the United States . . . Institutions* (New York: D. Appleton, 1879), 39–40. Manhart, *DePauw*, 1:80; Williamson, *Northwestern*, 23; Smith, *Allegheny*, 196; William Warren, *The Origin and Progress of Boston University* (Boston: Boston University, 1893), 42; Galpin, *Syracuse*, 33; Conkin, *Gone*, 10,55.

45. *WA* 23 Oct. 1872; *ZH* 16 Jan. 1873; Angie Warren Perkins to fellow alumnae, 16 Mar. 1908, vf for Warren '76; *WLM* 6(May 1898): 280; Bates College, *Catalogue*, 1872/73; Colby College, *Catalogue*, 1872/73; Mary E. Woodruff, "In Search of Usefulness: The University of Vermont's First Women Graduates" (M.A. thesis, University of Vermont, 1985), 35. One week after Wesleyan's term began, seven new women students, including one with sophomore standing, joined the one at the University of Vermont who had enrolled the year before (University of Vermont, *Catalogue*, 1872/73). And the first woman had enrolled at the University of Maine a few weeks earlier (see n38 above).

46. *WA* 6 Nov. 1872; *OP* '73, 15:4; College education for women in the 1870s was often viewed as an experiment (Patricia A. Palmieri, "From Republican Motherhood to Race Suicide: Arguments on the Higher Education of Women in the United States, 1820–1920," in Lasser, *Educating*, 55–56). Another eastern experiment began when Swarthmore opened as a coeducational college in 1869 (Swarthmore College, *Catalogue, 1869/70, 1870/71*). *ZH* 3, 17 Oct. 1872, 2 July 1874, 22 Apr. 1875, 6 July 1876. For a more reserved review, see *WA* 1 July 1876.

47. *WUC* 1872/73–1891/92. Special students are not included in this calculation. Other New England coeducational colleges in the 1870s and 1880s usually had only a small minority of women students. Boston University, where women became a majority in 1881, was an exception (Rosenberg, "Limits," 115; catalogues of these decades for Bates, Boston University, Colby, and Middlebury). Calculations on distance of home from Middletown are based on places of residence listed in *WUC* 1872/73–1890/91. Louise Wilby Knight, "The 'Quails': The History of Wesleyan University's First Period of Coeducation, 1872–1912" (Honors thesis, Wesleyan University, 1972), 19–21, 36. A woman elected class poet in 1876 was forced to resign (*WA* 12 Dec. 1876; *ZH* 21 Dec. 1876). Angie Warren Perkins to fellow alumnae, 16 Mar. 1908, vf for Warren '76; Knight, "Quails," 31–32; *OP* '75, 17:28; *WA* 2 Oct. 1875, 27 Mar. 1893. On the term *quail*, see wnrd 25 July 1864; *WA* 6 May 1869. *CA* 4 July 1889; *WA* 11 June 1873, 10 June 1874, 28 Oct. 1881, 10 June 1884.

48. *CA* 27 Jan. 1870; "Ladies at the University," *Home Journal* 28 Feb. 1883, 2; Stephen W. Dana, *Woman's Possibilities and Limitations: A Message to the Young Women of To-Day* (New York: F. H. Revell [ca. 1899]), 48; *WA* 30

June 1883, 10 Aug. 1882; Alice Hayes, "Can a Poor Girl Go to College?" *North American Review* 152(May 1891): 624. The four women graduates of Wesleyan in 1876 had only eight predecessors among women obtaining a B.A. from a New England college: two graduates of Bates (1869, 1873), one of Colby (1875), and five of the University of Vermont (two in 1875; three in 1876, one day before Wesleyan's commencement). See *General Catalogue of Bates College . . . , 1863–1915* (Lewiston, Maine: The College, 1915), 29, 35, 45; *General Catalogue of . . . Colby College . . . , 1820–1920* (Waterville, Maine: The College, 1920), 203; *General Catalogue of the University of Vermont, 1791–1900* (Burlington, Vt.: Free Press Association, 1901), 136. The first woman graduate of the University of Maine earned a B.S. in 1874, and the second woman graduate earned the same degree 2 Aug. 1876, a month after Wesleyan's commencement. Wesleyan elected women to Phi Beta Kappa less than a year after the University of Vermont became the first chapter in the nation to admit women (Vorhees, *History of PBK*, 262–63). For the larger context of women in Phi Beta Kappa, see Richard N. Current, *Phi Beta Kappa in American Life: The First Two Hundred Years* (New York: Oxford University Press, 1990), chap. 13. The chapters at Vermont and Wesleyan were the only active units of Phi Beta Kappa in the 1870s at coeducational institutions. Of the forty-three women graduates of Wesleyan, 1876–1892, sixty-three percent were members of Phi Beta Kappa. See *WAR* (1911).

49. *ZH* 23 Dec. 1880, 29 Nov., 20 Dec. 1882. The announcement for the 1883 dinner made no mention of excluding women (*ZH* 12 Dec. 1883). *ZH* 30 June 1886, 1 July 1891; AAM 23 June 1891, 27 June 1893.

50. Knight, "Quails," 19–29, 35–38. Wesleyan's percentage of woman graduates remaining single (53.5 percent) is just about equal to that for graduates of Bryn Mawr, 1889–1908, and is among the highest rates of nonmarriage found in the late nineteenth century at coeducational and women's colleges. See Roberta Frankfort, *Collegiate Women: Domesticity and Career in Turn-of-the-Century America* (New York: New York University Press, 1977), 54, 56, 73; Woodruff, "In Search," 37; Solomon, *In the Company*, 120. The calculation for Wesleyan is based on data reported by alumnae for the *WAR* (1911) and (1931). *ZH* 16 Jan. 1873, 19 Mar. 1890. As compared to the strong advocacy from *ZH* in Boston, the denomination's press in New York offered little support for coeducation and women's rights in general. The *Methodist* was lukewarm at best on women's rights in the 1870s (*M* 28 June 1873, 21 Mar., 8 Aug. 1874). Of the *Christian Advocate* editors, Daniel Curry (1864–76) had no sympathy for the women's movement (*CA* 27 Jan. 1870), and James M. Buckley (1890–1912) was "an unabashed woman hater" (Rowe, "Ordination," 62).

51. *CA* 23 Oct. 1873; ARP (1872):419–20, (1873):439–40, 447; BTM 24 June 1873; records of admittance, 1873–1892, 2–135, NCAR, box 11. For a

more detailed analysis, see Stuart G. Svonkin, "The Pluralistic Ideal at Wesleyan: Wesleyan's Orientation toward Race, Class, Gender, and Religion Within the Student Body, 1870–1970" (Honors thesis, Wesleyan University, 1989), chap. 1; ARP (1876):1; WA 10 June 1874, 17 June 1881, 10 June 1884; W. E. Woodruff '87, 1939; Peterson, New England, 77; ZH 5 Apr. 1882.

52. Cyrus D. Foss: "Our National Greatness," Ladies Repository 28(July 1868): 14; "The Mission of Our Country," CA 6 July 1876; "The Moral Element in Education," in Semi-Centennial of Wesleyan University . . . , 1881 (n.p., n.d.), 42, 37, 44; "Mundane versus Cosmic Culture," CA 4 July 1878; page proofs of baccalaureate sermons of 1879, 1880, CDFP, box 7; "The True Philosophy of Life," CA 26 July 1877. For a full expression of his Arminian beliefs, see Cyrus D. Foss, "The Spiritual Movement Cure," Ladies Repository 28(January 1868): 54–56. CA 6 July 1882; WA 7 July 1882; ZH 1 July 1885, 9 July 1884.

53. BTM 19 July 1871, 16 July 1872, 22 June 1875, 27 June 1876; William North Rice, "Wesleyan University," Scribner's Monthly 12(September 1876): 655. Wesleyan dropped daily evening prayers in 1874 (Burke, "Annals," cvi). WA 15 Nov. 1871; Rudolph, American, 75–77; Rudolph, Hopkins, 126; Ralph H. Gabriel, Religion and Learning at Yale . . . , 1757–1957 (New Haven: Yale University Press, 1958), 168–228; Le Duc, Piety, 453; Fuess, Amherst, 353–54. Harvard cautiously moved to a voluntary system in 1886 (Hawkins, Between, 133–35). Gabriel, Religion, 168–71; Rudolph, Hopkins, 126; WA 12 Mar. 1873, 15 Mar. 1881, 1 Feb. 1889, 16 Oct. 1883; ZH 8 Feb. 1888. These observances continued strongly throughout the nineteenth century (WA 2 Feb. 1898, 1 Feb. 1899). ZH 22 Apr. 1875, 26 Feb. 1880, CA 25 Mar. 1880, 14 Feb. 1895, 2 July 1891, 23 Apr. 1891, 5 Dec. 1901.

54. ARP (1882):1; Clarence P. Shedd, Two Centuries of Student Christian Movements: Their Origin and Intercollegiate Life (New York: Association Press, 1934), 120, 175, 179–80, chap. 9; C. Howard Hopkins, History of the YMCA in North America (New York: Association Press, 1951), 271–80. The initial effort to organize a YMCA at Wesleyan probably occurred in 1872 (WA 6 Nov. 1872). WA 26 Mar. 1878, 2, 12 Nov. 1880, 26 May 1885; Rudolph, Hopkins, 132. Campus YMCAs appeared at Yale in 1881 (Kelley, Yale, 304) and Amherst in 1882 (Le Duc, Piety, 141). The founding year for the campus Y group at Wesleyan is reported as 1885 in Yearbook of the Young Men's Christian Associations . . . , 1886 (New York: International Committee, 1886), 145.

55. Richard M. Cameron, Methodism and Society in Historical Perspective (New York: Abingdon Press, 1961), 244–48; ZH 1 Apr. 1875; NYT 7 Apr. 1875; James H. Timberlake, Prohibition and the Progressive Movement (Cambridge: Harvard University Press, 1963), 125; WA 10 Oct. 1876; Cyrus Foss, Jr., to CDF 24 Jan. 1888, CDFP, box 3.

56. Rudolph, Hopkins, 111; Fuess, Amherst, 193. Dates for the first chapter houses at Wesleyan are: Psi Upsilon (1878), Eclectic (1882), Delta

Kappa Epsilon (1883), Alpha Delta Phi (1884). From 1883 to 1893 Chi Psi used the Foss House, owned by Wesleyan. See *OP* '84, 26:1. *CA* 3 July 1884; *ZH* 9 July 1884; *WUC*, 1884/85–1889/90; *ZH* 4 July 1883; *OP* '84, 26:44, '85, 27:46; Le Duc, *Piety*, 121; Rice, "Wesleyan," 659; William North Rice, "Wesleyan University," in *The New England States*, ed. William T. Davis, vol. 2 (Boston: D. H. Hurd, 1897), 738; *CA* 7 July 1881; Daniel Steele to WNR 12 Aug. 1882, WNRP; *ZH* 1 July 1891.

57. The best source on this topic is F. B. Barrows and G. B. Munson, "The Douglas Cannon Scrap," *WLM* 24(May–June 1916): 326–39, 374–98. For examples of faculty and administrative attitudes, see FM 29 Jan. 1872; Cyrus Foss, Jr., to CDF, 24 Jan. 1888, CDFP, box 3. Barrows, "Douglas," 378.

58. On this form of hazing, see Cornelius H. Patton and Walter T. Field, *Eight O'Clock Chapel: A Study of New England College Life in the Eighties* (Boston: Houghton Mifflin, 1927), 238–41. *MP* 22 Feb. 1886; CDF to Jane C. Foss, 22 May 1877, Cyrus Foss, Jr., to Amelia R. Foss, 22 Sept. 1887, CDFP, boxes 3, 9.

59. Cyrus Foss, Jr., to Amelia R. Foss, 22 Sept. 1887, CDFP, box 9; *WUB* (November 1920):9; Karl P. Harrington, "'Doc Raymond'" *WUA* 34(May 1950): 11; *MP* 26 Nov. 1909. Usually practiced at alumni luncheons and dinners, the ritual began when a speaker asked: "Who was Doc Raymond?" The response then was chanted to a table-banging, dish-crashing percussive conclusion: "The man that cussed! The man that swore! The man that kicked in Sutherland's door! Bang! bang!—Bang! bang! BANG!" See [Arthur E. Sutherland], "'Open Door Policy' Inaugurated at Wesleyan—in 1882," *WUA* 36(January 1952): 13. Raymond had a remarkable memory for individual graduates, and they often made his home their first stop when returning to the campus. See *WUB* (November 1920):10; *Middletown Sun* 6 Apr. 1910. He even supervised preparation of the commencement-week dinner for alumni (*ZH* 6 July 1876). Class albums, 1865–91.

60. *CA* 29 Mar. 1871; Svonkin, "Pluralistic Ideal," 16–17, 23. This profile contrasts sharply with that for Williams College, where the students by 1872 tended to enter at age eighteen and come from wealthy urban families (Rudolph, *Hopkins*, 62–72).

61. *WA* 18 Oct. 1881; Nicolson, "Age," 45. Data on tuition at nineteenth-century New England colleges were gathered from their annual catalogues. Wesleyan's tuition went from $33 to $75 in 1874. See ARP (1874):468. This rate remained until 1906. *ZH* 25 July 1872, 10 June 1875. ARP (1882):1; schedule of beneficiaries of the New England Education Society, 1857–93, NEMHS; *Annual Reports of the Board of Managers of the New England Education Society* (1884–90), NEMHS; *CA* 28 July, 11 Aug., 29 Sept. 1881; *MP* 21 Aug. 1885; *CA* 29 July 1886. The highly competitive Seney scholarships drew frequent student criticism (*OP* '86, 28:8, 105, '87, 29:14, '88, 30:106), particularly when used in a financially threatening way to enforce rules of

conduct and class attendance (FM 30 Sept., 21 Oct. 1884). Record books of the Ladies University Education Society, September 1858–February 1877. On the concept of cultural currency in the form of diplomas and degrees issued by formal agencies such as schools and colleges, see Randall Collins, *The Credential Society: An Historical Sociology of Education and Stratification* (New York: Academic Press, 1979), 60–65.

62. ARP (1889):2; Caleb T. Winchester, "Wesleyan University," in *The College Book*, ed. Charles F. Richardson and Henry A. Clark (Boston: Houghton, Osgood, 1878), 318; Rice, "Wesleyan" (1876), 659; *ZH* 19 Feb. 1880, 25 July 1872; *CA* 26 July 1894.

63. *WUB* (November 1895):2; *WAR* (1911), 336–408; *WUB* (December 1902):22. Reasons offered for only about 20 percent of students in the 1830s becoming Methodist ministers were the need for employment with sufficient salary to pay large debts incurred for college expenses and the demand for teachers in "our literary institutions" (*CA* 7 June 1839). *WA* 3, 17, 31 May 1871; *WAR* (1883), 316; *WUA* 17(January 1933): 91. For similar trends at Amherst, see Fuess, *Amherst*, 423. *Wesleyan's Outposts* (n.p.: Wesleyan University, 1917), 7–12; ARP (1893):4, (1899):1–4.

64. *CA* 2 Sept. 1880; *ZH* 30 June 1886; *CA* 6 July 1876, 29 Jan. 1885. For a fascinating analysis of Yale's origins and their implications for its institutional identity, see George W. Pierson, *The Founding of Yale: The Legend of the Forty Folios* (New Haven: Yale University Press, 1988), esp. chap. 15.

65. The eleven accounts in order of appearance are: Gabriel P. Disosway, "The Wesleyan University: Dr. A. W. Smith," *MR* 49(January 1867): 93–99; [Caleb T. Winchester], "Historical," *WAR* (1869), 6–7; G. Brown Goode, "Wesleyan University," *CR* 2(September 1870): 6–9, and "History of Wesleyan University," *WA* 26 Oct., 9 Nov. 1870; [Caleb T. Winchester], "Historical Sketch of Wesleyan University," *WAR* (1873), xi-xiv; William North Rice, "Wesleyan University," *Scribner's Monthly* 12(September 1876): 648–61; [Morris B. Crawford], "Wesleyan University," *New England Journal of Education*, 28 Oct. 1876, 181–82; Caleb T. Winchester, "Wesleyan University," in *The College Book* ed. Charles F. Richardson and Henry A. Clark, (Boston: Houghton, Osgood, 1878), 301–19; Daniel Chase "Letters from Alumni—Birth and Infancy of Wesleyan" *WA* 7, 27 Nov., 8 Dec. 1879; Daniel Dorchester, "The Semi-Centennial of the Wesleyan University in 1881," *CA* 28 Oct., 4 Nov. 1880; [James M. Buckley], "1831. Wesleyan University. 1881," *CA* 16 June 1881. Disosway, Crawford, Rice, and Buckley begin with the Methodists. Goode, Chase, and Dorchester begin with Middletown or Partridge's academy. No connecting link between local and denominational events is made by Disosway, Crawford, Winchester (1867), or Buckley. Goode, Winchester, and Rice portray the link as accidental, or based on a trifling conversation or sportive suggestion. Their oldest source for this interpretation is probably Holdich, *Life*, 219–20. Chase and Dor-

chester see a substantive connection of important previous efforts by both parties. For a similar early account of Wesleyan's founding from a non-Methodist perspective, see John W. Barber, *Connecticut Historical Collections* (New Haven: John W. Barber, 1836), 510–11. A rare sequel to the Barber, Chase, and Dorchester renditions can be found in Arthur F. Goodrich, "Historical Wesleyan: Beginnings," *WLM* 6(October 1897): 24–26. For an outside history based largely on the accounts by members of the Wesleyan family, see Bernard C. Steiner, *The History of Education in Connecticut* (Washington, D.C.: GPO, 1893), 258–81.

66. Winchester, "Wesleyan" (1878), 307. Chase mentions Nehemiah Hubbard; Dorchester names the seven trustees appointed by academy trustees, and makes particular mention of Samuel D. Hubbard. On the state grants, see text at chap. 3 nn50–57.

67. On Clark's role, c.f. text at chap. 1 nn17–25. Goode, "Wesleyan," 6–7; Winchester, "Wesleyan" (1878), 306–7; Disosway, "Wesleyan," 99; Buckley, "Wesleyan," 1.

68. James M. King, "Historical Address," in *Semi-Centennial of Wesleyan University . . . , 1881* (n.p., n.d.), 15–29; *CA* 5 July 1877, 4 July 1878, 6 Oct. 1879; *ZH* 30 June 1886, 26 June 1889, 19 Mar. 1890; *CA* 14 Dec. 1899, 29 Mar. 1877; Rice, "Wesleyan" (1897), 732; William North Rice, "The History and Work of Wesleyan University," in *Celebration of the Seventy-Fifth Anniversary of the Founding of Wesleyan University* (Middletown: Wesleyan University, 1907), 48.

69. *Semi-Centennial*, 12–15, 42–48; *WAR* (1911), 846.

70. *Semi-Centennial*, 22; *FEx* 1902–3; *JGC* (1900), 830–33, 322, 465–67; *CA* 20 July, 14 Dec. 1899, 8 Mar. 1900, 25 Apr., 7 Nov. 1901; *WUB* (June 1899):1; ARP (1899):1–4; *FEx* 1899–1904; *CA* 17 Sept. 1903; BTM 30 June 1903, 15 Apr. 1904, 30 Mar. 1905. The $183,000 reported in 1905 was probably mostly in subscriptions. Subsequent financial exhibits show little actually paid in beyond the $41,000 received by June 1906. A mild recession from mid-1903 to mid-1904 probably created some difficulties for the second campaign (Mitchell, *Business Cycles*, 369).

71. *CA* 5 Dec. 1901; *WUB* (June 1902):1–3; *Celebration of the Wesley Bi-Centennial by Wesleyan University* (folded sheet dated March 1902), 3; William North Rice, "The Wesley Bicentennial," *North American Review* 176(June 1903): 831. In the selection of speakers, the program committee clearly opted for scholars more often than for celebrities. Even Woodrow Wilson was invited before his election as president of Princeton (CTW to WW, 3 Apr. 1902, *PWW* 12:314–15).

72. *Wesley Bicentennial, Wesleyan University* (Middletown: Wesleyan University, 1904), 44; Caleb T. Winchester, "John Wesley, the Man," in *Wesley Bicentennial*, 108, 99, 110, 103, 108; *Wesley Bicentennial*, 153; Woodrow Wilson, "John Wesley's Place in History," in *Wesley Bicentennial*, 165, 168–70.

73. *CA* 9 July 1903; William R. Hutchison, *The Modernist Impulse in American Protestantism* (Cambridge: Harvard University Press, 1976), 78, 102–3; Peterson, *New England*, 100, 138, 175–82; Tobias, *Old Dartmouth*, 112–13, chap. 6; Dartmouth College, *Catalogue* 1892/93, 1902/03, 1908/09; William Tucker, "Address," in *Wesley Bicentennial*, 188–89.

74. ʙᴛᴍ 15 May 1903. For information on Olin as an influential trustee, see chap. 6. *Wesley Bicentennial*, 131–54, 14–17.

75. Proceedings of the Electoral Conferences, 6 Apr. 1888; *WUB* (May 1901):1; *ZH* 6 July 1904. Fisk Hall was dedicated 28 June 1904, Scott Laboratory on 7 Dec. 1904 (*Celebration 75th*, 175–81). *Wesleyan University and the Wesley Bi-Centennial* (Middletown: Wesleyan University, 1902), 14.

Chapter 5 Methodist Professors

1. For biographical information on Van Vleck, see *WUB* (December 1912):8–13, (June 1911):29; *CA* 28 Nov. 1912; *WA* 7 Nov. 1912; Jane Van Vleck, *Ancestry and Descendants of Tielman Van Vleck of Niew Amsterdam* (New York: n.p., 1955), 284–85, 311–12. Van Vleck's two years at the Almanac Office, adjacent to Harvard and an important site in the early professionalization of American science, must have brought him into contact with such scholars as Benjamin Pierce, Maria Mitchell, Joseph Winlock, George Bond, and Benjamin Gould. No comments of Van Vleck on this experience can be located. But Simon Newcomb's testimony to the talent and intellectual vitality of this environment he entered as a young scientist just a few years after Van Vleck's departure indicates the important role the Almanac Office played in shaping scholarly outlooks and commitments for the young people it employed. See Simon Newcomb, *The Reminiscences of an Astronomer* (Boston: Houghton, Mifflin, 1903), 1–2, chap. 3; and Arthur L. Norberg, "Simon Newcomb's Early Astronomical Career" *Isis* 69(June 1978): 212–15. For biographical sketches of Atwater, Rice, and Winchester see text at nn76–100. Three of the four professors (Van Vleck was about to retire) led planning for the Wesley Bicentennial. William North Rice headed the program committee, upon which Caleb T. Winchester also served. Wilbur O. Atwater was a member of the committee on publications (minutes of the joint committee for celebration of the Wesley Bicentennial, 3 Jan. 1902, 22 Jan. 1903).

2. *WAR* (1911), 218; Charles E. Rosenberg, "Rationalization and Reality in Shaping American Agricultural Research, 1875–1914," in *The Sciences in the American Context: New Perspectives*, ed. Nathan Reingold (Washington, D.C.: Smithsonian Institution Press, 1979), 145; ᴡᴏᴀ to ᴡɴʀ, 2 Dec. 1872, 16 June 1873, ᴡɴʀᴘ. John Johnston, who had taught chemistry and other natural sciences at Wesleyan since 1835, retired on 24 June 1873 (ʙᴛᴍ 24 June 1873). Atwater was hired a few weeks later (ᴡᴏᴀ to ᴡɴʀ 2, 8 July 1873, ᴡɴʀᴘ).

3. FM 18 Feb. 1892; JBM 13–14 May 1831. The text of bylaws adopted in 1833 (JBM 27 Aug. 1833) apparently has not survived in manuscript or published form. The text published in 1859 was revised before final approval. The approved text appears only in the board minutes (JBM 21 June 1859). *Charter and By-Laws of Wesleyan University, Middletown, Conn.* (Bridgeport, Conn.: Gould and Stiles, 1884). Revisions bearing the same title were printed by Pelton and King in 1890 and 1894 and by Hartford Press in 1911.

4. For glimpses of the emerging concept of "permanent," "tenured," or senior faculty as compared to the lower differentiated ranks first appearing in the 1880s, see FM 12 Jan. 1886, 13 Mar. 1890, 18 Feb. 1892; RAC 2 Mar. 1893, 23 June 1894, 21 June 1899, 8 June 1908; FM 23 Nov. 1909. Recommendations of the Academic Council went to a companion committee of the board. This trustee committee evolved during the late 1880s, attaining full stature and form in 1890 as the committee on the board of instruction (BTM 20 Jan., 22 June 1886, 28 June 1887, 26 June 1888, 25 June, 15 Dec. 1889, 24 June 1890; *WUC* 1890/91, 6).

5. A breach in one of the three areas of full prerogative occurred in 1912, when a trustee committee assumed responsibility for recommending candidates for honorary degrees.

6. WNR in *Addresses . . . Foss*, 14–15. Action taken in 1886 gave a vote to those below the rank of full professor, except on matters of personnel or honorary degrees (FM 18 Jan. 1886).

7. Not included in these totals are the president (who chaired faculty meetings) and instructional staff, such as lecturers and course assistants, whose salaries clearly indicate part-time status. FM 7 Oct. 1890, 9 June 1896, 5 Jan., 2, 9, 30 Mar. 1897. Locations for the meetings were: 1870–80, North College (President's Room); 1881–92, Judd Hall (a classroom); 1892–95, South College; 1895–1904, North College; 1905–6, Fisk Hall; 1907–58, South College.

8. FM 13 Sept. 1871; *ZH* 22 Apr. 1875. By 1886/87 only two of the sixteen faculty members besides President Beach were ministers (*WUC* 1886/87, 7–8). FM 17 Sept. 1875, 23 May 1883, 4, 14, 15 Sept. 1874, 18 Nov. 1890. In 1876 and 1881 the faculty successfully continued their resistance to trustee desires for organization of a Methodist church on campus (FM 20 Sept., 31 Oct. 1876, 18 May 1881).

9. FM 1881–1908.

10. FM 30 June, 1 Oct. 1892, 26 Feb., 10 Mar. 1884, 17 Feb. 1885. Park H. Davis, *Football: The American Intercollegiate Game* (New York: Charles Scribner's Sons, 1911), 84, 88–90, 95. Wesleyan joined the new Intercollegiate Athletic Association of the United States (renamed the NCAA in 1910) in 1906. See FM 11 Dec. 1906; Ronald A. Smith, *Sports and Freedom: The Rise of Big-Time College Athletics* (New York: Oxford University Press, 1988),

chap. 14, 273n53. FM 14 Mar. 1899, 21 May 1900, 28 May 1901, 11 Mar. 1902, 31 Mar., 13 Oct. 1903. *Constitution and Bylaws of the Amherst College Athletic Board* (n.p. [ca. 1890]), 1–2; *Constitution and By-Laws of the Athletic Council and Association of Williams College, 1897–1906* (n.p., n.d.), 3–4. Wesleyan's council had broad responsibilities for fundraising, employing coaches, scheduling, and enforcing eligibility rules, but the faculty retained authority to exclude a student from a team for reasons of deficiency in scholarship or for misconduct. For the constitution and bylaws of the council, see *Wesleyan University: Handbook of Athletics* (Middletown: Wesleyan University Athletic Council, 1905), 9–15. FM 18, 24 Apr., 22 May 1906. Records of the council reflect considerable diplomacy in negotiating eligibility issues with Williams and Trinity (Athletic Council minutes, 29 Oct. 1903–29 June 1910).

11. FM 3 July 1877; W. E. Woodruff '87, R1939; FM 3 Sept. 1870, 7 Feb. 1893, 22 June 1891, 6 Dec. 1892. For a brief history of the honor system at Wesleyan, see John W. Spaeth, Jr., "Concerning the Honor System," *WUA* 35(January 1951): 3–4. FM 21 Mar. 1900, 21 Oct. 1872, 24 Feb. 1881, 25 Apr. 1910, 2 Mar. 1897, 10 Mar. 1896.

12. FM 27 Oct. 1890, 16 Oct. 1871; *WUC* 1895/96, 10; RAC 2 Mar. 1893; FM 29 Nov. 1898.

13. FM 1, 15 Oct. 1879, 7 Feb. 1893, 19 Jan. 1904, 19 Jan. 1909, 5 Oct. 1904.

14. FM 16 Nov. 1880, 2, 8 Nov. 1881, 1 Dec. 1885, 18 May 1886. The commission was spawned by the New England Association of Colleges and Preparatory Schools, established in 1885. See Edwin C. Broome, *A Historical and Critical Discussion of College Admission Requirements* (New York: Columbia University, 1903), 129. The Committee of Ten's report, completed in December 1893 and issued the following month, was both controversial and influential. It "represented a skillful compromise between traditional practices and the demands for change." See Theodore R. Sizer, *Secondary Schools at the Turn of the Century* (New Haven: Yale University Press, 1964), 143, chaps. 7–9. FM 30 Mar. 1897.

15. Yale's entrance examinations were oral and informal until 1871. See Claude M. Fuess, *The College Board: Its First Fifty Years* (New York: Columbia University Press, 1950), 5. FM 10 Feb. 1874, 29 Apr. 1879, 5 June 1883, 14 Apr., 10 May 1881, 14 Mar. 1902, 14 Jan. 1908. Harvard (1904) and Williams (1907) preceded Wesleyan in joining the CEEB; Yale (1909) and Amherst (1910) followed (Fuess, *College Board* 42, 52–53). FM 2 July 1887, 12 Mar. 1889, 21 May 1901, 25 Mar. 1902; *WUC* 1902/03, 33. The New England College Entrance Certificate Board (1902) did not include Harvard or Yale. See Edward A. Krug, *The Shaping of the American High School* (New York: Harper & Row, 1964), 156. Almost 77 percent of the students entering Wesleyan in 1906 were admitted by certificate. See ARP (1907):5–7. For

examples of faculty action on standards and recruiting, see FM 18 Nov. 1891, 23 Apr. 1895, 1 July 1901, 22 Nov. 1904, 25 Apr. 1893, 11 Jan. 1896. The faculty was also active in recommending students for financial aid. For examples, see FM 28 Sept. 1870, 10 Sept. 1873, 10 June 1884, 27 Mar. 1888, 17 Dec. 1895.

16. FM 17 Dec. 1873; *WUC* 1875/76, 42–43; FM 4 Dec. 1888; *WUC* 1888/89, 62–65; FM 21 Jan. 1896; *WUC* 1896/97, 87–91.

17. FM 19 June 1877. Wesleyan's action was well in advance of the national campaign against honorary Ph.D.'s, led by Nicholas Murray Butler in the 1890s. See Walter Crosby Eells, "Honorary Ph.D.'s in the Twentieth Century," *School and Society* 85(2 Mar. 1957): 74–75. FM 16 July 1872, 8, 24, 25 June 1878, 24 June 1879, 29 Apr., 20 May, 10 June 1884, 19 Oct. 1886, 14 June 1887; BTM 27 June 1888; *WUC* 1853/54, 21; FM 13 June 1890; BTM 24 June 1890. The nineteenth-century practice of granting the M.A. *in curso* three years after graduation for a fee (usually five dollars) persisted at most colleges until at least the 1870s. One of the last to end this custom was Hamilton College in 1918. By 1890 about one thousand earned master's degrees had been awarded in the United States. See Walter C. Eells, *Degrees in Higher Education* (New York: Center for Applied Research in Education, 1963), 76; [Frank K. Lorenz], "Academic Degrees at Hamilton," in *Hamilton College, 1985 Register* (Clinton, N.Y.: Hamilton College, 1986), xvii–xviii; Stephen H. Spurr, *Academic Degree Structures: Innovative Approaches* (New York: McGraw-Hill, 1970), 14. And having recommended in 1888 that the M.A. be conferred as an honorary degree "only in rare cases" (FM 14 June 1887), the senior faculty comprising the recently established Academic Council (1892) recommended in 1894 that the trustees institute a practice of granting the M.A. *ad eundem* to "those permanent members of the Faculty who are graduates of other colleges." Since only five faculty members at the time qualified for this honor (and one seems to have declined it), they may have been considered "rare cases" Among the "permanent" or full professors thus brought into the Wesleyan alumni-alumnae ranks *ad eundem gradum* in 1894 was Bradford P. Raymond, the first president of the university to hold a Ph.D. (RAC 23 June 1894; BTM 26 June 1894).

This particular degree usage is probably unique to Wesleyan. It borrows in part from customs found at Oxford, Cambridge, Harvard, and Yale in the eighteenth century for granting the B.A. and M.A. *ad eundem* as a form of academic reciprocity and courtesy. Holders of a degree from one of these institutions occasionally applied for and received the same degree and privileges from another of them. In 1900 Yale began a somewhat similar practice of awarding the M.A. *privatim* (and thus not at a public ceremony such as commencement) to full professors (and members of its corporation, Yale's nineteen trustees) who do not hold either a master's degree or doctorate from Yale (Eells, *Degrees*, 11–14).

18. FM 14 July 1870. This proposal probably originated with Gilbert Haven '46 (Gravely, *Gilbert Haven*, 174). Had Wesleyan recognized Douglass (1817–95) in this manner, it would have become the only white college to join Wilberforce and perhaps a few other black colleges in granting him an honorary degree (*DANB*, 186). FM 17 Apr. 1895, 21 Oct., 8 Dec. 1896, 22 Jan. 1901.

19. "To the Legislature of the State of Connecticut, Now in Session in the City of Hartford" (petition signed by Willbur Fisk et al., dated 19 May 1837) RG2 RSC-GA, Theatre Law Petitions, 1837. The law was sustained. See Morse, *Neglected*, 141. By the end of the century, faculty worried about students appearing as actors in dramatic performances "of questionable propriety" (FM 17 Mar. 1896). FM 19 Dec. 1871, 6 Mar. 1888, 20, 23 Mar. 1897.

20. FM 14 Sept. 1875. A similar committee was appointed in 1888 (FM 31 Jan. 1888). RAC 18 Oct. 1901; FM 5 Nov. 1901, 11, 25 Oct. 1887.

21. See text at chap. 2 n48.

22. Daniel Dorchester, "The Higher Educational Institutions of New England," *MR* 54(April, July 1872): 181–94, 399–413. Dorchester entered Wesleyan in 1843 and left during his junior year. At the time these articles were published his son was a member of the junior class at Wesleyan.

23. *WA* 26 Sept. 1872, 28 May 1873; FM 26 May, 16, 23 June 1873; ARP (1873):439–42, 445. The board approved replacing the ailing Johnston with a professor of analytical chemistry and appointing Caleb T. Winchester, who held the title of librarian, to be a full professor of rhetoric and English literature (report of the committee on the course of study, 24 June 1873, NCAR, box 1; BTM 24 June 1873).

24. Fuess, *Amherst*, 231–32; Peterson, *New England*, 53–54, 64–65; Lord, *History* 2:439. Yale took a half-step toward electives in 1876 (Kelley, *Yale*, 266–68).

25. *WUC* 1868/69, 20–23, 1869/70, 20–24, 1873/74, 21–24; *WA* 29 Sept. 1869, 24 Sept. 1873. For a detailed account of these curricular changes, see William North Rice, "The Curriculum of Wesleyan University," *WLM* 13(June 1905): 354–59.

26. *WUC* 1873/74, 25–30.

27. *WA* 24 Sep. 1873; report of the visiting committee of the board of trustees, June 1896, NCAR box 1; FM 18 May 1886; *WUC* 1885/86, 43–44, 1886/87, 4–41, 1899/1900, 68. A bit daunted by the array of choices in an elective system and mindful of an advising system just announced at Amherst, students called for a system of advising, at least for freshmen, in which each student "would be assigned to some member of the faulty to whom he might refer for the needed advice in the choice of electives" (*WA* 16 May 1900). Although an advising system was discussed by faculty in 1902, there is no record of one being established at this date (*WA* 16 May, 4 June 1902; FM 11 Mar., 13, 20 May 1902).

28. On the importance of specialization to development of the academic profession in late nineteenth-century America, see John Higham, "The Matrix of Specialization," in *The Organization of Knowledge in Modern America, 1860–1920*, ed. Alexandra Oleson and John Voss (Baltimore: Johns Hopkins University Press, 1979), 3–18. William North Rice, "Response of Professor Rice" in *Tributes to Professor William North Rice* (n.p.: Wesleyan Alumni Council, 1915), 34–35; *WUC* 1872/73, 1893/94, 29–53, 1884/85, 23–44. The evolution of departments (defined initially as areas of study to which a full faculty position is devoted) from 1870 to 1910 can be traced in the *WUC* and FM:

Moral and intellectual philosophy yielded:
>1. moral philosophy and Christian evidences (1884), which became ethics and Christian evidences (1886), then ethics and religion (1898), and
>2. mental philosophy (1884), which became philosophy (1886) and included a professor of psychology (1902) until psychology became a department in 1913. Arrangements for a psychology department were discussed as early as 1884 (FM 25 Apr. 1884).

Natural science yielded:
>1. chemistry (1873) and
>2. physics (1880).

Geology and natural history (part of natural science before 1867) yielded:
>1. geology (1884) and
>2. biology (1884).

Rhetoric and English literature yielded:
>1. English language (1890) and
>2. English literature (1890).

Modern languages (1873) yielded:
>1. German (1890) and
>2. Romance languages (1890).

History and political economy (1880, but known in its first year as political and social science) yielded:
>1. history (1890) and
>2. economics and social science (1890). (Economics and social science was staffed by a tutor, John R. Commons, in 1890/91 and by an instructor in 1891/92 before an associate professor was hired to head the department for 1892/93.)

Latin, Greek, mathematics and astronomy (not split until 1914), and elocution (after a hiatus of two years became public speaking in 1906) remained single departments throughout these forty years.

A faculty rank structure also evolved in the 1880s, particularly as some departments added staff beyond the original arrangement of one full professor for each subject area. In addition to the short-term appointments as tutor or departmental assistant, long-term prospects through promotion appeared in the form of initial appointments as instructor or as associate professor. See *WUB* (30 May 1891):2. Similar differentiated rank structure had evolved at Harvard and Dartmouth by 1880 (McCaughey "Transformation" 318–21; Tobias, *Old Dartmouth*, 150).

29. FM 17 Dec. 1873, 13 Sept. 1883, 19 Nov. 1889, 25 Nov. 1902; Wesleyan University [*Regulations*], [1873], [1883], [1889], [1902]; *WUC* 1886/87, 23. Although continuing until 1919 to list three terms separated by vacations, Wesleyan's calendar began to schedule midyear examinations (during the second term) in 1890 (*WUC* 1889/90, 73). In 1896 the faculty voted to formalize this practice, using midyear examinations to divide the academic year into two equal portions (FM 3 Nov. 1896). The word *semester* was first used in the calendar in 1925 (*WUC* 1925/26, 3), finally describing what, in terms of the smallest course-unit length, had been customary since 1886. FM 16 Feb. 1892; BTM 4 Mar. 1892; *WUC* 1870/71, 25, 1886/87, 40–43; FM 20 Mar. 1907; *WUC* 1908/09, 87. On the origin of credit hours, the "central piece of the American educational system," see Dietrich Gerhard, "The Emergence of the Credit System in American Education Considered as a Problem of Social and Intellectual History," American Association of University Professors *Bulletin* 41(Winter 1955): 647–68.

30. See text at chap. 1 n43 and chap. 2 nn40–43.

31. Caleb T. Winchester, Reporter, *Ceremonies and Speeches at . . . the Orange Judd Hall of Natural Science . . . 1870 . . . 1871* (n.p. [ca. 1871]), 8–9, 14–16, 20–21, 31, 45–54.

32. *OP '73*, 15:3–4; *CA* 6 July 1882; *WUB* (May 1892):2; *WA* 12 Dec. 1892.

33. Winchester, "Wesleyan" (1878), 310; *WUB* (April 1888):9–10, (November 1895):10. Rice, who assessed the academic atmosphere in 1895, is the best example of a faculty member embracing equally the mental discipline goal of the Yale *Reports* of 1828, the religious faith of Stephen Olin, and the research goals of late nineteenth-century science. See *WUB* (April 1888):4–6; *ZH* 20 Dec. 1899; *WUB* (November 1895):9–10. The theme of independent investigation by faculty and students runs throughout the articles on curriculum found in the *WUB* for November 1895. For an earlier and more detailed exposition that sounds much like the educational philosophy soon developed by John Dewey, see Herbert B. Conn "Original Research in the American College," *Science* 10(2 Sept. 1887): 109–12. When the elective system was fully developed and the lecture mode extensively used, a faculty member reminded listeners in 1913 that these devices, too, could be and were misused to the extent that students no longer thought as deeply and extensively as they did under the requirements and the recitation method of an earlier era. See Caleb T. Winchester, "Address by Prof. Winchester," in *Wesleyan University New York Alumni Association, Annual Banquet, January 10, 1913* (n.p., 1913), 5–6.

34. ARL 1871/72; *WUB* (November 1895):15. James was appointed librarian in 1891 and given a salary equal to that of a full professor in 1893; he also served as instructor in mathematics from 1890 to 1895. See *WUB* (May 1891):10; BTM 6 Mar. 1893; *WUB* (May 1893):1; *WAR* (1911), 358.

35. ARL 1887/88, 1889/90; *WUB* (January 1888):12, (May 1894):13. Library hours are listed in *WUC* 1873/74–1898/99. ARL 1898/99, 1870/71, 1891/92, 1909/10; Rider, "Growth," 4–6; *WUB* (May 1895):1–2, (May 1896):3, (June 1899):2, (November 1901):12, (November 1904):1; ARL 1909/10, 1904/05, 1906/07; ARP (1907):16–17; *WA* 9 Jan. 1907. From 1900 to 1912 receipts from bequests and annuities for endowed book funds from the estates of Rev. Albert S. Hunt, Harriet H. Wilcox, Elizabeth J. Mead, and Rev. Daniel Wise reached a total exceeding $60,000 (*FEx* 1900–12). Another source of growth in the collection was established in 1906, when Wesleyan's library was designated as a depository for public documents issued by the U.S. government. Documents in the Government Printing Office record that Wesleyan was so designated 30 Oct. 1906. Reports of an earlier date are probably premature. See *WA* 9 Mar. 1904; *WUB* (November 1904):13.

36. ARL 1868/69; Caleb T. Winchester, "Wesleyan University," *Library Journal* 2(October 1877): 70; Walter M. Whitehill, *Boston Public Library: A Centennial History* (Cambridge: Harvard University Press, 1956), 67, 69, 97, 77, 91, 103; ARL 1891/92, 1893/94; *WA* 14 Mar. 1894; ARL 1896/97; *WUB* (May 1897): 13, (November 1899): 11–13; ARL 1899/1900. Diefendorf (who before 1902 spelled her name without an *i*) was succeeded in 1904 by Ernestine Rose '02, B.L.S. New York State Library School '04, who stayed for one year before moving to a career of almost four decades in the New York Public Library system. Adrienne Van Winkle, who had worked with Cutter at the Forbes Library in Northampton, Mass., served from 1905 to 1907. Marguerite Van Benschoten '04, who had experience at the Brooklyn Public Library, served from 1907 to 1910. ARL 1907/08; *WUB* (May 1908):24; ARL 1909/10.

37. For information on Goode's career, see *DAB* 4:381–82; William North Rice, "George Brown Goode," *WUB* (November 1896):13–15; Paul H. Oehser, "George Brown Goode, 1851–1896," *Scientific Monthly* 64(March 1948): 195–205; Sally Gregory Kohlstedt, "History in a Natural History Museum: George Brown Goode and the Smithsonian Institution," *Public Historian*, 10(Spring, 1988): 7–26. *ARCM* (1878):7–9; *CA* 7 Mar. 1878; *ARCM* (1876):5–7.

38. *WUB* (May 1896):6; *ARCM* (1878):9–10, (1881):6, (1888):9; *WUB* (January 1888):8, (November 1894):12, (November 1897):10, WNR to G. Brown Goode, 22 Jan., 9 Dec. 1881, 23 Sept. 1882, 11 Feb., 26 July 1887, 6 Feb. 1888, 12 Nov. 1890, 11 June 1894, Smithsonian Institution Archives, record unit 54, box 106. Spencer F. Baird, secretary of the Smithsonian (1878–87), encouraged activities to build collections at colleges and acade-

mies. See Sally Gregory Kohlstedt, "Curiosities and Cabinets: Natural History Museums and Education on Antebellum Campuses," *Isis* 79(Sept. 1988): 425. Ties with Goode also brought published United States documents to Wesleyan's library. See ARL 1872/73. *WUB* (May 1910):16–17, (November 1896):11–12, (November 1897): 10, (May 1901),14.

39. Sally Gregory Kohlstedt, "Natural History at Dickinson and Other Colleges in the Nineteenth Century," *John and Mary's Journal* 10(Winter 1985): 42–44; W. O. Atwater and E. B. Rosa, "A New Respiration Calorimeter and Experiments on the Conservation of Energy in the Human Body," *Physical Review* 9(September, October 1899): 129–63, 214–51; *WUB* (May 1900):9–10, (December 1902):13, (May 1906):25; *WA* 20 Apr. 1904; A. A. Roback, *History of American Psychology* (New York: Library Publishers, 1952), 129–34; *WUB* (November 1895): 4. The psychology laboratory moved to the second floor of the new Fisk Hall in 1904 (*WA* 25 Jan. 1905). *WUB* (December 1905):25, (May 1906):26, (December 1906):22; *ARCM* (1892):5; *WUB* (May 1919):37–38, 33.

40. Data on graduate students are drawn primarily from *WUC* 1873/74–1909/10. *WUB* (November 1895):13–14; FM 11 June, 1 Oct. 1889; *WUB* (May 1894):5; *CA* 12 Aug. 1886; FM 28 Mar., 14, 20, 22, 27 May 1870, 2, 18 Dec. 1891, 26 Jan. 1892; *WUB* (November 1890):2. Almost everyone who applied for graduate study was admitted (minutes of the committee of the faculty on graduate instruction, 3 Oct. 1889–11 July 1910). Yale awarded its first earned M.A. in 1876, Trinity in 1889. The number of such degrees awarded nationally multiplied rapidly in the several decades after 1890 (when the total was seventy). Whereas Wesleyan's graduate enrollments held at about a dozen per year in the 1890s, Trinity's stayed at two or three per year. See Walton C. John, *Graduate Study in Universities and Colleges in the United States* (Washington, D.C.: GPO, 1935), 6–15; Weaver, *Trinity*, 233.

41. Examining committees in the early 1870s were nominated by the faculty and approved by the executive committee of the board (FM 29 May 1871, 6, 13 May 1874). *ZH* 2 July 1874; *CA* 12 Aug. 1886.

42. FM 9 Dec. 1872, 11 Nov. 1873, 21 Apr. 1891. For information on examining committees from 1831 to 1870, see text at chap. 2 n54. The honor system instituted in 1893 to govern written exams, as well as the exams themselves, can be viewed as related to the high premium placed on independent investigation. The pledge signed by students stated: "I have neither used nor given any assistance during this examination." See FM 7 Feb. 1893. ww to J. Franklin Jameson, 12 June 1889, *PWW* 6:321.

43. FM 23 Feb., 3 Mar. 1891, 8 Nov. 1892, 2 Mar. 1893; BTM 6 Mar. 1893, 13–14 May 1831; report of the visiting committee . . . , 1896.

44. The new curriculum was approved in 1907 (FM 14 June 1907; BTM 6 Dec. 1907) after two years of "leisurely" debate. Dutcher, *Historical*, 27–28, 39. The idea of a major began to acquire advocates around the turn of

the century. A curricular revision in this direction at Williams preceded Wesleyan's by five years, putting somewhat more emphasis on distribution and less on the major. Amherst moved to a system in 1911 that continued to emphasize breadth by requiring three majors. The system of a single major of substantial depth plus a distribution system framed by three divisions did not appear at Amherst until the late 1930s. See Rudolph, *Curriculum*, 227–29; Williams College Catalogue 1903/04; Lawrence A. Babb et al., *Education at Amherst Reconsidered: The Liberal Studies Program* (Amherst, Mass.: Amherst College Press, 1978), 15, 17.

45. Dutcher, *Historical*, 28. Harvard's system of concentration and distribution was approved in 1909. Hawkins, *Between*, 272–78. Reforms to institute requirements for a concentration, or what would soon be called the major, occurred at Princeton in 1904 and Yale in 1908. See Alexander Leitch, *A Princeton Companion* (Princeton: Princeton University Press, 1978), 513; *PWW* 15:252–63, 277–95; Pierson, *Yale*, 262–63, 309–10). *WUC* 1907/08, 76. Until 1858 Wesleyan's curriculum required mathematics study in all four years (and up through calculus). Required mathematics departed from the junior year in 1869 and the sophomore year in 1892. The Greek requirement went from four years to three (except for a brief reappearance in 1852/53) in 1850. It was relegated to freshman and sophomore years in 1869 and to freshman year in 1892. Required study of Latin (with the exception of 1853/54 and 1858/59) remained at four years until 1869, when it dropped to just the freshman and sophomore years. Required only in the freshman year as of 1892, it remained a staple of freshman year for most students even after 1908, when a choice was provided between Latin and Greek (*WUC* 1831–1910).

46. Increasing the level of academic rigor across the curriculum was probably another important issue. The revision of 1908, for example, eliminated the weak Latin-scientific course leading to a bachelor of philosophy degree. It also instituted Saturday morning classes (*CA* 4 June 1908; Dutcher, *Historical*, 21, 30). *WUB* (December 1907):9; William North Rice, "The Curriculum of Wesleyan University," *WLM* 13(June 1905): 360; data compiled from *WUC* 1875/76– 1909/10; Rice, "Curriculum," 362. It was a short step from the link between curriculum and faculty professional values to specialized courses providing preparation for other careers. A few curriculum modifications in this direction appeared in 1907. See *WUB* (December 1908:5–6. A degree in electrical engineering based on courses taught by Walter Cady in the physics department was even considered. See ARP (1908):11.

47. Data on Wesleyan faculty are from *WAR* (1921). McCaughey, "Transformation," 331; Le Duc, *Piety*, 13–15, 49–50; Rudolph, *Hopkins*, 128, 131. Dartmouth was moving in the same direction, but at a slower pace (Tobias, *Old Dartmouth*, 153). Johns Hopkins awarded its first Ph.D.'s in 1878. See

Hugh Hawkins, *Pioneer: A History of the Johns Hopkins University, 1874–1889* (Ithaca, N.Y.: Cornell University Press, 1960), 122, 291.

48. Morris B. Crawford to WNR, 7 Apr. 1879, WNRP; William Rice to WNR, 24 Mar. 1880, WNRP.

49. Henry L. Osborn to WNR, 28 Aug. 1885, WNRP. Osborn was a biologist who received his Ph.D. from Johns Hopkins, as did Dewey, in 1884. Dewey was happily teaching at the University of Michigan in 1885 and had met Harriet Alice Chipman, whom he married when she graduated in 1886.

50. *WAR* (1881), 227; *NCAB* 14:138–39; *WA* 30 June 1885; *DAB* 6:199–200; *NCAB* 33:137–38; FM 20 May 1885; BTM 23 June 1885; *WA* 12, 30 June 1885; *PWW* 6:555–556; diary of John Franklin Jameson, 25 June 1885, John Franklin Jameson Papers, Manuscript Division, Library of Congress; *The Biographical Record of the Class of '79, Yale College* (New York: White, Stokes, and Allen, 1885), 57.

51. FM 10 May 1886; *WAR* (1911), 117; FM 26 May 1886; *WAR* (1911), 347; *DAB* 11:453–54; FM 27 May, 4 June 1886; *WAR* (1911), 285; *DAB* 10:4; *WA* 17 June 1886. Merrill joined the Episcopal church in 1891 and was ordained a priest in 1895, but his affinity for this denomination probably started to develop soon after the death of his first wife in 1885 (W. E. Woodruff '87, R1939). For a similar struggle between president and faculty at Dartmouth in 1881, see Tobias, *Old Dartmouth*, 31–42.

52. FM 19 July 1872; *ZH* 13 Nov. 1912; *CA* 12 June 1879; *ZH* 15 May 1879; *CA* 28 Nov. 1912. Van Vleck's distaste for public speaking and lack of clerical credentials precluded a candidacy for election to the presidency of Wesleyan, yet he was ranked with Willbur Fisk in having "an influence so widespread, so deep, so permanent" (*ZH* 21 Dec. 1887; *CA* 28 Nov. 1912). ARP (1888):3, (1889):4; *WUB* (15 Oct. 1888):11; John Van Vleck to C. C. Skilton, 5 Feb. 1912, Van Vleck Papers.

53. Herbert W. Conn to Albert Shaw, 13 Apr. [1888], Albert Shaw Papers, box 54, Rare Books and Manuscripts Division, New York Public Library; Elizabeth Donnan and Leo F. Stock, eds., *An Historian's World: Selections from the Correspondence of John Franklin Jameson* (Philadelphia: American Philosophical Society, 1956), 45n8; Lloyd J. Graybar, *Albert Shaw of the Review of Reviews: An Intellectual Biography* (Lexington: University Press of Kentucky, 1974), 5, 20; Donnan, *Historian's* 44n2; WW to James E. Rhoads, 7 June 1888, *PWW* 5:736. Wesleyan's offer of $2,500 compared favorably with Wilson's $2,000 salary at Bryn Mawr and the same amount offered to Jameson by Brown. See Henry W. Bragdon, *Woodrow Wilson: The Academic Years* (Cambridge: Harvard University Press, 1967), 160; Donnan, *Historian's*, 44n2. Bragdon, *Wilson*, 160, 150–151.

54. *PWW* 5:752n1, 6:16. Information on the denominational affiliation of Wesleyan faculty in 1887 and 1900 was obtained primarily from Record Book #9, First Methodist Episcopal Church, Middletown, Conn. Faculty

lists in the catalogues for fall 1887 and fall 1900 were also used to determine alumni percentages.

55. Bragdon, *Wilson*, 113, 124, 233; *PWW* 6:473, 326n1, 61–76; Bragdon, *Wilson*, 112, 124, 242; Hubert B. Goodrich, "Research Experiences and Problems at a Small College," *Science* 65(8 April 1927): 342–45; *WUB* (January 1899):3. Interest in scholarly productivity found expression at Wesleyan during the 1880s in the bibliography of writings by alumni and faculty published in *WAR* (1883), 529–668; the article in 1887 on "Original Research" by Herbert W. Conn; and the call for alumni to send copies of their books and other publications to the library in *WUB* (15 Oct. 1888):10. *PWW* 6:4,397.

56. Only two members of the faculty continuing from 1887/88 to 1888/89 were under forty. Cyrus Foss, Jr., to CDF, 2 Oct. 1888, CDFP; George H. Opdyke, "Woodrow Wilson's Relation to 'Art and Nature Appreciation,'" *WUA* 24(October 1939): 14. Among the collection of reminiscences on his teaching style, see those by George H. Opdyke and Charles Eggleston (papers relating to Woodrow Wilson at Wesleyan). Though Wilson disliked teaching women at Bryn Mawr and came to Wesleyan in part because he was "hungry for a class of men" (*PWW* 5:764,619, 6:11), surviving recollections from the tiny minority of women in his classes at Wesleyan make no comment suggesting bias against them (papers relating to Woodrow Wilson at Wesleyan). Hawkins, *Pioneer*, 277–78; *WA* 18 Jan. 1889; *WUB* (May 1889):10–11; Bragdon, *Wilson*, 172–73; Carl F. Price, "When Woodrow Wilson Was at Wesleyan," *CA* 7 Aug. 1919.

57. Van Vleck said he would advocate Wilson's appointment by the trustees "even with the risk of losing you soon" (*PWW* 5:735). Wilson's wife looked back on "poor Wesleyan" in 1892 as a college where trustees and faculty were destined to see "the best men . . . slip through their fingers" due to insufficient resources and reputation (*PWW* 7:608). Wilson attributed this inferiority of Wesleyan students to "a parentage, for the most part, of narrow circumstances and of correspondingly narrow thought" (*PWW* 6:481). When serving as a reader for examinations written by students competing for a prize, however, Wilson's friend Jameson found the Wesleyan students did very well compared to those he knew at Brown (*PWW* 6:643,673). ww to Robert Bridges, 26 Aug. 1888, *PWW* 5:763–64. Wilson told Williams that he would stay at Wesleyan if Princeton did not make an offer (*PWW* 6:454–57). His starting salary at Princeton was $3,000. This was $500 more than his salary at Wesleyan (*PWW* 6:526, 528–29, 542–43). While Wilson bargained with Princeton, Van Vleck worked to retain him at Wesleyan (*PWW* 6:537, 540).

58. ww to Azel Hazen, 8 Mar. 1890, ww to J. Franklin Jameson, 20 Mar. 1890, ww to Frederick Jackson Turner, 23 Aug. 1889, Frederick Jackson Turner to ww, 5 Feb. 1890, ww to Charles Homer Haskins, 27 May 1890,

PWW 6:545, 557, 369–71, 521–22, 632–33. Herbert W. Conn to Albert Shaw, 13 Apr. [1888], John Van Vleck to Albert Shaw, 14 Apr. 1888, Albert Shaw Papers, box 54, Rare Books and Manuscripts Division, New York Public Library; ww to Albert Shaw, 29 Apr., 5 May 1890, Albert Shaw to ww, 6 June 1890, *PWW* 6:617–18, 623–25, 640–41. In making this prediction, Wilson was greatly encouraged by the recent gift of $250,000 from Daniel Ayres (*PWW* 6:453–54).

59. The committee, appointed 29 June 1887, included three wealthy laymen (W. Hoyt, W. Ingraham, G. Reynolds), three ministers connected with literary pursuits (J. Buckley, J. King, W. Rice), and a bishop (E. Andrews). On Hunt (a Wesleyan trustee, 1888–98) and his candidacy, see William Rice to WNR, 29 Jan. 1888, WNRP; *WUB* (November 1899):5–6; *NCAB* 4:416; *MR* 82(March 1900): 177–95. Three of the candidates held Ph.D.'s from Boston University: Raymond, Ensign McChesney (pastor of St. Paul's in New York City), and James Bashford (about to accept the presidency of Ohio Wesleyan). George McGrew held a law degree from Harvard and published several books, Charles Little became a well-published scholar, and George Reed became president of Dickinson. Regarding their candidacies, see William Rice to WNR, 8 Nov. [1888], 19 Nov. 1888, WNRP. On Van Vleck's trip and counsel, see William Rice to WNR, 14 Feb., 19 Nov. 1888, WNRP; BTM 19 Nov. 1888. For a profile of Van Vleck and the respect he inspired, see W. E. Woodruff '87, R1939.

60. Because data in ARP (1903):3 and *WUB* (May 1896):1 are somewhat misleading, annual faculty lists in *WUC* were used to analyze the addition of positions and the student-faculty ratio for 1890–95. *WUB* (October 1889):8. Raymond studied at Leipzig and Göttingen in 1880/81 (*NCAB* 9:431) and received his Ph.D. in 1882. Boston University awarded its first Ph.D. in 1877, and had granted a total of eight before 1882. See *Historical Register of Boston University, 1869–1901* (Boston: Boston University, 1901), 52–69. For his fullest expression of pride in faculty research achievements, see ARP (1907):8–13. *Bradford Paul Raymond, 1846–1916* (Middletown: Wesleyan University, 1916), 10.

61. *CA* 9 Mar. 1916; *Raymond*, 3; WNR to G. Brown Goode, 1 Dec. 1875, 20 Sept. 1887, George Brown Goode Papers, Smithsonian Institution Archives, record unit 54, box 107, folder 1; *Raymond*, 12, 18; Francis G. Benedict, "Autobiographical Statements" (typescript of recollections dictated September and October 1920), 68, Francis G. Benedict Papers, Countway Library of Medicine, Boston; *CA* 2 Mar. 1916; *Raymond*, 24; *MNYEC* (1916), 136–37; *Raymond*, 18, 12. Faculty affection for Raymond was similar to that expressed toward Foss (WNR to CDF, 12 May 1880, George Prentice to CDF [13 May 1880], CDFP, box 3).

62. *WA* 13 July 1889; *MP* 26 June 1889; *Raymond*, 7–9; *NYTr* 27 June 1889; "Wesleyan University," 1044; *NCAB* 9:431. Frank Creamer, "Rev.

Bradford Paul Raymond," *University* 2(May 1889): 4–6. There is no complete text of Raymond's inaugural address, given with only occasional reference to an extended outline (*NYTr* 27 June 1889; *CA* 4 July 1889). The fullest text reported, based on the manuscript outline, appeared in *Zion's Herald* 17 July 1889.

63. All references to Raymond's inaugural address are from *ZH* 17 July 1889. Since the early 1850s Methodist writers had been addressing issues raised by the founder of positivist philosophy, Auguste Comte, and finding ways to reconcile his emphasis on scientific knowledge with their Christian faith in spiritual realities (Cashdollar, *Transformation*, 124–34). Raymond came into contact with this enterprise during his years of part-time graduate study at Boston University (1875–81). Borden Parker Bowne, the young Methodist philosopher appointed there in 1876, probably had a deep influence on Raymond. As Bowne had in the early 1870s, Raymond went to Germany during the 1880/81 academic year to study at Göttingen with the idealist metaphysician Hermann Lotze. See Francis J. McConnell, *Borden Parker Bowne: His Life and His Philosophy* (New York: Abingdon Press, 1929), 37, 115; *NCAB* 4:431. Only the title of Raymond's doctoral dissertation ("Materialism") has survived, but presumably it was a dissenting critique. Bowne was a leader in the battle against positivism (Cashdollar, *Transformation*, 423–26). Raymond was a loyal footsoldier, using Bowne's central focus on personality in his inaugural address. Raymond opposed excessive empiricism derived from science (*WA* 30 June 1896) and other positivist heresies in his baccalaureate sermons (summaries of which appear in the *Argus*) and in his book, *Christianity and the Christ: A Study of Christian Evidences* (New York: Hunt and Eaton, 1894), 232. It is appropriate that another "confronter of positivism," the former president of Princeton, James McCosh, pronounced the benediction at Raymond's inauguration (Cashdollar, *Transformation*, 434; *WA* 13 July 1889). Whereas Peterson sees the "whole man" concept used by college presidents in the late nineteenth century to celebrate gentlemanly taste and virtues (Peterson, *New England*, 38), Raymond's use gave primary emphasis to philosophical and religious issues. For the role that Bowne and German idealism's optimistic view of history played in liberal Protestantism of the 1890s, see Hutchison, *Modernist*, 121–29. Raymond carried this idea to the point of embracing Josiah Strong's belief that the chief agents of God working in history were Anglo-Saxons (Raymond, *Christianity*, 222). Raymond regularly commented on social issues (such as urban poverty and trade unionization), and he often urged students to serve the kingdom of God in ways that "soften the brutality of progress." See *WA* reports on his baccalaureate sermons of 1893, 1896, 1898, 1903, 1904, and 1906. Like Bowne, however, he would not qualify as a social gospel minister, except possibly in terms of some affinity with the message of individual meliorism espoused by the movement's conservative wing (Henry F. May, *The Protestant*

Churches and Industrial America (New York: Harper & Row, 1949), 195–96; Hutchison, *Modernist*, 165n36; *CA* 5 Dec. 1901). A similarly mild social reform message could be heard from Amherst's president, George Harris (Le Duc, *Piety*, 139–48). Raymond once indicated that his references to manhood and service were not oblivious to a widening field for social action by women (baccalaureate sermon of 1895). The clearest statement of Raymond's effort to reconcile science with denominational values is in his baccalaureate sermon of 1901: "Scientists are advancing religion since they show [the] unity and integrity of the universe." The "obligation incumbent upon us as a denomination," Raymond told Methodist conferences, is to provide resources for "work of the highest grade, and to contribute a much larger number of scholars for the highest places, both in thought and in literature." See ARP (1892):3.

    64. *Addresses . . . Foss*, 14–15; *WUB* (May 1910):7; *WA* 13 July 1889.

    65. ARP (1860):243–44, (1866):347, (1868):376–77, (1872):418, (1873):435–36; JBM 19 June 1860; BTM 24 June 1873, 22 Jan., 24 June 1874; FM 13 Mar. 1890. The five-year-term system was probably dropped as part of a bylaws revision in 1873–74. No copies of the new bylaws text have survived. BPR to Max Farrand, 9 Feb. 1898 Max Farrand Papers, Henry E. Huntington Library, Pasadena, Calif.; BTM 27 June 1899; RAC 15 Apr. 1902, 8 June 1907. For a sketch of the late nineteenth-century trend in higher education from short-term to "indefinite" appointments without legal protection, see Walter P. Metzger, "Academic Tenure in America: A Historical Essay," in Commission on Academic Tenure in Higher Education, *Faculty Tenure* (San Francisco: Jossey-Bass, 1973), 123–35. On establishment of the Academic Council, see FM 18 Feb. 1892; BTM 28 June 1892; RAC 13 July 1892. Concurrence of the faculty on appointments was required from the beginning of Wesleyan's history, but was threatened by John W. Beach in the mid-1880s (see text at chap. 5 nn50–51). Establishment of the Academic Council in 1892 gave renewed legitimacy to this professional prerogative.

    66. William North Rice, "Middletown Scientific Association" (Paper presented to the Middletown Scientific Association, 8 Mar. 1927), 4–7; Male undergraduates were elected to membership beginning in 1871 and women in 1880. Minutes of the Middletown Scientific Association, 17 Mar. 1871–14 Mar. 1967. On the hegemony of national professional scientific associations by 1900 over the host of local societies founded in nineteenth-century America to promote "vernacular science," see Thomas Bender, "Science and the Culture of American Communities in the Nineteenth Century," *HEQ* 16(Spring 1976): 63–77. Lectures at meetings of the MSA were "as free from technicalities as possible that everyone may understand them" (*WA* 21 Nov. 1906). Growth in faculty participation in national scholarly communities can be traced in reports on faculty activities in *WUB*

1888–1911. Beginnings of such membership go back to the 1850s, when Augustus Smith and John Van Vleck joined the American Association for the Advancement of Science. See Sally Gregory Kohlstedt, *The Formation of the American Scientific Community: The American Association for the Advancement of Science, 1848–60* (Urbana: University of Illinois Press, 1976), app. *ZH* 2 Sept. 1880; minutes of the Apostles Club 7 Dec. 1894–8 May 1967; *WUB* (May 1895):10.

67. [William Graham Sumner], "The 'Ways and Means' for Our Colleges," *Nation* 11(8 Sept. 1870): 153; *CA* 9 Mar. 1871; BTM 18 July 1871; minutes of the board of trustees of Amherst College 11 July 1871, Amherst College Archives; Frank Stricker, "American Professors in the Progressive Era: Incomes, Aspirations, and Professionalism," *Journal of Interdisciplinary History* 19(Autumn 1988): 347, 338–39. Faculty at Bucknell, Franklin and Marshall, Princeton, and Swarthmore lived very comfortably in the small college towns of the 1880s. See W. Bruce Leslie, "When Professors Had Servants: Prestige, Pay, and Professionalization, 1860–1917," *History of Higher Education Annual* 10(1990): 19–30. FM 29 Mar. 1876; BTM 26 June 1877, 26 June 1879, 24 June 1884, 23 June 1885, 22 Apr. 1879. Roger L. Geiger, *To Advance Knowledge: The Growth of American Research Universities, 1900–1940* (New York: Oxford University Press, 1986), 10–12; *PWW* 7:189–90; *OP* '92, 34:5, 117; BTM 20 Mar. 1891. The raise for Winchester forced upward adjustments of salary for the president and the senior professor (BTM 23 June 1891). Atwater started receiving offers in the late 1880s (*WA* 12 Oct. 1888). Evidence of offers and the salary increases they stimulated is drawn from: BTM and *WUB* 1891–1910; *PWW* 10:317, 16:68, 80; Max Farrand to A. Lawrence Lowell 22, 27, 30 Mar., 9, 13 Apr. 1901, A. Lawrence Lowell Papers, Harvard University Archives. Entry-level salaries for those lacking a Ph.D., however, were meager. John R. Commons was paid $1,000 as a tutor in economics and social science in 1890/91. (He was later fired for poor teaching.) See John R. Commons, *Myself: The Autobiography of John R. Commons* (Madison: University of Wisconsin Press, 1964), 45. And inflation eroded the purchasing power of average salaries at Wesleyan and elsewhere after 1900. See *WUB* (December 1909):4; Stricker, "American," 246–48.

68. *WUB* (November 1900):13, (November 1892):9, (May 1893):7–9, (December 1905):25, (May 1901):4–8, (June 1911):27–56, (November 1901):14–15, (November 1900):13. In 1906 the first edition of James M. Cattell's *American Men of Science* would designate eight Wesleyan faculty as among the nation's thousand leading scientific scholars (*WA* 4 Apr. 1906).

69. *WA* 6, 13, 20 Nov., 4, 11, 18 Dec. 1894; *Brooklyn Eagle* 8 Nov. 1894; *WA* 13 Nov. 1884; H. W. Conn, *The Outbreak of Typhoid Fever at Wesleyan University* (n.p., n.d. reprinted from the report of the state board of health for 1894).

70. Finkelstein, "From Tutor," 100. In 1888 Wesleyan offered Woodrow Wilson use of a room in the chapel for an office if he paid an annual charge of twenty dollars for steam heat (*PWW* 5:753). BTM 22 June 1896, 26 Mar., 29 June 1897, 21 Feb., 28 June 1898. The census of leaves is based primarily on BTM, *FEx*, and FM for 1880–1910. Sabbaticals were granted selectively to established scholars at a dozen major research universities by 1900 (Geiger, *To Advance*, 75). Yale began to grant them systematically to full professors in 1910 (Kelley, *Yale*, 329).

71. Photograph of the faculty, 1900/1901, VF for faculty photographs; George Prentice, "Prof. C. S. Harrington" *OP* '86, 28:15–17; "George Prentice" *OP* '94, 36:101–4; *WUB* (November 1893):10–12; *ZH* 18 Oct. 1893; *WUB* (June 1902):4–5; C. T. Winchester, "Address on J. C. Van Benschoten," CTW Papers; *WUB* (December 1912):11. Farrand cultivated colleagueship with such prominent academicians as A. Lawrence Lowell of Harvard (Max Farrand to A. Lawrence Lowell, 22, 27, 30 Mar. 1901, 15 June 1910, A. Lawrence Lowell Papers, Harvard University Archives). C. R. Smith '99, R1939. Use of academic caps and gowns (long common in British universities) by all faculties of Harvard University first occurred in 1886 at the celebration of its 250th anniversary (Morison, *Three Centuries*, 362), but the Harvard College faculty may have begun to wear academic regalia a decade earlier (*WA* 6 May 1876). An intercollegiate commission met at Columbia in 1895 to develop a uniform code for academic costume in America. Leading universities quickly adopted its standards. See Gardner C. Leonard, *The Cap and Gown in America* (Albany, N.Y.: Cotrell and Leonard, 1896), 10–13. Wesleyan seniors first wore caps and gowns at commencement in 1892 (see chap. 6 n106). As part of a faculty effort "to add to the dignity and impressiveness of the Commencement exercises" (FM 1 July 1897, 8, 15 Mar. 1898), specifications based on those of the commission were approved in 1900 for caps and gowns to be worn by graduating seniors, faculty, and trustees for all appropriate occasions at Wesleyan. See RAC 19 June 1900; *WUB* (November 1900):12–13. Implementation awaited additional stimuli. An observer of faculty assembled on the commencement platform in 1902 reported "all sorts of fashion in clothing, from the dignified and appropriate Prince Albert coat, with its fitting accompaniments, down to a gray sack suit and red necktie." He thought even John Wesley would have disapproved of this disarray and urged faculty to join the seniors in wearing academic garb (*CA* 3 July 1902). Acting upon a faculty recommendation, the trustees decided that the practice of assembling faculty in academic regalia should begin with the commencement season of 1903, which included celebration of the Wesley Bicentennial. (RAC 28 May, 23 Dec. 1902; BTM 1 May 1903).

72. For denominational encouragement in the 1860s, see text at chap. 2 n40. *CA* 1 Dec. 1853, 21 Apr. 1870; *Semi-Centennial*, 13–15; *ZH* 28 Nov.,

5 Dec. 1883, 26 Sept. 1888; *CA* 9 Nov. 1893, 26 July 1894, 2 July 1896, 6 July 1893.

73. *CA* 4 Nov. 1875, 6 Oct. 1879, 5 Aug. 1880, 29 Mar. 1877, 12 June 1879, 29 Jan. 1885.

74. Stevenson, *Scholarly Means*, 7; *Semi-Centennial*, 44. For a discussion that finds more confrontation and a more rapid shift from ideals of the orator to those of the philosopher in the late nineteenth century than can be supported by Stevenson's research or mine, see Kimball, *Orators*, chap. 6. Stevenson, *Scholarly Means*, 12. Carlos Storrs '87, R1939. Traditional providential explanations can be found in student resolutions reprinted in *WA* 6, 13 Nov., 4, 11 Dec. 1894. H. William Conn, "Study of Science and the Christian Faith," *MR* 72(January 1890): 79, 92; Oscar Kuhns, "Dante as a Tonic for Today," *The Dial* 23(September 1897): 110 and "The Many and the One," *MR* 88(May 1906): 456. Conn, Kuhns, and several other faculty members regularly contributed articles to the *MR* from 1890 to 1910, often linking their scholarly findings to a religious message. *CA* 4 July 1888.

75. George M. Marsden, *Fundamentalism and American Culture: The Shaping of Twentieth-Century Evangelicalism, 1870–1925* (New York: Oxford University Press, 1980), 102–4; *MR* 79(January 1897): 131. Winchester, Atwater, and Rice were born in the mid-1840s and began teaching at Wesleyan between 1868 and 1873. By the fall of 1904 they were the only members of Wesleyan's second faculty generation still teaching at the University.

76. *ZH* 31 Mar. 1920; *DAB* 10:376; [George M. Dutcher, ed.], *A Memorial to Caleb Thomas Winchester, 1847–1920, Professor of English Literature in Wesleyan University* (Middletown: Wesleyan University, 1921), 204. Although primarily engaged in arranging and cataloguing the library in its new building, Winchester assumed responsibility for teaching a few courses from 1869 to 1873 (Dutcher, *Memorial*, 106–7).

77. *CA* 29 Mar. 1877; Dutcher, *Memorial*, 25, 65, 83; Rudolph, *Curriculum*, 134; BTM 26 June 1879; *WA* 22 Feb. 1881.

78. *WUB* (January 1888):4, (May 1889):6, (May 1890):6; Dutcher, *Memorial*, 150, 169; Carl F. Price, "Winchester: Twenty Years After," *WUA* 24(May 1940): 6; Dutcher, *Memorial*, 27, 134, 27, 150; W. E. Woodruff '87, R1939; Dutcher, *Memorial*, 145–47, 262; "Professor Winchester's Address," *MR* 95(April 1913): 277–84. Winchester was more pious than most of his contemporaries advocating "liberal culture" at universities studied by Laurence Veysey. Like many of them, however, he remained a strong believer in mental discipline. See Laurence R. Veysey, *The Emergence of the American University* (Chicago: University of Chicago Press, 1965), chap. 4; *MR* 95(March 1913): 277–84.

79. Dutcher, *Memorial*, 92, 183–86, 48; Caleb T. Winchester, "Literature as an Agent of Christian Culture," *ZH* 2 Apr. 1890. Showing his high

esteem for hymns and for the ability of great literature to stir noble emotions, Winchester asked in this address before the Boston Methodist Social Union: "Has not Shakespeare glorified God as truly as Dr. Watts?"

80. Dutcher, *Memorial*, 271–75. Kittredge carried more of the load in producing this series, but Winchester had a major role. See Clyde K. Hyder, *George Lyman Kittredge: Teacher and Scholar* (Lawrence: University of Kansas Press, 1962), 74; CTWP, box 4, folder 6. The offer from Chicago came just a few years after another member of the Wesleyan faculty contrasted such colleagues as Winchester with professors at Yale who "teach for money only." Winchester, Rice, and others at Wesleyan, he asserted, work "for God and the church, not for Wesleyan on a salary basis" (Carlos H. Storrs '87, R1939). When Winchester was offered double his salary to teach at a university founded primarily with Baptist money, however, he gave it careful consideration (*PWW* 7:189–90). Dutcher, *Memorial*, 166. Winchester lectured at such other institutions as Brown, Princeton, Smith, Wisconsin, and Yale (Dutcher, *Memorial*, 287–88). He advised Woodrow Wilson in 1891 that "in moderate doses lecturing, like sherry, is pleasant and . . . profitable . . . to the pocket . . . in a moderate degree" (*PWW* 7:315). *PWW* 8:209, 9:580–81; Dutcher, *Memorial*, 165; *Nation* 69(28 Dec. 1899): 488. *Some Principles* went through at least a dozen printings from 1900 to 1950, including a translation into Japanese.

81. Caleb T. Winchester, "Narrow Methodism or Broad?" *ZH* 4 May 1898; Mudge, *History*, 321.

82. [Charles Parkhurst], "The Scholar in the Church," *ZH* 4 May 1898; *DAB* 7:244; Mudge, *History*, 370–71. In the early 1890s Winchester had offered liberal views on the Bible without provoking controversy: "Some Remarks on the Bible as Literature," *ZH* 12 Oct. 1892. And others had objected in the early and mid-1890s to the amusements prohibitions enacted in 1872 (*JGC* [1872], 379–80), without either rebuttal or effect. See *MR* 74(May 1892): 375–89, 78(March 1896): 384–92. Winchester seems to have sensed that by 1898 protofundamentalism was becoming a sufficient force in the denomination to be challenged. He expected to "provoke decided opposition," and did (*ZH* 4 May 1898). Winchester's colleague Rice engaged the Methodist denomination on this issue two years later, leading a substantial group of ministerial allies in an unsuccessful attempt to have the General Conference drop from the *Discipline* the list of prohibited amusements (*CA* 19 Apr., 7 June 1900).

83. *HC* 23 Sept. 1907; *DSB* 1:325; *Catalogue of the Officers and Graduates of Yale . . . , 1924* (New Haven: Yale University, 1924), 453. In the 1860s Johnson was "America's leading authority on agricultural chemistry" (*DSB* 1:325). On Johnson's career, see Margaret W. Rossiter, *The Emergence of Agricultural Science: Justus Liebig and the Americans, 1840–1880* (New Haven: Yale University Press, 1975), chaps. 8–9.

84. In addition to the brief biographical sketch by Charles E. Rosenberg in *DSB*, two scholarly studies place Atwater's career in the context of nutritional research in late nineteenth-century America: Edward C. Kirkland, "'Scientific Eating': New Englanders Prepare and Promote a Reform, 1873–1907," *Proceedings of the Massachusetts Historical Society* 86(1974): 28–52; Naomi Aronson, "Nutrition as a Social Problem: A Case Study of Entrepreneurial Strategy in Science," *Social Problems* 29(June 1982): 474–86. Supplementary biographical information can be found in *DAB* 1:417–18, Leonard A. Maynard, "Wilbur O. Atwater—A Biographical Sketch," *Journal of Nutrition* 78(September 1962): 2–9. On Atwater's "well-honed political skills" in lobbying for government funds, see Harvey A. Levenstein, *Revolution at the Table: The Transformation of the American Diet* (New York: Oxford University Press, 1988), 73–76. Rossiter, *Emergence*, 161–71; *SAC* (1875), 156; Aronson, "Nutrition," 479. Atwater obtained volunteer help for his dietary surveys from organizations such as Hull House and Tuskegee Institute. For an example of the procedure, see WOA to Booker T. Washington, *BTWP* 3:546. *WUB* (October 1888):10. On the tension between pure science and agricultural technology in the work of experiment stations, see Charles E. Rosenberg, "Science, Technology, and Economic Growth: The Case of the Agricultural Experiment Station Scientist, 1875–1914," *Agricultural History* 45(October 1971): 1–20.

85. *WUB* (May 1896):13–14, (November 1901):14–15; Atwater and Rosa, "New Respiration," 239–40. In 1907 the calorimeter was moved to Boston and installed in the nutrition laboratory (near the Harvard Medical School) recently funded by the Carnegie Institution of Washington. See *WUB* (May 1908):10–11. Francis G. Benedict, who served from 1896 to 1907 as Atwater's close colleague in Wesleyan's chemistry department, arranged for this move as he left to become director of the new laboratory. Much of the experimental success with the calorimeter at Wesleyan is attributed to Benedict, who directed the Carnegie Institution laboratory until his retirement in 1937. See Russell H. Chittenden, *The First Twenty-Five Years of the American Society of Biological Chemists* (New Haven: n.p., 1945), 12–13.

86. Rather than maintaining a well-stocked experimental bar in the basement of Judd Hall, Atwater used ethyl alcohol, the characteristic ingredient of alcoholic beverages, in almost all of his experiments. It was mixed with either water or coffee before being ingested. His calculations of caloric values for specific beers, wines, and liquors were based on published data from chemical analyses done by others. See John S. Billings, ed., *Physiological Aspects of the Liquor Problem*, vol. 2 (Boston: Houghton, Mifflin, 1903), 231, 328–42. For praise of Atwater from members of the denomination, see *ZH* 18 Mar. 1880, 4 July 1894; BTM 14 May 1895. Atwater was an active member of First Methodist Church in Middletown from 1874 until his death (First Methodist Church, Record Books 7–9, Storage Room, First

United Methodist Church) and a speaker at Methodist gatherings. On Atwater's father, William Warren Atwater, see *MVtC* (1867), 17; *MTyC* (1879), 54–55. For writings by Atwater that show his desire for successful temperance reform, see "Abstract of Professor Atwater's Report," *Outlook* 62 (29 July 1899): 706; "False and True Teaching in Our Schools Concerning Alcohol," *Journal of Social Science* 37 (December 1900): 112–13; "Alcohol, Physiology, and Temperance Reform," *Harper's* 101 (November 1900): 853–58.

87. W. O. Atwater, "Foods and Beverages," *Century Magazine* 36(May 1888): 137–40; Norton Mezvinsky, "Scientific Temperance Instruction in the Schools," *HEQ* 1(March 1961): 49–50; Atwater, "False," 109–10. On Atwater's stature as a scientist by the late 1890s, see "The People's Food—A Great National Inquiry: Professor W. O. Atwater and His Work," *Review of Reviews* 13(June 1896): 679–90. And his reputation continued to grow. In 1902 Atwater achieved recognition as one of the first "exceptional men" whose research received funding from the new Carnegie Institution of Washington. See Charles D. Walcott to WOA, 4 Dec. 1902, WOAP, box 6; *WUB* (June 1903):9; Nathan Reingold, "National Science Policy in a Private Foundation: The Carnegie Institution of Washington," in *The Organization of Knowledge in Modern America, 1860–1920*, ed. Alexandra Oleson and John Voss, (Baltimore: Johns Hopkins University Press, 1979), 318, 333–34; Kirkland, "Scientific Eating," 40.

88. Minutes of the Middletown Scientific Association, 13 June 1899; Timberlake, *Prohibition*, 48–50; Billings, *Physiological*, 2:169–343. For the most extensively researched and broadly contextual account of Atwater's encounter with the WCTU, see Philip J. Pauly, "The Struggle for Ignorance about Alcohol: American Physiologists, Wilbur Olin Atwater, and the Woman's Christian Temperance Union," *Bulletin of the History of Medicine* 64(1990): 366–92.

89. C. T. Winchester, "Wilbur Olin Atwater, An Appreciation," *WLM* 16(November 1907): 46–47; *CA* 3 Oct. 1907; W. E. Woodruff '87, R1939; *WUB* (December 1907):14; ARP (1908):5; Atwater, "False," 116; Arthur W. Browne, "The Sciences at Wesleyan," in Price, *Wesleyan's First*, 297–98; *WUB* (June 1898):4. For the content of his MSA talk, see Atwater, "Abstract," 703–6. For a report on the discussion following the talk, see *CA* 29 June 1899.

90. WOA to F. M. Barber, 13 June 1899, WOAP, box 8; *MP* 16 Jan. 1900; *NYH* 14 June 1899; *NYT* 14 June 1899; *CA* 29 June, 13 July 1899. Efforts to explain careful and precise distinctions that would render Atwater's research less offensive continued for many years. See William North Rice, "Alcohol in the Light of Recent Scientific Research," *Federation* (March 1903), 12–19. For evidence of Atwater being cited in liquor advertisements, see J. S. Dickerson to WOA, 13 Feb. 1900, WOAP, box 5; *CA* 1 Mar. 1900; WOA to Duffy Malt Whiskey Co., 6 Mar. 1900, WOAP, box 8.

91. *An Appeal to Truth: An Analysis of Professor Atwater's Statements* . . . *Investigation* (Boston: n.p., 1900), 2–3, 6. Dr. William H. Welch, chief "Influential" in the late nineteenth-century effort to strengthen scientific research as the basis for modern medicine, served with Atwater on the Committee of Fifty. As Welch's career and the 1910 report on medical education by Abraham Flexner show, few physicians in 1900 were well trained in science. See Donald Fleming, *William H. Welch and the Rise of Modern Medicine* (Boston: Little, Brown, 1954), 119, 131, 174, 196. *Appeal*, 6–12, 1; *JGC* (1872), 379–80; Ruth Bordin, *Woman and Temperance: The Quest for Power and Liberty, 1873–1900* (Philadelphia: Temple University Press, 1981), 168–70; Benjamin, "Methodist," 326; K. Austin Kerr, *Organized for Prohibition: A New History of the Anti-Saloon League* (New Haven: Yale University Press, 1985), 75; Jack S. Blocker, Jr., *Retreat from Reform: The Prohibition Movement in the United States, 1890–1913* (Westport, Conn.: Greenwood Press, 1976), 199; Timberlake, *Prohibition*, 20; Cameron, *Methodism*, 248. The ironic observation from the *Wine and Spirit Gazette* is quoted in *Appeal*, 15.

92. For a few examples of Atwater's many efforts, see *WUB* (May 1900):7, (May 1901):5; "Alcohol, Physiology, and Superintendence," *Educational Review* 20(June 1900): 1–29; National Education Association, *Proceedings of the Department of Superintendence* (1900), 72–88; "Temperance Reform," *Outlook* 65(22, 29 Nov. 1902): 678–83, 732–37. Atwater even had to defend his position to his uncle, a retired Methodist minister in Michigan (WOA to George S. Barnes, 16 Feb. 1901, WOAP, box 9). *WA* 12 Jan. 1898; *CA* 13 June 1898, 8 Mar. 1900; Bordin, *Woman*, 137; WOA to C. T. Winchester, 20 Apr. 1904, WAOP, box 10; Thomas D. Crothers to Mary H. Hunt, 16 Mar., 17 Apr., 1 Aug., 17 Dec. 1901, Scientific Temperance Federation Records, box 1 Rare Books and Manuscripts Division, New York Public Library; *NAW* 2:237–38; *MR* 81(September 1899): 797.

93. WOA to BPR, 20 July 1901, WOAP, box 9; *WUB* (June 1903):12; *OP* '99, 41:189–91, '03, 45:190. For continuing criticism of Atwater in the Methodist press, see *CA* 23 Jan., 12, 19 June 1902. New York *Sun* 21 Oct., 9 Dec. 1902; *WA* 29 Oct., 17 Dec. 1902. *Life* magazine defended Atwater against the Methodist preachers "who rail so absurdly," see *Life* 40(6 Nov. 1902): 388. Atwater's talk on "Food for the Poorer Classes" at the New York Preachers' Meeting in 1896 had been "received with great satisfaction" (*CA* 5 Mar. 1896). *Reply to the Physiological Sub-Committee of the Committee of Fifty* (n.p., 1904), 21; Mezvinsky, "Scientific," 53; H. A. White '04, R1939; William E. Mead, diary, 28 Nov. 1904; *DSB* 1:325.

94. The most extensive sources of biographical information on WNR are "Rice Memorial Number," *WUB* (January 1929); *MNYEC* (1929), 124–27; and *DAB* 8:547–48. Rice's father, William, saw only limited service in the pulpit after 1857 due to poor health. He served as librarian of the Springfield Public Library, 1861–97, and as trustee of Wesleyan, 1875–97.

See William North Rice, ed., *William Rice: A Memorial* (Cambridge: n.p., 1898), 3–13. WNR, diary, 19 May 1864; Rice, *Personal History*, 20. For an assessment of Dana's work in relation to theistic goals pursued by his Yale colleagues, see Stevenson, *Scholarly*, chap. 5. *Catalogue . . . Yale*, 453. Due to the required three-year period between the B.A. and the M.A. in course, Rice obtained his Ph.D. from Yale one year before receiving his M.A. from Wesleyan. Rice's leave was without salary (JBM 16–17 July 1867). On three occasions, for a total of almost two years, Rice served as acting president of Wesleyan. He had close association with several influential trustees. See *WUB* (January 1929):14–15, 39–40.

95. William North Rice, "James Dwight Dana, Geologist, 1813–1895," in *Leading American Men of Science*, ed. David Starr Jordan (New York: Henry Holt, 1910), 233, 265; Ronald L. Numbers, *Creation by Natural Law: Laplace's Nebular Hypothesis in American Thought* (Seattle: University of Washington Press, 1977), 111; Jon H. Roberts, *Darwinism and the Divine in America: Protestant Intellectuals and Organic Evolution, 1859–1900* (Madison: University of Wisconsin Press, 1988), chaps. 2, 3, 5; Rice's doctoral research was published as "The Darwinian Theory of the Origin of Species," *New Englander* 26(October 1867), 603–35. For Rice's view of his scientific pilgrimage, see William North Rice "Twenty-Five Years of Scientific Progress," *Bibliotheca Sacra* 50(January 1893): 1–29. Rice, "Darwinian," 634–35; Lewis G. Westgate, "Memorial of William North Rice," *Bulletin of the Geological Society of America* 40(30 March 1929): 54. Rice thought that Darwin had "made possible for us a larger and nobler faith in God." See William North Rice, *The Return to Faith and Other Addresses* (New York: Abingdon Press, 1916), 102; Rice, "James Dwight Dana," 266.

96. *WUB* (June 1911):29–31, (January 1929):7–8; *Tributes to Professor William North Rice* (Middletown: Wesleyan Alumni Council [ca. 1915]), 40; William North Rice, "The Pastoral Opportunity of the College Professor," *Christian Student* 6(February 1905): 7–9; Westgate, "Memorial," 51; W. E. Woodruff '87, R1939; *WUB* (January 1929):8; H. A. White '04, R1939; M. E. Culver '75, R1939. Culver and others note that Rice's popularity with students was diminished by his lack of interest in athletics. *MNYEC* (1929), 124. Rice also had close ties with the New England Conference (Mudge, *History*, 335). Rice's standing among Methodists probably was reinforced by his support for the temperance movement and the Anti-Saloon League (Westgate, "Memorial," 54). WNR to Edward L. Rice, 25 Jan. 1900, WNRP; *WUB* (January 1929):34.

97. Rice, *Return*, 7; *MNYEC* (1929), 126; Westgate, "Memorial," 52; *WUC* 1895/96, 50; William North Rice, *Twenty-Five Years of Scientific Progress and Other Essays* (New York: Thomas Y. Crowell, 1894), 171; William North Rice, "Scientific Thought in the Nineteenth Century," *Science* 10(29 Dec. 1899): 13; *ZH* 20 Dec. 1899.

98. WNR to Edward L. Rice, 27 May 1902, WNRP.

99. Ibid.; Hutchison, *Modernist*, 113–14; Marsden, *Fundamentalism*, chap. 12; Gerald O. McCulloh, "The Theology and Practices of Methodism," in *HAM* 2:596–98; William Warren Sweet, *Methodism in American History* (New York: Methodist Book Concern, 1933), 390–91; BTM 25 June 1901; *CA* 9, 30 Nov. 1905; Williamson, *Northwestern*, 103; *CA* 30 Jan. 1902; Forenc M. Szasz, *The Divided Mind of Protestant America, 1880–1930* (University: University of Alabama Press, 1982), chaps. 2–6; WNR to Edward L. Rice, 22 July 1902, WNRP.

100. George P. Mains to WNR 22 July 1902, WNRP. Mains may still have been in the process of some delicate financial negotiations between the Book Concern and the General Conference. See *MR* 82(January 1900): 34–49. Kelley was under fire from conservatives for permitting articles by liberal authors to appear in the *Methodist Review* (George P. Mains to WNR, 22 July 1902, WNRP). He even decided not to have Rice's book reviewed in this journal, lest it incite "certain prowlers about Zion who are eager to become accusers" (William V. Kelley to WNR, 3 Mar. 1905, WNRP). Edward G. Andrews to WNR, 27 Jan. 1903, WNRP. Rice's book, *Christian Faith in an Age of Science*, was published in New York in December 1903 by A. C. Armstrong. There are several allusions to Rice coming "very near being brought . . . before a tribunal of his church for heresy," but they do not specify if such threats occurred before (perhaps in response to several challenges to "an inerrant Bible" he published in the 1890s, e.g., *ZH* 20 Dec. 1899 or "Scientific Thought," 13) or after publication of *Christian Faith*. See *WUB* (January 1929):9, 33; W. E. Woodruff '87, R1939.

101. See the collection of Rice's articles in WNRP. Younger faculty by 1905 were publishing almost entirely in journals of their disciplines. See *WUB* (May 1905):8–12, (May 1908):19–22. Rice was recruited by Clarence Darrow to serve as an expert witness in the Scopes trial (*HC* 19 July 1925), but restrictions Judge John T. Raulston put on the amount of such testimony prevented Rice from appearing. See Ray Ginger, *Six Days or Forever: Tennessee v. John Thomas Scopes* (Boston: Beacon Press, 1958), 154. Rice's critical review of Bryan's *In His Image* (*CA* 20 Apr. 1922) may have brought him to the attention of Darrow. Winchester went to the General Conference armed with a long memo from Atwater providing information to be used in defending Atwater's position on the nutritional value of alcohol (WOA to CTW, 20 Apr. 1904, WOAP, box 10). *CA* 27 Oct. 1904; Hutchison, *Modernist*, 114; Robert E. Chiles, *Theological Transition in American Methodism, 1790–1935* (New York: Abingdon Press, 1965), 71; McCulloh, "Theology," 598; Sweet, *Methodism*, 391–93.

1. Bradford P. Raymond, *Twenty-Five Years of Wesleyan's History* (n.p. [1903]),
2. Except where otherwise noted, financial assessments in this and succeed-
ing paragraphs are based on analysis of the annual financial exhibits for
1890–1910. Morrill *Multimillionaire*, 95–97; BTM 22–23 June 1902. On
dwindling Methodist support, especially with reference to endowment
funds, see text at chap. 4 n70. Raymond, *Twenty-Five Years*, 2.

2. Raymond, *Twenty-Five Years*, 2; *WUB* (May 1889):1, (31 May 1890):7,
(November 1890):2; *CA* 19 July 1894; *WUB* (November 1895):23–24. Data
on enrollments, faculty and staff size, and courses obtained from the annual
catalogues of Wesleyan, Williams, and Amherst.

3. Tuition and enrollment data obtained from the annual catalogues of
Wesleyan, Williams, and Amherst. *FEx* 1895–1905. Within the Methodist
context, Boston University's freshman enrollments fared no better than
Wesleyan's from 1895 through 1910, although those at Syracuse quadrupled.
Data obtained from catalogues for 1895–1910.

4. *FEx* 1870–1910; *WUB* (November 1901):1, (May 1905):1, (December
1906):2–3. Data on annual market values of the Williams endowment
supplied to the author by Office of the Treasurer, Williams College. King,
History of Endowment, 142.

5. Raymond consistently carried grim financial news to the board from
1900 through 1903. See *WUB* (November 1900):1–2; BTM 25 Nov. 1901;
WUB (November 1901):3–4; BTM 29–30 June 1903. For a statistical review
of Raymond's nineteen-year presidency at Wesleyan, see *WUB* (December
1907):16–17. For somewhat varied assessments of Raymond's presidency at
Lawrence University (1883–89), see *Lawrentian* 5(November 1888): 72; Marguerite E. Schumann, *The Creation of a Campus* (Appleton, Wis.: Lawrence
College Press, 1957), 18–19; Samuel Plantz, "Lawrence College," *Wisconsin
Magazine of History* 6(1922–23): 162–63; William F. Rainey, *The History of
Lawrence University, 1847–1925* (Appleton, Wis.: Lawrence University,
1984), 105–7; E. C. Dixon, "President Bradford P. Raymond," in *Lawrence
University Alumni Record, 1857–1905* (Appleton, Wis.: Lawrence University,
1906), 71–72; James Arneil, "Lawrence in My Time," in *Lawrence College
Alumni Record, 1857–1922* (Appleton, Wis.: Lawrence University, 1923),
169–71.

6. *WA* 13 July 1889. For examples of Raymond's addresses, see those on
"Education and Citizenship" and "What Signs of Improvement Are Visible
in the Undergraduate Life of American Students?" in National Education
Association, *Proceedings* 31(1892): 344–48, 32(1893): 142–46. *WUB* (October
1889):11, (May 1890):5, (May 1893):8. For examples of Raymond's writings
for denominational readership, see "The Scantiness of Literary Production
in Our Church," in *The Present State of the Methodist Episcopal Church: A Symposium*, ed. George R. Crooks (Syracuse, N.Y.: Hunt and Eaton, 1891),

73–82; "Christian Ethics," *MR* 82(July 1900): 513–23; "Wesley's Religious Experience," *MR* 86(January 1904): 28–35; "Our Southern Schools," *ZH* 3 Feb. 1904. Burke, *American*, 216; *MYB* (1892), 82–83, (1901), 78–79.

7. Amherst's George Harris, president from 1899 to 1911, established a pleasing public image for the college (Le Duc, *Piety*, 138) and a new urbane tone on campus (Fuess, *Amherst*, 266–69). Enrollments grew at a steady pace and endowment, with much help from the president of the board, increased by about $1 million (King, *History of Endowment*, 200). Facilities as well as enrollments and endowment expanded substantially at Williams during the presidencies of Franklin Carter (1881–1901) and Henry Hopkins (1902–8). See Spring, *History*, 244, 256–57. Brown's William Faunce (1899–1929) quickly raised $2 million in endowment and launched a major building era to improve the campus (Bronson, *History*, 469–71). Dartmouth's William Tucker (1893–1909) was probably the most dynamic of these contemporaries (Lord, *History* 2:504–5). *FEx*, 1903; WOA to Marcia Atwater, 29 Sept., 6 Oct. 1901, WOAP, box 12; H. Loranus Davis to WNR, 11, 27 Oct. 1904, WNRP. Consideration of large-scale enrollment increases accompanied the call for endowment growth. See *WUB* (November 1901):4–5; BTM 30 June 1903. The trustees also appointed a committee to work on reducing expenses (BTM 28 Oct. 1903). Raymond's health was never robust. He took a leave of absence in 1896/97 for "a much needed rest." See *WUB* (November 1896):1. By 1908, when he was "seriously broken in health" (WNR to Edward L. Rice, 26 July 1908, WNRP), a newspaper reported that "he has not been in good condition for several years" (*Brooklyn Eagle* 21 Mar. 1908).

8. In the 1870s New York City Methodists began to think of a metropolitan unit defined by a "circle of at least fifty miles radius from New York as a centre" (*M* 26 July 1872). For background on configurations of culture and influence with reference to late nineteenth-century New York, see Thomas Bender, *New York Intellect: A History of Intellectual Life in New York City from 1750 to the Beginnings of Our Time* (New York: Knopf, 1987), chap. 5; Lawrence A. Cremin, *American Education: The Metropolitan Experience, 1876–1980* (New York: Harper & Row, 1988), 9, 523, 606, 675; Robert Stern et al., *New York, 1900: Metropolitan Architecture and Urbanism, 1890–1915* (New York: Rizzoli, 1983), 11–24. Rudolph, *Hopkins*, 65–72; Story, *Forging*, chaps. 2–8; Fuess, *Amherst*, chap. 20; Tobias, *Old Dartmouth*, 10.

9. Cremin, *Metropolitan*, 5; Stern, *New York*, 11. On Foss's preaching, see chap. 4 n25. *M* 1 May 1875; Cyrus Foss, *Wesleyan University* (single folded sheet, ca. 1876), 2; *MP* 20 Jan. 1888; Gregg M. Turner and Melancthon W. Jacobus, *Connecticut Railroads . . . An Illustrated History* (Hartford: Connecticut Historical Society, 1986), 125, 188, 192; *WUB* (November 1895):4. A straight line drawn on a road map to connect Central Park with the Boston Common runs through Middletown approximately 3 miles south of the city center. Middletown is 88 miles along this line from New York City and 98

miles from Boston. The actual rail distance from Middletown to New York City was 98 miles and to Boston was 115 miles. See *WUB* (April 1888):7. In addition to the three runs daily (connecting in New Haven with the Boston express) to and from New York City, Middletown in 1870 was served by the older trunk line to Berlin, connecting with what became in 1872 the New York, New Haven, and Hartford, and by the Connecticut Valley connecting at Saybrook with the Shore Line route. See George P. Baker, *The Formation of the New England Railroad Systems: A Study of Railroad Combination in the Nineteenth Century* (Cambridge: Harvard University Press, 1937), chaps. 3–4. For their schedules, see *MC* 7 Dec. 1870. Three trains per day left Middletown for New York and three for Willimantic (*WA* 17 Dec. 1873). Service from New York to Boston on the Air Line began in 1876, and introduction of a faster train, the New England Express, in 1884 lowered travel time between these cities to six hours. From 1895 to 1902, the Air Line Limited, which stopped only in Middletown, made this run in five hours (Harrington, *Autobiography*, 158–59; Baker, *Formation*, 58).

10. *WUC* 1868/69, 32; *OP* '79, 22:96, '95, 37:132; *WA* 31 Jan. 1882, 26 Jan. 1891; *NYH* 26 May 1884; *NYTr* 23, 25 Feb. 1889; *WA* 18 Dec. 1888, 1 Feb. 1889, 14 May 1895; *CA* 14 Aug. 1879.

11. *WA* 3 Mar. 1894. Data on residences are taken from *WAR* (1883) and supplements to it published in 1893, 1903, and 1909. *WA* 24 Feb. 1904.

12. *WA* 24 Feb. 1904; *WLM* 14(March 1906): 259. In the 1860s New York City spawned a host of annual alumni dinners and supporting associations, societies, and clubs to represent New England colleges such as Dartmouth (1864), Williams (1867), and Amherst (by 1869). See Tobias, *Old Dartmouth*, 183; Patricia H. Hans, "The Growth and Influence of the Alumni Movement on the Governance of Four Private Colleges: Williams, Union, Hamilton, and Amherst, 1821–1925" (Ph.D. diss., State University of New York at Buffalo, 1983), 38. *Amherst Student* 23 Jan. 1869. *WA* 18 Mar. 1869, 14 Jan. 1869, 22 Feb. 1871, 20 Jan. 1882, 26 Jan. 1894, 3 Mar. 1897; *WUB* (December 1902):2. Names of the Wesleyan clubs varied. Sometimes they were called associations.

13. *CA* 14 Dec. 1882; Stephen Henry Olin, *Response of Stephen Henry Olin, Class of 1866 . . . , 1919* (New York: New York Wesleyan University Club, 1919), 4; Stephen Henry Olin, *Three Addresses* (n.p. [ca. 1923]), 18. For reports on annual alumni club meetings from 1870 to 1910, see December, January, and February issues of *WA*. By 1901 the New York club often dined at the Waldorf-Astoria.

14. *WA* 3 July 1894. The alumni visiting committees came at the invitation of the board (BTM 6 Mar. 1893). *WA* 1 July 1903; *WLM* 12(June 1904): 399; *WA* 18 Dec. 1907; *WLM* 16(February 1908): 218, 16(May 1908): 357–61; AAM 20 June 1911; *WUB* (May 1908):3. Amherst and Williams established alumni councils in 1914. Williams began publication of an

alumni journal in 1909 and Amherst in 1911 (Hans, "Growth," 42, 45, 139, 162).

15. *Annual Banquet of the New England Wesleyan Alumni* (single folded sheet, 1912); *WLM* 13(January 1905): 170; *WA* 14 June 1882; Nightingale, *Handbook*; *WA* 5 Feb. 1880, 2 Dec. 1892, 3 July 1893, 1 July 1903. Stanford's president put Wesleyan in a league with Brown, Amherst, Williams, Colgate, and Bryn Mawr. See David Starr Jordan, *The Voice of the Scholar: With Other Addresses on the Problems of Higher Education* (San Francisco: Paul Elder, 1903), 53. On the Cattell rankings, see chap. 5 n68; David S. Webster, "James McKeen Cattell and the Invention of Academic Quality Ratings, 1903–1910," *Review of Higher Education* 8(Winter 1985): 107–21. On the intensity of concerns about rank, see David S. Webster, "The Bureau of Education's Suppressed Rating of Colleges, 1911–1912," *HEQ* 24(Winter 1984): 499–511. Babcock placed Wesleyan among the fifty-nine institutions in his top category. See Richard W. Lykes, *Higher Education and the United States Office of Education, 1867–1953* (Washington, D.C.: U.S. Office of Education, 1975), 224.

16. *WA* 6 Nov. 1901, 16 Dec. 1896, 2 Nov. 1904, 20 Nov. 1901; *WLM* 16(December 1907): 123–29; *WA* 20 Nov. 1901.

17. *WA* 29 Jan. 1902; AAM 24 June 1902, 27 June 1905; *WLM* 14 (December 1905): 128; *FEx* 1910; Raymond, *Twenty-Five Years*, 2; James A. Develin to BPR, 13 June 1904, correspondence regarding contributions, 1904–05, NCAR, box 5A; AAM 27 June 1905; *WUB* (December 1907):27, (May 1908):6; AAM 25 June 1907; *WUB* (May 1910):5. Amherst began an alumni fund with annual solicitations in 1906, initially seeking contributions only from the re-union classes. It became a comprehensive annual fund in 1922. The Williams Loyalty Fund (1919) grew out of annual solicitations to meet special needs during World War I. (Hans, "Growth," 165, 47).

18. *WA* 29 Mar., 11 Oct. 1890; AAM 24 June 1902; *WA* 24 May 1905. The trustees heard from an alumnus in publicity work (James S. Judd '85) in 1901 and decided to establish a "Bureau of Publicity," but little was done about this matter before 1910. See BTM 24 June, 25 Nov. 1901; Henry M. Wriston, *Academic Procession: Reflections of a College President* (New York: Columbia University Press, 1959), 5.

19. *WA* 2 Dec. 1885, 26 Oct., 14 Dec. 1886, 15 Jan. 1887; *WLM* 13(March 1905): 257–58; *WA* 24 Apr. 1883, 18 Nov. 1892, 1 Apr. 1903, 5 Feb. 1884, 5 Nov. 1886; *WLM* 13(January 1905): 168, 13(February 1905): 215. Discussion of Methodist identity in 1905 began when the alumni editor for a new section in the *WLM* invited responses to the question: "In what sense is Wesleyan, and in what sense should Wesleyan be, a Methodist insti-tution?" See *WLM* 13(October 1904): 39. The founding of American University in Washington, D.C., raised new questions about denomina-tional loyalty to Wesleyan, especially when Mark Hoyt and then John

Andrus, both millionaire trustees of Wesleyan, were tapped to serve as chairs of American's board in the 1890s (*WA* 1 Mar. 1890, 1 July 1891, 7 Mar. 1900; Morrill, *Multimillionaire*, 105).

20. For references to occasional proposals in the 1860s to adopt a new name, see chap. 3, n83. *M* 23 Aug. 1873; *WA* 7 May 1880; *ZH* 9 Feb. 1871, 19 Mar. 1874; *CA* 16 June 1881; *M* 23 Aug. 1873; *WA* 14, 22 Dec. 1885; Moses Scudder, Jr., to S. F. Upham, 26 May 1874, NCAR, box 1, folder 10; BTM 24 June 1874; *CA* 5 July 1877; *WA* 2 June 1880, 29 Apr., 10 June 1874, 18 May 1880; *ZH* 11 June 1874; *WA* 14 Dec. 1885.

21. AAM 25 June 1879, 23 June 1880; BTM 28 June 1887, 26 June 1888, 24 June 1890, 23 June 1891; AAM 29 June 1887, 25 June 1889, 24 June 1890, 23 June 1891; *WA* 14 July 1888; ARP (1874):473; *WA* 4 Mar. 1874, 24 Sept. 1873; *WUB* (November 1891):11–12; *WA* 16 May 1891; BTM 23 June 1891; AAM 23 June 1891.

22. *CA* 2 July 1891; AAM 23 June 1891, 23 June 1896; *WA* 17 Mar. 1897; John B. Scott et al., *Wesleyan University* (single sheet dated 22 Oct. 1891); *WA* 19 Feb. 1895; *WLM* 2(October 1893): 34; *WUB* (December 1905):16; *WA* 16 Jan. 1907; *WLM* 17(November 1908): 82.

23. The Raymond presidency seems to have reached its peak in the mid-1890s (*WA* 9 Apr. 1895). *WA* 5 Apr. 1895, 20 Nov. 1901; *WLM* 12(June 1904): 360. From the mid-1890s to 1910 there were many variations in nomenclature for these groups. In 1901 they were known as the Wesleyan Young Alumni Club of New York and the Boston Young Alumni Club. *WA* 1 Mar., 4 Oct. 1905, 28 Feb., 9, 16 May, 24 Oct. 1906, 3 July 1907, 18 Jan. 1905, 6 Nov. 1907.

24. *WA* 20 Nov. 1901, 6 Nov. 1907; BTM 27 June 1894; *CA* 21 June 1894. These meetings occurred from 1894 to 1899, after which the board found itself too busy to spare the time for such gatherings (AAM 26 June 1894, 25 June 1895, 23 June 1896, 29 June 1897, 28 June 1898, 27 June 1899). *WUB* (May 1894):9–11. The movement to obtain balloting by mail took fourteen years. See AAM 23 June 1880, 27 June 1883; BTM 24 June 1884; *WA* 10 Oct. 1884; *WUB* (April 1888):2–3, (May 1891):3–4. About 45 percent of the living graduates cast ballots (AAM 26 June 1894). AAM 26 June 1900. Williams began electing alumni trustees in 1868. By 1872 alumni representation on Williams's board reached the authorized limit: five of seventeen members. Election permitting ballots by mail began in 1875. Amherst revised its charter in 1874 to provide for alumni-elected trustees. They were to succeed the five trustees elected by the state legislature, as each of those incumbents resigned or died. This process, begun in 1875 and completed in 1897, gradually achieved a full complement of five alumni-elected trustees on the seventeen-member board. Balloting by mail began in 1930. See Hans, "Growth," 29–31, 141–42; William J. Newlin, ed., *Amherst College: Biographical Record of the Graduates and Non-Graduates*, rev. ed. (Amherst, Mass.:

Amherst College, 1939), xxi. The Wesleyan Alumni Association requested larger representation in 1900 and 1909 (AAM 26 June 1900, 29 June 1909), but the alumni-elected proportion did not change until the board's size went from fifty-five to twenty-six in 1959, with six of the twenty-six elected by alumni. Alumni had called for a smaller board in closer touch with the campus in 1907 (WA 29 May 1907).

25. SAC 6:796, 8:140; WA 20 Nov. 1901. For evidence of sustained efforts by alumni clubs to endorse trustee candidates who were businessmen or lawyers, and usually non-Methodists, see WA 26 Mar. 1902, 13 Mar. 1907. Data on composition of the board are drawn from TDB. After the election of Wallace (AAM 27 June 1893), the trustees retained Andrews as a board member by electing him to fill a vacancy (BTM 27 June 1893). All five non-Methodists—Wallace, Olin, and Baker (each with ties to the Episcopal denomination) plus Smith (Congregational) and Knapp (Unitarian)—came from Methodist families. Among the other five, only Reynolds and Whitney seem to have been active in affairs of the Methodist denomination. By 1910, 42 percent of the board were businessmen, and 23 percent were lawyers. Almost twenty percent were non-Methodists. The percentages of businessmen and lawyers are almost identical with averages for fifteen private institutions of the East and Midwest for 1910/11 (McGrath, "Control," 264). In addition to Reynolds, fellow metropolitan lawyers Olin and William M. Ingraham '46 were alumni-elected trustees serving on the general executive committee (BTM 6 Mar. 1893). Upon the death of Oliver Hoyt, Reynolds became the first alumnus to serve as president of the board (BTM 28 June 1887).

26. Much of the information in this and the next paragraph comes from TDB. BTM 22 Apr. 1879, 26 June 1879; William H. Wallace, a millionaire iron manufacturer, stopped renting a pew at Summerfield Methodist Church in 1884 and resigned from Wesleyan's board in June 1884. This is probably the time when he became an Episcopalian. See pew rental account books of Summerfield Methodist Church, MECR, vol. 484; BTM 24 June 1884; CA 12 Sep. 1901. On the expulsion of William J. Hutchinson from the stock exchange, see NYT 7 June 1882 and New York World 7 June 1882. Serving on the investigating committee that found Hutchinson "guilty of improper and illegal practices" was a fellow Wesleyan trustee, Joseph S. Stout. See Report of the Special Committee of Investigation . . . May 5, 1882 . . . Hutchinson & Co. (n.p., 1882), 16. Pursued by law suits and creditors, Hutchinson made a speedy departure for Paris in 1884 (NYT 1 Mar. 1885). Andrew C. Fields, another Methodist trustee, was involved in the insurance industry scandal of 1905. He was an Albany lobbyist for the Mutual Life Insurance Company. Pursued by detectives, Fields fled in a private railroad car and established a secret residence in Los Angeles. He was not a board member, however, when the scandal broke, having been booted for nonattendance in 1903. See NYT 12 Feb. 1911; Morton Keller, The Life Insurance Enterprise, 1885–1910:

A Study in the Limits of Corporate Power (Cambridge: Harvard University Press, 1963), 214–18, 245, 252; втм 30 June 1903. The move by Amherst's board in the 1890s to elect a few wealthy businessmen from New York City yielded substantial gifts to increase endowment and no reported brushes with embarrassment (Harris, *History*, 87–96). Wesleyan application dated 7 Feb. 1910, p. 2, cfatr.

27. E. Digby Baltzell, *Philadelphia Gentlemen: The Making of a National Upper Class* (Glencoe, Ill.: Free Press, 1958), 236. On increasing wealth among Methodists and on defections to other denominations, see McChesney, "Effect," 5–7; *CA* 10 Jan., 7 Feb. 1901. On Rand, see *NCAB* 28:26; records of the Grace Episcopal Church, Medford, Mass., 1888. On Wallace, see *CA* 12 Sep. 1901; *Brooklyn Eagle* 4 Sept. 1901, 20 July 1915; *OP* '00, 42:3. On Baker, see *NCAB* 33:204; records of First Methodist Church, 1890, and of Emmanuel Episcopal Church, 1895, Newport, R.I., Newport Historical Society, On Ingraham and Stout, see *WA* 16 Feb. 1911 and *NYT* 30 June 1904.

28. Francis G. Fairfield, *The Clubs of New York . . . Club-Men* (New York: Henry L. Hinton, 1873), 9, 11, 15, 28; Henry L. Nelson, "Some New York Clubs," *Harper's Weekly* 34(15 March 1890): 211. For additional commentary on metropolitan men's clubs, see Baltzell, *Philadelphia Gentlemen*, 336–45; David C. Hammack, *Power and Society: Greater New York at the Turn of the Century* (New York: Russell Sage Foundation, 1982), 72–77; John Tauranac and Christopher Little, *Elegant New York: The Builders and the Buildings, 1885–1915* (New York: Abbeville Press, 1985), 123–27.

29. Frank Mason North, "Stephen Henry Olin," *WUA* 10(August-October 1925): 10–11; M. Eugene Culver, "Reminiscences of the Seventies," *WLM* 6(May 1898): 278; *OP* '95, 37:frontispiece; *WA* 1 July 1903; John C. Clark, "Memorial of Stephen H. Olin," *Yearbook of the Association of the Bar of the City of New York* (New York: Association of the Bar, 1926), 470; Addison L. Green, Address at the service in memory of Stephen Henry Olin, 8 Nov. 1925, typescript, ofp, box 6, p. 11; *OP* '95, 37:185.

30. Green, Address, 18; North, "Olin," 8–10; *CM*, 679–80. Descended from the Livingston family, Julia M. Olin (1814–79) was owner and summer resident of the estate from the time of her youth. See J. Theodore Hughes, *An Historical Sketch of . . . Freeborn Garrettson . . . Preacher*, 2d ed. (Rhinebeck, N.Y.: Rhinebeck United Methodist Parish, 1984), 34, 44. Stephen Henry's father was first married to Mary Bostick, a "distinguished belle" from Georgia who "had considerable means." She died in 1839. See *Life of Olin*, 1:139, 258–67; Arthur H. Harrop, *The Story of Ammi Bradford Hyde* (Cincinnati: printed for the author, 1912), 31–32. Julia M. Olin to Mary Garrettson, 18 Nov. 1849, ofp, box 3; sho to Julia M. Olin, 22 Feb. 1862, early October 1864, ofp, box 6. Olin was an honors student but did not achieve election to Phi Beta Kappa until 19 July 1871 (list of members of the Connecticut Gamma of Phi Beta Kappa, Wesleyan University, 1845–75).

31. *CM* 679–80; North, "Olin," 9; *Memorial Service in Honor of the Late Julia M. Olin . . . , 15 May 1879* (n.p., n.d.), 5–8, 12–19; Julia M. Olin belonged to the Episcopal church prior to her marriage to Stephen Olin. See *Twentieth-Century Biographical Dictionary of Notable Americans* (Boston: Biographical Society, 1904), vol. 8; *Memorial Service . . . , 1879*, 4, 10; Julia M. Olin to Margaretta Lynch, 17 Feb. 1844, OFP, box 3. The Flushing Institute, which served in the 1830s as a prototype for the Episcopal boarding school, came under new ownership in the mid-1840s. See James McLachlan, *American Boarding Schools: A Historical Study* (New York: Charles Scribner's Sons, 1970), 105–6, 133; *Catalogue of Officers and Students of the Flushing Institute* (July 1859). SHO to Julia M. Olin, 22 Dec. 1862, 22 Feb. 1863, 4 Jan. 1864, 22 June 1865, OFP, box 6; Olin considered transferring to Columbia for his senior year (Julia M. Olin to SHO, 24 June 1865, OFP, box 6). Toward the end of Olin's senior year, his mother lamented his lack of church membership (Julia M. Olin to SHO, 2 May 1866, OFP, Box 6). WNRD 7 Sept. 1862; WNR to Frank Mason North, 29 Aug. 1925, WNRP. A devoted Methodist, Rice critiqued his friend Olin's acting presidency of Wesleyan in 1922/23 by stating that the president of Wesleyan ought "to have religion, and not merely a distant respect for it" (WNR to Edward L. Rice, 23 Sept. 1923, WNRP). Alice Barlow, daughter of millionaire corporate lawyer S. L. M. Barlow, died in 1882, three years after the marriage. See *New York Evening Post*, 24 Oct. 1879; *Harper's Weekly* 26(25 November 1882): 739; *NYT* 11, 13 July 1889; *NCAB* 3:259; *DAB* 1:613–15. Emeline Harriman Dodge was the daughter of Oliver Harriman, a wealthy merchant who loaned $3,000 to his nephew, E. H. Harriman, to launch the career of this railroad magnate. When she married Olin in 1903, Emeline was the widow of W. Earl Dodge, whose father made his fortune with Phelps, Dodge & Co. See *NYT* 21, 22 March 1903, 14 Aug. 1938; Lloyd J. Mercer, *E. H. Harriman: Master Railroader* (Boston: Twayne, 1985), 9; *NYT* 13 Mar. 1904; *DAB* 3:353. *NYT* 12 Dec. 1902, 12 Nov. 1903, 9 Aug. 1925.

32. North, "Olin," 10; *WAR* (1883), 215; *NCAB* 1:181, 22:152; Clark, "Memorial," 467–69.

33. *WAR* (1911), 231; Clark, "Memorial," 469; Carl Price, "Stephen H. Olin, Litt. D.," *CA* 14 June 1923; Stephen H. Olin, *Suggestions Upon the Strategy of Street Fighting* (New York: privately printed, 1886), 1, 3, 4–10, 14–16. Olin thus participated in the movement of the 1880s and 1890s to turn national guard units into "more centralized and professional military organizations." This movement was in harmony with views of most Americans on use of force to maintain order. See Robert M. Fogelson, *America's Armories: Architecture, Society, and Public Order* (Cambridge: Harvard University Press, 1989), 29–40. North, "Olin," 10; Clark, "Memorial," 469; Phyllis Dain, *The New York Public Library: A History of Its Founding and Early Years* (New York: New York Public Library, 1972), 80–82.

34. Butler was an Episcopalian and a Republican who served as dean at Columbia from 1890 until the start of his forty-three-year presidency in 1902 (*DAB* Supplement 4:133–38). He was fifteen years younger than Olin. Butler and Olin traveled together, with their wives, in Europe. They shared membership in the Round Table Club. Each received an honorary doctorate from the other's institution (Butler from Wesleyan in 1916; Olin from Columbia in 1923). Butler arranged for the inscription on Olin's tombstone, designed by McKim, Mead, & White. See Nicholas Murray Butler, *Across the Busy Years*, vol. 2 (New York: Charles Scribner's Sons, 1940), 247, 430; SHO to Nicholas Murray Butler (3 Apr. 1916, 7 June 1923), Butler to SHO (4 Apr. 1916, 11 May 1923), Emeline H. Olin to Butler (9 Sept. 1925), Butler to Emeline H. Olin (3 Dec. 1925), Nicholas Murray Butler Papers, Rare Book and Manuscript Library, Columbia University. Stephen H. Olin, "Public School Reform in New York," *Educational Review* 8(June 1894): 1–6; Stephen H. Olin, "The New York Common Schools," *Harper's* 90(March 1895): 584–89; Hammack, *Power*, 278–93, 310–13. Similar movements to centralize urban education and put it under the control of "business and professional elites" occurred soon afterward in St. Louis (1897), Baltimore (1898), Philadelphia (1905), Boston (1905), and other cities. See David B. Tyack, *The One Best System: A History of American Urban Education* (Cambridge: Harvard University Press, 1974), pt. 4; Joseph M. Cronin, *The Control of Urban Schools: Perspectives on the Power of Educational Reformers* (New York: Free Press, 1973), chaps. 4–5. Hammack, *Power*, 115–16; *WAR* (1911), 231. There were close ties between the University Settlement Society and the reform-oriented mayoral campaigns of Strong (1894) and Low (1897, 1901). By 1902 the University Settlement residents were "one of the most remarkable collections of young reformers and writers ever assembled." See Allen F. Davis, *Spearheads for Reform: The Social Settlements and the Progressive Movement, 1890–1914* (New York: Oxford University Press, 1967), 180–84, 99. Olin's early interest in civic reform is indicated by his membership on the executive committee of the Young Men's Reform Association of New York in 1873 and his efforts for improved city government a year earlier. See *WAR* (1883), 216; Stephen H. Olin, *Argument Upon the Charter . . . New York* (New York: Citizen's Association of New York, 1872).

35. Stephen H. Olin, *Occasional Addresses by Stephen Henry Olin* (n.p.: printed for private distribution, 1911), 3, 7. On Olin as one of sixteen original incorporators of the Players (1888), see *The Players* (New York: n.p., 1897), 5. He joined the Century Association in 1875, Round Table in 1877, and University in 1879, serving as secretary, 1891/92. He also belonged to the City and the Down-Town. See Allan Nevins et al., *The Century, 1847–1946* (New York: Century Association, 1947), 396; Stephen H. Olin, *The Round Table Club, 1868–1918* (n.p. [ca. 1918]), 4; *Charter, Constitution, House Rules, and List of Officers and Members of the University Club* (New York:

University Club, 1892), 45; James W. Alexander, *A History of the University Club of New York, 1865–1915* (New York: Charles Scribner's Sons, 1915), 192; *OP* '95, 37:185. Characteristics emphasized for membership are delineated for three of Olin's clubs in Hammack, *Power*, 72–74. Nicholas Murray Butler to Emeline H. Olin, 2 Jan. 1931, NMBP; *OP* '95, 37:185; *WA* 18 Jan. 1889; *NYT* 16 Feb. 1892. Lacking great wealth and having a somewhat attenuated knickerbocker lineage, Olin's presence on the McAllister list demonstrates the permeability of New York elites as compared with those of Boston or Philadelphia. These characteristics, his professional success, and his interest in civic and cultural enterprises also make Olin an atypical member of the New York "400." See Frederic C. Jaher, "Style and Status: High Society in Late Nineteenth-Century New York," in *The Rich, the Well Born, and the Powerful: Elites and Upper Classes in History*, ed. Frederic C. Jaher (Urbana: University of Illinois Press, 1973), 258–84.

36. Committee for the Wesleyan University Club of New York, *A Tribute* (large single sheet printed in 1925), OFP; *NYT* 7 Aug. 1925; Clark, "Memorial," 461; Stephen Henry Olin, "The Founders and Builders," *WUA* 7(February 1923): 6. For the deathbed story, see *Life of Olin* 2:455–56. *Semi-Centennial*, 48; *WA* 19 Dec. 1910; North, "Olin," 10; Olin, *Response*, 7.

37. Price, "Olin," 754. There was talk of Olin becoming an alumni-trustee candidate, at age twenty-seven, who would be "progressive" in "proposing and urging reforms" (Moses L. Scudder to WNR, 2 June 1874, WNRP). AAM 25 June 1879 and at five-year intervals thereafter; *ZH* 8 Feb. 1877; *WA* 4 Feb. 1879, 19 Dec. 1889; *ZH* 3 July 1873; *WA* 18 Mar. 1903; *Wesley Bicentennial*, 131–34. Olin helped to found the New York Wesleyan alumni club (*WA* 25 Feb. 1869). Green, Address, 16; BTM 27 June 1882, 28 June 1887, 26 June 1894. The committee on the board of instruction was not recognized as a standing committee of the board in *WUC* until 1890, but its evolution as a committee, under the chairmanship of Olin, began in 1886 (see chap. 5 n4). BTM 6 Mar. 1893; *OP* '95, 37:184; *WA* 28 Mar. 1906; *WUA* 10(August–October 1925): 13.

38. North, "Olin," 10. Olin wrote this poem, "Tele Mystica," as a song for his fraternity, sung to the tune of Fleming's "Integer Vitae." See *Songs of the Eclectic Fraternity, Wesleyan University* (Middletown: n.p., 1876), 9; *WUA* 10(August–October 1925): 12; Green, Address, 1.

39. James L. McConaughy, typescript of a tribute to Stephen H. Olin delivered at the service in memory of Olin, 8 Nov. 1925, p. 2. On the complex connections between urbanization and the development of organized athletics, see Steven A. Riess, *City Games: The Evolution of American Urban Society and the Rise of Sports* (Urbana: University of Illinois Press, 1989). Melvin L. Adelman, *A Sporting Time: New York City and the Rise of Modern Athletics, 1820–70* (Urbana: University of Illinois Press, 1986), 193–97; Smith, *Sports*, chaps. 3–4. Smith's book lacks factual accuracy in several of its references to Wesleyan.

40. *WA* 1, 15 May, 26 Sept. 1872; *NYH* 16 July 1872, 16 July 1873; *WA* 5 Nov. 1873, 26 Sept. 1872; *NYH* 18 July 1873. On contributions from Olin, Squire, and others in New York and Boston, see *WA* 2 July, 5 Nov. 1873, 29 Apr., 30 Sept. 1874, 2 Oct. 1875, 6 May 1876. The story of Squire's major gift is told by Harry C. Heermans '75 in R1939. H. C. M. Ingraham to WNR, 19 Mar. 1874, WNRP.

41. On early racing days in Saratoga, see George Waller, *Saratoga: Saga of an Impious Era* (Englewood Cliffs, N.J.: Prentice Hall, 1966), 126–27. For accounts of the 1874 regatta, see Harry C. Heermans '75, R1939; *NYH* 16–19 July 1874. An estimated thirty thousand spectators were on hand in 1875 to watch thirteen crews compete (Smith, *Sports*, 47). *NYTr* 17 June 1875; *NYT* 14 July 1875; *Harper's Weekly* 19(24, 31 July 1875): 598, 618. For a detailed account of how the New York City press made the 1875 race "the most newsworthy item of the day," see Guy M. Lewis, "America's First Intercollegiate Sport: The Regattas from 1852 to 1875," *Research Quarterly* 38(December 1967): 644–46. Smith, *Sports*, 48–50; *WA* 12 Nov. 1876; *OP* '98, 40:143. In 1876 the Wesleyan crew, despite encouragement from a toast at the New York alumni club (*WA* 13 Jan. 1876), finished sixth at Saratoga, beating only Princeton (*WA* 24 Oct. 1876). *WA* 14 June 1882.

42. *WLM* 17(March 1909): 236; *CA* 26 Sept. 1872, 24 July 1873, 5 Dec. 1872; *ZH* 24 July 1873, 9 Apr. 1874.

43. *CA* 5 Dec. 1872; *ZH* 24 July, 7 Aug. 1873; *WA* 26 Feb. 1873, 28 Apr. 1874; *ZH* 7 Aug. 1873; *OP* '74, 16:2; *WA* 28 Oct. 1874, 29 Jan. 1873. On muscular Christianity, see Adelman, *Sporting*, 279–86. *CA* 6 July 1893, 19 July, 11 Oct. 1894.

44. Smith, *Sports*, 70. For the rules used by Wesleyan, see *WA* 18 Dec. 1875. *WA* 20 Nov., 4 Dec. 1875; Riess, *City*, 4, 271n8; *NYH* 1 Dec. 1876; Riess, *City*, 56.

45. *OP* '85, 27:70, '98, 40:114; *WA* 16 Nov. 1883. Wins over the University of Pennsylvania came in 1885, 1887, and 1889. *WA* 2 Dec. 1885; Tom Perrin, *Football: A College History* (Jefferson, N.C.: McFarland, 1987), 5. Olin had watched Wesleyan defeat Rutgers in New York in 1884 (*WA* 25 Nov. 1884).

46. Nicolson, *Athletics*, 168. Games against Amherst, Williams, and Trinity often were played on fields in the small cities of Springfield and Hartford. Wesleyan was admitted to the Intercollegiate Football Association League in 1885 (*WA* 17 Feb. 1885); Harvard withdrew in 1889 (Smith, *Sports*, 80). *WA* 16 Nov. 1883; *OP* '92, 34:102; Smith, *Sports*, 78–79; *WA* 2 Dec. 1892, 5 Dec. 1890. Numbers were not worn by college football players until decades later (Rudolph, *American*, 386). *WA* 10 Oct. 1884.

47. Smith, *Sports*, 88–91; *OP* '98, 40:115; *WA* 19 Nov. 1887, 16 Nov., 2 Dec. 1886, 19 Dec. 1887; *MP* 30 Oct., 2, 4 Nov. 1893; *WA* 2, 13 Nov. 1893; *OP* '94, 36:152–53.

48. *WA* 6 Oct. 1894. A typhoid epidemic canceled play against Trinity, and a game against Brown replaced that scheduled with Dartmouth. *WA* 4 Dec. 1894; *OP* '98, 40:116. The only previous contests with Williams were four scattered through the 1880s; from 1882 to 1893 there were six games with Amherst (*WA* 5 Dec. 1900). *WA* 9 Nov., 21 Dec. 1898, 25 Jan. 1899. This arrangement, sometimes referred to as the Tri-Collegiate League or the New England Tri-Collegiate League, lasted from 1899 to 1902. Amherst, Williams, and Dartmouth competed in an earlier Triangular League from 1892 to 1898 (*WA* 23 Dec. 1893, 2 Mar. 1898). *WLM* 8(October 1899): 38; *WA* 25 Jan. 1899.

49. *WA* 13 Nov. 1893; Smith, *Sports*, 55; *WA* 16 Oct. 1883; *OP* '90, 32:117; *WA* 20 May, 6 July 1892, 26 Jan. 1893; *WLM* 2(October 1893): 34; *WA* 30 June 1898, 15 Jan. 1895. Reiter served as a seasonal coach for a fee of $650 in 1903 and 1904 (*WA* 28 Oct. 1903, 5 Oct. 1904, 12 Apr. 1905). Having studied at Princeton Theological Seminary for two years, he was praised by alumni as "not only an effective athlete but an influential Christian." See *WA* 8 Mar. 1905; *WAR* (1931), 76; *CA* 2 July 1908. On the hiring of coaches by the day, week, or season at many institutions in the late nineteenth century, including a crew coach at Wesleyan in the mid-1870s, see Smith, *Sports*, 35, 148–49, chap. 11.

50. Football budgets appear annually in *WA*. Faculty also made contributions and helped raise additional funds to support intercollegiate teams (exchange of letters between Seward V. Coffin and CTW, 7, 8 Oct. 1895, CTWP, box 4; *CA* 21 Apr. 1887). Lack of a high fence to enclose the football field and baseball diamond hurt gate receipts up to 1897 (AAM 25 June 1889, 23 June 1896; BTM 25 June 1889; *WA* 6 Oct. 1891). For a description of the new system, see *OP* '92, 34:97–98. A copy of the system's constitution in its fully evolved form appeared in *WA* 11, 18, 25 Jan. 1899. Seward V. Coffin to WW, 1 Mar. 1891, *PWW* 7: 171–72. The faculty kept control of eligibility. See *WUB* (November 1892): 11. On fund-raising efforts, see circular letter from J. B. Scott et al., 22 Oct. 1891, NCAR, box 7; *WA* 19 Feb. 1895. *WA* 11 Mar. 1903; *WUB* (November 1903):12–13; Howard J. Savage, *American College Athletics* (New York: Carnegie Foundation for the Advancement of Teaching, 1929), 24. For the constitution of the Athletic Council, see *WA* 18 May 1904. The first meeting was one day after authorization by the board (BTM 28 Oct. 1903; Athletic Council minutes, 29 Oct. 1903). For the constitution of the Alumni Athletic Association, see *WA* 20 Apr. 1904. *WA* 27 June 1906, 16 Jan. 1907, 12 Oct. 1908; *WUB* (December 1908):20–21.

51. *WA* 23 Feb. 1898, 29 Oct. 1902; Smith, *Sports*, 200–8. Wesleyan was involved in a rough-play incident with Columbia in 1905 (*NYH* 8 Oct. 1905; *NYTr* 8, 9, 10 Oct. 1905; *WA* 11 Oct. 1905). ARP (1907):8. The National Collegiate Athletic Association was known from 1906 to 1910 as the Intercollegiate Athletic Association of the United States (Smith, *Sports*,

272n52). Wesleyan's dean, Frank W. Nicolson, a charter representative and secretary-treasurer of the NCAA (1909–39), was a leader in the movement against professionalism in college athletics (FM 11 Dec. 1906; *WAR* [1941], 21; *WA* 4 Mar. 1908). The pass from Samuel B. Moore '08 to Irvin Van Tassell n1910 gained twenty yards against Yale, 3 Oct. 1906 in New Haven. See *WA* 3, 10 Oct. 1906; Nicolson, *Athletics*, 50–51, 157; *WUA* 40(February 1956): 5–6. The major college season opened on Saturday, September 29, with Princeton completing a long forward pass from a halfback to an end (probably after a lateral) in a game against Villanova (*NYT* 30 Sept. 1906). On 3 October, Princeton and Williams completed forward passes in games played at about the same time as Wesleyan's against Yale (*NYT* 4 Oct. 1906; *Boston Globe* 4 Oct. 1906). Despite Riley Ondek's claim that the "first *legal* forward pass" occurred in a game between two Kansas colleges (Washburn and Fairmount) in December 1905, this was only an experimental game played months before the new rules were adopted and published. See Riley Ondek, "Birth of the Bomb," *Sports History* 1(March 1988): 39; Smith, *Sports*, 204–6. The other major claim for first use, in a game on 5 Sep. 1906 between Saint Louis University and Carroll College at Lake Beulah, Wisconsin, is flawed by the fact that it took place during preseason conditioning camp for the Saint Louis team and was clearly described as a practice game by the *Carroll Echo* 15(October 1906): 9. Saint Louis University was a pioneer in use of the forward pass that season, but there is no mention of completed passes in accounts of its first or second regular season games (29 September, 4 October). See *Fleur de Lis* 7(November 1906): 51–52; *St. Louis Post Dispatch* 30 Sept. 1906.

52. Rudolph, *Hopkins*, 71–72, 164–65; Smith, *Sports*, 52–53; Adelman, *Sporting*, 92, 114, 136–37, 121; *OP* '64, 5:43; SHO to Julia M. Olin, [early October 1864], [June 1865], OFP, box 6. Olin served as president of the Agallian Base Ball Club (see text at chap. 2 n60) from his sophomore through senior year and played positions ranging from catcher to third base to left field (*OP* '65, 6:37, '66, 7:34; Agallian Base Ball Club scorebook).

53. *WA* 28 June 1871. Students, too, were quick to argue that "conquests on the lake or ballground" were a means "to have Wesleyan raised to greater eminence" (*WA* 28 June 1871, 14 Dec. 1880). Edgar Fauver, "A History of Wesleyan Athletics," *OP* '31, 73:184; *WA* 11 May 1888, 20 May 1892, 28 Apr. 1896. Another contact with alumni came in the late 1880s. A varsity versus alumni baseball game occurred during commencement and reunion week (*WA* 7 July 1887). Probably not until 1898 did alumni win one of these contests (*CA* 14 July 1898). *WA* 3 July, 11 Oct. 1893. About eight hundred spectators watched Yale's defeat (*WA* 12 May 1893). In 1897 another win over Yale also produced a large celebration (*WA* 14 Apr. 1897). *WA* 12 May 1893.

54. *WA* 11 June 1868; Smith, *Sports*, 125, chap. 11; *WA* 2 Dec. 1892;

FM 17 May 1898; *WA* 8 May 1901; *Harper's Weekly* 40(23 May 1896): 526; *OP* '98, 40:109.

55. Jack Falla, *NCAA, The Voice of College Sports: A Diamond Anniversary History 1906–1981* (Mission, Kan.: NCAA, 1981), 37–39; Smith, *Sports*, 62–66.

56. *WA* 5, 15 Feb. 1884; *MP* 2 Feb. 1889; *WA* 14 Jan. 1896; 2 Mar., 21 Dec. 1898, 25 Jan., 26 Apr., 7 June, 5 July, 6 Dec. 1899.

57. *WA* 28 Feb. 1900, 27 Feb., 8 May 1901; FM 26 Mar., 30 Apr., 14 May 1901; *MP* 1, 3 May 1901; Williams College *Vidette* 3, 10, 31 May 1901; *WA* 8 May 1901, 26 Feb. 1902; Le Duc, *Piety*, 133; *WA* 28 May, 4 June 1902. A full set of eligibility rules for the league had only recently been adopted (FM 11 Mar. 1902). Williams resumed baseball competition with Amherst in 1904 and Wesleyan followed suit in 1905 (*WA* 26 Oct. 1904, 8 Mar., 31 May 1905). Wesleyan did not return to playing football against Amherst, however, until 1910 (*WA* 10 Oct. 1910).

58. *WA* 2 Mar. 1904, 29 Nov. 1905; Athletic Council minutes 3 June 1905–14 Dec. 1907; *WA* 25 Feb. 1903, 15 Oct. 1902; *WLM* 9(May 1901): 351, 14(June 1906): 425–28; *WA* 11 Mar. 1908.

59. *WUB* (November 1895):22; Raymond, "What Signs," 143–44. The *OP* of '98 was dedicated to athletics. Track competition from 1887 to 1896 was limited to an annual intramural field day and the spring meet of the New England Intercollegiate Athletic Association. Both gatherings included a bicycle race. For the first of these meets, see *WA* 27 May, 8 June 1887. Dual meets in track began with one against Trinity in 1895 (*WA* 21 May 1895). For an interesting account of an early intramural cross-country race, see *WA* 28 Nov. 1906. Jesse Hurlbut '00 briefly held the world record in the pole vault during the spring of 1898 (*WA* 25 May 1898, 4 Mar. 1903). Tennis courts appeared on the back campus during the early 1880s (*WA* 14 June 1882, 13 May 1884, 1 May 1885). Competition beyond the campus began in 1900, when Wesleyan sent a representative to the first tournament of the New England Intercollegiate Tennis Association (*WA* 23 May 1900). A tournament for three teams in 1903 preceded the first dual match, against Brown, in 1906 (*WA* 10 June 1903, 16 May 1906). One year after the nation's first intercollegiate basketball game (Hamline versus Minnesota in 1895), a Wesleyan group engaged the local YMCA team. The first intercollegiate basketball game for Wesleyan was against Yale on 10 Dec. 1896. After this 39-4 defeat, Wesleyan eschewed intercollegiate competition until a game with Amherst on 28 Feb. 1902. See Smith, *Sports*, 220; *WA* 22 Jan. 1895, 14, 28 Jan., 4 Feb. 1896. *Yale Daily News* 11 Dec. 1896. *WA* 27 Jan. 1897, 5 Mar. 1902. Wesleyan's first intercollegiate hockey game was 28 Jan. 1910 against the Massachusetts Agricultural College at Pratt Rink, Amherst (*WA* 31 Jan. 1910).

60. *WA* 29 Jan. 1895; *OP* '95, 37:185; Riess, *City*, 57; Patton, *Eight*,

60–61. This was a second generation of gymnasiums, replacing structures that were crude by comparison. Brown's new facility cost nearly $66,000 (Bronson, *History*, 459).

61. The motion to appoint this committee was made by John B. Scott '81 of Philadelphia, another leader in the gym movement among Wesleyan alumni (AAM 25 June 1889). *WUB* (15 Oct. 1889):12; *WA* 26 Oct. 1889; *MP* 28 Sept. 1889; *CA* 17 Oct. 1889; *WA* 26 Oct. 1889, 16 May 1889, 7 Jan. 1890; BTM 20 Mar. 1891; *WA* 19 Dec. 1890, 11, 23 Mar. 1891; BTM 20 Mar., 23 June 1891. Plans included provision for endowed maintenance; a fund of $25,000 was established for this purpose (Van Vleck, *Historical Sketch*, 55). AAM 23 June 1891; *WA* 11 Mar. 1892; BTM 28 June 1892; *WA* 20 Feb. 1892; BTM 27 June 1893, 23 Mar., 14 Dec. 1894. The building committee studied gyms at Harvard, Yale, and Cornell in making plans for the new building (*NYTr* 6 Oct. 1894).

62. *WA* 3 July 1893, 11 June 1868; Adelman, *Sporting*, 173–74; *OP* '86, 28:70; Smith, *Sports*, 83–84, 96; Riess, *City*, 56; Bruce Haley, *The Healthy Body and Victorian Culture* (Cambridge: Harvard University Press, 1978), chap. 5; Harvey Green, *Fit for America: Health, Fitness, Sport, and American Society* (New York: Pantheon Books, 1986), 182–83; J. A. Mangan and James Walvin, eds., *Manliness and Morality: Middle-Class Masculinity in Britain and America, 1800–1940* (New York: St. Martin's Press, 1987), 2–6; *WA* 10 Feb. 1886; *ZH* 4 July 1894. About five hundred friends and alumni of Wesleyan attended the dedication on 5 Oct. 1894 (*CA* 11 Oct. 1894). *DAB* 1:290; *WA* 16 Oct. 1894; *MP* 6 Oct. 1894; *HC* 6 Oct. 1894; *WUB* (November 1894):5. Andrews was an athletic enthusiast on his own campus (Patton, *Eight*, 134). Fayerweather Gymnasium cost about $50,000 (*FEx* 1894–96).

63. An earlier push for fencing and grading the field in 1892 led to only minor improvements (*WA* 2 Mar., 6 July 1892; BTM 27 June 1893). AAM 23 June 1896, 29 June 1897; BTM 22 June 1896, 29 June 1897; *WA* 31 Mar. 1897; *WUB* (November 1898):5; *OP* '98, 40:108; *WA* 31 Mar. 1897, 18 May, 8 June 1898. The new diamond in the southwest corner of the field replaced one in the northeast corner. The new track, also relocated from a northeastern site, enclosed the diamond and football field. Andrus supplied $2,000 of the $3,371 used to construct the grandstand behind home plate. See *WUB* (November 1891):11, (December 1902):15; *WA* 30 Apr. 1902.

64. FM 8 Nov. 1894; *WUB* (November 1895):16–18; ARP (1896):2; *WA* 5 Mar. 1895; *OP* '96, 38:170–71, '97, 39:170, '10, 52:204. Gymnastic competition ended in 1911 (Fauver, "History," 187). *WA* 13 Nov. 1893; FM 30 June, 1 Oct. 1892; *WA* 14 Oct. 1903; ARP (1908):33–34; FM 25 May 1909, 20 June 1910; *WA* 13 Dec. 1909; *WUB* (May 1910):8–9; *WLM* 18(June 1910): 362–69; SHO to Julia M. Olin, 27 Sept. 1865, OFP, box 6; Stephen H. Olin, "At a Dinner of the National Collegiate Athletic Association . . . December

Twenty-eighth, 1922," in Olin, *Three*, 10; *WUA* 2(October 1917): 4; *OP '94*, 36:186–87; *CA* 11 Oct. 1894; *NYTr* 6 Oct. 1894.

65. BTM 23 June 1891, 27 June 1893, 1 Nov. 1912. From 1886 to 1913, Olin led the committee on the board of instruction (see chap. 5 n5), supporting the growth of a strong faculty while he worked to develop attractive campus facilities. For Olin's interest in a scholarly faculty, see SHO to Julia M. Olin, 15 Dec. [internal evidence demonstrates that the correct date of this letter is 15 Jan. 1865], OFP, box 6; report of the visiting committee to the board of trustees, June 1896, NCAR, box 1.

66. On construction of Fayerweather, see *WUB* (May 1893):12, (November 1893): 8–9. On Cady, see Montgomery Schuyler, "The Works of Cady, Berg & See," *Architectural Record* 6(June 1897): 517–56; Stern, *New York*, 14–15, 370–73; *BDAA*, 104; *MEA* 1:364. A devoted member of his Presbyterian church (*NYT* 18 Apr. 1919), Cady belonged to one of Olin's clubs, Century. See *WWA* (1910–11), 83, 291. One of Cady's designs at Yale was for Fayerweather Hall. See *Buildings and Grounds of Yale University*, ed. Richard C. Carroll (New Haven: Yale University, 1979), 105. Architects for urban armories thought their designs for a medieval castle or fortress "inspired awe and fear and fostered respect and obedience" (Fogelson, *America's Armories*, chap. 4). *WA* 29 May 1893; *WUB* (May 1893):12; *CA* 11 Oct. 1894. Construction of the boiler house was completed in January 1891 (*WA* 26 Jan. 1891). The heating apparatus began bringing steam heat to all campus buildings 5 December, before roofing was finished (*WA* 5 Dec. 1890, 26 Jan. 1891; *MP* 19 Dec. 1890). The building also had a dynamo room from which Wesleyan gradually supplied some of its own electricity to campus buildings in the 1890s. See *WUB* (November 1898):9; BTM 24 June 1890, 18 Apr. 1902; *WA* 5 Nov. 1891, 18 Nov. 1892, 30 June 1898, 14 Mar. 1900; *WAR* (1911), xix–xxi. Amherst supplied steam heat to its dormitories in 1893 and electricity shortly thereafter (King, *Consecrated*, 112).

67. *ZH* 4 July 1894, 2 July 1902; *CA* 3 July 1902; AAM 24 June 1902; BTM 24 June 1902.

68. *WUB* (May 1908):3. Acquisition of the land parcels that comprise Harvard Yard, a square campus of about the same size as Wesleyan's, proceeded over almost two centuries (1637–1835). See Bainbridge Bunting, *Harvard: An Architectural History* (Cambridge: Harvard University Press, 1985), 17. *WUB* (May 1890):2. On the shanty, see *WLM* 5(January 1897): 114–16; *WA* 18, 28 Nov., 19 Dec. 1882. On the billboard, see *WA* 12 Oct., 12 Nov. 1880, 28 Oct. 1881, 3 Mar., 17, 28 Nov. 1882, 16 Nov., 7 Dec. 1883, 27 May 1884, 5 May, 3 June, 16 Nov. 1886, 7 Apr. 1888; Harrington, *History*, 141; George W. Gardner '89, R1939; *WA* 10 Oct. 1884; *ZH* 24 June 1885. The lawn mower was given in 1876 by William H. Wallace, the parent of a senior (*WA* 20 May 1876). *WA* 21 Apr. 1882; *CA* 10 July 1879. On the back campus, however, the overgrown condition of the college ceme-

tery caused some concern. See *WLM* 6(November 1897): 61–62; ᴀᴀᴍ 24 June 1902. Some thought had even been given to moving it (ᴇxᴄᴍ 27 Dec. 1883).

69. ʙᴛᴍ 24 June 1902; *WA* 8 Oct. 1902. *CA* 14 July 1904. The building cost $114,000 (*Celebration 75th*, 175).

70. This building memorialized a graduate of 1881 who died from illness contracted during service in the Spanish-American War. Construction was funded by his father, Charles Scott, a trustee from Philadelphia (see text at chap. 4 n19), and brother, Charles Scott, Jr., '86. Total cost was $118,000. See *WA* 1 July 1903; *Celebration 75th*, 178–81, 201–9. *WUB* (November 1891):13, (November 1898):1–2; *WA* 8 Oct. 1902; *WUB* (June 1903):4; Stern, *New York*, 294, 410–19; *BDAA*, 506.

71. *WA* 13 Apr. 1891; *ZH* 21 July 1892. Examples of club men include George S. Coleman '76 of New York, contributor and fund-raiser for the 1893 Psi Upsilon chapter house; Olin, one of the original incorporators for Eclectic alumni; J. B. Thomas '70 of Boston and New York, one of the original incorporators for the Alpha Delta Phi alumni. William R. Baird, *Baird's Manual of American College Fraternities*, 7th ed. (New York: College Fraternity Publishing, 1912), 677. Eclectic's alumni incorporated in 1870 as the Socratic Literary Society; Alpha Delta Phi's in 1881 as the Adelphic Literary Society of Wesleyan University, of Middletown, Connecticut; Delta Kappa Epsilon's in 1881 as the Kent Literary Club of Wesleyan University of Middletown; Psi Upsilon's in 1889 as the Xi Chapter of the Psi Upsilon Fraternity (preceded by a voluntary association of the same name established in 1867—records in the Psi Upsilon archives, Middletown, Conn.); Chi Psi's in 1889 as the Alpha Alpha Literary Society; Delta Tau Delta's in 1899 as the Phi Rho Literary Society. See *SAC* 6:848; 9:30; 9:186–87; 10:910; 10:1256; 13:341. Beta Theta Pi relied on two corporations. The Wooglin Associates, incorporated in 1897, may have started as an undergraduate group. It held title to the chapter house purchased that year at the corner of Washington and Park streets. Title for the new chapter house at High and Church streets was held by the Raimond Duy Baird Memorial Association, alumni who incorporated in 1912. Articles of incorporation for both groups are on file with the secretary of state, Hartford, Conn. Wesleyan even provided mortgage funding for Alpha Delta Phi in 1905 as part of the college's endowment investments (*FEx* 1907). *WUC* 1907/08; *WA* 28 Oct. 1908.

72. Harrington, *History*, 140–44; *WA* 18 Nov. 1892; *WUB* (May 1893):2. The total cost of building and lot came to about $40,000 (*NYTr* 22 May 1893).

73. *WA* 12 Nov. 1902; Stern, *New York*, 98, 153; *NCAB* 29:321–22. Cost of the building was about $40,000. See *WUB* (November 1903):13. This building suffered serious damage in a fire 28 May 1912 (*WA* 30 May 1912) and was replaced with a totally remodeled brick structure in 1927 (*WA* 17 Feb. 1927).

74. *To the Members of the Middletown Chapter of Alpha Delta Phi* (folded sheet

dated 7 July 1894); *CA* 14 July 1904; the house cost about $40,000. *WUB* (May 1905):17–18. On Princeton's clubs, see Wheaton J. Lane, ed., *Pictorial History of Princeton* (Princeton: Princeton University Press, 1947), 153–55; Constance M. Greiff et al., *Princeton Architecture: A Pictorial History of Town and Campus* (Princeton: Princeton University Press, 1967), 168–69.

75. *MEA* 1:123–24; *WUA* 8(March 1924): 38; *DAB* 1:477–78. For a full-scale study of Bacon, see Christopher A. Thomas, "The Lincoln Memorial and Its Architect, Henry Bacon (1866–1924)" (Ph.D. diss., Yale University, 1990). Amherst began its relations with McKim, Mead & White in 1891. William R. Mead was an Amherst graduate (King, *Consecrated*, 107–8). *NYT* 17 Apr. 1912; *WA* 2 Dec. 1912. One of Bacon's first tasks in this advisory capacity would be to design the new wing that added a swimming pool to Fayerweather Gymnasium in 1913 (*WA* 19 Jan. 1914), thus completing this work by Wesleyan's first New York City architect, J. C. Cady. At the time he designed Eclectic, Bacon was working on his most important building in New York, the Union Square Savings Bank (1907). See Stern, *New York*, 178. *WA* 17 Oct. 1906; *The Eclectic House* (Middletown: Eclectic Society, 1908), 4. The lot for Eclectic cost about $20,000 and construction about $40,000. See H. C. M. Ingraham, "The New Club House and Its Relation to Our Society" (typescript of an address delivered at the dedication of the Eclectic Club House 11 Oct. 1907), 10. Delta Kappa Epsilon House (acquired by the fraternity in 1888, renovated in the mid-1890s and replaced in 1929) occupied a position just outside the new circle (Stiles, *Seventy-Five*, chap. 3). The Beta Theta Pi House (1913) was constructed in a similar location (*WA* 22 Sept., 15 Dec. 1913). Delta Tau Delta leased a building farther north on High Street from 1903 to 1913 and acquired an adjacent residence in 1915. See Orliff van Heik Chase, "Fifty Years at Wesleyan: Gamma Zeta of Delta Tau Delta, Phi Rho Literary Society, 1891–1941" (typescript, ca. 1941), chap. 2. Kappa Rho Sigma, a fraternity denied recognition by the college body senate, leased a house at 11 College Place during its brief existence (ca. 1907–10). See *WA* 10 Oct. 1906; *Middletown City Directory*, 1908–10.

76. This house was owned by Samuel D. Hubbard, a key founding trustee of Wesleyan, until his death in 1855, and by his widow, Jane, until her death in 1885. It stayed in the family by bequests, first to Samuel Hubbard's niece, Susan Carrington Clarke, until her death in 1895, and then to her daughter, Jennie M. Clarke. Jennie Clarke sold the property to Wesleyan in 1904 for $20,000, plus an annuity of $10,000 that, upon her death in 1910, endowed the Samuel Dickinson Hubbard Scholarship. See Middletown Probate Records 20:260–62, 30:564–68; *WA* 29 Oct. 1895, 9 Mar. 1904; *MP* 21 Oct. 1895, 11 Jan. 1910; agreement between Jennie M. Clarke and Wesleyan University for purchase of property and provision of an annuity, dated 19 Jan. 1904, NCAR, box 5A.

77. For a detailed description of North College in the 1880s, see W. E. Woodruff '87, R1939; *WUB* (May 1893):13, (November 1893):1, 10; *WA* 11 Oct. 1893. The work on North College cost about $25,000. Chapel renovation was directed by J. C. Cady and cost about $8,000. See *WUB* (June 1898):9; *WA* 20 Apr. 1898.

78. *WA* 7 Mar. 1906; BTM 23 Mar. 1906. On remodeling South College at a cost of about $15,000, see *WA* 28 Mar., 9 May 1906, 9 Jan. 1907; *WUB* (6 Dec. 1906):2, 6–7; ARP (1907):14. Plans were drawn by William D. Johnson of Hartford and New York City. Johnson was known locally as architect for the Middletown High School (1896) and for the first six of sixteen buildings designed for the Connecticut Hospital for the Insane. See Yale University, *Obituary Record* 98(1940): 178–79; *HC* 11 May 1939; *Geer's Hartford City Directory* (1906), 638. It was proposed in 1909 to rename this building Clark Hall in honor of Laban Clark. See *WUB* (May 1909):8. On the fire and the reconstruction of North College at a cost of about $130,000, see *WA* 7 Mar., 16 Oct. 1906, 15 Jan. 1908; *WUB* (May 1906):6–14, (December 1906), 4–6, (December 1907), 7–8; ARP (1907):14–15. About $35,000 toward the new building came from insurance on the old, with the balance paid almost entirely from permanent funds of the college. See EXCM 16 March 1906; *FEx* 1907, 1908; *CA* 6 Feb. 1908. On Harrie T. Lindeberg, who became known for his work on country club buildings, embassies, and residences for the very wealthy, see *NCAB* 47:527; *BDAA*, 12–13; *NYT* 11 Jan. 1959; Russell J. Whitehead, "Harrie T. Lindeberg's Contribution to American Domestic Architecture," *Architectural Record* 55(April 1924): 309–72. Lindeberg was just starting his career in 1906 as a new partner in Albro and Lindeberg. He belonged to one of Olin's clubs, the Players. In a similar incident at Dartmouth in 1904, Dartmouth Hall (1791), the oldest surviving building, burned and was rebuilt as a replica in 1906 (Lord, *History*, 489–90). The new North College had several ties with Wesleyan's past in addition to its general resemblance to the structure of 1825. Doc Raymond, who supervised construction of Judd Hall (1871), directed excavation for the North College basement in mid-1906. He also saved from the ruins all the stones marked with class numerals at the time of ivy plantings on Class Day. These stones were restored to comparable positions in the new foundation. The "Old Laboratory" behind North College, built in 1825 by Captain Partridge as a gun house, was demolished to provide brick for the new building. See *WUB* (May 1909):7; *WLM* 14(May 1906): 364; *WUB* (May 1908):34, (May 1907):8–9; *WA* 24 Apr. 1907.

79. The series of prints by Littig & Company included all eight Ivies, the "Little Three," such major state universities as Michigan and Virginia, such independent universities as Chicago, and several dozen other institutions of higher education. Seven private preparatory schools were also represented. See *Catalogue of Prints by Paul Victorius*, (New York: Paul Victorius Prints,

1985), 46–66. *WUB* (May 1908):8. The Wesleyan print measured 15 by 28 inches. Little is known about Rummell (1848–1924), who lived in Brooklyn. For examples of his bird's-eye views of New York City, see Moses King, *King's Views of the New York Stock Exchange* (New York: Moses King, 1897), 1; Phelps Stokes, *The Iconography of Manhattan Island, 1498–1909*, vol. 3 (New York: Robert H. Dodd, 1918), plate 172. On use of the perspective drawing and painting technique known as bird's-eye view, see John Reps, *Views and Viewmakers of Urban America* (Columbia: University of Missouri Press, 1984), chap. 2. From 1875 to 1895 Wesleyan used woodcuts and engravings of College Row in advertisements and as a letterhead for college stationery (EXCM 3 Sept. 1875; *WA* 16 Oct. 1894). Photographs of the front campus and College Row were used for the next six years (*WA* 30 Apr. 1895, 3 Oct. 1900, 5 June 1901). Wesleyan had used photography booklets for promotional purposes since the mid-1890s. See *Souvenir of Wesleyan University, Published in the Interests of the Athletic Association of the College by the Wesleyan Argus* (n.p., 1896). Where newer campuses such as those of Columbia, Stanford, and Chicago achieved a "general unity of effect" through formal designs influenced by the Beaux Arts system of architectural planning, a New England campus such as Wesleyan's had more loosely developed architectural configurations before 1910. See A. D. F. Hamlin, "Recent American College Architecture," *Outlook* 74(May–August 1903): 792; Turner, *Campus*, chap. 5. There was, however, a movement for better college architecture, often led by "enlightened" graduates and their architect friends, on several campuses of older colleges, including Amherst and Williams. See "The College Beautiful," *Nation* 77(6 August 1903): 108–9. A leading architectural critic found most of Wesleyan's buildings in 1911 to be "seemly edifices." See Montgomery Schuyler, "The Architecture of American Colleges, VII; Brown, Bowdoin, Trinity and Wesleyan," *Architectural Record*, 29(February 1911): 161–66. Another measure of campus enlargement and modernization might have been noted in 1910 by Doc Raymond, as he retired after forty-five years as superintendent of buildings and grounds. One of Raymond's duties over these decades was to ring the chapel bell calling students to morning chapel and classes. In 1910 a new system of electric bells in all classroom buildings signaled the beginning and end of class periods. See *WUB* (May 1910):5; *WA* 3 Mar., 14 Apr. 1910.

80. *WA* 10 June 1884; *OP* '95, 37:184; Olin, *Response*, 7; *WA* 1 Mar. 1889; *WUB* (November 1895):20.

81. These data are taken from Svonkin, "Pluralistic Ideal," chap. 1 and from his student data base. See also *WA* 22 Nov. 1899, 21 Jan. 1903; *WUA* 17(October 1932): 91; *WUB* (June 1922):30. The percentage of entering students from public high schools increased rapidly in the 1890s, moving from 36 percent in 1893 to 60 percent in 1901. See W. A. Wetzel, "Ten Years of High School Growth," *Educational Review* 24(December 1902): 521. Wesleyan

made a very modest start during the 1890s in drawing students from preparatory schools outside the Methodist ranks, beginning with the Mount Hermon School. See "Preparatory Schools, 1888–1908," 96, 184, NCAR, box 11.

82. John A. Porter, "College Fraternities," *Century* 36(September 1888): 755; *Eclectic*, 3–4; *OP* '09, 51:224–25. Dates of completion and locations for the first generation of chapter houses are: Psi Upsilon (1878), Broad St.; Eclectic (1882), College Place; Delta Kappa Epsilon (1883), current site; Alpha Delta Phi (1884), current site. Beta Theta Pi leased a housed on Washington Street for five years before purchasing it in 1897. Chi Psi and Delta Tau Delta used leased facilities. On construction of the second generation of fraternity houses, see text at nn72–75.

83. Eugene H. L. Randolph, "Greek Letter Societies in American Colleges," *New England Magazine* 17(September 1897): 81. Michael S. Kimmel, "Men's Responses to Feminism at the Turn of the Century," *Gender and Society* 1(September 1987): 262; *WA* 6 July 1892, 9 June 1897; *WLM* 12(October 1903): 36; *WA* 9 June 1897, 9 Oct. 1889.

84. *WA* 15 Feb. 1889; *OP* '06, 48:70–78; *WA* 15 Feb. 1889.

85. *WA* 16 Nov. 1898; BTM 30 Mar. 1899; *WA* 26 Apr. 1899, 10 June, 3 Oct. 1900; *WUB* (November 1899):14 (November 1900), 11; *WA* 2 Oct. 1902; *OP* '02, 44:77, '10, 52:101, '05, 47:74, '06, 48:93, 78; *WLM* 7(June 1899): 362; minutes of the College Commons, 5 Jan.–6 Apr. 1900.

86. The recruiting brochure published in 1899, *A Circular of Information Concerning Wesleyan University, Middletown, Conn.*, included on pages describing the academic program large pictures of all seven fraternities. *WA* 20 Feb. 1894, 16 Dec. 1896; *WLM* 5(January 1897): 121–22; *CA* 2 July 1891; *ZH* 7 July 1897. For worry that Wesleyan was "overdoing the social side of education," see *ZH* 3 July 1895. James Bryce, *The American Commonwealth*, rev. ed., vol. 2 (New York: Macmillan, 1911), 733; *WUB* (June 1899):19; Raymond, "What Signs," 144; ARP (1908):12.

87. *WUB* (November 1895):20; *WA* 19 Dec. 1882.

88. *CA* 3 July 1902; Benjamin, "Methodist," 341; *OP* '91, 33:81–82; *WLM* 7(May 1899): 302–7. The Harvard glee club was founded in 1858, and Yale's appeared in 1861. See Elliot Forbes, *A History of Music at Harvard to 1972* (Cambridge: Department of Music, Harvard University, 1988), 3; *The First Hundred Years, 1861–1961: A Short History of the Yale Glee Club* (n.p., n.d.), 4.

89. *OP* '91, 33:84–86, '90, 32:106; *WA* 13 Oct. 1869; "Wesleyan University," *CR* 1(May 1870): 138; *WA* 19 June 1872, 20 Jan., 7 Nov. 1882, 6 Nov. 1883, 4 Nov. 1884, 21 Apr. 1886; *CA* 9 July 1885; *NYTr* 3 Apr. 1886; *WA* 5 June 1888. Members of the sixteen-man 1888 club returned to give concerts at Wesleyan's seventy-fifth anniversary and at their fortieth class reunion. See *ZH* 4 July 1906; *WUA* 13(July 1928): 33. The Chicago performance was

in "the magnificent, unapproachable Auditorium," a 4,237-seat theater designed by Adler and Sullivan that had opened the year before. See *WA* 3 May 1890; Robert Twombly, *Louis Sullivan: His Life and Work* (New York: Viking, 1986), 187–95. For information on some representative tours, see *WA* 9 Dec. 1893, 15 Jan. 1895, 13 Jan. 1897, 11 Jan. 1899, 9 Apr. 1902, 14 Jan. 1903, 21 Apr. 1909. With a bit of hyperbole, the *Argus* reported that "Wesleyan is known throughout the East as the singing college" (*WA* 9 May 1906).

90. The analytical approach developed by Sandra Sizer in her work on revival hymns might be similarly employed with regard to college songs. She explores the ways in which gospel hymns "represent a general description of the world" and define the singers as "belonging to the same group, and especially to *this* group and not to *that*." See Sandra S. Sizer, *Gospel Hymns and Social Religion: The Rhetoric of Nineteenth-Century Revivalism* (Philadelphia: Temple University Press, 1978), 16–17. Wesleyan songs used for the brief description in this paragraph appear in *OP* '91, 33:87–104.

91. *WA* 10 Mar. 1885, 10 Feb. 1886, 11 June 1888; *OP* '91, 33:87–104; *WA* 26 Feb. 1895, 31 May 1905; *WLM* 13(February 1905): 210; *OP* '09, 51:26. Frederick L. Knowles '94, a well-published poet and son of a Methodist minister (*WA* 4 Oct. 1905), wrote the lyrics for "Come Raise the Song." William B. Davis '94, choirmaster and organist of the Episcopal church in Middletown (1894–1927) and director of the glee club (1892–1917) composed the music. A song written or later recognized as the alma mater appeared at Harvard in 1836, Williams in 1859, Yale in 1880, and Amherst in 1903. See Mason Hammond, "Notes on the Words and Music Used in Harvard's Commencement Ceremonies," *Harvard Library Bulletin* 24(July 1978): 299–301; Rudolph, *Hopkins*, 161; Kelley, *Yale*, 228; Fuess, *History*, 350. For other institutions, see Dee Baily, "College Songs," in *The New Grove Dictionary of American Music*, vol. 1 (New York: Macmillan, 1986), 470–72. The earliest texts of Wesleyan songs can be found in class day programs of the 1860s. Singing at alumni club gatherings began in the late 1860s (*WA* 14 Jan. 1869, 19 Jan. 1870). The alumni sing first appeared as part of the alumni reunion schedule in 1903 (*Wesley Bicentennial*, 12). Regarding weekly college sings, see *CA* 14 July 1901; *WA* 22 May 1901, 30 Apr. 1902, 5 Apr. 1905, *OP* '06, 48:214. *WLM* 11(June 1903): 354.

92. The predecessor organization that appeared sporadically in the 1890s was known as Wesleyan Mask (*WA* 3 July 1893, 27 Mar. 1894, 13 Jan. 1897, 16 Mar. 1898; *OP* '95, 37:131, '98, 40:185). *WA* 12, 20, 27 Apr. 1904, 18 Oct. 1905. Excluded from drama, as from all other extracurricular activities after 1900, women staged an occasional production of their own. In 1902 they performed "As You Like It" at the Middlesex Opera House (*ZH* 2 July 1902). *WA* 22 Jan., 5 Feb. 1907, 8 Apr., 6 May 1908.

93. *WA* 2 June 1896; Peterson, *New England*, chap. 7; *WA* 27 Mar., 24 Apr. 1894; *OP* '96, 38:121. The citizenship club was enthusiastically

endorsed by the trustees and by Bradford Raymond. Faculty members such as Atwater helped procure the speakers (BTM 26 July 1894; *WA* 27 Mar., 11 Dec. 1894). The club lasted for three years (*OP* '95, 37:133, '96, 38:120–21, '97, 39:118). *WA* 19 Nov. 1895; Egbert R. Nichols, "A Historical Sketch of Intercollegiate Debating: I," *Quarterly Journal of Speech* 22(April 1936): 213–16. At the club level, debates occurred between the Peithessophian Society of Rutgers University and the Philomathaen Society of New York University in 1881 and 1887. See David Potter, *Debating in the Colonial Chartered Colleges: An Historical Study, 1642 to 1900* (New York: Teachers College, Columbia University, 1944), 96–101. *WA* 10 Mar. 1896. Despite a call for a course in argumentation (*WA* 27 Jan. 1897) and occasional mention of possible league formation (*WA* 22 Dec. 1897), intercollegiate debate at Wesleyan was dormant from fall 1896 to fall 1900. *OP* '01, 43:108, '04, 46:176. The varsity debating society, established in 1901, and its successors sustained intercollegiate debating at Wesleyan for subsequent decades. *WA* 30 May 1906; *WUB* (May 1908):25; *OP* '09, 51:173.

94. *OP* '91, 33:7, '92, 34:5, '97, 39:20–21, '99, 41:5; *WA* 28 Apr. 1896, 1 July 1903, 3 Nov. 1892, 26 Oct. 1898, 8 Nov. 1899. For an example of campus news exchanges with Williams and Amherst, see *WA* 21 Mar. 1900. *WA* 24 Mar. 1909; *WLM* 1(June 1892): 29–30; *WA* 13 Jan. 1894. For a survey of early Wesleyan journalism, see *WLM* 2(February 1894): 172–77. The earliest student publication, *The Classic*, was a literary monthly that appeared from July 1840 to July 1842. The *Olla Podrida* appeared in 1858 as a four-page newspaper but became a substantial pamphlet in 1862. It steadily increased in size, becoming a hardcover book in 1887. The first photograph appeared in 1886, and individual pictures of seniors were included beginning in 1899. Responsibility for producing *OP* was assumed by the fraternities, 1858–72 (except for 1861 and 1862), by committees from the *Argus*, 1873–76, by a transition committee in 1877, and by a board of editors from the junior class (including a representative from each fraternity), 1878–1918. Beginning in 1882, covers bear the class year of the junior class. The year of publication can thus be obtained by subtracting one year from that on each cover. Yearbooks appeared at Williams in 1853 (Rudolph, *Hopkins*, 79) and at Amherst in 1855 (Fuess, *Amherst*, 196–97). The student newspaper at Williams dates from 1867 (Spring, *History*, 308–9) and that at Amherst from 1 Feb. 1868 (Fuess, *Amherst*, 196). The *Argus* acquired an office (in North College) during the spring of 1884 (*WA* 2 May 1884). The *Argus* was published every three weeks, 11 June 1868–15 July 1869, every two weeks, 29 Sept. 1869–1 July 1879, and every ten days, 15 Oct. 1879–3 July 1894. Weekly issues began 6 Oct. 1894 and semi-weekly issues began 7 Oct. 1909. The *Wesleyan Literary Monthly* (1892–1917) was started by several disaffected members of the *Argus* board (*WA* 27 Mar. 1893).

95. *WUB* (May 1893):13, (June 1899):12; *WA* 12 May 1893, 11 May 1898,

19 Mar. 1902, 15 Oct. 1886; *WUB* (January 1888):9, (November 1895):20–21; *CA* 7 July 1892; *WA* 17 Jan. 1892, 12 Apr. 1899, 31 Mar. 1909. A similar shift from Bible study to social service projects occurred at Amherst's campus YMCA by 1910 (Le Duc, *Piety*, 141–43). On links between urban and campus aspects of the YMCA movement, see Hopkins, *History*, 277, 283, 286–87, 629. *WLM* 3(June 1895): 311; *WUB* (May 1897):12, (May 1901:11–12; *CA* 23 June 1892; AAM 28 June 1892; *WA* 6 July 1892; Kelley, *Yale*, 304. In 1890 Wesleyan hosted the annual meeting of college YMCAS in New England (*WA* 1 Feb. 1890). Delegates from Wesleyan regularly attended the national summer YMCA conferences, hosted initially by Dwight L. Moody, at Mount Hermon and Northfield, Mass. (*WA* 6 Oct. 1896, 3 Oct. 1900, 8 Oct. 1902). Efforts to obtain new members included an annual reception for the entering class and publication of the *Freshman Handbook* (first issue in 1890), containing much useful information about the college. See, *WUB* (November 1895):21. BTM 27 June 1910; *WA* 22 Sept. 1910.

96. ARP (1908):6–8; *WA* 1 Feb. 1889, 4 June 1892. For occasional early dissent regarding compulsory services see *WA* 22 Mar. 1871, 22 Feb. 1881, 12 May 1885; *WLM* 2(December 1893): 110. Such dissent at Amherst in 1893 was short-lived (Le Duc, *Piety*, 140). *WA* 5 May 1897, 19 Mar. 1902; FM 16 Dec. 1902, 17 Feb., 3 June 1903; BTM 30 June 1903, 28 June 1904; FM 7 July 1904; *WA* 5 Oct. 1904; *WUB* (November 1904):2, (May 1909):13–14; FM 20 Dec. 1907, 4, 25 Feb. 1908; BTM 9 Apr., 22 June 1908, 26 Feb. 1909; *WA* 27 Feb., 26 Oct. 1883; *WUB* (May 1910):5, 26–27. A large majority of the vesper service preachers in 1909/10, however, were Methodist. Regulations for chapel cuts permitted unexcused absences for about 10 percent of the morning chapel services per term in the 1870s and 1880s (FM 17 Dec. 1873), 15 percent from 1889 to 1893 (FM 19 Nov. 1889), about 25 percent from 1893 to 1909 (FM 11 Apr. 1893), and more than 37 percent from 1909 until abolition of the daily chapel requirement in 1928 (FM 3 Nov. 1908). Absence from a Sunday church service counted as five chapel absences. Wesleyan's cut policy in the 1890s was considerably more liberal than the level of 10 percent at Williams in the mid-1890s (*Williams College Catalogue* 1894/95, 54). *WUB* (May 1909):4–5.

97. *WA* 12 Dec. 1892, 16, 26 Jan., 6, 21 Feb., 6, 16 Mar. 1893; FM 14 Mar., 4 Apr., 2 May 1893. The ten students were four seniors, three juniors, two sophomores, and one freshman (*WA* 25 Nov. 1893). John Bigham, "An Instructive Experiment in College Government, *Educational Review* 3(February 1892): 162–67; Peterson, *New England*, 230n20, 145; Louis C. Hatch, *The History of Bowdoin College* (Portland: Loring, Short and Harmon, 1927), 203–09. For some earlier experiments at state universities in the 1870s and 1880s, see Henry D. Sheldon, *The History and Pedagogy of American Student Societies* (New York: Appleton, 1901), 256–59. Proposals made in the mid-1880s ran up against an unreceptive president (*WA* 9,

23 Dec. 1884, 3 Feb. 1885, 4 Mar. 1886). *WA* 12 Dec. 1892, 21 Feb., 16 Mar. 1893, 26 Jan., 18 Dec. 1894, 20 Jan. 1886; *WUB* (May 1893):2; Patton, *Eight*, 58; *WLM* 8(Dec. 1899): 130–33; FM 17, 21 December 1903, 7 Jan., 29 Mar., 24, 28 June 1904; *WA* 16 Mar. 1904, 22 Mar. 1905. For the constitution of the college body, adopted 11 June 1904, see *WA* 1 Nov. 1905. Authority for discipline continued to rest with the faculty, but placing "the entire control of the student body in the hands of the college senate" (*WA* 26 Oct. 1904) meant that "recommendations of the College Senate within reasonable limitations will be accepted" (*WA* 25 Jan. 1905). During its second year the college body instituted a student activities tax of one dollar per term (*WA* 18 Oct. 1905). In 1907 the organization established rules for the new North College and assumed responsibility for maintaining order in the building. See *WUB* (May 1908):27. Records of the proceedings of the college body and the senate were not kept until 1911. Although there does not appear to be a high level of student government activity, Wesleyan students seem to have sustained more interest in this enterprise than those at other New England colleges studied by Peterson (Peterson, *New England*, 145–46).

98. *WA* 6, 21 Feb. 1893; FM 7 Feb. 1893, Thomas J. Wertenbaker, *Princeton, 1746–1896* (Princeton: Princeton University Press, 1946), 363–64; Bird T. Baldwin, *Present Status of the Honor System in Colleges and Universities* (Washington, D.C.: GPO, 1915), 24–26; *WA* 3 Mar. 1896; *Report of Franklin Carter, President of Williams College . . . , 1896*, 9–10; *Amherst Student* 17 June, 13 Sept. 1905; *WA* 27 Oct. 1897; *WLM* 8(December 1899): 130; *WA* 3 July, 6 Mar. 1893; 25 Nov. 1908. The first constitution for the honor system was adopted in 1896 (*WA* 17 Dec. 1895, 14 Jan. 1896). Penalties of suspension or expulsion included the posting of violators' names (*WA* 12 Mar. 1902, 15 June 1907, 2 Mar. 1909).

99. *Shall I Go to College?* (n.p.: Wesleyan University [ca. 1888]); *WUB* (May 1889):12–15. This pamphlet was a special issue of *WUB* prepared by a committee of four faculty members. *WUB* (November 1895):2, 20–22, 4–5; *WA* 6 Nov. 1872, 12 Mar. 1873.

100. *WUB* (November 1897):12–14. The percentage of Episcopalians at Trinity in 1905 was a bit higher, 69 percent (Weaver, *Trinity*, 343n60). For reports on the portion of students from Methodist families, see *CA* 6 Oct. 1879; *WA* 17 June 1881, 10 June 1884, 26 Oct. 1888, 6 Feb. 1893, 20 Nov. 1901, 6 Nov. 1907. ARP (1908): 15. The percentage would stay in the 60 to 70 percent range until about 1920 and then drop sharply in the 1920s to approximately one-third by 1931, when Episcopalians in the freshman class outnumbered Methodists. For examples of recruiting interest and effort, see *WA* 17 June 1891, 23 Dec. 1893, 3 Mar. 1896, 18 May 1898, 28 Feb. 1900; BTM 14 Dec. 1894; *WUB* (May 1907):2. *WA* 25 Feb. 1896, 1 Feb. 1905, 26 Feb. 1908; *OP* '07, 49:208; *WLM* 18(March 1910): 260.

101. Most faculty in 1884, however, supported the Democratic candidate, Grover Cleveland (*WA* 23 Oct. 1884). *WA* 19 Oct. 1904, 20, 27 Oct., 11 Nov. 1896, 13 Jan. 1897. A Wesleyan chapter of the Intercollegiate Socialist Society, organized in 1906, was small and short-lived (*OP* '06, 48:184, '07, 49:191). *WUA* 17(January 1933): 91; *WAR* (1911), 454–63; Fuess, *Amherst*, 243. For data on the class of 1905, see *WA* 15 Mar. 1905; *WAR* (1921), 418–29. In the class of 1908 about 19 percent stated (as freshmen) that their intended vocation was business. By spring of their senior year this choice had increased to 28 percent. About 40 percent actually entered the business world. See *WA* 15 Mar. 1905, 18 Mar. 1908; *WAR* (1931), 613–25. William North Rice, "A Danger Arising from the Popularization of the College," *Science* 29(5 March 1909): 373–74.

102. For examples of the frequent use of *earnest* by students describing themselves and of its use by other observers of Wesleyan student life, see *WA* 17 Oct. 1882, 14 Nov. 1884; *CA* 6 July 1893; *WA* 27 Mar. 1894, 24 Feb. 1904. On Thorndike, a leading American psychologist, see Jeraldine Joncich, *The Sane Positivist: A Biography of Edward L. Thorndike* (Middletown: Wesleyan University Press, 1968). Beech was a missionary and educator in China (*WA* 30 Apr. 1902). About 100 graduates of 1891 to 1911 became college professors and about 120 became ministers. See *WUA* 17(January 1933): 91. Two particularly interesting graduates of this period are Frederick L. Knowles '94, a poet whose death in 1905 cut short a promising career (*WA* 4 Oct. 1905) and Charles Ellis '00, designer of the Golden Gate Bridge. See Jesse B. Rittenhouse, *The Younger American Poets* (Boston: Little, Brown, 1904), chap. 11; Caleb T. Winchester, *An Appreciation of Frederick Lawrence Knowles* (Boston: Wesleyan Young Alumni Club, 1906); John W. Paton, "Two Men and a Bridge," *WUA* 70(Fall 1987): 1–9. This was the first year that students from the United States were selected as Rhodes scholars. Nixon earned a M.A. in classics during his undergraduate years and was a member of the football and track teams (*WA* 29 June 1904). He was the grandson of a Methodist bishop, Edward G. Andrews (*CA* 23 June 1904). Rules for the cannon scrap, published in 1901, elicited commentary regarding "the comfort of the spectators" (*WA* 9 Jan. 1901). The rules were revised in 1906 to create a contest more interesting for spectators (*WA* 19 Dec. 1906). *WA* 3 Oct. 1906, 27 Apr. 1898. The faculty decided that seniors in good standing who enlisted would qualify for degrees awarded in absentia (FM 23 Apr. 1898). Initial interest in enlisting was expressed by 275 students (*MP* 18, 22, 25, 29 Apr. 1898). A dozen undergraduates actually enlisted (*ZH* 6 July 1898). One of them and a graduate student died as a result of typhoid fever contracted during military service. (*WA* 12, 19 Oct. 1898). For a roster of Wesleyan volunteers, see *OP* '99, 41:183–84. *WA* 2 Dec. 1903. A cheer leader and five assistants were appointed in 1905 (*WA* 5 Apr. 1905). *CA* 26 July 1894.

103. *OP* '92, 34:157; *WLM* 14(November 1905): 65, 16(October 1907): 28, 16(April 1908): 301; ARP (1907):9; *WLM* 17(June 1909): 395–99. The Latin-scientific course for the Ph.B. was eliminated in the curricular revision of 1908. About 27 percent of the graduates from 1892 to 1908 took degrees in this "resort of the weakest students." See *WUB* (June 1922):26; Dutcher, *Historical*, 21; *OP* '10, 52:218. With the honor system functioning effectively, there was little room for "skidding" (cheating) in exams. *WLM* 16(April 1908): 301; *WA* 7 Oct. 1903.

104. *WA* 27 Feb. 1877, 16 Oct. 1883, 6 Dec. 1887, 26 Oct. 1888; *OP* '93, 35:108; BTM 25 June 1895; *OP* '00, 42:159, '04, 46:194; *WA* 3 Mar. 1897; *WLM* 8(February 1900): 232, 12(May 1904): 345; *WA* 24 Feb. 1904, 27 Feb. 1907, 22 Feb. 1908, 24 Feb. 1909, 13 May, 16 Dec. 1912, 6 Feb. 1913, 9 Dec. 1903, 1 Mar. 1905, 13 Nov. 1907. In 1906 "junior week" appeared, with a schedule of events from Thursday to Sunday (*WA* 2 May 1906).

105. Up to at least 1900, Wesleyan probably remained "the cheapest college in New England" or close to it (*WA* 19 Jan. 1872, 9 Dec. 1893, 9 Apr. 1895). *WA* 8 Oct. 1895; *WUC* 1890/91–1909/10; Svonkin, "Pluralistic Ideal," 62; *WUB* (June 1899):16, (November 1895):18–19; *WLM* 10(December 1901): 126; *WA* 17 June 1891; Bryce, *American Commonwealth*, 2:747.

106. *WLM* 2(February 1894): 187; Carlos H. Storrs '87, R1939. A tradition of sophisticated applause by finger snapping began in the early 1870s and persisted for about a century. Wesley E. Woodruff '87, R1939; *WUB* (May 1896):12–13. In the freshman class that enrolled fall 1899, 58 percent had "lived mostly in cities" (*WA* 22 Nov. 1899). *WA* 24 Feb. 1904. For a similar analysis, see Louise L. Stevenson, "Preparing for Public Life: The Collegiate Students at New York University, 1832–1881," in *The University and the City: From Medieval Origins to the Present*, ed. Thomas Bender (New York: Oxford University Press, 1988), 151, 171–73. Wesleyan students first used caps and gowns in 1892. The practice had begun at a few American colleges in the 1870s and became widespread in the 1890s. After a five-year interval, Wesleyan seniors began regular use of caps and gowns for commencement exercises in 1897. See *WA* 6 July 1892; *MP* 29 June 1892; *WA* 6 Nov. 1877, 2 Nov. 1893, 20 Feb. 1894, 20 Oct. 1897. *WLM* 16(April 1908): 303, 12(June 1904): 362–65.

107. Panunzio prepared at Maine Wesleyan Seminary. See Constantine Panunzio, *The Soul of an Immigrant* (New York: Macmillan, 1921), chap. 10; interview with Louis O. LaBella '21, 7 Dec. 1988; *WUC* 1908/09–1910/11. A few Catholics are identified in the student body of the mid-1880s (*WA* 12 June 1885, 1 July 1886, 7 July 1887), and seven were attending in 1907 (*WA* 6 Nov. 1907). Fannie Myerson '02 and Annie Fisher '04 probably were the first persons of Jewish faith to graduate from Wesleyan (Seigfried Kristeller '65 had converted to Methodism prior to entering Wesleyan [*CA* 14 Feb. 1884]). On Fisher's Wesleyan experiences, see Andra Miriam Rose, "Vision

of a New Profession: Annie Fisher and Educational Wisdom" (Honors thesis, Wesleyan University, 1982), 56–59. Pedro Ramon Gillot y Fernandez '92 of Cuba (later known as Pedro Ramon Gillot) probably was Wesleyan's first Latin-American graduate, followed by Julian Aznar '94 of Mexico. Jewsuki Shimata '92 of Japan probably was Wesleyan's first Asian graduate (Ayskeh Kabayama n1889 entered in 1885 and attended for two years before transferring to Amherst, where he graduated in 1889).

108. Isaac N. Cardozo n1879 entered from Columbia, S.C., as a sophomore (spring 1876), lived alone in a North College room normally occupied by two students, and left after the next winter term (merit record book, 1861–85, North College vault). He continued his studies at Amherst and then Oberlin. William L. Bulkley n1888 entered from Orangeburg, S.C., as a junior (fall 1886), roomed with a sophomore in North College, and left before the end of term. He had previously acquired a B.A. at Claflin University, and he earned a Ph.D. from Syracuse University in 1893. He was the fourth African-American to earn a Ph.D., the first being Edward Bouchet at Yale in 1876. See Harry W. Greene, *Holders of Doctorates among American Negroes . . . , 1876–1943* (Boston: Meador Publishing, 1946), 26, 117, 140, 166, 187. Bulkley became a faculty member at Claflin and then was a public school principal in New York City (*NYT* 18 Feb. 1901). In 1890 he wrote a letter to the *Argus* concerning lynching in the South (*WA* 15 Feb. 1890). For basic biographical information on black students named in the text and notes of this chapter, see *WAR*. For room assignments, see *WUC*.

109. *Plattsburgh Daily Press* 26 June 1902. Data on father's occupation and on preparatory schools are drawn from: records of examinations, 1882–1909; transcript cards, classes of 1909–1911, North College vault. Interview with John W. E. Bowen III, 5 Dec. 1988, *DANB*, 52–53. Wesleyan might have been known among African-Americans in Baltimore through the presidency of J. Emory Round '55 at Morgan College (now Morgan State University). From 1872 to 1887 Round served as the first president and then as a faculty member at this institution, founded by local Methodists with help from Richard S. Rust '41 of the Freedman's Aid Society. See *WA* 28 Jan. 1892; *WOR* (1892), 15–16; Edward N. Wilson, *The History of Morgan State College: A Century of Purpose in Action, 1867–1967* (New York: Vantage Press, 1975), 29–33, 47, 109–13. Connections among Wesleyan, Booker T. Washington, and Exeter Academy suggest other possibilities. Atwater worked with Washington on a nutrition survey at Tuskegee in the mid-1890s (*BTWP* 3:546; *WA* 11 Feb. 1896). Atwater's son graduated from Exeter in 1902. Harlan P. Amen, headmaster of Exeter, was an admirer of Washington, whose son enrolled there in 1907. Among the Exeter graduates of 1907 was Bowen, whose father was a longtime ally of Washington (*BTWP* 2:361, 4:79, 7:339, 364).

110. *WA* 9 April 1895; *BTWP* 3:583–87; Louis R. Harlan, *Booker T. Wash-*

ington in Perspective: Essays of Louis R. Harlan (Jackson: University Press of Mississippi, 1988), 83–84. Washington spoke at Williams in 1898 and at Amherst in 1903 (*BTWP* 4:435, 8:103). *WA* 29 Oct. 1895; *CA* 6 Feb. 1896. Career information comes from various editions of *WAR*. *ZH* 3 Feb. 1904.

111. Ray Stannard Baker, *Following the Color Line: American Negro Citizenship in the Progressive Era* (New York: Doubleday, Page, 1908), 38, 146; Walter G. Muelder, *Methodism and Society in the Twentieth Century* (New York: Abingdon Press, 1961), 43–44; Handy, *Christian America*, 151–58; *WA* 22 Nov. 1888, 4 Nov. 1889; *WLM* 10(April 1902): 277–82; *ZH* 4 July 1906. Wilson spoke often on blacks and the South (*WA* 29 Apr., 27 May 1903, 22 Mar. 1905). *OP* '99, 41:174, '01, 43:183, 218, '03, 45:123. Four African-American students belonged to the Commons Club before 1906. Before 1907 they occasionally appeared in class pictures. See *OP* '02–'11.

112. Arthur B. Haley to Norman J. Daniels, 24 Mar. 1959, vf for Haley '07. Haley's letter recalls his experiences on the baseball team more than a half century earlier, but almost every detail in the letter can be verified. It serves as the principal source for this episode at Wesleyan and as the only source regarding a college body vote in 1905. *Daily Princetonian* 26, 27 Apr. 1905, 25, 26 Apr. 1906; *WA* 3 May 1905, 2 May 1906; Edwin E. Slosson, *Great American Universities* (New York: Macmillan, 1910), 104–5; Marcia Graham Synnott, *The Half-Opened Door: Discrimination and Admissions at Harvard, Yale, and Princeton, 1900–1970* (Westport, Conn.: Greenwood Press, 1979), 174; Steven A. Riess, *Touching Base: Professional Baseball and American Culture in the Progressive Era* (Westport, Conn.: Greenwood Press, 1980), 194–95. From 1890 to 1898 Wesleyan played annually against the Cuban Giants, a touring team of black players. For reports on the first and last of these games, see *WA* 17 May 1890, 30 May 1898. On the Cuban Giants, see Robert Peterson, *Only the Ball Was White: A History of Legendary Black Players and All-Black Professional Teams* (Englewood Cliffs, N.J.: Prentice Hall, 1970), 34–39, 48–49, 59. On Taylor playing in the 1906 season, see baseball stories in *WA* on games through 21 Apr. 1906; on Smith, see *WA* 9, 16, 23 May 1906; *MP* 1, 16 May 1906. Two blacks entered in 1923, two in 1924, and one in 1929. Charles Blake '33 earned election to PBK. Student efforts to exclude an African-American from the football team at Amherst in 1907 were thwarted by the swift action of President George Harris. Compared to the six blacks entering Wesleyan from 1909 through 1928, more than twenty enrolled at Amherst. See Harold Wade, Jr., *Black Men of Amherst* (Amherst, Mass.: Amherst College Press, 1974), 29–30, 111–12.

113. The notion of graduating from the extracurriculum is not used with the intention to suggest that the average Wesleyan undergraduate was less than seriously inclined toward the curriculum. The picture of student life at major universities of this period studied by Veysey, for example, is far more hedonistic and anti-intellectual than conditions I find at Wesleyan (Veysey,

Emergence, 268–94). Wesleyan had only limited immunity, however, to growth on American campuses of what Bryce termed "social life and its amusements." Skills that American college students thought were needed to prosper in the metropolitan milieu are suggested by one of Bryce's comments on American higher education around 1910. He notes that "intellectual distinction in the work of the college is little sought by ambitious spirits, and little valued by their companions" (Bryce, *American Commonwealth* 2:757). Wesleyan students were somewhat slower to develop the metropolitan orientation than those at such other New England colleges as Dartmouth, where Tobias finds that students by 1881 "consciously linked their ambitions to men like the New York alumni who represented the metropolitan culture and success in business" (Tobias, *Old Dartmouth*, 11). Olin had employed a Wesleyan graduate as early as 1890 (*WA* 15 Feb. 1890).

114. Majority report submitted to the board, June 1900, CF; BTM 26 Feb. 1909; Stephen H. Olin, *An Argument against the Woman's Suffrage Amendment to the Constitution of New York* (n.p., 1915), 3–8.

115. For a more detailed account and pathbreaking analysis of coeducation at Wesleyan, 1890–1912, see Knight, "'Quails,'" chaps. 2–15. Three articles by Knight report much of this research: *WUA* 59(Winter 1975): 22–24, 59(Spring 1975): 17–19, 60(Winter 1976): 21–23. On the national context for coeducation and for developments at New England colleges, see Lynn D. Gordon, *Gender and Higher Education in the Progressive Era* (New Haven: Yale University Press, 1990), chap. 1; Rosenberg, "Limits," 115, 120; Joan G. Zimmerman, "Daughters of Main Street: Culture and Female Community at Grinnell, 1884–1917," in *Woman's Being, Woman's Place: Female Identity and Vocation in American History* (Boston: G. K. Hall, 1979), 154, 168; Stameshkin, *Town's College*, 217–22; Marilyn Mavrinac, "Genteel Conflict: The Early Years of Coeducation at Colby College," *Colby Alumnus* 76(December 1986): 12–15; Eisenmann, "Women." *WUC* 1891/92–1898/99. For comparatively supportive male responses to women students up to 1893, see *WA* 17 Oct. 1882, 10 June 1884; *WLM* 1(December 1892): 123–24, 2(October 1893): 37–38. For contemporary views that hostilities began to grow significantly from the 1893/94 academic year onward, see W. F. Sheldon to WNR, 11 June 1900, WRNP; *ZH* 4 July 1894. *WA* 21 Oct. 1893, 9 Dec. 1893, 3 Mar. 1894; *WLM* 2(October 1893): 33.

116. *OP* '94, 36: 33, 76; Steiner, *History*, 271; *OP* '96, 38: 37 '97, 39: 14, 22, 28, 34; Burton H. Camp, "1897," typescript of an address to the Conversational Club, 8 Apr. 1968, 15, VF for Camp '01; *CA* 3 July 1902. Class day exercises began in 1863. See *WLM* 6(April 1898): 247. For signs of participation by women before 1901, see *WA* 4 Nov. 1889; *WLM* 1(October 1892): 48–50, 1(March 1893): 228. Regarding use of the gym, see FM 8 Nov. 1894; *WA* 2 Apr. 1895; *ZH* 3 July 1895. In addition to contributions toward construction of the gym (*WA* 26 Oct. 1889), women contributed to support of the football

team (*WA* 25 Nov. 1893). William North Rice, "Coeducation at Wesleyan" *Springfield Daily Republican* 10 Aug. 1908, clipping in WNRP. For a similar pattern of exclusion at Cornell in the 1880s and 1890s, see Charlotte W. Conable, *Women at Cornell: The Myth of Equal Education* (Ithaca, N.Y.: Cornell University Press, 1977), 116–18.

117. A poll taken in 1890 seemed to indicate that most alumni began the decade in favor of coeducation at Wesleyan (*WA* 29 Mar. 1890). *WA* 26 Jan., 14 Mar. 1894, 25 Feb. 1896, 26 Feb. 1897, 12 Oct. 1898. Smith had written in 1893 that "lovers of football" hoped for the "abandonment of co-education" (*WA* 13 Nov. 1893). Daniel Chase observed in 1899: "This athletic craze would gladly banish female students and fill their places with athlete males" (*ZH* 4 Jan. 1889). Evidence of alumni reluctance to send sons to a coeducational Wesleyan can be found as early as the mid-1880s (W. P. Hubbard '63 to WNR, 3 June 1885, WNRP). Hubbard's son, Nelson, did enroll, however, in 1888. Fear of feminization was also expressed in reactions to proposals for reducing brutality in the cannon rush (*WA* 1 Feb. 1899). *WA* 5 Oct. 1898.

118. Developments mentioned in this paragraph are consistent with general patterns of "women's collegiate culture" in the 1890s. See Lynn D. Gordon, "The Gibson Girl Goes to College: Popular Culture and Women's Higher Education in the Progressive Era, 1890–1920," *American Quarterly* 39(Summer 1987): 211–15. Woodrow Wilson also sensed a change in the early 1890s, with an influx "of young women who go to college of *course*, as young men have long done." These "easy going and sociable students" would be different from the previous generation of "women who were pioneers, examples, missionary adventurers," according to Wilson (ww to John Franklin Jameson, 21 Feb. 1892, *PWW* 7:444). *OP* '93, 35:153–55; *ZH* 21 July 1892; *WA* 21 Dec. 1892. Clara Van Vleck '81, secretary to the president, was an adult presence in Webb Hall during the 1890s (BTM 27 June 1893, 27 June 1905). In 1901 Anna Fisher became the first dean of women (BTM 6 June 1901). *ZH* 4 July 1894; *WA* 3 July 1893, 17 Nov. 1897; *WA* 16, 27 Mar., 9 Dec. 1893; *OP* '94, 36:75,81,78, '98, 40:78; *WA* 23 Apr. 1895, 10 Mar. 1897. Since women's activities were excluded from the yearbook and other student publications after 1898, few records exist to trace the continuation of these organizations. The Delta Delta Delta chapter remained active until June 1912. And a chapter of Alpha Gamma Delta existed from 1906 to 1912. See Bessie Leach Priddy, *A Detailed Record of Delta Delta Delta, 1888–1931* (Menasha, Wis.: George Banta, 1932), 396–99. *ZH* 1 July 1908; Rice, "Coeducation." Wives of faculty members and local trustees formed an organization to serve their separate sphere in 1892. The Monday Club (started as the Wednesday Club) fostered serious literary discussion and some social events (Monday Club minutes, 1892–1910).

119. *OP* '97, 39:20–21. For another example of threatening language, see *WLM* 3(July 1895): 313. *WA* 4 May, 5 Oct. 1898; *OP* '99, 41:5. On the more

general pattern of backlash against women's education after 1900, see Palmieri, "From Republican," 57–59.

120. BTM 22 June 1896, 26 Mar. 1897; *ZH* 7 July 1897; *WUB* (November 1896), 2; *WLM* 7(October 1898): 30, 33–34, 7(November 1898): 70; *WA* 26 Oct. 1898. For the steady drumbeat against coeducation sounded in student publications, see *WA* 26 Jan. 1898, 8 Nov. 1899, 7, 28 Mar. 1900; *WLM* 7(May 1899): 318 8(October 1899): 40, 8(February 1900): 232–33, 8(March 1900): 280–86. Walter N. Hill '01 to Catherine R. C. Smith, 11 Dec. 1898, Smith-Childs Family Papers; press clippings of the coeducation controversy at Wesleyan University (1898), scrapbook assembled by Sarah Carrie Hallock '02; FM 15 Nov., 10 Dec. 1898; *WA* 21 Dec. 1898.

121. BTM 30 Mar. 1899; AAM 27 June 1899; *CA* 6 July 1899; *WA* 5 July 1899; WNR to Edward L. Rice, 14 June 1898, 3 May 1901, WNRP; FM 13 June 1899; *Papers on the Relation of Wesleyan University to the Higher Education of Women* (Middletown: Wesleyan University, 1900), 5; minute of a report of the coeducational committee of the Wesleyan Young Alumni Association of New York (typescript of a report adopted 27 Oct. 1899), 4–6, CF; *Papers*, 3.

122. BTM 20 Mar. 1900; AAM 26 June 1900; *To the Board of Trustees of Wesleyan University* (petition from the women graduates with covering letter dated 2 June 1900), CF; *CA* 3 May 1900; *To the Board of Trustees of Wesleyan University*, (text of resolutions adopted at a meeting of undergraduates on 19 June 1900), CF; WNR to Edward L. Rice, 3 March 1909, WNRP; *To the Board of Trustees of Wesleyan University* (dissenting statement of C. T. Winchester, Herbert Welch, and Seward V. Coffin dated 23 June 1900), CF; *To the Board of Trustees of Wesleyan University* (dissenting statement of J. M. Van Vleck dated 25 June 1900), CF.

123. BTM 26 June 1900. Limits on admission of women were also established at Colby (1901) and Middlebury (1902). A limit was proposed at Dickinson in 1909. See Mavrinac, "Genteel Conflict," 17; Stameshkin, *Town's College*, 221; Sellers, *Dickinson*, 302. A motion to abolish coeducation received only the vote of its maker, George S. Coleman '76. New York City lawyer, Episcopalian, longtime member of the New York Wesleyan Alumni Club, and president of the intercollegiate Psi Upsilon Club of New York, Coleman helped to raise money for the Fayerweather Gymnasium (TDB; *WA* 21 Jan. 1881, 20 Feb. 1892).

124. *WA* 27 June 1900; *WLM* 10(November 1901): 84; *WA* 25 June 1902; FM 2 July 1900. Women had been integrated in the alphabetical class lists since 1892 (FM 12 Oct. 1886; *WUC* 1892/93); RAC 19 Nov. 1900, 11 Jan., 22, 24 June 1901; *ZH* 4 July 1900; *CA* 5 July 1900.

125. *WUC* 1892/93–1908/09. Almost 40 percent of the women entering 1882–98 were from out of state. More than 90 percent of students at the Women's College in Brown University came from within a twenty-five-mile radius of Providence (Eisenmann, "Women," 147a). For detailed

examination of the social boycott and harassment, see Knight, "'Quails,'" chap. 10.

126. FM 10 June 1902; *WA* 25 June 1902; Knight, "'Quails,'" 123–24; FM 6 Mar. 1904; *WA* 23 Mar. 1903. By 1906 women had started a Young Women's Christian Association (Rice, "History," 50). *WA* 16 Dec. 1903; *WLM* 14(May 1906): 361–62; *Collier's* 41(12 Sept. 1908): 13; *WLM* 17(November 1908): 82; Harrington, *Autobiography*, 143.

127. The few influential voices raised on behalf of coeducation seemed to come from the West. See, e.g., David Starr Jordan, "The Question of Coeducation," *Munsey's Magazine* 34(March 1906): 683–88. On Goode, see *WAR* (1911), 552; *WLM* 17(December 1908): 125. On Van Vleck as the faculty member respected above all others by alumni and friends of Wesleyan, see *ZH* 26 June 1889. Rice, "History," 50; *WA* 28 June 1890; Bradford P. Raymond, "Why We Are Methodists," in Charles H. Small, *Corner-Stones of Faith* (New York: E. B. Treat, 1898), 242–43; BPR to WNR, 23 Dec. 1907, WNRP. After a long struggle, women had gained "equal laity rights" within the denomination in 1900, but full clergy rights would not be obtained until 1956. See Rosemary Skinner Keller, "Creating a Sphere for Women," in *Historical Perspectives on the Wesleyan Tradition: Women in New Worlds*, ed. Hilah F. Thomas and Rosemary Skinner Keller (Nashville, Tenn.: Abingdon Press [ca. 1981]), 250; Elaine Magalis, *Conduct Becoming a Women: Bolted Doors and Burgeoning Missions* (n.p.: Woman's Division, Board of Global Ministries, United Methodist Church [ca. 1973]), 138. Raymond may also have had in mind the fact that longtime foes of women's rights continued to occupy influential positions within the denomination. James Buckley, editor of *CA*, for example, would publish a book in 1909 entitled *The Wrong and Peril of Woman Suffrage*. See Ruth Bordin, *Frances Willard: A Biography* (Chapel Hill: University of North Carolina Press, 1986), 166.

128. For a brief sketch of the General Education Board and a comparison of its role to that of the Carnegie Foundation for the Advancement of Teaching, see Potts, "American Colleges," 374–75. BPR to Wallace Buttrick, 15, 21 Mar. 1905, Buttrick to BPR, 18, 22 Mar. 1905, GEBF. The new campus would border on a ravine with a "beautiful stream." With similar negative results, Raymond had approached the General Education Board for $10,000 in 1905 and for $100,000 in 1906 to build a chemistry building (BPR to Starr J. Murphy, 16 Oct. 1905, 24 Jan. 1906, GEBF). H. C. M. Ingraham to WNR, 7, 21 Jan., 22 Feb. 1909, WNRP; Morrill, *Multimillionaire*, 100; Harrington, *Autobiography*, 146. Andrus may also have been displeased that Wesleyan did not offer the presidency to his son-in-law, Frederick Davenport. WAS to WNR, 22 Feb., 6 Mar. 1909, WNRP.

129. Tufts, where women first entered in 1892, was in a similar bind. See Russell E. Miller, *Light on the Hill: A History of Tufts College, 1852–1952*, vol. 1 (Boston: Beacon Press, 1966), 179–91. RAC 3, 17 Dec. 1907. This position was

reaffirmed by a vote of 12–3 in 1908 (RAC 11 Nov. 1908). Trustees on the committee were Andrus, Buckley, Downey, Kelley, and Pearne (BTM 6 Dec. 1907). Faculty on the committee were Bradley, Fife, Harrington, Rice, and Winchester (RAC 17 Dec. 1907). BTM 22 June 1908; *WAR* (1921), 225; BTM 16 June 1923.

130. BTM 23 June 1908; *WA* 22 Jan. 1908; WNR to Vida F. Moore, 9 Jan. 1909, WNRP; *WA* 4 Nov. 1908. In describing male undergraduate attitudes, journalists were probably alluding to the celebration of masculinity by Teddy Roosevelt. Frank Putnam, "A College for Women in Prospect," *New England Magazine* 37(November 1907): 284; *Meriden Weekly Republican* 19 Dec. 1907; BTM 26 Feb. 1909.

131. *WA* 3 Mar. 1909; *WLM* 17(March 1909): 256–59; *OP* '09, 51:248. Harold J. Conn '08 recalled in a manner directly linked to racial attitudes the way men treated women students: "Mostly they ignored them—much as they did the few negro students in those days." See the questionnaire he returned to Lucy Knight in 1972, Knight research materials. *CA* 4 Mar. 1909; *NYT* 1 Mar. 1909; *NYTr* 27 Feb. 1909; *NYH* 27 Feb. 1909. The *Tribune* did have a satirical jibe for Wesleyan males when the last four women graduated (*NYTr* 18 June 1912). *Independent* 66(25 Mar. 1909): 648–49. For responses to this criticism, see subsequent issues of 25 Mar., 15 Apr.; *WLM* 7(April 1909): 296–300. Moving quickly to eradicate all traces and reminders of coeducation, Wesleyan changed Webb Hall to a men's dormitory in the fall of 1909 and renamed it East Hall (*WA* 7 Oct. 1909). By 1911 an elderly denominational leader in Boston, James Mudge '65, looked back on the decision and concluded: "We are not inclined to regret that the college has swung back into line with the institutions with which it must necessarily compete" (*CA* 10 Aug. 1911).

132. WNR to Edward L. Rice, 3 March 1909, WNRP; Solomon, *In the Company*, 55. Instruction of women at Brown began in 1891, but the women's college was not fully and officially established until 1897 (Bronson, *History*, 457). WNR to Vida F. Moore, 9 Jan. 1909, WNRP; Stameshkin, *Town's College*, 217–22; Mavrinac, "Genteel Conflict," 15–17; Miller, *Light*, 182–98. "All matters relating to a Coordinate College for Women" were referred to a committee chaired by the new president, William A. Shanklin, whose chief task was to increase Wesleyan's endowment and eliminate persistent annual deficits (BTM 28 June 1909). WNR to Mrs. L. S. Cummings, 4 Mar. 1909, 14 July 1910, WNR to Elizabeth C. Wright, 21 July 1910, Wright to WNR, 26 July 1910, WNRP; Gertrude E. Noyes, *A History of Connecticut College* (New London, Conn. Connecticut College, 1982), 9–16, 29; *NYT* 12 December 1902, 12 November 1903; *NCAB* 24:273, 49:263.

133. BTM 24 June 1907; *WA* 3 July 1907. Although appointed professor of the English Bible, Raymond was in too poor health to assume this position. See *WUB* (May 1909):26. He died in 1916. BTM 13 Nov. 1908; SHO to WNR, 14 Nov. 1908, WNRP.

134. *WUB* (December 1906):2–3, (December 1908):4, (June 1903):1–2; btm 15 Apr. 1904; rac 8 Nov. 1904; btm 30 Mar. 1905; *WUB* (May 1905):1; *ZH* 5 July 1905; *WUB* (December 1908):4, (December 1909):19, 4. Striker finds contemporary claims a bit high; he estimates an inflation increase of 20 to 40 percent (Striker, "American Professors," 247–49). *WUB* (May 1905):1, (May 1907):2–3. From 1903 to 1912 Amherst's endowment grew by almost $1,000,000. (King, *History*, 124).

135. Henry M. Wriston, "The Selection of Presidents," *WUA* 50(May 1966): 3; *CA* 21 Nov. 1907; *WLM* 16(January 1908): 170; *WA* 5 Feb. 1908; btm 24, 25 June 1907, 23 June 1908. When Wesleyan's search began in 1907, the presidents of Amherst, Williams, Dartmouth, and Bowdoin were clergymen. Laymen had previously occupied the presidency at all but Dartmouth, and each would select a layman as its next president: Williams in 1908, Dartmouth in 1909, Amherst in 1912, Bowdoin in 1918, and Wesleyan in 1924. *WLM* 16(January 1908): 170; *WA* 26 Feb. 1908.

136. Francis J. McConnell, "Introduction," in Fred Hamlin, *S. Parkes Cadman: Pioneer Radio Minister* (New York: Harper, 1930), x. For additional commentary and information on Cadman's career, see *DAB* 11:85–86; *NCAB* 28:192–94. Cadman relinquished his Methodist ordination in 1901, but retained his membership in the Methodist chapel of his boyhood in Britain (*CA* 23 July 1936). *CA* 10 Jan. 1901; *Brooklyn Eagle* 24 Mar., 4, 6 Apr. 1908; *MP* 8 Apr. 1908; wnr to Edward L. Rice, 28 Apr. 1908, wnrp. It is unlikely that Wesleyan could have made a salary offer even approximating the $10,000 per year paid to Cadman at Central. Shanklin was hired at $4,500. See *Reports of the Prudential Committee . . . of the Central Congregational Church* (1908), 29, Brooklyn Historical Society; btm 13 Nov. 1908. Cadman was well known to Wesleyan's faculty, having received an honorary D.D. and preached a highly acclaimed university sermon during commencement week in 1898 (*ZH* 6 July 1898; *CA* 14 July 1898). While considering the Wesleyan presidency, Cadman received a reserved and courteous pledge of encouragement and support from the senior faculty (rac 24 Mar. 1908), but their first choice was clearly Frederick M. Davenport '89 (ctw to Frederick M. Davenport, 28 Apr. 1908, pfmd).

137. *WAR* (1911), 401–2; *WA* 18 Dec. 1907; H. C. M. Ingraham to wnr, 22 Mar. 1908, wnrp; Charles O. Judkins to K. P. Harrington, 16, 25 Nov., 20, 27 Dec. 1907, 2 Jan. 1908, K. P. Harrington Papers; letters to Frederick M. Davenport from Rowland Miles '89 (1 Oct. 1907), George S. Coleman '76 (12 Feb. 1908), John Gowdy '97 (13 Apr. 1908), Caleb T. Winchester (28 Apr. 1908), pfmd. Davenport was offered a professorship at Wesleyan in 1906 (rac 1 Mar. 1906; wnr to Frederick M. Davenport, 13 Apr. 1906, pfmd). wnr to Edward L. Rice, 25 Apr. 1908, wnrp; John Gowdy to Frederick M. Davenport, 13 Apr. 1908, pfmd. Although Davenport did not actively seek the Wesleyan presidency, he was ready to "carefully consider"

an offer (Frederick M. Davenport to Charles O. Judkins, 24 Dec. 1907, PFMD). He won the state senate seat in November 1908 (*WA* 11 Nov. 1908). *NCAB* 46:210–11. *NYT* 28 Dec. 1956.

138. BTM 13 Nov. 1908; WNR to Edward L. Rice, 22 Nov. 1908, H. C. M. Ingraham to WNR, 2, 4 Nov., 22 Mar. 1908, WNRP. Ingraham was a Brooklyn lawyer highly active in the Methodist church (*CA* 15, 23 Feb. 1911). Because he and his wife were traveling in Europe from June through September 1908, he probably relied heavily on his classmate, Kelley, to conclude the search. Shanklin had been a candidate since at least the beginning of 1908 (WAS to Elihu Root, 14 Jan. 1908, Elihu Root Papers, Manuscript Division, Library of Congress). BTM 13 Nov. 1909.

139. Kelley and Bennett, who went to Chicago to meet and interview Shanklin (BTM 13 Nov. 1908), were probably the most active and influential members of the search committee (Charles O. Judkins to K. P. Harrington, 16 Nov. 1907, K. P. Harrington to William V. Kelley, 6 Jan. 1908, K. P. Harrington Papers). *MR* 111(March 1928): 273–75, 108(January 1925): 35–36; *CA* 22 Dec. 1927; WNR to Edward L. Rice, 22 Nov. 1908, WNRP. Kelley helped prepare the trustee minute on Shanklin's resignation and, though feeble, offered a prayer at the house on the day of Shanklin's funeral. See BTM 8 Dec. 1923; *MR* 108(January 1925): 30–31. The childless Kelley noted that Cadman was "one of my boys" (comment written by Kelley on S. Parkes Cadman to William V. Kelley, 25 Feb. 1924, William V. Kelley Papers, UMA). *CA* 25 June 1908.

140. Circumstantial evidence for Olin's disappointment with the selection begins with his resignation the day after Shanklin's election and ends with Olin playing a major role in forcing Shanklin's resignation in 1923. Evidence along the way (SHO to WNR, 25 Feb. 1918, WNR to Edward L. Rice, 8 Sept. 1923, WNRP) and an interview 23 Feb. 1989 with Mrs. John Ewing, daughter of Wesley Rich '11, suggests that Olin is the unidentified person described in the memoirs of Henry Wriston '11 as "perhaps the bitterest critic" of Shanklin. See Wriston, *Academic Procession*, 18. Presidents of academic stature were selected by Williams (Harry A. Garfield, professor of politics, Princeton University) in 1907 and Amherst (Alexander Meiklejohn, professor of philosophy, Brown University) in 1912. There is a paucity of accurate and readily available information concerning Shanklin's life before his Wesleyan presidency. See the brief, flawed sketches in *NCAB* 14:292; *MNYEC* (1925), 121–23; *WA* 18 Nov. 1909; *WUB* (December 1908):8–9; S. K. Turner and S. A. Clark, *Twentieth Century History of Carroll County, Missouri* (Indianapolis, Ind.: B. F. Bowen, 1911), 565–67; E. V. Claypool, "Career of Dr. Shanklin," *Upper Iowa Collegian* 30 Sept. 1905. In data Shanklin submitted to WWA from 1910 to 1925, as well as all biographical sketches, he was described as a graduate of Hamilton College in 1883. Shanklin also obtained from the Hamilton chapter of Phi Beta Kappa in

1907 election as an alumnus member. Information on Shanklin at Hamilton College supplied by Frank K. Lorenz, curator of special collections. For information on Hamilton's seldom-practiced award of the B.A. *ex gratia* (by favor), see Lorenz, "Academic," xvi–xvii. Shanklin's ties to the Root family began in his teenage years, when he attended high school in Carrollton, Missouri, with Edwin B. Root, son of Oren Root, Jr. (Hamilton '56), and nephew of Elihu Root (Hamilton '64). Edwin Root and Shanklin enrolled at Hamilton in 1879 and became members of Sigma Phi, the fraternity of Oren and Elihu. Oren returned to Hamilton a year later to succeed his father as professor of mathematics. Shanklin seems to have been considered almost a member of the Root family. Speaking at Shanklin's inauguration, Elihu Root noted with "personal affection" that he had "known him since as a boy he entered Hamilton." See *The Installation of William Arnold Shanklin, L.H.D. LL.D., as Ninth President of Wesleyan University* (Middletown: Wesleyan University, 1909), 43. Root was a key trustee at Hamilton, 1883–1937, and chair of the board 1909–37 (*DAB* suppl. 2:581). On Oren Root, Jr., see Win Winship, "Oren Root, Darwinism and Biblical Criticism," *Journal of Presbyterian History* 62(Summer 1984): 111–23. Information on Shanklin at Garrett supplied from institutional records by David Himrod, reference librarian. Shanklin is listed in the 1891/92 Garrett catalogue as having a B.A. Regents and other records at the University of Washington checked by staff members, Manuscripts and University Archives Division, University of Washington Libraries. Information on Shanklin at the University of Missouri supplied by D. J. Wade, reference specialist, University Archives. Information on Shanklin in Kansas supplied by Zoe Nell Nading from a file of the *Chetopa Advance* 10, 17 Apr., 11 Dec. 1884, 1 Jan., 22 Oct. 1885. *Upper Iowa Collegian* 7 Dec. 1908; *History of the Peru United Methodist Church* (Peru, Kans.: n.p., 1971), 1; *WWAM*, 197; M. H. Alderson, "Upper Iowa University," *The Palimpsest* 46(March 1965): 154; *Upper Iowa Collegian* 18 Jan. 1909. WAS to Arthur T. Hadley, 28 Sept. 1906, Arthur T. Hadley Presidential Records, YRG 2-A-13, Manuscripts and Archives, Yale University Library.

141. Olin had glowing praise for Butler's presidency of Columbia (1901–45) and asked Butler to send a copy of his annual report for 1910 to Shanklin. See Stephen H. Olin, *For President, Nicholas Murray Butler* (n.p. [ca. 1920]), 7–9; SHO to Nicholas Murray Butler, 15 Feb. 1911, NMBP. BTM 26 Feb. 1909; *WA* 24 Mar. 1909; enrollment data taken from catalogues of Upper Iowa University, 1905/06–1908/09; *WUB* (May 1909):6; *Upper Iowa Collegian* 18 Jan. 1909; WAS to William C. Levere, 8 Aug. 1914, VF for fraternities; H. C. M. Ingraham to WNR, 18 Mar. 1909, WNRP; WAS to WNR, 6 Mar. 1909, WNRP. Shanklin knew William Howard Taft as well as Elihu Root (see text at n145). Olin knew Taft well enough to invite him and his wife to the wedding of Olin's youngest daughter in 1902 and to urge Taft to speak at Wesleyan's seventy-fifth anniversary celebration in 1906 (SHO to William H.

Taft, 11 Dec. 1902, 27 Oct. 1905, William Howard Taft Papers, Manuscript Division, Library of Congress, reels 37, 53). Throughout Shanklin's career, his "charm of personality" is cited by observers as his outstanding characteristic. For the phrases quoted, see *WUB* (October 1928):15, 23. Henry Wriston found Shanklin well suited to perform "a vital service of promotion" for Wesleyan (Wriston, "Selection," 3).

142. All constituencies were "keyed up to the highest level of expectancy." See, *WLM* 17(February 1909): 107. WNR to Edward L. Rice, 22 Nov. 1908; WNRP; FM 18 Nov. 1908; ARP (1908):1; *WA* 18 Nov., 9 Dec. 1908; *WLM* 17(December 1908): 124–28; *CA* 24 Dec. 1908. Two months prior to his campus visit, Shanklin attended the New York Alumni Club dinner, where he "won the heart of every man and his reception was cordial beyond measure" (*CA* 16 Dec. 1909). *ZH* 30 June 1909; *CA* 18 Feb. 1909. The best accounts of Shanklin's visit are: *Meriden Morning Record* 12 Feb. 1909 (by Dudley Harmon '09); *WA* 24 Feb. 1909.

143. "The ruling theme of the day was that of personality" (*Boston Evening Transcript* 12 Nov. 1909). *WA* 18 Nov. 1909; *CA* 18 Nov. 1909. Shanklin had previously announced his presidential agenda: increased enrollment to five hundred and increased resources through a fund drive for $1 million (*WA* 7 July 1909). For examples of Shanklin's prose, see *CA* 20 May 1904, 24 Dec. 1908; *WA* 23 Dec. 1908. Shanklin's lack of much training in Latin forced a change in the commencement ritual where the president spoke briefly in Latin before awarding degrees. Burton Camp reports that initially Shanklin's "Latin pronunciation was so atrocious and he said it badly with so much assurance and vigor" that this speech was soon translated into English for his subsequent use (Camp, "1897," 13). *Installation of Shanklin*, 51–63. Shanklin's emphasis on service, "a sense of social responsibility and a passion for social justice" echoed Harry A. Garfield's inaugural address at Williams a year earlier in which emphasis was placed on education for citizenship (Spring, *History*, 259) and Nicholas Murray Butler's inaugural address at Columbia in 1902, entitled "Scholarship and Service." See, William Summerscales, *Affirmation and Dissent: Columbia's Response to World War I* (New York: Teachers College Press, 1970), 36–37. *WLM* 18(November 1909): 77; *WUB* (October 1928):31.

144. For a richly detailed account of the Shanklin inauguration, see Willard M. Wallace, "A Tale of Two Presidents" *WUA* 70(Winter 1988): 17–21. *Installation of Shanklin*, 43–47, 100; Wesleyan had considerable contact with the Republican party before Taft's visit. Bradford Raymond and a majority of the faculty during his presidency were Republicans. See BPR to WW, 11 Nov. 1910, *PWW* microfilm, series 2, reel 23; *MP* 19 Sept. 1888. President McKinley agreed to attend the commencement ceremonies in 1901 but had to cancel because his wife was ill. See *CA* 16 May, 4 July 1901; *WA* 26 June 1901. His postmaster general, Charles E. Smith, came,

however, and delivered with "patriotic eloquence" the Phi Beta Kappa oration, "American Development and Destiny." See *WUB* (May 1901):1, 9; *ZH* 3 July 1901, *CA* 4 July 1901. President Theodore Roosevelt was approached concerning an appearance at the Wesley Bicentennial celebration in 1903 (BTM 23 June 1902), and William Tucker, president of Dartmouth, a key speaker at this event, was a loyal Republican. See William J. Tucker, *My Generation: An Autobiographical Interpretation* (Boston: Riverside Press, 1919), 389. Although the famous social gospel minister, Washington Gladden, was nominated for an honorary degree that year by the faculty, his name was quietly removed from the list by Stephen Henry Olin's trustee committee (RAC 14 May 1903; BTM 15 May 1903). Gladden's progressive Republican views on trade unions, race issues, and municipal ownership of utilities may well have grated conservative sensibilities among trustees. On Gladden's views as of 1903, see Jacob Henry Dorn, *Washington Gladden: Prophet of the Social Gospel* (Columbus: Ohio State University Press, 1967), 200–1, 216–17; Ronald C. White, Jr., and C. Howard Hopkins, *The Social Gospel: Religion and Reform in Changing America* (Philadelphia: Temple University Press, 1976), 103–4; Robert T. Handy, ed., *The Social Gospel in America 1870–1920* (New York: Oxford University Press, 1966), 24–29. Speakers at the Wesley Bicentennial identified Wesley's traits as a scholar, humanitarian, and Methodist; Olin noted that he was a Tory (*Wesley Bicentennial*, 131). Horace S. Merrill and Marion G. Merrill, *The Republican Command, 1897–1913* (Lexington: University Press of Kentucky, 1971), 19, 92, 272.

145. *HC* 13 Nov. 1909; *Minneapolis Journal* 27 Sept. 1908; *NCAB* 14:292–93; WAS to WHT, 8 Dec. 1908, and fifteen subsequent letters relating to Taft's visit on 12 Nov. 1909, WHTP, Manuscript Division, Library of Congress, reels 112, 480, 495, 351. Taft later agreed to continue on to Hartford that evening to dedicate a new armory. *WUB* (December 1909), 12; *Installation of Shanklin*, 47, 40–44, 100. Root, Sherman, Stryker, and Shanklin belonged to the Hamilton chapter of Sigma Phi. Taft was a Psi U at Yale and made time to stop briefly at the Wesleyan chapter house to sign its guest register (*MP* 12 Nov. 1909).

146. The day began for Olin when he met Taft's train and rode beside him in the parade through Middletown (*MP* 12 Nov. 1908). *WUB* (December 1909):12; *Installation of Shanklin*, 34, 51, 63. Shanklin moved vigorously through the Methodist conference circuit as well as traversing the alumni club trail, eliciting warm receptions from both constituencies. See *WUB* (May 1910):23; *MNYEC* (1910), 29; *MNYC* (1910), 75. BTM 22 Apr. 1910; H. C. M. Ingraham to WNR, 22 Feb. 1909, WNRP. The installation cost $4,500, an amount equal to Shanklin's annual salary (*FEx* 1910, 23; BTM 13 Nov. 1908). WNR to Raymond Dodge, 24 Aug. 1910, WNR to Edward L. Rice, 16 Nov. 1910, WNRP; *CA* 2 Dec. 1909; *Leslie's Weekly* 108(28 January 1909): 76; *Outlook* 93(27 Nov. 1909): 943–44. For examples of extensive cov-

erage in the urban press, see articles appearing 13 Nov. 1909 in *Philadelphia Public Ledger*, *NYT*, and *NYTr*. An article in *NYH* said the inauguration "is thought to presage an era of great prosperity for the university." An article in *Boston Evening Transcript* (12 Nov. 1909) said "a brilliant future was bespoken for the institution under the new regime."

147. On the development of this role for the Carnegie Foundation for the Advancement of Teaching, see the analysis of Henry Pritchett and his board by Ellen Condliffe Lagemann, *Private Power for the Public Good: A History of the Carnegie Foundation for the Advancement of Teaching* (Middletown: Wesleyan University Press, 1983), 37–41 and Theron F. Schlabach, *Pensions for Professors* (Madison: State Historical Society of Wisconsin, 1963), 11–17. Regarding work with similar effects by Frederick T. Gates and Wallace Buttrick via Rockefeller's General Education Board, see Raymond B. Fosdick, *Adventure in Giving: The Story of the General Education Board* (New York: Harper & Row, 1962), chap. 10.

148. Stephen H. Olin, *Correspondence Concerning the Application of Wesleyan University for Acceptance by the Carnegie Foundation for the Advancement of Teaching, October 7 1908–April 26, 1909* (n.p., 1909), 2; Joseph F. Wall, *Andrew Carnegie* New York: Oxford University Press, 1970), 871–72; CFAT, *First Annual Report* (1906), 21–22; Schlabach, *Pensions*, 29–31.

149. BTM 15 Apr. 1904. Exercising its prerogative to grant pensions to selected individuals and their widows at institutions not on the accepted list, Carnegie began supplying a retirement allowance to Atwater (and then his widow) in mid-1907, and to Raymond (and then his widow) in mid-1909. See CFAT *Second Annual Report* (1907), 115; *Fourth Annual Report* (1909), 12. Raymond had lost almost all his invested financial assets in a fire that destroyed the paper mill owned by his son and son-in-law (WNR to Edward L. Rice, 26 July 1908, WNRP; BPR to WNR, 14 June 1909, WNRP; *WA* 7 July 1909). Only two faculty retired prior to 1904, both in poor health. John Johnston received a college pension of $1,500 per year from 1873 to his death in 1879, and Calvin S. Harrington received $1,250 per year from 1885 until his death in 1886 (BTM 24 June 1873, 23 June 1885). Data on church membership of faculty as of 1906 compiled from Record Book #9, Record of the First Methodist Church, Middletown, Conn., 1892–1909, Storage Room, First United Methodist Church. For estimates and calculations of Methodist presence on the faculty, see *CA* 5 Dec. 1901; CTW to WW, 24 Oct. 1908, CTWP, box 4.

150. *Celebration 75th*, 4; *WUB* (May 1905):4; *WLM* 13(June 1905): 391; *Celebration 75th*, 4–6, 167–69, 145–52. Regarding the alumni fund, see *Celebration 75th*, 4; *WUB* (May 1906):29–31, 2, 5–6. About $183,000 had been raised toward a goal of $1 million in the preceding Wesley Bicentennial campaign (BTM 30 Mar. 1905). By 1910 Wesleyan had fifteen regional alumni associations. See *WUB* (December 1909):6. Sports events in 1903 included a

varsity versus alumni baseball game and a victory over Williams. Singing included a glee club concert and a campus rally. In 1906, after a two-year lapse, the campus illumination and organized alumni sing became regular events at alumni reunion weekends (*Celebration 75th*, 8; *WA* 27 June 1906). *WUB* (May 1906):1; *Celebration 75th*, 49. Raymond led the board through charter revision with similar use of Wesleyan's history. See ARP (1907):15. Speakers at events after the Alumni Association vote reinforced this interpretation and action taken to delete the Curry amendment of 1870 (*Celebration 75th*, 58–59, 77). *WAR* (1911), 189; AAM 26 June 1906; *ZH* 4 July 1906.

151. BTM 1 May 1903, 30 Mar., 26 June 1905; *WUB* (December 1907):17–19; Olin, *Correspondence*, 14; BPR to Henry S. Pritchett, 22 Mar. 1907, CFATR; *ZH* 3 July 1907; *SAC* 15:292–95. Formal acceptance of the legislative action came at the annual board meeting 25 June 1907. *WUB* (December 1907):3; BTM 6 Dec. 1907; *CA* 23 Jan. 1908; *Brooklyn Eagle* 4 Apr. 1908.

152. BPR to trustees of CFAT, 9, 25 Nov. 1907, CFATR; Robert A. Hohner, "Southern Education in Transition: William Waugh Smith, the Carnegie Foundation, and the Methodist Church," *HEQ* 27(Summer 1987): 186–98. The case of Bowdoin College and several other institutions had raised similar issues by late fall 1907 (undated internal memorandum of early 1909, in response to Olin's petition, summarizing actions of the executive committee on formal relations with a denomination, CFATR). CFAT, *Second Annual Report* (1907), 40–61. Henry S. Pritchett to BPR, 28 Dec. 1907, CFATR.

153. BTM 9 Apr., 22 June 1908; Wall, *Andrew Carnegie*, 877; David S. Webster, *Academic Quality Rankings of American Colleges and Universities* (Springfield, Ill.: Charles C. Thomas, 1986), 80–83.

154. Olin, *Correspondence*, 1, 7, 8; Lagemann, *Private Power*, 22–24. Olin and Pritchett even counted Nicholas Murray Butler, key member of the Carnegie executive committee, as a mutual friend. Pritchett joined Olin and Butler as a member of Olin's favorite club, the Round Table, in 1915 (Nicholas Murray Butler to Henry S. Pritchett, 2 Dec. 1915, Henry S. Pritchett Papers, Manuscript Division, Library of Congress, box 2). Correspondence between Pritchett and Butler in these papers stretches over forty years. Olin probably discussed Wesleyan's case with his friend Butler, and Winchester made a private appeal to his former colleague Woodrow Wilson, who served with Butler on Carnegie's executive committee (CTW to WW, 24 Oct. 1908, CTWP, box 4). Olin sent his concluding letter to Pritchett in late April 1909 and probably published the correspondence in mid-1909.

155. SHO to WNR, 13 Apr. 1909, WNRP; *The General Education Board: An Account of its Activities, 1902–1914* (New York: General Education Board, 1915), 3, 15–16, 156–59; Webster, *Academic*, 72. In addition to his requests of 1905 and 1906 (see n128 above), Raymond made similarly unsuccessful grant requests for $200,000 and then $50,000 in 1907. Shanklin started with a request for $250,000. Wesleyan raised the $900,000 and received its

$100,000 grant in 1912. Information concerning Wesleyan and the General Education Board obtained from substantial correspondence in GEBF.

156. Henry S. Pritchett to WAS, 26 Jan. 1910, CFATR; CFAT, *Fifth Annual Report* (1910), 28; SHO to WNR, 6 May 1910, WNRP; SHO to Nicholas Murray Butler, 5 May 1910, NMBP.

157. *CA* 6 Aug. 1908, 4 Aug. 1910; *WA* 24 Feb. 1910; *WUB* (May 1908), 34; Olin, *Correspondence*, 2; *WA* 4 Apr. 1906. Full-time undergraduate enrollments at Wesleyan grew from 294 in 1907/08 to 473 in 1915/16. Tuition and enrollment data are taken from catalogues of the three colleges. The faculty had also built a level of instruction placing Wesleyan's curriculum in the top quality category of Babcock's national survey in 1911 and had linked Wesleyan with "the best colleges and universities in the country" by joining the College Entrance Examination Board. See Lykes, *Higher Education*, 47; *WUB* (December 1908):5. BTM 22 Apr. 1910; 17 June 1912; *MNYC* (1887), 72. By the 1890s some wealthy and prestige-minded Methodists began to send their sons to Yale rather than Wesleyan. See *MR* 72(January 1890): 124. Even in Curry's era (he died in 1887) there were no appropriations to colleges from the Methodist General Conference. See Paul M. Limbert, *Denominational Policies in the Support and Supervision of Higher Education* (New York: Teachers College, Columbia University, 1929), 124–25. Whereas Wesleyan in 1881 was viewed as below the second rank of New England colleges, occupied by such institutions as Amherst, Brown, and Dartmouth (Tobias, *Old Dartmouth*, 93), it was equipped to fare better in any ranking done in 1910. Finding pretentious the use of *university* to describe "a good old college," an alumnus in 1910 asked, "Why not ally ourselves, therefore, in name as well as spirit with our natural associates, Williams and Amherst?" See *WA* 28 Oct. 1910. BTM 28 June 1910.

Index of
First Citations
in Notes

A guide to full reference information for works cited in more than one chapter, by chapter and note number

Mudge, *History*, 1:41
New England, 2:40
Nicolson, *Athletics*, 2:60
Nightingale, *Handbook*, 4:44
Norwood, "More Letters," 1:22
Palmieri, "From Republican," 4:46
Patton, *Eight*, 4:58
Peterson, *New England*, 2:48
Pierson, *Yale*, 3:19
Potts, "American Colleges," 1:34
Potts, *Baptist Colleges*, 1:36
Potts, "College Enthusiasm!" 1:34
Prentice, *Wilbur Fisk*, 1:45
Public Statute Laws, 1:30
Rice, "History," 4:68
Rice, *Personal*, 2:38
Rider, "Growth," 3:77
Rosenberg, "Limits," 4:34
Royall, *Black Book*, 1:10
Rudolph, *American*, 1:28
Rudolph, *Curriculum*, 1:37
Rudolph, *Hopkins*, 2:22
Scanlon, *Randolph-Macon*, 1:36
Sellers, *Dickinson*, 2:32
Semi-Centennial, 4:68
Smith, *Allegheny*, 1:35

Smith, *Sports*, 5:10
Solomon, *In the Company*, 4:34
Spring, *History of Williams*, 3:82
Stameshkin, *Town's College*, intro.:2
Steiner, *History*, 4:65
Stiles, *Seventy-Five*, 2:58
Story, *Forging*, intro.:1
Stricker, "American Professors," 5:67
Svonkin, "Pluralistic," 4:51
Swift, "Heartless," 2:63
Swift, "Sense," 2:63
Timberlake, *Prohibition*, 4:55
Tobias, *Old Dartmouth*, intro.:1
Tolles, "College Architecture," 1:41
Tributes . . . Rice, 2:32
Turner, *Campus*, 1:41
Tyler, *History of Amherst*, 2:35
Van Vleck, *Historical Sketch*, 3:8
Vesey, *Emergence*, 5:78
Voorhees, *History*, 2:51
Weaver, *Trinity*, 1:3
Wesley Bicentennial, 4:72
Williamson, "Willbur Fisk," 1:44
Williamson, *Northwestern*, 4:23
Winchester, "Wesleyan" (1878), 4:62
Works of Olin, 2:10

Index

Academic Council, 120, 134, 138, 144
Adams, John Quincy, 25
Adelphian Society, 41
Adelphi College (became Adelphi University in *1963*), 137
African-American students, 47, 53–54, 55, 209–11
Agallian Base Ball Club, 46, 184
Air Line Railroad, 52, 94, 164
Allegheny College, 56, 103
Almirall, Raymond F., 194
Alpha Delta Phi, 45, 194–95, 199, 334n71, 338n82
Alpha Gamma Delta, 348n118
Alpha Kappa Upsilon, 214
Alumnae
  and Alumni Association, 105
  and coeducation, 214, 216
Alumni
  annual fund, 169
  athletics supported by, 170, 178, 183–84, 188, 330n53, 358n150
  careers of, 164–65. *See also* Students, career expectations and choices
  class reunions, 48, 63
  clubs, 48, 64, 165–66, 357n150. *See also by name*
  and dances, 207
  and election of trustees, 63, 64–65, 81, 87, 105, 171–72
  and fund-raising, 64, 70, 76–77, 162, 167, 169, 229

influence of, 63–64, 65, 166, 170–71, 221, 229
  prayer meetings, 108
  publication of news and opinions, 166
  and public relations, 169
  reunion sing, 339n91, 358n150
  as trustees, 64
  visiting committees, 166
  and women's education, 101, 213–14
Alumni Association, 48, 64, 81, 101, 105, 165, 167, 169, 170, 171, 187, 190, 216, 229
Alumni Athletic Association, 170, 184
Alumni Council, 166, 271n36
Alumni Fund, 169
Alumni Record, 49–50, 64, 65, 77, 81
Amenia Seminary, 29, 95, 96
American Agriculturalist, 77, 152
American Association for the Advancement of Science, 157
American Colonization Society, 55
American Literary, Scientific, and Military Academy (ALS&MA), 3–6, 9, 11, 14, 277n77
American Museum of Natural History, 189
American Society of Naturalists, 157
American University, 321n19
Amherst College, 221, 231, 261n44, 271nn28,36, 273n51, 282n16, 296n15, 345n107, 359n157

as teacher and scientist, 119, 145,
    152–53, 154, 309n67, 345n109
and temperance, 153–56
Augusta College, 15
Ayres, Daniel, 90, 142, 162, 306n58

Bacon, Henry, 195, 335n75
Baker, Darius, 171, 173
Baltzell, E. Digby, 172
Bangs, Heman, 8
Bangs, Nathan
    and curriculum, 25
    and discipline of students, 33
    education and early career, 24, 25
    election as president, 24
    health problems, 255n9
    inaugural address, 25
    and mental discipline, 31
    as Methodist leader, 70, 255n7
    personal characteristics, 24
    resignation and subsequent
        career, 25, 33, 255n9
Barnard College, 192, 220
Barnes, Jonathan, 9, 271n36
Barnswell, Thomas F., 55, 265n63
Barnum, Phineas T., 201
Bates College, 99, 100, 103
Beach, John W.
    and alumni, 97
    and Arminianism, 106
    and coeducation, 104
    dismissal of, 97–98, 137–38, 141
    education and early career, 96
    election as president, 96
    and faculty, 97, 137–38, 141, 142
    as fund-raiser, 96, 97
    personal characteristics, 96
    and George Seney, 96, 97–98
    and students, 96–97
Beech, Joseph, 206
Beecher, Henry Ward, 60, 99, 201
Beers, Henry A., 150
Beman, Amos, 54, 265n63, 267n10

Benedict, Francis G., 145, 313n85
Bennett, George S., 222
Beta Theta Pi, 199, 334n71,
    335n75, 338n82
Billboard, 191
Blakeslee, Olin S., 153
Boarding Hall. See Observatory Hall
Boiler plant, 189
Boston, 52, 56–57, 63, 75, 84, 93,
    164
Boston Public Library, 131
Boston University, 84, 202, 209,
    306nn59,60
    and coeducation, 103, 214, 288n47
    competition with Wesleyan, 105,
        127, 167, 180
    enrollments, 318n3
    founding of, 56, 57, 84, 85, 93,
        269n19, 279n85, 283n22
    and Hinckley Mitchell case, 159
    and Bradford Raymond, 142,
        306n60, 307n63
Boston Wesleyan alumni club, 64,
    104–05, 165, 166
Boston Wesleyan young alumni
    club, 165, 169, 170
Bowdoin College, 13, 35, 44, 55,
    99, 202, 204, 231, 286n37,
    358n152
Bowen, John W. E., Jr., 209
Bowne, Borden P., 159, 307n63
Bradley, Walter P., 145
Brice, Calvin S., 88
Bridgeport, Conn., 10
Brooklyn, N.Y., 146, 164, 178, 181,
    184, 197, 221
    and alumni, 165, 172, 178
    and architecture, 194
    and Methodist institutions, 90,
        94, 146, 169
    and trustees, 84, 88–89, 90, 92,
        172
Brooklyn Eagle, 146

and curriculum reform, 17–19
day of prayer for, 108
and discipline of students, 32,
122
elective systems, 127
faculty as professionals, 259n35
fraternities, 200
governance structures, 13
gymnasiums, 187
as local enterprises, 15, 56,
250n21
and major field of study,
302nn44,45
and master's degree, 124–25,
297n17, 302n40
metropolitan orientation of, 163,
167
as nonsectarian, 15
and professionalism in sports,
185–86
proliferation of (*1820–60*), 15
removal controversies at, 275n60
state aid to, 68, 248n10, 273n51
and traditions of liberal learning,
17, 129
and new urban wealth, 73
and women's education, 98–100
and YMCA movement, 108
Columbia University, 43, 122,
178–79, 181
Commission of Colleges in New England, 123
Committee of Fifty, 154, 156
Committee of Ten (NEA), 123,
296n14
Commons, John R., 309n67
Commons Club, 200, 208–09, 210,
277n75
Comte, Auguste, 307n63
Conferences, 279n83
New England, 10, 12, 14, 19, 25
New Hampshire and Vermont,
12

New York, 8, 10, 12, 14, 24, 25,
30
New York East, 8, 94, 106, 117,
158
Conn, Herbert W., 136, 145, 146,
149
Connecticut College for Women,
220
Connecticut General Assembly, 14,
68–70, 113, 125
Conwell, Russell H., 164
Cornell University, 148, 178, 181
Crawford, Morris B., 136
Crooks, George R., 72
Cummings, Joseph
and alumni relations, 62, 64, 65
and buildings maintenance, 59,
80
and campus improvement, 61, 62,
80
as candidate for governor, 108
and coeducation, 101, 104
and curriculum revision, 127
and discipline of students,
33–34, 61, 283n23
education and early career, 29–30
election as president, 29, 67, 93
evangelical views, 30, 106
and faculty scholarship, 38, 93,
142
as fund-raiser, 53, 57, 58, 73, 93
honorary degree from Harvard,
275n63
and mental discipline, 31, 32,
261n43
and Methodist relationship, 62,
65, 72, 80, 105, 275n63
and name change for Wesleyan,
170
personal characteristics of, 30,
31, 32, 33
as president, 30–31, 47, 61–62,
77, 142

and amusements, 125, 298n19
and athletics, 121–22
breadth of responsibilities,
  35–36, 123, 128
caps and gowns worn by, 61, 116,
  148, 271n30
and chapel services, 121, 204, 295n8
committees, 121
and curriculum, 120, 123,
  126–30, 134–35
departments, 128, 299n28
and discipline of students,
  122–23, 204
and examining committees, 120,
  133–34
financial contributions, 67, 145
Fisk's view of, 20, 34
generations, 146–48
and German universities, 37–38,
  119, 130, 136, 137, 138, 142,
  150, 152, 156, 306n60
and governance, 120, 204
graduate degrees of, 37, 136, 152,
  156
and graduate students, 133
and honorary degrees, 120,
  124–25, 271n29
and honors for students, 124
and library, 123
meetings, 121, 295n7
and Methodism, 34–35, 135,
  136–39, 148–60, 228
offices for, 146, 310n70
and orator and philosopher traditions, 19–20, 38, 39, 129, 149
pensions, 228, 230, 231
piety of, 34, 38, 106, 149
and political issues, 125
and presidents, 93–94, 137–38,
  142, 143, 163, 221, 225
as professionals, 36–38, 119–21,
  143, 144, 146, 148, 259n35
and publicity for Wesleyan,

125–26, 145–46
and Raymond, 141–42, 143
research and publications, 36–38,
  135–46, 231
recruitment by major universities,
  145
sabbatical leaves, 146
salaries of, 36, 87, 89, 139,
  144–45, 221, 259n35, 309n67
and selection of colleagues, 36,
  120, 136–38
size of, 53, 121, 162
and tariff on books, 125
teaching load, 139
teaching methods, 39, 130
tenure, 144, 295n4, 308n65
and tutors, 122, 261n42
voting rights, 295n6
and Wesley Bicentennial, 115,
  118
and women's education, 101, 216,
  219
Fairchild, James H., 98–99
Farrand, Max, 148
Faust, Albert B., 148
Fayerweather, Daniel B., 90, 91,
  142, 162, 187, 282n16
Fayerweather Gymnasium, 91,
  187–90, 202
First Church of Christ (Congregational), Middletown, Conn., 9,
  116, 139
First Methodist Church, Middletown, Conn., 6, 8, 18, 43, 92,
  115, 156, 189, 203
Fisher, Anna, 348n118
Fisk, Ruth Peck, 77, 95, 191
Fisk, Willbur, 231
  and abolition vs. colonization,
    54–55, 268n12
  academic Arminianism of, 20, 23
  and admission of African-
    American students, 54

and Taft, 354n141
as trustee, 116–17, 177
Olla Podrida, 42, 202, 214–15, 219, 340n94
Orator and philosopher traditions, 19–20, 38, 39, 129, 149

Palestine Garden, 6
Paley, William, 24
Panic of *1837*, 53, 56, 67
Panic of *1857*, 53
Panic of *1873*, 87, 88, 93, 127
Panic of *1884*, 89
Panic of *1893*, 90
Panunzio, Constantine M., 208
Parkhurst, Charles, 151
Partridge, Alden, 3–6, 12, 21, 59, 77, 79
Pearson, Charles W., 159
Peithologian Society, 41
Pembroke College. *See* Women's College in Brown University
Pennington, Perry D. G., 209
Perkins, Angie Warren, 103, 105
Peters, John, 14–15
Phi Beta Kappa, 42, 104, 200, 289n48
Phillips Exeter Academy, 209
Philorhetorian Society, 41
Phi Nu Theta. *See* Eclectic
Phi Rho, 199
Phi Sigma, 214
Plattsburg State Normal and Training School, 209
Players Club, 176
Porter, Noah, 94
Portland, Conn. (formerly Chatham), 3, 4, 67
Prentice, George, 146
Presidents, 284n28
as administrators, 61
health of, 56, 255n9
inaugural addresses, 17–21, 25,

29, 30, 95, 143, 225–26, 284n26
salaries of, 94, 259n35, 309n67, 352n136
searches for, 24, 25, 28, 29, 141–42, 220–22. *See also by name*
President's House: (*1837–1904*), 53, 79, 104; (*1904–*), 195
Princeton University, 90, 122, 124, 140–41, 145, 179, 181, 195, 205, 210–11, 305n57
Pritchett, Henry S., 229–31
Prohibition party, 108, 155
Psi Upsilon, 42, 45, 191, 193–94, 334n71, 338n82, 356r145
Purvis, Augustus G., 209

Radcliffe College, 99, 220
Railroads
Berlin branch line, 52
Boston and New York Air Line, 52, 94, 164
Hartford and New Haven, 52
New York, Chicago, and St. Louis, 88
Shore Line, 52
Rand, John C., 172, 178, 185
Randolph-Macon College, 15, 27, 85, 279n85
Randolph-Macon Woman's College, 229–30
Ray, Charles B., 53–54
Raymond, Bradford P.
and African-American students, 209–10
alumni criticism of, 163, 171
and athletics, 187
and coeducation, 215, 218
and early career, 142, 162–63, 224
election as president, 141–42
and enrollments, 142, 162, 167

as major donor, 88–89, 97, 282n13

as Methodist, 88–89, 93, 113, 115

and scholarships, 104, 111, 282n13, 291n61

as trustee, 97–98

Seventy-fifth anniversary celebration, 229

Seymour, Thomas H., 60

Shanklin, William Arnold

education and early career, 224

election as president, 220, 222

and fraternities, 224

as fund-raiser, 224–25, 231

inauguration, 225–27

as Methodist, 222, 224, 227

personal characteristics, 222, 224–26

and Republican party, 225, 226–27

and students, 225, 226

and William H. Taft, 226

and women's education, 218, 224–25, 351n132

Shaw, Albert, 139, 141

Sheffield Scientific School, 119

Sherman, James S., 226

Sigma Phi, 224

Sigma Pi, 104

Sigma Rho, 104

Silliman, Benjamin, 18, 43, 60

Skull and Serpent, 42

Sleeper, Jacob, 57, 75, 84

Smith, Augustus D.

as acting president, 24

and admissions standards, 53

and discipline of students, 33

education and early career, 28, 35

election as president, 28

as fund-raiser, 29, 58, 257n18

as layman, 29, 72, 256n17

and mental discipline, 31, 32

and ministerial courses, 40

personal characteristics, 28–29

as president, 29, 40, 53, 59, 61

resignation, 29, 33, 63–64, 67, 72, 256n18

as scholar, 37, 260n36

subsequent career, 257n18

Smith, Edwin O., 214

Smith, John D., 209, 210–11

Smithsonian Institution, 132, 152

South College, 4, 11, 14, 78–79, 131, 133, 196, 208

Spanish-American War, 92, 206, 343n102

Springfield, Mass., 178, 180

Squire, Watson C., 178

Stamford Bank, 69

Stanford University, 145, 167

Stanley, George W., 9, 14, 271n36

State agricultural experiment station, 152

State bacteriological laboratory, 133

Stone, Lucy, 286n38

Stone, Phebe, 286n38

Storrs, William L., 9, 40, 271n36

Stout, Andrew V., 84, 88, 93, 94, 96

Stout, Joseph S., 173

Stryker, Melancthon W., 226

Students. *See also* African-American students; Women students

and academic advising, 298n27

activities, function of, 41–43, 45–46, 48, 197, 199, 201

ages of, 32, 44, 197, 263n55

cane rush, 110

cannon scrap, 109–10, 122, 206

caps and gowns worn by, 208

career expectations and choices, 34, 48–49, 112, 164–65, 206, 212, 292n63

characteristics of, 44, 45, 47–48, 111–12, 139–40, 197, 199,

University Press of New England

publishes books under its own imprint and is the publisher for Brandeis University Press, Dartmouth College, Middlebury College Press, University of New Hampshire, Tufts University, and Wesleyan University Press.

Library of Congress Cataloging-in-Publication Data

Potts, David B. (David Bronson)
    Wesleyan University, 1831–1910 : collegiate enterprise in
New England / David B. Potts
       p.   cm.
    Originally published: New Haven: Yale University Press,
© 1992.
    "Wesleyan University Press paperback"—T.p. verso.
    Includes bibliographical references (p.   ) and indexes.
    ISBN 0–8195–6360–9 (pbk.: alk. paper)
    1. Wesleyan University (Middletown, Conn.)—History.
I. Title.
LD5901.W32P68 1999
378.746'6—dc21   98–54280